# THE BEST

# AMERICAN

# MAGAZINE

# WRITING

# 2017

# THE BEST AMERICAN MAGAZINE WRITING

## 2017

**Edited by Sid Holt for the American Society of Magazine Editors**

Columbia University Press    New York

Columbia University Press
*Publishers Since 1893*
New York    Chichester, West Sussex
cup.columbia.edu
Copyright © 2017 Columbia University Press
All rights reserved

Library of Congress Cataloging-in-Publication Data
ISSN 1541-0978
ISBN 978-0231-18159-4 (pbk.)

Cover design: Nancy Rouemy

# Contents

Nicholas Thompson

# Introduction

The protagonists of Mac McClelland's essay, "Delusion Is the Thing with Feathers," about the hunt for an ivory-billed woodpecker in Cuba, are two ornithologists, Tim Gallagher and Martjan Lammertink. They've traveled far past the place where the road ends; they've exhausted themselves going up and down mountain ridges. The car they came in gave up long ago, even after two oxen helped pull it from a ditch. They've looked everywhere they wanted to look and talked to everyone they came to talk to. But they haven't found the darn bird. Their journey is at its end, and it's time to give up and head to the airport to go home.

Then they realize there's one last person who might be able to help, one more person who might have seen the bird. And so they sneak away from the rest of their group to head back into the jungle. As McLelland writes: "There's hope! Gallagher thinks, perking up out of his dire exhaustion, in which he barely staggered out of the woods just yesterday. We can still do this!"

I won't tell you what they learn or if they find the bird. McClelland, who accompanied the ornithologists on the quest, risked her health for the story in a hundred ways, and her essay is a marvel of storytelling. It would be a shame to spoil any of the drama. But I tell the beginning of the anecdote because it's a way to illustrate the type of reporting that you'll find in this collection and that you always find in the best magazine writing. The journalists here are like Gallagher and Lammertink: they're obsessed. They keep calling and writing and revising and talking. There's always one more person to talk to or one more thing to try to do better. There's always a chance that they'll find the unseen bird or uncover the secret document or maybe just craft the perfect line.

Think about Gabriel Sherman, the author "The Revenge of Roger's Angels." Through dedication and years of diligent reporting, he exposed secrets at Fox News that no one expected would come out—or, certainly, secrets that no one at Fox wanted to come out. The company compiled a 400-page opposition research file on Sherman as he worked. But because of his tenacity, and his reputation for probity and accuracy, sources kept calling him. Roger Ailes, the most powerful man at perhaps the most powerful news organization in the country, lost his job because of the persistence of a magazine reporter.

Or think about Shane Bauer. He spent four months working as a guard at Winn Correctional Center, in Louisiana, and then fourteen more months reporting on what he learned. Life inside a private prison is violent and often unjust, but it's also mostly kept hidden. To explain it, you need to commit. You need to be there at the training session where the employees are told that when two inmates start to stab each other, the guards should just holler, "Stop," and then lean back and watch.

The writers in this collection, of course, weren't all trying to shine flashlights in dark corners. Becca Rothfeld, in her marvelous essay about what it means to wait for someone, is working to explain a state of mind. "Waiting is consuming. At times it is terrible, a wound that cannot be mitigated but must instead be mutely survived," she writes. "And sometimes waiting is an insult, an indignity, as pointlessly pathetic as refusing to take off the wedding dress in which you were abandoned years ago by someone who no longer cares and probably doesn't remember."

This kind of storytelling is deeply satisfying, but I sometimes ponder why we, as humans, are so attached to it. Writing, of course, has clear evolutionary value. The societies that first learned to write kept better records and planned smarter expeditions. But it's not immediately apparent that the forces of natural selection would favor people who sit around telling tales about one another. If one village was filled with farmers and the other with storytellers, wouldn't Darwin predict that the farmers would thrive while the raconteurs would get eaten by tigers? We know that didn't happen, though, and surely part of the reason is instruction. Read about the mistakes of others, and you won't make the same mistakes yourself. Or, maybe more pertinently, learn when to plant your crops and why to keep your children out of the river where the alligators live. But the virtues of storytelling are much deeper than that: they help us forge social identities; they let our imaginations develop; they give us pleasure; they let us connect with one another. They make us feel good. And they make us feel outraged at things that are wrong.

All of that is true today. Storytelling, particularly when combined with great journalism and thinking, helps us to understand and to make decisions for society. Read Sarah Stillman's piece in this collection, "The List," and try not to boil with outrage at the lives our nation throws away when it classifies children as sex offenders. Reading Nikole Hannah-Jones on the intense complexities of school choice in Brooklyn will surely change the way you think about how we educate our kids.

·     ·     ·

Of course, as you've surely heard, the craft is under threat. It's hard to go a day without encountering the argument that our attention spans are shortening. We're too distracted by Instagram or Facebook, by texts and by sexts. The entire Internet will have turned into short-form videos by the time the sun rises tomorrow. If that wasn't enough, the decline of advertising revenue has been starving the journalism business for at least the last decade. And it surely doesn't help to have the president of the United States hate-tweeting against the free press every morning when the rooster crows.

But, actually, if you examine all these issues, one by one, it's possible to be hopeful about the future of great magazine writing. As someone with inside information from my previous job at *The New Yorker*, I can assure you that the two essays from that publication in this collection were read, beginning to end, by an astonishing number of people. The same is true at *Wired*, where I work now. A good rule of thumb, the editors of the website Longform once told me, is that roughly 90 percent of readers on their site who get through the first 15 percent of the best long stories reach the end. (The founders of that site also told me that they get traffic referrals form OK Cupid, meaning people were trying to get dates by touting their love of long-form journalism.)

If that doesn't persuade you, look at other fields, like television. The shows we watch today are infinitely more complex than even the best of what people watched twenty years ago. Compare, say, *Game of Thrones* to *M\*A\*S\*H*. And then remember, too, that the series is based upon a series of books, written by George R. R. Martin, that cumulatively run about 4,500 pages. If we can get through all of that, our attention spans are surely not shrinking.

That's not to say, of course, that business models aren't truly threatened. But the question of whether great magazine writing survives is quite different from the question of whether every magazine survives. Advertising is shifting, and the newsstand business is declining. As this happens, however, new sources of support arise. *The Atlantic*, which published Jeffrey Goldberg's extraordinary essay on Obama's foreign policy, now supports itself in no small part through conferences. *The New Yorker*, in the last few years, built a successful digital subscription model. It's hard to make a business work now just packaging information, but you can definitely make a business work by presenting knowledge.

And last, of course, there is the question of our president, the subject of quite a few essays in this collection—and perhaps an incorrect prediction or two as well. He does pose a threat to magazine writing in ways that we will no doubt understand far better when the historians start to look back. By riling up his supporters against the press, he can do damage to the institutions that critique him or, in the darkest scenarios, to the whole notion of a free press—though, for the moment, his attacks serve mainly to launch subscription drives.

Even leaving aside politics, Donald Trump stands against many of the values that the work in this collection stands for: rigorous thinking, attention to detail, craft, and prose. The day after the election, I remember talking to a group of colleagues about how to respond to Trump. The best way, we decided, was just to do our jobs well. To report fairly and accurately, to fact-check everything, to make sentences beautiful. Presidents serve four-year terms, and great writing lasts much longer.

There's another moment in McClelland's essay where she and the photographer sit at the side of the path, watching as their travel companions whack the oxen trying to pull their jeep out of a ditch. The journey seems both miserable and futile. "Do you ever wonder if this is all worth it? For a bird?" the photographer asks. The subtext is clear: is obsession worth it? Is it worth making all those extra calls and traveling to ever-more-absurd locales for one's craft?

The answer, of course, is a resounding yes.

# Acknowledgments

In mid-January hundreds of journalists meet on the campus of Columbia University in New York City to judge the National Magazine Awards for Print and Digital Media. After two days of reading magazines, exploring websites, and watching videos, the judges make their decisions and send the results to the National Magazine Awards Board for approval. Two weeks later the finalists are announced on Twitter. Four weeks later the winners are honored at the National Magazine Awards Gala (this year hosted by Lester Holt). Less than a year later you buy this book.

*Best American Magazine Writing* gathers together the most notable stories from the current year's National Magazine Awards. The American Society of Magazine Editors partnered with the Columbia School of Journalism to establish the awards in the early 1960s. The first award was presented to *Look* in 1966; the first award for digital journalism was presented to *Money* in 1997. Known as the Ellies for the elephant-shaped statuette presented to each winner, the awards now include twenty categories, ranging from Reporting and Feature Writing to Photography and Design.

This year, 280 publications participated in the Ellies, submitting 1,376 entries. The awards were judged by 282 journalists and educators, who chose 5 to 7 finalists in each category. Sixty-four media organizations were nominated for National Magazine

Awards. Nineteen titles received multiple nominations, led by *New York* with ten, the *New York Times Magazine* with seven, and *The New Yorker* with five. *New York* and the *New York Times Magazine* also won the most awards, both with three. Complete lists of the judges, finalists and winners are posted on the ASME website at http://www.magazine.org/asme/national-magazine-awards/winners-finalists.

Many of the writers included in *Best American Magazine Writing 2017* are repeat finalists. The nomination in Feature Writing of George Saunders's "Trump Days" for *The New Yorker* marked the seventh time Saunders's work has been honored with an Ellie nomination or award. His short stories won awards for *Harper's Magazine* in 1994 and 1996, *The New Yorker* in 2000, and *Esquire* in 2004. His fiction was also nominated for awards for *The New Yorker* in 1999 and 2010.

One of the most honored reporters in the history of the Ellie Awards, Pamela Colloff, was nominated in Feature Writing for her story "The Reckoning" for *Texas Monthly*. Her work for *Texas Monthly* was previously nominated in Public Interest in 2001 and 2011; in two separate categories, Reporting and Feature Writing, in 2013; and again in Feature Writing in 2015. Her two-part series "The Innocent Man"—about Anthony Graves, who was wrongfully convicted of murdering his family and freed from prison only after the publication of Colloff's story—won the award for Feature Writing in 2013.

The nomination of Sarah Stillman's story "The List" for *The New Yorker* was her fourth in Public Interest in the last six years. Her story "The Invisible Army" for *The New Yorker* won the award for Public Interest in 2012. The nomination of Mac McClelland's story "Delusion Is the Thing With Feathers" for *Audubon* was her third in Feature Writing in the last seven years. She was previously nominated for her work for *Mother Jones* in 2011 and 2013.

Other repeat Ellie finalists included Jeffrey Goldberg (finalist this year in Reporting for *The Atlantic*), who won Reporting for *The New Yorker* in 2003; Andrew Sullivan (finalist in Essays and Criticism for *New York*), who as the editor of *The New Republic* won the award for Public Interest in 1995; and Rebecca Traister (finalist in Feature Writing for *New York*), who was nominated in Columns and Commentary for *The New Republic* in 2015. Matt Taibbi, who won the award for Columns and Commentary for *Rolling Stone* in 2008, was nominated in the same category for the same magazine this year.

David Quammen, whose essay for *National Geographic*'s "Yellowstone: Wild Heart of a Continent" was nominated this year in the Single-Topic Issue category, has won three National Magazine Awards: in 1987 for Essays and Criticism for *Outside*; in 1994 for Special Interests, again for *Outside*; and in 2005 for Essays for *National Geographic*.

Two 2017 award winners were also repeat honorees. Nikole Hannah-Jones, whose story "Worlds Apart" for the *New York Times Magazine* won Public Interest this year, was nominated for her story "Segregation Now" for *The Atlantic*, also in Public Interest, in 2015. Rebecca Solnit won Columns and Commentary for *Harper's Magazine* after her work was nominated in the same category in 2016.

The members of ASME want to thank these and the other writers whose work is included here—Shane Bauer, Siddhartha Mukherjee, Zandria F. Robinson, Becca Rothfeld, and Gabriel Sherman—for making this edition of *Best American Magazine Writing* possible. Also to be thanked are the many editors and judges who participate in the National Magazine Awards every year. The Ellie Awards were established to advance the practice of journalism by honoring excellence, enterprise, and innovation. Only with the support of dedicated editors and writers can this goal be achieved.

Each of the sixteen members of the ASME board of directors is responsible for overseeing the administration, judging, and presentation of the Ellie Awards but especially deserving of thanks is Dana Points, who as president of the board in 2016–2017 brought the same passion to the awards that she showed during her distinguished tenure as editor in chief of *Parents*. In addition to Dana, I also want to thank Lester Holt, anchor of *NBC Nightly News with Lester Holt* and *Dateline NBC*, for hosting this year's awards presentation.

ASME has cosponsored the awards with the Columbia Journalism School for more than half a century. The members of ASME thank Steve Coll, the Pulitzer Prize–winning reporter who now serves as the dean of the journalism school, for his continuing support of the National Magazine Awards. ASME would also like to thank Abi Wright, the executive director of professional prizes at Columbia for her help in organizing the Ellies judging every year and for her valuable service as a member of the National Magazine Awards Board.

David McCormick of McCormick Literary has long represented ASME as its agent. For his work on our behalf, the members of ASME are truly thankful. The editors of *BAMW* at Columbia University Press are Philip Leventhal and Michael Haskell. They both deserve more than thanks. I especially want to acknowledge Philip's high regard for literary journalism and Michael's skill and determination.

The members of ASME thank our colleagues at MPA, the Association of Magazine Media, for their support not only of the Ellies but also of ASME. Deserving of special recognition are the chair of the MPA board of directors, Steve Lacy of Meredith Corporation, and Linda Thomas Brooks, the president and CEO of MPA. For nearly a decade now, I've been trying to come up with new and witty ways to thank my associate at ASME, Nina Fortuna, for her inestimable contributions to the Ellies. This year I give up. Nina—thanks again.

Finally, on behalf of ASME, I want to thank Nicholas Thompson for writing the introduction to this year's edition of *BAMW*. At a time when the challenges facing media seem ever more daunting, Nick reminds us why journalists and readers both are sticking with magazines. I look forward to seeing him onstage soon, accepting an Ellie for his work as editor in chief of *Wired*.

# THE BEST
# AMERICAN
# MAGAZINE
# WRITING
# 2017

## Audubon

FINALIST—FEATURE
WRITING

*"This is* birding. *Go dangerous or go home." So writes Mac McClelland in this account of two ornithologists' search for the elusive, perhaps extinct ivory-billed woodpecker. Deep in the forests of eastern Cuba, readers soon find themselves part of a disaster-prone and evidently deranged venture. "McClelland writes with wry confidence as the expedition goes bad, then worse, then worse still," said the Ellie judges. "Delusion Is the Thing with Feathers" is McClelland's third Ellie-nominated story. "For Us Surrender Is Out of the Question," her report on the Karen rebellion against the Burmese government, was nominated in 2011; "I Was a Warehouse Wage Slave" was nominated in 2013. Both were published by* Mother Jones.

Mac McClelland

# Delusion Is
# the Thing
# with Feathers

"Here ends our happiness," the driver says, approaching the end of the pavement and stopping the government truck. It has no seatbelts or roll bar, and apparently very little in the way of shocks, but the two birders on board are happy, now and these past six days, despite how the particulars of their expedition may have struck others—say, the writer and photographer also on board—as uncomfortable. Or, frankly, miserable. Tim Gallagher, sixty-five, and Martjan Lammertink, forty-four, went through worse in their searches for *Campephilus* woodpeckers in other countries before they landed in Cuba to look for the granddaddy of all finds, the elusive and by most accounts extinct ivory-bill. No one has looked hard here for a long time, in this last half-plausible place. *Someone should really look in Cuba*, people who know and care about such things have been saying, and so here Gallagher and Lammertink are. With, as it happens, not much they aren't willing to do—suffer; die—to get that done.

There was the crush of last-minute getting-ready, Gallagher tying up loose ends as editor in chief of *Living Bird* at his office in the Cornell Lab of Ornithology. There was Lammertink on a twenty-two-hour bus to a Brazilian airport from interior Argentina, where the Dutch ornithologist works for the National

Scientific and Technical Research Council, followed by nineteen hours of airports and planes to Ithaca, New York. There were the two of them at Walmart together buying pots and pans and tents and staying up late packing and waking up early to drive, along with the writer, more than four hours to Toronto and then landing late in Holguín, east Cuba, Gallagher more than two personal airline bottles of prosecco deep, to deal with the even later arrival of the photographer. No sooner had they had breakfast at their budget homestay the next morning, after four hours of sleep for Lammertink and maybe five for Gallagher, than maps were spread open across a table and Carlos Peña, a Cuban natural history specialist, stopped by to help strategize. *This is where the paved road ends.* Pointing, leaning. *This is where any road ends. This is where you might be able to pick up some mules to help with transport.* Then it was out to a grocery store for rice and pasta and eggs and water before a quick lunch and into the car for the first leg of the long trip, to Farallones de Moa. Toward the mountains. Into the woods.

The rented car was a 1955 Willys: two and a half seats in the front and two very narrow benches bolted longways into the back. The group's hundreds of pounds of gear, food, and luggage were piled up in between and on top of half of them, leaving Gallagher and the photographer to squeeze onto the ends of opposite little pews, hunching over to keep their heads off the low metal roof. At breakfast the writer again expressed her wish that there were seatbelts, which she generally tries to secure on work trips when she is in charge of logistics; while the photographer kindly validated her feelings by saying this was a normal human desire, Lammertink did not deign to respond. Gallagher, maybe a bit tipsily, had slapped her knee and laughed about it the night before as their young driver sped the proto-jeep away from the airport around the proliferation of horse-drawn carts on the street in the dark. Now, as they prepared to drive the first three of the many, many hours they'd spend on Cuban roads over two weeks,

Lammertink invited the writer to cram herself into the only place she would fit, between him and the driver. "It'll just be much more fatal in an accident," he said of sitting in the front, then laughed, the fact that car accidents cause the most American deaths abroad being funny.

Ha ha!

But of course, this is *birding*. Go dangerous or go home.

The target destination was Ojito de Agua, an area beyond Farallones in the mountains of Parque Nacional Alejandro de Humboldt. In 1986, Cuban biologists Giraldo Alayón and Alberto Estrada found ivory-bills there, and a few weeks later they and the eminent woodpecker specialists Lester Short and Jennifer Horne confirmed the sightings there. Lammertink himself spent eight months in 1991 and 1993 looking for them there. Ojito de Agua has been protected for thirty years now—since the sightings—so maybe, Lammertink hopes, the habitat might now be more hospitable to ivory-bills.

In the car to Farallones, Gallagher bounced his old bones about in the back with zero complaints and inhuman patience. Dust swirled in through the open and broken windows, more as they got farther from the city, five miles an hour and less when the pavement expired and the road turned uphill and rocky and deeply, deeply rutted. He cheerfully schlepped in his Wellingtons through mud and across narrow planks over ravines to a jungle shack lent to them by a coffee farmer who never, ever buttons his shirt—then back out again after the regional Protected Areas official told the foreigners by phone that he wouldn't allow them into the forest from there. And that nor were they allowed in Farallones at all. As a tiny muddy village, it has no amenities or services for visitors, including—most importantly—permission to host them.

So it was on to Baracoa, a lovely if mildly shabby beach town four and a half hours of mostly jolting non-road farther east, to meet with the evicting regional Protected Areas official, whereupon he sent them back again some two hours west, to the national park's visitor's center on Bahía de Taco, a parking-lot-size patch of grass separating the non-road from the ocean where the group was to sleep for two nights in a different, more official jungle shack while the Protected Areas agency considered whether to allow them to venture deep into the national park.

At Taco Bay, the sand flies were savage. There was no plumbing but a vat of carried-up river water from which the group could draw buckets to bathe beside the non-road. Everyone, even the birders, hated the bathroom, a multiperson outhouse that did not enjoy much in the way of maintenance. When the supply of potable water they'd hauled in ran out, the writer taught herself how to use the $250 worth of water-filtration and UV-sterilization equipment she had bought before embarking (she and the photographer, who are accustomed to hardships but of a different kind, have discovered that they are wearing matching new pairs of technical wicking antimicrobial quick-drying underpants). Gallagher helped her purify water for the group, impressed with how much more convenient it was than a camping straw, which filters bacteria one sip at a time and does not filter viruses and which was all he carried in his bag, though he has neither a naiveté about waterborne illness nor an ironclad digestive tract. A partial list of places where Gallagher has suffered severe gastrointestinal distress includes: Mexico, Costa Rica, and Peru. In Mexico, he also got Hepatitis A. Which is a virus.

But this wasn't a "hard" trip. A hard trip, that would be something like—speaking of—Mexico, where in 2010 Gallagher and Lammertink, in quest of imperials, a possibly also extinct and even larger—the largest—woodpecker species, were headed into cartel lands so dangerous that every one of the Mexican biologists who had been recruited to go with them dropped out. Gallagher and Lammertink went anyway, and in one of the villages on the way, three houses were burned to the ground, one man kidnapped for ransom; as they drove through the area, they passed locals fleeing the other way. But they pressed on, crossing paths with armed traffickers and enlisting smugglers and Uzi-carrying locals as guides, Gallagher praying that if he got killed his wife would find his notes and finish the book he was working on, and when they emerged from those mountains alive, the forest ranger who had—under great protest—helped them get in broke down crying.

Or, a hard trip would be something like Argentina, where Gallagher and Lammertink trekked high and low and high and higher and low and high again following radio-tagged helmeted woodpeckers (a species that indisputably exists) over the jungle hills starting at four a.m. daily and for fourteen hours a day while it poured relentlessly and mosquitos infected with botfly eggs bit them and dropped maggot larvae onto their bodies, where they burrowed and grew and thrived. Lammertink said nothing about the pain, but Gallagher caught him flinching once as one crunched away at the shoulder tissue under his skin. (Gallagher himself finally reached a breaking point and dug his infestation, and his skin and thigh tissue, out wholesale with a knife.) Living in Argentina and tramping often into the jungles after helmeted woodpeckers, Lammertink averages forty botfly cases per year. In the shower on the first morning here in Cuba, he squeezed a mass of yellow pus and partly liquefied dead-botfly parts out of a hole in his forearm.

Cuba is nothing. They don't even have botflies in Cuba!

Still, the driver of the government truck is right. Things do get worse. By the time they do, the team has driven back east again to Baracoa, and then south through the mountains and switch-backs to the ocean clear on the other side of the island and west again from there, the views gorgeous with beach to the left and dramatic desert rock to the right on the way to Guantánamo, to another Protected Areas office to beg, barter, and finally secure the coveted clearance into Ojito de Agua. They have left the rented Willys and loaded more provisions into this government jeep driven by this government employee, though after a too-brief stint at the mechanic's it is barely or in the opinion of at least one national park staffer not at all ready to complete the trip up the half-road on the mountain ahead. In even the best scenario, it is unlikely that the group will reach their destination, a manned national park station seven miles up deep mud and rock, before dark; twilight approaches, and the forecast calls for rain, which will render the way unpassable by jeep for sure.

The government driver tries anyway. He takes a deep breath and gathers himself when the pavement ends, and they crash forward through the uneven landscape, jeep rocking violently and Gallagher and the media trying to keep from slamming into one another in the backseat. Until they stop. Stuck. Mired in a deep mud trench. Everyone ejects, and rocks are collected and thrown under the tires and into the muck ahead, and after a while the truck is dislodged. And then more crashing—and some very near tipping—and then they get stuck again. And the driver kills the battery trying to drive out. And everyone again decamps, and the gear and luggage and provisions are offloaded, splayed around the muddy clearing, and the driver runs away, and after a long time he returns leading two yoked oxen from a farm somewhere and they're tied to the truck and everybody pushes and rocks it while the farmer beats the oxen relentlessly, breaking branches and then entire small trees over their backs and across their faces until they break free and escape and don't trample anybody but have to be chased down and wrangled and retied to the truck.

After a couple of hours of this, Gallagher turns to the writer and remarks, "This gives you a little idea of how hard it is to study these birds. And why nobody's doin' it."

It grows dark.

It starts to pour.

Really, she has no idea.

·    ·    ·

In photographs, the ivory-bill has something human about it. There's a sentience to the weirdly alert yellow eyes, an intensity to its regard that, combined with a wide stance—rare in the bird world—reads almost like standoffishness. In pictures from 1938 of a large juvenile perched on naturalist J. J. Kuhn's arm in Louisiana's Singer Tract, the bird's big, slightly opened beak looks a breath away from expressing fully formed sentences.

In stuffed specimen form, the ivory-bill looks like a raggedy nightmare. Dead-eyed or eyeless and old, the ones in the Cornell Ornithology Lab's vault were only depressing to behold when Gallagher and Lammertink brought them out past multiple security doors for the writer to inspect before heading to Cuba. One specimen there, mounted on a piece of wood, was previously a decoration out on someone's smoking porch or something, the feathers weathered and broken down. In the collections manager's office, another mounted specimen has its serrated tongue intact and extending between open bills, but when the thing was gingerly lifted up for the writer's closer review, one long toe-claw fell off.

No wonder Gallagher was so thrilled to see a live one tear through the sky in the Arkansas bottomland swamp in 2004. He had been obsessed with birds for as long as he could remember, once in his early teens lying facedown on the ground in the sun of the California mountains for hours looking dead so a turkey vulture would land on him. (By the time the experiment was reluctantly abandoned as a failure, he was so burned and dehydrated that he barely had the strength to ride his bike back down the hill and home.) And then there he was, after so much searching, rediscovering the bird world's most coveted and iconic ghost species. Or so he, and several other searchers whom the Lab of Ornithology subsequently enlisted to scour swamp forests across the South for five years, spending several million dollars, maintains—though the only video they captured is highly contested as proof.

As a teenager, Lammertink, too, tried to attract the close attention of a vulture, attempting first to buy a dead sheep but ultimately resorting to sprinkling a doll in tomato-sauce blood and leaving it under the raptors' flight path. (This experiment also failed.) He was one of Cornell's ivory-bill searchers ten years ago but not a beholder of one of the six other sightings named in the paper the lab eventually published. He still believes his colleagues, but he thinks the bird or birds they saw have probably since died. He is highly skeptical that any ivory-bills still survive in Cuba, the only other place besides the Southeast United States they've ever been known to live: The title of the paper he published after searching here in the nineties is "Status of Ivory-Billed Woodpecker *Campephilus principalis* in Cuba: Almost Certainly Extinct." He wrote another piece for the journal of the Neotropical Bird Club called "No More Hope for the Ivory-Billed Woodpecker *Campephilus principalis*." But maybe, he thinks now, the birds weren't there then, in the few remaining patches of pine forest where American researcher George Lamb *definitely* saw (and obtained photographic proof of) them in 1956, the last such universally accepted records on Earth. Maybe they found suitable habitat in the lowland hardwoods nearby, where maybe they held on until the newly protected pine forest regenerated enough for them to return.

On that note: The national park guide assigned to the group at Bahía de Taco, who goes by El Indio, said he saw an ivory-bill with his father just twenty-four years ago, right in those lowland hardwoods, where the birds would generally not be expected to live.

And so the group looked there, in the lowland hardwoods. From Bahía de Taco they set out on what Gallagher invariably calls a "death march": twelve hours and, according to the photographer's iPhone, ninety-nine flights of stairs' worth of elevation over often extraordinarily slippery red clay scouring for ivory-bill markings or oval nest cavities in trees. It was on that day that they first broke out the double-knocker.

The double-knocker is an innovation of Lammertink's own design and construction. An online video documents him using it to attract another *Campephilus* woodpecker, the pale-billed, which exists from Mexico to Panama, strapping the small wooden box to a tree with rope, pulling out a contraption made of two dowel rods that he sways back then swings into the box, one dowel and then the other making contact, mimicking the distinctive *Campephilus* sound: *BAM-bam*. In the video, recorded in Costa Rica, he does this, and then, from a distance: a pale-billed knocks back.

!

In the forest near Bahía de Taco, Lammertink trudged off the path beaten for park visitors and through the brush up an incline, finding a pine tree in a growth of quebrahachas, the type of tree El Indio said were dominant where he had his sighting not far from there. Everyone stood silently as Lammertink prepared. He pulled out the box. He strapped it up. He set the dowel contraption on top of it. He opened his notebook. He marked down the time and GPS coordinates. He pulled out an MP3 player attached to a speaker wrapped in camouflage. And then, after much such settling in, he swayed back, and struck.

*BAM-bam.*

Everyone was silent.

Lammertink looked around slowly.

He waited twenty-two to twenty-three seconds, checking his watch, then struck again.

*BAM-bam.*

He waited.

He struck again.

And again.

After ten double-knocks, he put the dowels down, picking up his MP3 player and speaker. He scrolled through his playlist, then pressed play, holding the speaker aloft as the recording of an ivory-bill, the only existing recording of an Ivory-bill, from

1935, played, underlain by heavy static. People say it sounds like a horn. Or a baby goat. *Kent. Kent-kent.* Lammertink turned in slow circles blasting it, and Gallagher kept his ears alert as the sound played for ninety seconds. Then he turned it off, and waited.

He put his hands on his hips. He checked his watch.

Gallagher didn't move.

Then they started the process over, in the same spot.

*BAM-bam.*

A double-knock session takes about thirty minutes. With other *Campephilus* species, Lammertink has waited as long as twenty minutes afterward for them to respond to a call. When he thought they'd waited long enough this time, the group all sitting and standing silently there in the forest, they picked up the bags and waters and cameras they'd set down and took off again, hiking 500 meters farther into the forest to try again. The call carries at least half that far, so to maximize exposure in the limited amount of time available to any one man, Lammertink spaces them out thusly. After the second session, they hiked another 500 meters and tried again.

Those thirty minutes, knocking and waiting the third time, it was getting late in the day. It was hot, and mosquitoes landed on the motionless party. At some point, the photographer wandered off a bit. Gallagher sat down farther back on the path and rested. The writer practiced her yogic Mountain Pose. A huge bird suddenly broke through the trees and soared into view, sweeping and grand and even with some white underside. But it was only a turkey vulture, buzzing close to remind them that life is fleeting.

There have been times when Lammertink used the double-knocker in places where he knew for a fact *Campephilus* woodpeckers were nearby (-slash-existed), and they didn't respond. To get one to do so on this trip in a territory this large, he conceded to the photographer, would be very lucky. To not get one proves nothing.

So: There is not a moment to waste. Not in Bahía de Taco double-knocking, and especially not after Lammertink walked to El Indio's father's house and interviewed him and asked him what sound the ivory-bill had made when he saw the bird with his son twenty-four years ago and the man made the wrooong, very wrong sound of a different bird, and the wrong wing description to boot. As El Indio was only seven at the time, his recollection likely colored by his father's identification of the species, both of the accounts of these two—the only two—witnesses to the exciting possibility that the ivory-bill did or could live in non-pine forest in eastern Cuba were therefore called into question.

It was a disappointing development, one that Lammertink would henceforth refer to as "The Twist."

So not a moment to waste getting out of Bahía de Taco—though the forest there was chockful of other species sightings: scaly-naped Pigeon and Cuban trogon and stygian owl; Cuban Amazon, Cuban pewee, West Indian woodpecker, Cuban tody, Cuban solitaire, great lizard-cuckoo, black-and-white warbler, Cuban green woodpecker. Not a moment to waste getting to Guantánamo and getting permission—no time to care or alert the authorities about the endangered parrot being kept illegally caged on the floor of the kitchen in the restaurant where they ate in town—and getting back out to push up the mountain, not a moment to wait for a new day with more light remaining and less chance of rain or a fully fixed vehicle that might not die when it gets stuck.

That night, after hours of human pushing and oxen pulling, the jeep is freed. And with more pushing and pulling, it is rolled backward, and pop-started. But it cannot make it up the now rain-slicked mountain rock, though the driver tries for a terrifying twenty minutes with all the equipment and group again loaded inside. There is a Cuban military outpost a ways back down; the group makes its way there in the downpour, in the dark, and begs a patch of concrete floor to sleep on in a dwelling containing what Gallagher will refer to for the rest of the trip and maybe the rest of his life as The Worst Toilet in the World.

"This will be a great story to tell later," he keeps saying. He's been saying this for six days. He will continue to say it for eight more. But the writer is in no mood to agree with the principle that a good story is better than a good time, partly because she has become afflicted with diarrhea—the group has concluded that there must have been an accidental ingestion of a drop from the Bahía de Taco vat of river water—but also because people (read: men) who constantly tell stories of bad times are tedious, and she is basically certain she could write an equally compelling scene if this Cuban restricted-jungle military outpost in the mountains above Guantánamo had turned out to be home to a team of scrappy dogs attired in miniature formalwear and trained to serve cocktails to visitors—which would be a good time—rather than a toilet that in addition to being The Worst has no door to separate anyone who's using it from her comrades.

Earlier, the photographer sidled next to the writer and asked, as they both turned their faces away from the merciless beating of the oxen, a patch of protected Cuban forest being deforested with the tearing down of ever-larger branches and trees with which to assault them, "Do you ever wonder if this is all worth it? For a bird?" The two of them snickered darkly. Just moments before, a chunk of wood had cracked off an oxen-beating club as it broke over the animal's hide and shot past the photographer's head, missing him by maybe an inch. "One that almost definitely doesn't exist?"

.     .     .

"There is definitely a subset of people who are driven to this," famed birder and Pulitzer finalist Scott Weidensaul will later explain to the writer. There are birders (and other field biologists), he will say, who are driven to the extent of, "Let's save forty-five minutes of field time tomorrow by finishing this hike tonight in the dark, even though we may fall and break our necks." He has himself made "really bad decisions," he says, for which he could have died. Even in the absence of bad decisions, outcomes can be fatal. Ted Parker, another famed birder, did die, along with premier neotropical botanist Alwyn Gentry and leading Ecuadoran conservationist Eduardo Aspiazu Estrada, in a plane crash doing a treetop survey; so did Phoebe Snetsinger, then the most prolific birder in history, when her van rolled in Madagascar. Nathaniel Gerhart died in 2007 in a car accident in Indonesia—three years after he discovered previously unknown habitat of the Selva cacique—and so did Siarhei Abramchuk in 2010, from an encephalitis-bearing tick bite in Belarus. Subramanian Bhupathy, head of conservation biology at the Sálim Ali Centre for Ornithology and Natural History in India, died in 2014 after slipping down a hill and landing with a bamboo spike in his eye.

"I'm not saying that that's a decision I would necessarily make," Weidensaul will say of the hypothetical dangerous night hike. Though "part of that just becomes if you've gotten away with it in the past, you assume you're gonna get away with it in the future," he's taking fewer risks now. But "I certainly understand what drives somebody to make that kind of a decision. Just this driving passion to push yourself to the limit because you don't know what's on the other side of the next hill. Because you don't know what you're gonna find, and if at the end of the day you haven't done everything you possibly can, you leave yourself wondering: Well, what if I had?" Of Parque Nacional Alejandro de Humboldt, Weidensaul says, "If there's a reason there's an ivory-bill anywhere, it's there, it's because those are the places that are most difficult to get into."

When the group wakes up at dawn in the military outpost below Ojito de Agua, Lammertink secures four mules to carry gear. Two national park guards also arrive to accompany them. The sun comes out blazing. They climb uphill. When they make it to the manned station several miles up in the afternoon, they stop for a moment—but then continue on, five miles more to the clearing at Ojito de Agua, where Lammertink wants to make camp and mount searches. The writer, who has been ingesting food but has effectively not eaten in two days because of the diarrhea, becomes too weak to stand; they put her on a mule. They put Gallagher, who is growing increasingly tired, on another one. They reach Ojito de Agua shortly before dark, and it starts to rain as they set up their tents. The Cubans fill the designated treated-water receptacle with untreated water; Lammertink, the only fluent Spanish speaker, has not explained to them that the Americans are designating such a receptacle or why because he personally is not bothering with water treatment from this mountain spring. A partial list of untreated-water tragedies that have occurred in Lammertink's previous fieldwork includes: the death of a human man. That time even Lammertink didn't trust the water, so sketchy were the sources they were pulling it from in the Bornean jungle, but the field assistant, a local, wouldn't listen to anyone's warnings. Diphtheria came on fast after he went back home and turned worse quickly; by the time his family went for medical help, there was nothing anyone could do.

The photographer almost drinks the untreated water before the mistake is discovered.

The writer has already drunk a liter of it.

At Ojito de Agua, everyone in the small camp bathes and washes their hands and dishes in a stream that the mules are pissing and shitting in and near. The second night, one of the mules awakens the camp, moaning and thrashing and crashing around; it lies down, and then, to the great astonishment and helplessness of its Cuban masters, violently dies.

"This is not what normal birding is like," Gallagher clarifies at some point to the writer, in case this has been lost on her.

It starts to pour again. In the morning, they break dead-mule camp for fear of infection and rotting-mule smell and hike three miles to another, smaller clearing, perched on the side of a cliff where mosquitoes are swarming in great clouds. It rains again when they arrive to set up for three nights among the trees and underbrush, which in this area are covered with sharp thorns and spikes of varying lengths. When Lammertink stayed here twenty-five years ago, he brushed up against a plant that turned his forearm into a bloated, oozing, yellow-pus-seeping rash of open blisters that didn't close for five months and then didn't fade from scarring for "years." He doesn't know which plant it was, so he can't point it out.

But.

In between the moving, and machete-swinging through non-trails, and basic surviving:

Silence.

Between sweating and getting snagged and rained on, slipping over wet rocks in the middle or right on the side of a mountain, twenty flights of elevation before even seven-thirty a.m. one day (the writer climbing under her own power, as her stool has miraculously solidified):

They stop. They strap up the double-knocker. They turn on recorders, and write down coordinates, and call to the ivory-bill.

*BAM-bam.*

They wait, collectively, for hours, sitting or standing quietly, for a response. *BAM-bam.* Waiting. *Kent-kent* through the speakers; waiting. Hiking and trudging and starting over. In all that stillness and hard staring, it's easy to understand how an anticipation broken by a bird finally bursting forth would evoke sobs, as it immediately did in the guy Gallagher saw the ivory-bill with in 2004—after they'd dodged countless close calls with poisonous water moccasins in the southeastern American swamp.

But in Cuba, one never does burst forth. Worse, there are not even any signs in this place, the last place in the country where ivory-bills lived, that they were here anytime recently. There are no foraging signs, none of the bark-scaling and bark-stripping ivory-bills do. No recent cavities. The forest is not even as ivory-bill-friendly as Lammertink would like. Though protected, it's dense. The regrowth pines don't have enough light and space to grow into big ivory-bill habitat. There are no reports among locals, not even crappy secondhand rumors that one has been seen or heard in decades, excepting one witness who they will go check out when they leave the woods. All of the interviews with potential witnesses they've tracked down so far have been hopeless: The one with El Indio's father that contained The Twist, the one with the former logger they passed on the way to the national park station who said no one had seen the bird after the eighties, the one with the ninety-one-year-old in Farallones who said ivory-bills were everywhere when he was a kid but not since and kept trying to steer the conversation away from extinct birds ("He says, 'We're all made out of dust and to dust we will return,'" Lammertink translated. "His wife passed away three years ago, and he believes she now lives in eternity, or something") as Lammertink mightily steered it toward extinct birds again and again ("There's probably at this age more pressing questions than ivory-bills," he said as he finally gave up).

Sitting down in camp on the final night, Lammertink pronounces that the worst day in the field is better than the best day in the office. He became captivated by woodpeckers in general and ivory-bills in specific when he picked up a book on the bird family by chance in a library at age eleven. When he graduated high school, he worked at a dairy factory to save money to finance his trip to come here and look for them, and this time, he is satisfied with how much ground he's covered. He is hungry, since he ate only a handful of stale crackers for lunch on another hard-charging day of traveling and double-knocking, and thirsty, since he lost his water bottle at some point in doing so. Having observed the character of his interactions with the other members of the group for almost two weeks, the writer has circled in her notes to ask him if he likes birds better than people, but on this last night she sits down next to him and asks instead if he cares more about birds than he does about himself.

He pauses for a long, long time, and stutters. He allows when pressed that the botflies are a gross and painful annoyance but a small one and maybe he should put more DEET on his clothes. But when you're getting up close on a bird and you feel a mosquito land, you can't just be swatting around like a maniac. No. You can barely dare to breathe. He doesn't think he would kill himself over a bird. Not deliberately. Yes he's had dengue fever and malaria, and he died once. Well didn't quite die, but came close to dying, when he and a field assistant were swarmed by thousands of bees in Borneo. They were in and out of consciousness after, ferocious puking and diarrhea while some villagers tried to pluck thousands of stingers from their faces and backs and arms, and others stood around saying they wouldn't make it for sure. It was an oriental honey-buzzard, which rips open bees' nests, that had whipped them up and caused the whole event; Lammertink had never seen one of the birds, and he was pretty excited until the bees attacked. He and the field assistant are married now and have two children. "I've been doing this now for, let's see, twenty-five years, fieldwork in tropical areas, and you know, I'm still alive," he says. He laughs. "So, why not do it for another twenty-five years?" He is not a thrill seeker. Not even a risk seeker, he says. He acknowledges that some of the work he does is risky, "but it's always for some kind of conservation project, and if something goes terribly wrong, at least in my last moments, I know it was for some greater cause."

In the morning, Lammertink, who can endure almost anything but cannot abide an unshaven face, shaves by feel beside the cold creek. The group packs up camp. They march eight miles over a mountain ridge and out of the forest, stopping for a last double-knock session, finally coming out the side opposite the one they entered—north, back up in Farallones. Both birders say, as they emerge filthy from the trees, that it does seem like the ivory-bill is dead in Cuba. Lammertink's earlier conclusions, he reconcludes, are confirmed. The little bit of hope he was holding is squashed.

But.

Wait.

The ivory-bill is not given up so easily.

After a night of sleep back at the first jungle shack, the birders decide, while the photographer and writer are out of earshot, that they will go back into the woods. Today. There is still that last witness, who someone said saw one in 2008 and heard one in 2011. They haven't interviewed him yet. They are on their way to interview him this morning. If he seems credible, they will ditch the writer and photographer and round up some mules and hike right back into the mountains for another double-knock session tonight, and another at dawn, and then try to race back out and to a driver and to the airport hours away over barely-roads to make their flight tomorrow.

*There's hope!* Gallagher thinks, perking up out of his dire exhaustion, in which he barely staggered out of the woods just yesterday. *We can still do this!*

.   .   .

The witness says he saw ivory-bills, all right.

He saw them in 1971.

Gallagher is crushed. His throat is thick with grief and near-crying when he comes into the writer's hotel room the next day to confess the plan to jettison her and continue the expedition, foiled only by the confirmation of a faulty report. "I just suddenly . . ." he says. "I thought: These birds are really gone." His swallows are heavy. "I mean, I'm the most optimistic person in the world, and it was just . . . inescapable to me. And I almost felt guilty, as though, like, me giving up made it so. It was really like having a loved one on a ventilator or something, and they're already gone, and you just have to make that decision to give up."

He thinks other people should keep looking here. Even though he feels sure the birds aren't here. He doesn't know why. He says it's hard to say. He himself won't come back, though, unless there's a solid sighting. This is it for him.

Here in Cuba, anyway! He's talking about the *Cuban* ivory-bill. He will continue to float the rivers and bayous of the American Southeast looking—Oh yes! he says. Because that's who he is. He will never give up the dream of finding one in America, though he's been mired in controversy since the first time he proclaimed that he had—the catalyst of the highest-profile birder fight in modern history. Weidensaul, when saying on the record that he considers Gallagher's sighting "persuasive," equates that admission to "driving nails into the coffin of my professional reputation."

"I need to go, to exclude the possibility that they're there," Lammertink had said at the Toronto airport, before they left. "It's too important not to check."

"Of course, it's a real long shot, and probably nothing will happen," Gallagher had said the same day. "But as in fishing, if you don't put your fly in the water, there's no chance you're gonna catch anything. You could go to some stream and go, This is a terrible-looking stream, or whatever, or unlikely to have trout, but I'll cast the fly out there. And I've caught trout in some really unusual places." If he can keep that kind of hope up for trout, what can't he do for birds, with which he's been in love since he was talking to them out on his grandmother's porch as a three-year-old while his father, a sailor who was sunk three times in World War II and came back a scary drunk, knocked her around inside. "Someone's gotta do it, or it's not gonna get done."

The writer and the photographer don't understand, haven't understood, the risks the birders take. But one could argue that the writer and photographer do—that they are on this very trip doing—the same for their own work. The birders' passion does bring maybe balance but certainly conservation successes sometimes to this planet. The sightings in the eighties got the forest they've just exited protected, and perhaps not a moment too soon—three of the areas where George Lamb photographed the ivory-bills in the fifties are completely logged and mined out, in a country that is really just now opening up and increasing infrastructure and investment. Gallagher's alleged 2004 sighting helped get more of a singular and threatened American landscape preserved. It's hard to argue that it was a bad outcome, regardless of whether there were ivory-bills in it. Back in the day, early explorers did outrageous things to discover the world when it was still wild and unknown. So do their modern counterparts, who are trying to prove it still is, and to keep little pieces of it that way.

On the way to Farallones, back on the first day, the group stopped by the side of the road for a bathroom break. Though it's currently the only road connecting all the cities in Cuba's northeast, they didn't bother to properly pull over. They climbed out, dusty and jeep-shook. Not a car passed. After they'd all returned from their visits to the surrounding woods, they stood stretching their legs quietly until Gallagher intoned, in his best voiceover impression as he gazed toward the trees, "And they stopped for a bathroom break, and suddenly, there was an ivory-bill!" his face lit brighter than two bottles of prosecco at the possibility.

## New York Times Magazine

**WINNER—PUBLIC INTEREST**

*"This category honors magazine journalism that illuminates issues of local, national or international importance." So reads the description of the National Magazine Award for Public Interest published annually in the call for entries. Rarely is the winner of the Ellie in this category as surprisingly personal as it was in 2017. In "Worlds Apart," Nikole Hannah-Jones described the effects of modern-day school segregation on her own family as she explored the legacy of decades of misguided policies affecting both housing and education. Hannah-Jones's story "Segregation Now," published in* The Atlantic, *was nominated as a finalist in Public Interest two years ago. She joined the* New York Times Magazine *as a staff writer in 2015.*

## Nikole Hannah-Jones

# Worlds Apart

In the spring of 2014, when our daughter, Najya, was turning four, my husband and I found ourselves facing our toughest decision since becoming parents. We live in Bedford-Stuyvesant, a low-income, heavily black, rapidly gentrifying neighborhood of brownstones in central Brooklyn. The nearby public schools are named after people intended to evoke black uplift, like Marcus Garvey, a prominent black nationalist in the 1920s, and Carter G. Woodson, the father of Black History Month, but the schools are a disturbing reflection of New York City's stark racial and socioeconomic divisions. In one of the most diverse cities in the world, the children who attend these schools learn in classrooms where all of their classmates—and I mean, in most cases, every single one—are black and Latino, and nearly every student is poor. Not surprisingly, the test scores of most of Bed-Stuy's schools reflect the marginalization of their students.

I didn't know any of our middle-class neighbors, black or white, who sent their children to one of these schools. They had managed to secure seats in the more diverse and economically advantaged magnet schools or gifted-and-talented programs outside our area or opted to pay hefty tuition to progressive but largely white private institutions. I knew this because from the moment we arrived in New York with our one-year-old, we had many conversations about where we would, should, and definitely should not send our daughter to school when the time came.

My husband, Faraji, and I wanted to send our daughter to public school. Faraji, the oldest child in a military family, went to public schools that served army bases both in America and abroad. As a result, he had a highly unusual experience for a black American child: He never attended a segregated public school a day of his life. He can now walk into any room and instantly start a conversation with the people there, whether they are young mothers gathered at a housing-project tenants' meeting or executives eating from small plates at a ritzy cocktail reception.

I grew up in Waterloo, Iowa, on the wrong side of the river that divided white from black, opportunity from struggle, and started my education in a low-income school that my mother says was distressingly chaotic. I don't recall it being bad, but I do remember just one white child in my first-grade class, though there may have been more. That summer, my mom and dad enrolled my older sister and me in the school district's voluntary desegregation program, which allowed some black kids to leave their neighborhood schools for whiter, more well off ones on the west side of town. This was 1982, nearly three decades after the Supreme Court ruled in *Brown v. Board of Education* that separate schools for black and white children were unconstitutional, and near the height of desegregation in this country. My parents chose one of the whitest, richest schools, thinking it would provide the best opportunities for us. Starting in second grade, I rode the bus an hour each morning across town to the "best" public school my town had to offer, Kingsley Elementary, where I was among the tiny number of working-class children and the even tinier number of black children. We did not walk to school or get dropped off by our parents on their way to work. We showed up in a yellow bus, visitors in someone else's neighborhood, and were whisked back across the bridge each day as soon as the bell rang.

I remember those years as emotionally and socially fraught but also as academically stimulating and world-expanding. Aside from the rigorous classes and quality instruction I received, this was the first time I'd shared dinners in the homes of kids whose parents were doctors and lawyers and scientists. My mom was a probation officer, and my dad drove a bus, and most of my family members on both sides worked in factories or meatpacking plants or did other manual labor. I understood, even then, in a way both intuitive and defensive, that my school friends' parents weren't better than my neighborhood friends' parents, who worked hard every day at hourly jobs. But this exposure helped me imagine possibilities, a course for myself that I had not considered before.

It's hard to say where any one person would have ended up if a single circumstance were different; our life trajectories are shaped by so many external and internal factors. But I have no doubt my parents' decision to pull me out of my segregated neighborhood school made the possibility of my getting from there to here—staff writer for the *New York Times Magazine*—more likely.

Integration was transformative for my husband and me. Yet the idea of placing our daughter in one of the small number of integrated schools troubled me. These schools are disproportionately white and serve the middle and upper-middle classes, with a smattering of poor black and Latino students to create "diversity."

In a city where white children are only 15 percent of the more than one million public-school students, half of them are clustered in just 11 percent of the schools, which not coincidentally include many of the city's top performers. Part of what makes those schools desirable to white parents, aside from the academics, is that they have some students of color, but not too many. This carefully curated integration, the kind that allows many white parents to boast that their children's public schools look like the United Nations, comes at a steep cost for the rest of the city's black and Latino children.

The New York City public-school system is 41 percent Latino, 27 percent black, and 16 percent Asian. Three-quarters of all students are low-income. In 2014, the Civil Rights Project at the University of California, Los Angeles, released a report showing that New York City public schools are among the most segregated in the country. Black and Latino children here have become increasingly isolated, with 85 percent of black students and 75 percent of Latino students attending "intensely" segregated schools—schools that are less than 10 percent white.

This is not just New York's problem. I've spent much of my career as a reporter chronicling rampant school segregation in every region of the country and the ways that segregated schools harm black and Latino children. One study published in 2009 in *The Journal of Policy Analysis and Management* showed that the academic achievement gap for black children increased as they spent time in segregated schools. Schools with large numbers of black and Latino kids are less likely to have experienced teachers, advanced courses, instructional materials, and adequate facilities, according to the United States Department of Education's Office for Civil Rights. Most black and Latino students today are segregated by both race and class, a combination that wreaks havoc on the learning environment. Research stretching back fifty years shows that the socioeconomic makeup of a school can play a larger role in achievement than the poverty of an individual student's family. Getting Najya into one of the disproportionately white schools in the city felt like accepting the inevitability of this two-tiered system: one set of schools with excellent resources for white kids and some black and Latino middle-class kids, a second set of underresourced schools for the rest of the city's black and Latino kids.

When the New York City Public Schools catalogue arrived in the mail one day that spring, with information about Mayor Bill de Blasio's new universal prekindergarten program, I told Faraji that I wanted to enroll Najya in a segregated, low-income school. Faraji's eyes widened as I explained that if we removed Najya, whose name we chose because it means "liberated" and "free" in Swahili, from the experience of most black and Latino children, we would be part of the problem. Saying my child deserved access to "good" public schools felt like implying that children in "bad" schools deserved the schools they got, too. I understood that so much of school segregation is structural—a result of decades of housing discrimination, of political calculations and the machinations of policy makers, of simple inertia. But I also believed that it is the choices of individual parents that uphold the system, and I was determined not to do what I'd seen so many others do when their values about integration collided with the reality of where to send their own children to school.

One family, or even a few families, cannot transform a segregated school, but if none of us were willing to go into them, nothing would change. Putting our child into a segregated school would not integrate it racially, but we are middle-class and would, at least, help to integrate it economically. As a reporter, I'd witnessed how the presence of even a handful of middle-class families made it less likely that a school would be neglected. I also knew that we would be able to make up for Najya anything the school was lacking.

As I told Faraji my plan, he slowly shook his head no. He wanted to look into parochial schools or one of the "good" public schools or even private schools. So we argued, pleading our cases from the living room, up the steps to our office lined with books on slavery and civil rights, and back down, before we came to an impasse and retreated to our respective corners. There is nothing harder than navigating our nation's racial legacy in this country, and the problem was that we each knew the other was right and wrong at the same time. Faraji couldn't believe that I was asking him to expose our child to the type of education that the two of us had managed to avoid. He worried that we would be hurting Najya if we put her in a high-poverty, all-black school. "Are we experimenting with our child based on our idealism about public schools?" he asked. "Are we putting her at a disadvantage?"

At the heart of Faraji's concern was a fear that grips black families like ours. We each came from working-class roots, fought our way into the middle class, and had no family wealth or safety net to fall back on. Faraji believed that our gains were too tenuous to risk putting our child in anything but a top-notch school. And he was right to be worried. In 2014, the Brookings Institution found that black children are particularly vulnerable to downward mobility—nearly seven of ten black children born into middle-income families don't maintain that income level as adults. There was no margin for error, and we had to use our relative status to fight to give Najya every advantage. Hadn't we worked hard, he asked, frustration building in his voice, precisely so that she would not have to go to the types of schools that trapped so many black children?

Eventually I persuaded him to visit a few schools with me. Before work, we peered into the classrooms of three neighborhood schools, and a fourth, Public School 307, located in the Vinegar Hill section of Brooklyn, near the East River waterfront and a few miles from our home. PS 307's attendance zone was drawn snugly around five of the ten buildings that make up the Farragut Houses, a public-housing project with 3,200 residents across from the Brooklyn Navy Yard. The school's population was 91 percent black and Latino. Nine of ten students met federal poverty standards. But what went on inside the school was unlike what goes on in most schools serving the city's poorest children. This was in large part because of the efforts of a remarkable principal, Roberta Davenport. She grew up in Farragut, and her younger siblings attended PS 307. She became principal five decades later in 2003, to a low-performing school. Davenport commuted from Connecticut, but her car was usually the first one in the parking lot each morning, often because she worked so late into the night that, exhausted, she would sleep at a friend's nearby instead of making the long drive home. Soft of voice but steely in character, she rejected the spare educational orthodoxy often reserved for poor black and brown children that strips away everything that makes school joyous in order to focus solely on improving test scores. These children from the projects learned Mandarin, took violin lessons and played chess. Thanks to her hard work, the school had recently received money from a federal magnet grant, which funded a science, engineering, and technology program aimed at drawing middle-class children from outside its attendance zone.

Faraji and I walked the bright halls of PS 307, taking in the reptiles in the science room and the students learning piano during music class. The walls were papered with the precocious musings of elementary children. While touring the schools, Faraji later told me, he started feeling guilty about his instinct to keep Najya out of them. Were these children, he asked himself, worthy of any less than his own child? "These are kids who look like you," he told me. "Kids like the ones you grew up with. I was being very selfish about it, thinking: I am going to get mine for my child, and that's it. And I am ashamed of that."

When it was time to submit our school choices to the city, we put down all four of the schools we visited. In May 2014, we learned Najya had gotten into our first choice, PS 307. We were excited but also nervous. I'd be lying if I said I didn't feel pulled in the way other parents with options feel pulled. I had moments when I couldn't ignore the nagging fear that in my quest for fairness, I was being unfair to my own daughter. I worried—I worry still—about whether I made the right decision for our little girl. But I knew I made the just one.

·     ·     ·

For many white Americans, millions of black and Latino children attending segregated schools may seem like a throwback to another era, a problem we solved long ago. And legally, we did. In 1954, the Supreme Court issued its landmark *Brown v. Board of Education* ruling, striking down laws that forced black and white children to attend separate schools. But while *Brown v. Board* targeted segregation by state law, we have proved largely unwilling to address segregation that is maintained by other means, resulting from the nation's long and racist history.

In the Supreme Court's decision, the justices responded unanimously to a group of five cases, including that of Linda Brown, a black eight-year-old who was not allowed to go to her white neighborhood school in Topeka, Kan., but was made to ride a bus to a black school much farther away. The court determined that separate schools, even if they had similar resources, were "inherently"—by their nature—unequal, causing profound damage to the children who attended them and hobbling their ability to live as full citizens of their country. The court's decision hinged on sociological research, including a key study by the psychologists Kenneth Clark and Mamie Phipps Clark, a husband-and-wife team who gave black children in segregated schools in the North and the South black and white dolls and asked questions about how they perceived them. Most students described the white dolls as good and smart and the black dolls as bad and stupid. (The Clarks also found that segregation hurt white children's development.) Chief Justice Earl Warren felt so passionate about the issue that he read the court's opinion aloud: "Does segregation of children in public schools solely on the basis of race, even though the physical facilities and other 'tangible' factors may be equal, deprive the children of the minority group of equal educational opportunities? We believe that it does." The ruling made clear that because this nation was founded on a racial caste system, black children would never become equals as long as they were separated from white children.

In New York City, home to the largest black population in the country, the decision was celebrated by many liberals as the final strike against school segregation in the "backward" South. But Kenneth Clark, the first black person to earn a doctorate in psychology at Columbia University and to hold a permanent professorship at City College of New York, was quick to dismiss Northern righteousness on race matters. At a meeting of the Urban League around the time of the decision, he charged that though New York had no law requiring segregation, it intentionally separated its students by assigning them to schools based on their race or building schools deep in segregated neighborhoods. In many cases, Clark said, black children were attending schools that were worse than those attended by their black counterparts in the South.

Clark's words shamed proudly progressive white New Yorkers and embarrassed those overseeing the nation's largest school system. The New York City Board of Education released a forceful statement promising to integrate its schools: "Segregated, racially homogeneous schools damage the personality of minority-group children. These schools decrease their motivation and thus impair their ability to learn. White children are also damaged. Public education in a racially homogeneous setting is socially unrealistic and blocks the attainment of the goals of democratic education, whether this segregation occurs by law or by fact." The head of the Board of Education undertook an investigation in 1955 that confirmed the widespread separation of black and Puerto Rican children in dilapidated buildings with the least-experienced and least-qualified teachers. Their schools were so overcrowded that some black children went to school for only part of the day to give others a turn.

The Board of Education appointed a commission to develop a citywide integration plan. But when school officials took some token steps, they faced a wave of white opposition. "It was most intense in the white neighborhoods closest to African American neighborhoods, because they were the ones most likely to be affected by desegregation plans," says Thomas Sugrue, a historian at New York University and the author of *Sweet Land of Liberty: The Forgotten Struggle for Civil Rights in the North*. By the mid-1960s, there were few signs of integration in New York's schools. In fact, the number of segregated junior-high schools in the city had quadrupled by 1964. That February, civil rights leaders called for a major one-day boycott of the New York City schools. Some 460,000 black and Puerto Rican students stayed home to protest their segregation. It was the largest demonstration for civil rights in the nation's history. But the boycott upset many white liberals, who thought it was too aggressive, and as thousands of white families fled to the suburbs, the integration campaign collapsed.

Even as New York City was ending its only significant effort to desegregate, the Supreme Court was expanding the *Brown* ruling. Beginning in the mid-1960s, the court handed down a series of decisions that determined that not only did *Brown v. Board* allow the use of race to remedy the effects of long-segregated schools, it also *required* it. Assigning black students to white schools and vice versa was necessary to destroy a system built on racism—even if white families didn't like it. "All things being equal, with no history of discrimination, it might well be desirable to assign pupils to schools nearest their homes," the court wrote in its 1971 ruling in *Swann v. Charlotte-Mecklenburg Board of Education*, which upheld busing to desegregate schools in Charlotte, N.C. "But all things are not equal in a system that has been deliberately constructed and maintained to enforce racial segregation. The remedy for such segregation may be administratively awkward, inconvenient and even bizarre in some situations, and may impose burdens on some; but all awkwardness and inconvenience cannot be avoided."

In what would be an extremely rare and fleeting moment in American history, all three branches of the federal government aligned on the issue. Congress passed the 1964 Civil Rights Act,

pushed by President Lyndon B. Johnson, which prohibited segregated lunch counters, buses, and parks and allowed the
Department of Justice for the first time to sue school districts to
force integration. It also gave the government the power to with-
hold federal funds if the districts did not comply. By 1973, 91 percent of black children in the former Confederate and border
states attended school with white children.

But while Northern congressmen embraced efforts to force
integration in the South, some balked at efforts to desegregate
their own schools. They tucked a passage into the 1964 Civil Rights
Act aiming to limit school desegregation in the North by prohibiting school systems from assigning students to schools in order to
integrate them unless ordered to do so by a court. Because Northern officials often practiced segregation without the cover of law,
it was far less likely that judges would find them in violation of
the Constitution.

Not long after, the nation began its retreat from integration.
Richard Nixon was elected president in 1968, with the help of a
coalition of white voters who opposed integration in housing and
schools. He appointed four conservative justices to the Supreme
Court and set the stage for a profound legal shift. Since 1974,
when the *Milliken v. Bradley* decision struck down a lower court's
order for a metro-area-wide desegregation program between
nearly all-black Detroit city schools and the white suburbs surrounding the city, a series of major Supreme Court rulings on
school desegregation have limited the reach of *Brown*.

When Ronald Reagan became president in 1981, he promoted
the notion that using race to integrate schools was just as bad as
using race to segregate them. He urged the nation to focus on
improving segregated schools by holding them to strict standards, a tacit return to the "separate but equal" doctrine that was
roundly rejected in *Brown*. His administration emphasized that
busing and other desegregation programs discriminated against
white students. Reagan eliminated federal dollars earmarked to

help desegregation and pushed to end hundreds of school-desegregation court orders.

Yet this was the very period when the benefits of integration were becoming most apparent. By 1988, a year after Faraji and I entered middle school, school integration in the United States had reached its peak and the achievement gap between black and white students was at its lowest point since the government began collecting data. The difference in black and white reading scores fell to half what it was in 1971, according to data from the National Center for Education Statistics. (As schools have since resegregated, the test-score gap has only grown.) The improvements for black children did not come at the cost of white children. As black test scores rose, so did white ones.

Decades of studies have affirmed integration's power. A 2010 study released by the Century Foundation found that when children in public housing in Montgomery County, Md., enrolled in middle-class schools, the differences between their scores and those of their wealthier classmates decreased by half in math and a third in reading, and they pulled significantly ahead of their counterparts in poor schools. In fact, integration changes the entire trajectory of black students' lives. A 2015 longitudinal study by the economist Rucker Johnson at the University of California, Berkeley, followed black adults who had attended desegregated schools and showed that these adults, when compared with their counterparts or even their own siblings in segregated schools, were less likely to be poor, suffer health problems, and go to jail and more likely to go to college and reside in integrated neighborhoods. They even lived longer. Critically, these benefits were passed on to their children while the children of adults who went to segregated schools were more likely to perform poorly in school or drop out.

But integration as a constitutional mandate, as justice for black and Latino children, as a moral righting of past wrongs, is no longer our country's stated goal. The Supreme Court has effectively sided with Reagan, requiring strict legal colorblindness even if it leaves segregation intact and even striking down desegregation programs that ensured integration for thousands of black students if a single white child did not get into her school of choice. The most recent example was a 2007 case that came to be known as Parents Involved. White parents in Seattle and Jefferson County, Kentucky, challenged voluntary integration programs, claiming the districts discriminated against white children by considering race as a factor in apportioning students among schools in order to keep them racially balanced. Five conservative justices struck down these integration plans. In 1968, the court ruled in *Green v. County School Board of New Kent County* that we should no longer look across a city and see a "'white' school and a 'Negro' school, but just schools." In 2007, Chief Justice John Roberts Jr. wrote: "Before Brown, schoolchildren were told where they could and could not go to school based on the color of their skin. The school districts in these cases have not carried the heavy burden of demonstrating that we should allow this once again—even for very different reasons. . . . The way to stop discrimination on the basis of race is to stop discriminating on the basis of race."

Legally and culturally, we've come to accept segregation once again. Today, across the country, black children are more segregated than they have been at any point in nearly half a century. Except for a few remaining court-ordered desegregation programs, intentional integration almost never occurs unless it's in the interests of white students. This is even the case in New York City, under the stewardship of Mayor de Blasio, who campaigned by highlighting the city's racial and economic inequality. De Blasio and his schools chancellor, Carmen Fariña, have acknowledged that they don't believe their job is to force school integration. "I want to see diversity in schools organically," Fariña said at a town-hall meeting in Lower Manhattan in February. "I don't want to see mandates." The shift in language that trades the word "integration" for "diversity" is critical. Here in this city, as in many, diversity functions as a boutique offering for the children of the privileged but does little to ensure quality education for poor black and Latino children.

"The moral vision behind *Brown v. Board of Education* is dead," Ritchie Torres, a city councilman who represents the Bronx and has been pushing the city to address school segregation, told me. Integration, he says, is seen as "something that would be nice to have but not something we need to create a more equitable society. At the same time, we have an intensely segregated school system that is denying a generation of kids of color a fighting chance at a decent life."

.      .      .

Najya, of course, had no idea about any of this. She just knew she loved PS 307, waking up each morning excited to head to her pre-K class, where her two best friends were a little black girl named Imani from Farragut and a little white boy named Sam, one of a handful of white pre-K students at the school, with whom we carpooled from our neighborhood. Four excellent teachers, all of them of color, guided Najya and her classmates with a professionalism and affection that belied the school's dismal test scores. Faraji and I threw ourselves into the school, joining the parent-teacher association and the school's leadership team, attending assemblies and chaperoning field trips. We found ourselves relieved at how well things were going. Internally, I started to exhale.

But in the spring of 2015, as Najya's first year was nearing its end, we read in the news that another elementary school, PS 8, less than a mile from PS 307 in affluent Brooklyn Heights, was plagued by overcrowding. Some students zoned for that school might be rerouted to ours. This made geographic sense. PS 8's zone was expansive, stretching across Brooklyn Heights under the Manhattan bridge to the Dumbo neighborhood and Vinegar Hill, the neighborhood around PS 307. PS 8's lines were drawn when most of the development there consisted of factories and warehouses. But gentrification overtook Dumbo, which hugs the East River and provides breathtaking views of the skyline and a quick commute to Manhattan. The largely upper-middle-class and white and Asian children living directly across the street from PS 307 were zoned to the heavily white PS 8.

To accommodate the surging population, PS 8 had turned its drama and dance rooms into general classrooms and cut its pre-K, but it still had to place up to twenty-eight kids in each class. Meanwhile, PS 307 sat at the center of the neighborhood population boom, half empty. Its attendance zone included only the Farragut Houses and was one of the tiniest in the city. Because Farragut residents were aging, with dwindling numbers of school-age children, PS 307 was underenrolled.

In early spring 2015, the city's Department of Education sent out notices telling fifty families that had applied to kindergarten at PS 8 that their children would be placed on the waiting list and instead guaranteed admission to PS 307. Distraught parents dashed off letters to school administrators and to their elected officials. They pleaded their case to the press. "We bought a home here, and one of the main reasons was because it was known that kindergarten admissions [at PS 8] were pretty much guaranteed," one parent told the *New York Post*, adding that he wouldn't send his child to PS 307. Another parent whose twins had secured coveted spots made the objections to PS 307 more plain: "I would be concerned about safety," he said. "I don't hear good things about that school."

That May, as I sat at a meeting that PS 8 parents arranged with school officials, I was struck by the sheer power these parents had drawn into that auditorium. This meeting about the overcrowding at PS 8, which involved fifty children in a system of more than one million, had summoned a state senator, a state assemblywoman, a City Council member, the city comptroller and the staff members of several other elected officials. It had rarely been clearer to me how segregation and integration, at their core, are about power and who gets access to it. As the Rev. Dr. Martin Luther King Jr. wrote in 1967: "I cannot see how the Negro will totally be liberated from the crushing weight of poor education, squalid housing and economic strangulation until he is integrated, with power, into every level of American life."

As the politicians looked on, two white fathers gave an impassioned PowerPoint presentation in which they asked the Department of Education to place more children into already-teeming classrooms rather than send kids zoned to PS 8 to PS 307. Another speaker, whose child had been wait-listed, choked up as he talked about having to break it to his kindergarten-age son that he would not be able to go to school with the children with whom he'd shared play dates and Sunday dinners. "We haven't told him yet" that he didn't get into PS 8, the father said, as eyes in the crowd grew misty. "We hope to never have to tell him."

The meeting was emotional and at times angry, with parents shouting out their anxieties about safety and low test scores at PS 307. But the concerns they voiced may have also masked something else. While suburban parents, who are mostly white, say they are selecting schools based on test scores, the racial makeup of a school actually plays a larger role in their school decisions, according to a 2009 study published in *The American Journal of Education*. Amy Stuart Wells, a professor of sociology and education at Columbia University's Teachers College, found the same thing when she studied how white parents choose schools in New York City. "In a postracial era, we don't have to say it's about race or the color of the kids in the building," Wells told me. "We can concentrate poverty and kids of color and then fail to provide the resources to support and sustain those schools, and then we can see a school full of black kids and then say, 'Oh, look at their test scores.' It's all very tidy now, this whole system."

I left that meeting upset about how PS 307 had been characterized, but I didn't give it much thought again until the end of summer, when Najya was about to start kindergarten. I heard that the community education council was holding a meeting to discuss a potential rezoning of PS 8 and PS 307. The council, an elected group that oversees twenty-eight public schools in District 13, including PS 8 and PS 307, is responsible for approving zoning decisions. School was still out for the summer, and almost no PS 307 parents knew plans were underway that could affect them. At the meeting, two men from the school system's Office of District Planning projected a rezoning map onto a screen. The plan would split the PS 8 zone roughly in half, divided by the Brooklyn Bridge. It would turn PS 8 into the exclusive neighborhood school for Brooklyn Heights and reroute Dumbo and Vinegar Hill students to PS 307. A tall, white man with brown hair that flopped over his forehead said he was from Concord Village, a complex that should have fallen on the 307 side of the line. He thanked the council for producing a plan that reflected his neighbors' concerns by keeping his complex in the PS 8 zone. It became clear that while parents in Farragut, Dumbo, and Vinegar Hill had not even known about the rezoning plan, some residents had organized and lobbied to influence how the lines were drawn.

The officials presented the rezoning plan, which would affect incoming kindergartners, as beneficial to everyone. If the children in the part of the zone newly assigned to PS 307 enrolled at the school, PS 8's overcrowding would be relieved at least temporarily. And PS 307, the officials' presentation showed, would fill its empty seats with white children and give all the school's students that most elusive thing: integration.

• • •

It was hard not to be skeptical about the department's plan. New York, like many deeply segregated cities, has a terrible track record of maintaining racial balance in formerly underenrolled segregated schools once white families come in. Schools like PS 321 in Brooklyn's Park Slope neighborhood and the Academy of Arts and Letters in Fort Greene tend to go through a brief period of transitional integration, in which significant numbers of white students enroll, and then the numbers of Latino and black students dwindle. In fact, that's exactly what happened at PS 8.

A decade ago, PS 8 was PS 307's mirror image. Predominantly filled with low-income black and Latino students from surrounding neighborhoods, PS 8, with its low test scores and low enrollment, languished amid a community of affluence because white parents in the neighborhood refused to send their children there. A group of parents worked hard with school administrators to turn the school around, writing grants to start programs for art and other enrichment activities. Then more white and Asian parents started to enroll their children. One of them was David Goldsmith, who later became president of the community education council tasked with considering the rezoning of PS 8 and PS 307. Goldsmith is white and, at the time, lived in Vinegar Hill with his Filipino wife and their daughter.

As PS 8 improved, more and more white families from Brooklyn Heights, Dumbo, and Vinegar Hill enrolled their children, and the classrooms in the lower grades became majority white. The whitening of the school had unintended consequences. Some of the black and Latino parents whose children had been in the school from the beginning felt as if they were being marginalized. The white parents were able to raise large sums at fund raisers and could be dismissive of the much smaller fund-raising efforts that had come before. Then, Goldsmith says, the new parents started seeking to separate their children from their poorer classmates. "There were kids in the school that were really high-risk kids, kids who were homeless, living in temporary shelters, you know, poverty can be really brutal," Goldsmith says. "The school was really committed to helping all children, but we had white middle-class parents saying, 'I don't want my child in the same class with the kid who has emotional issues.'"

The parents who had helped build PS 8, black, Latino, white, and Asian, feared they were losing something important, a truly diverse school that nurtured its neediest students, where families held equal value no matter the size of their paychecks. They asked for a plan to help the school maintain its black and Latino population by setting aside a percentage of seats for low-income children, but they didn't get approval.

PS 8's transformation to a school where only one in four students are black or Latino and only 14 percent are low-income began during the administration of Mayor Michael Bloomberg, known for its indifference toward efforts to integrate schools. But integration advocates say that they've also been deeply disappointed by the de Blasio administration's stance on the issue. In October 2014, after the release of the UCLA study pointing to the extreme segregation in the city's schools, and nearly a year after de Blasio was elected, Councilmen Ritchie Torres and Brad Lander moved to force the administration to address segregation, introducing what became the School Diversity Accountability Act, which would require the Department of Education to release school-segregation figures and report what it was doing to alleviate the problem. "It was always right in front of our faces," says Lander, a representative from Brooklyn, whose own children attend heavily white public schools. "Then the UCLA report hit, and the segregation in the city became urgent."

The same month that Lander and Torres introduced the bill, Fariña, the schools chancellor, took questions at a town-hall-style meeting for area schools held at PS 307. A group of four women, two white, two black, walked to the microphone to address Fariña. They said that they were parents in heavily gentrified Park Slope and that Fariña's administration had been ignoring their calls to help their school retain its diminishing black and Latino populations by implementing a policy to set aside seats for low-income children. Fariña, a diminutive woman with a no-nonsense attitude, responded by acknowledging that there "are no easy answers" to the problem of segregation and warned that there were "federal guidelines" limiting "what we can do around diversity." What Fariña was referring to is unclear. While the Supreme Court's 2007 ruling in Parents Involved tossed out integration plans that took into account the race of individual students, the court has never taken issue with using students' socioeconomic status for creating or preserving integration, which is what these parents were seeking. In addition, the Obama administration released guidelines in 2011 that explicitly outlined the ways school systems could legally use race to integrate schools. Those include drawing a school's attendance zone around black and white neighborhoods.

At another town-hall meeting in Manhattan last October, Fariña said, "You don't need to have diversity within one building." Instead, she suggested that poor students in segregated schools could be pen pals and share resources with students in wealthier, integrated public schools. "We adopt schools from China, Korea, or wherever," Fariña told the room of parents. "Why not in our own neighborhoods?" Integration advocates lambasted her for what they considered a callous portrayal of integration as nothing more than a cultural exchange. "Fariña's silly pen-pal comment shows how desensitized we've become," Torres told me. "It could be that the political establishment is willfully blind to the impact of racial segregation and has led themselves to believe that we can close the achievement gap without desegregating our school system. At worst it's a lie; at best it's a delusion." He continued, "The scandal is not that we are failing to achieve diversity. The scandal is we are not even trying."

Fariña would only talk to me for fifteen minutes by phone. She told me in May that her pen-pal comments had been taken out of context. "If you hear any of my public speeches, this has always been a priority of mine," she said. "Diversity of all types has always been a priority." She went on to talk about the city's special programs for autistic students and about how Japanese students have benefited from the expansion of dual-language programs. But Asian American students are already the group most integrated with white students. When pressed about integration specifically for black and Latino students, Fariña said the city has been working to support schools that are seeking more diversity and mentioned a socioeconomic integration pilot program at seven schools. "I do believe New York City is making strides. It is a major focus going forward."

On May 30, four days after our interview, the Department of Education said in an article in the *Daily News* that it was starting a voluntary systemwide "Diversity in Admissions" program and would be requesting proposals from principals. In 2014, several principals said they had submitted integration proposals and had not gotten any response from Fariña.

The announcement of the new initiative caught both principals and parents by surprise. Jill Bloomberg, principal at Brooklyn's Park Slope Collegiate, which teaches sixth through twelfth grade, says she learned about the initiative from the news article but otherwise had heard nothing about it, even though the deadline to submit proposals is July 8, about a month away. "I am eager for some official notification for exactly what the program is," she told me.

David Goldsmith, who has been working on desegregation efforts as a member of the community education council, says he found the initiative, its timing, and the short deadline for submitting proposals "puzzling." "We could be very cynical and say, 'They are not serious,'" he says.

Last June, de Blasio signed the School Diversity Accountability Act into law. But the law mandates only that the Department of Education report segregation numbers, not that it do anything to integrate schools. De Blasio declined to be interviewed, but when asked at a news conference in November why the city did not at least do what it could to redraw attendance lines, he defended the property rights of affluent parents who buy into neighborhoods to secure entry into heavily white schools. "You have to also respect families who have made a decision to live in a certain area," he said, because families have "made massive life decisions and investments because of which school their kid would go to." The mayor suggested there was little he could do because school segregation simply was a reflection of New York's stark housing segregation, entrenched by decades of discriminatory local and federal policy. "This is the history of America," he said.

Of course, de Blasio is right: Housing segregation and school segregation have always been entwined in America. But the opportunity to buy into "good" neighborhoods with "good" schools that de Blasio wants to protect has never been equally available to all.

●　　　●　　　●

To best understand how so many poor black and Latino children end up in neglected schools, and why so many white families have the money to buy into neighborhoods with the best schools, you need to look no further than the history of the Farragut Houses and PS 307. Looking at PS 307 today, you might find it hard to imagine that the school did not start out segregated. The low-slung brick elementary school, which opened in 1964, and the Farragut public-housing projects right outside its front doors once stood as hopeful, integrated islands in a city fractured by strict color lines in both its neighborhoods and its schools.

The ten Farragut buildings, spread across roughly eighteen acres, opened in 1952 as part of a scramble to house returning GIs and their families after World War II. When the first tenants moved in, the sprawling campus—named for David Farragut, an admiral of the United States Navy—was considered a model of progressive working-class housing, with its open green spaces, elevators, modern heating plant, laundry, and community center.

In 1952, a black woman named Gladys McBeth became one of Farragut's earliest tenants. Nearly three generations later, when I visited her in November, she was living in the same four-teenth-floor apartment, where she paid about $1,000 a month in rent. Back then, she said, Farragut was a place for strivers. "I didn't know nothing about projects when I moved in," she said. "It was veteran housing." The project housed roughly even num-bers of black and white tenants, including migrants escaping hardship from Poland, Puerto Rico, and Italy and from the feu-dal American South. To get in, everyone had to show proof of marriage, a husband's military-discharge papers, and pay stubs.

Robert McBeth, Gladys's husband, drove a truck while she stayed home raising their four children. In the years before the *Brown* decision, the oldest of the McBeth children went to a nearby school where the kids were predominantly black and Latino because the New York City Board of Education bused white children in the area to other schools, according to the NAACP. School officials at the time, as today, claimed the racial makeup of the schools was an inevitable result of residential segregation. Though Farragut was not yet segregated, most of the city was. And that segregation in housing often resulted from legal and open discrimination that was encouraged and condoned by the state, and at times required by the federal government.

Nowhere would that become more evident than in Farragut, which by the 1960s was careering toward the same fate overtak-ing nearly all public housing in big cities. White residents used Federal Housing Administration–insured loans to buy their way out of the projects and to move to shiny new middle-class subdi-visions. This subsidized home-buying boom led to one of the broadest expansions of the American middle class ever, almost exclusively to the benefit of white families. The FHA's explicitly racist underwriting standards, which rated black and integrated neighborhoods as uninsurable, made federally insured home loans largely unavailable to black home seekers. Ninety-eight percent of these loans made between 1934 and 1968 went to white Americans.

Housing discrimination was legal until 1968. Even if black Americans managed to secure home loans, many homes were off-limits, either because they had provisions in their deeds prohibiting their sale to black buyers or because entire communities—including publicly subsidized middle-class developments like Levittown on Long Island and Stuyvesant Town in Manhattan—barred black home buyers and tenants outright. The McBeths tried to buy a house, but like so many of Farragut's black tenants, they were not able to. They continued to rent while many of their white neighbors bought homes and built wealth. Scholars attribute a large part of the yawning wealth gap between black and white Americans—the typical white person has thirteen times the wealth of a typical black person—to discriminatory housing policies.

But before Farragut's white tenants left, parents of all colors sent their children to PS 307. Gladys McBeth, who died in May, sent her youngest child across the street to PS 307 and worked there as a school aide for twenty-three years. "It was one of the best schools in the district," she reminisced, sitting in a worn paisley chair. But by 1972, Farragut was more than 80 percent black, and to fill the vacant units and house the city's growing indigent population, the city changed the guideline for income and work requirements, turning the projects from largely working-class to low-income.

At some point, PS 307's attendance zone was redrawn to include only the Farragut Houses, ensuring the students would be black, Latino and poor. The New York City Department of Education does not keep attendance data before 2000, but as McBeth remembered it, by the late 1980s, PS 307 was also almost entirely black and Latino. McBeth, who sent all four of her children to college, shook her head. "It all changed."

.    .    .

PS 307 was a very different place from what it had been, but Najya was thriving. I watched as she and her classmates went from struggling to sound out three-letter words to reading entire books. She would surprise me in the car rides after school with her discussions of hypotheses and photosynthesis, words we hadn't taught her. And there was something almost breathtaking about witnessing an auditorium full of mostly low-income black and Latino children confidently singing in Mandarin and beating Chinese drums as they performed a fan dance to celebrate the Lunar New Year.

But I also knew how fragile success at a school like PS 307 could be. The few segregated, high-poverty schools we hold up as exceptions are almost always headed by a singular principal like Roberta Davenport. But relying on one dynamic leader is a precarious means of ensuring a quality education. With all the resources Davenport was able to draw to the school, PS 307's test scores still dropped this year. The school suffers from the same chronic absenteeism that plagues other schools with large numbers of low-income families. And then Davenport retired last summer, just as the clashes over PS 307's integration were heating up, causing alarm among parents.

Najya and the other children at PS 307 were unaware of the turmoil and the battle lines adults were drawing outside the school's doors. Faraji, my husband, had been elected copresident of PS 307's PTA along with Benjamin Greene, another black middle-class parent from Bed-Stuy, who also serves on the community education council. As the potential for rezoning loomed over the school, they were forced to turn their attention from fund raising and planning events to working to prevent the city's plan from ultimately creating another mostly white school.

It was important to them that Farragut residents, who were largely unaware of the process, had a say over what happened. Faraji and I had found it hard to bridge the class divides between the Farragut families and the middle-class black families, like ours, from outside the neighborhood. We parents were all cordial toward one another. Outside the school, though, we mostly went our separate ways. But after the rezoning was proposed, Faraji and Benjamin worked with the Rev. Dr. Mark V. C. Taylor of the Church of the Open Door, which sits on the Farragut property, and canvassed the projects to talk to parents and inform them of the city's proposal. Not one PS 307 parent they spoke to knew anything about the plan, and they were immediately worried and fearful about what it would mean for their children. PS 307 was that rare example of a well-resourced segregated school, and these parents knew it.

The Farragut parents were also angry and hurt over how their school and their children had been talked about in public meetings and the press. Some white Dumbo parents had told Davenport that they'd be willing to enroll their children only if she agreed to put the new students all together in their own classroom. Farragut parents feared their children would be marginalized. If the school eventually filled up with children from high-income white families—the median income for Dumbo and Vinegar Hill residents is almost ten times that of Farragut residents—the character of the school could change, and as had happened at other schools like PS 8, the results might not benefit the black and Latino students. Among other things, PS 307 might no longer qualify for federal funds for special programming, like free after-school care, to help low-income families.

"I don't have a problem with people coming in," Saaiba Coles, a Farragut mother with two children at PS 307, told those gathered at a community meeting about the rezoning. "I just don't want them to forget about the kids that were already here." Faraji and Benjamin collected and delivered to the education council a petition with more than 400 signatures of Farragut residents supporting the rezoning, but only under certain conditions, including that half of all the seats at PS 307 would be guaranteed for low-income children. That would ensure that the school remained truly integrated and that new higher-income parents would have to share power in deciding the direction of the school.

In January of this year, the education council held a meeting to vote on the rezoning. Nearly four dozen Farragut residents who'd taken two buses chartered by the church filed into the auditorium of a Brooklyn elementary school, sitting behind a cluster of anxious parents from Dumbo. Reporters lined up alongside them. In the months since the potential rezoning plan was announced, the spectacle of an integration fight in the progressive bastion of Brooklyn had attracted media attention. Coverage appeared in the *New York Times*, in the *Wall Street Journal*, and on WNYC. "Brooklyn hipsters fight school desegregation," the news site *Raw Story* proclaimed. The meeting lasted more than three hours as parents spoke passionately, imploring the council to delay the vote so that the two communities could try to get to know each other and figure out how they could bridge their economic, racial, and cultural divides. Both Dumbo and Farragut parents asked the district for leadership, fearing integration that was not intentionally planned would fail.

In the end, the council proceeded with the vote, approving the rezoning with a 50 percent low-income set-aside, but children living in PS 307's attendance zone would receive priority. But that's not a guarantee. White children under the age of five outnumber black and Latino children of the same age in the new zone, according to census data. And the white population will only grow as new developments go on the market. Without holding seats for low-income children, it's not certain the school will achieve 50 percent low-income enrollment.

David Goldsmith, president of the council, told me he didn't believe that creating low-income set-asides in only one school made sense; he is working to create a plan that would try to integrate the schools in the entire district that includes PS 8 and PS 307. But Benjamin Greene, who voted against the rezoning because it did not guarantee that half of the seats would remain for low-income children, said: "We cannot sit around and wait until somebody decides on this wonderful formula districtwide. We have to preserve these schools one at a time."

In voting for the rezoning, the council touted its bravery and boldness in choosing integration in a system that seemed opposed to it. "With the eyes of the nation upon us," Goldsmith began. "Voting 'yes' means we refuse to be victims of the past. We are ready to do this. The time is now. We owe this to our children."

But the decision felt more like a victory for the status quo. This rezoning did not occur because it was in the best interests of PS 307's black and Latino children but because it served the interests of the wealthy, white parents of Brooklyn Heights. PS 8 will only get whiter and more exclusive: the council failed to mention at the meeting that the plan would send future students from the only three Farragut buildings that had been zoned for PS 8 to PS 307, ultimately removing almost all the low-income students from PS 8 and turning it into one of the most affluent schools in the city. The Department of Education projects that within six years, PS 8 could be three-quarters white in a school system where only one-seventh of the kids are white.

PS 307 may eventually look similar. Without seats guaranteed for low-income children, and with an increasing white population in the zone, the school may flip and become mostly white and overcrowded. Farragut parents worry that at that point, the project's children, like those at PS 8, could be zoned out of their own school. A decade from now, integration advocates could be lamenting how PS 307 went from nearly all black and Latino to being integrated for a period to heavily white.

That transition isn't going to happen immediately, so some Dumbo parents have threatened to move or enroll their children in private schools. Others are struggling over what to do. By allowing such vast disparities between public schools—racially, socioeconomically, and academically—this city has made integration the hardest choice.

"You're not living in Brooklyn if you don't want to have a diverse system around your kid," Michael Jones, who lives in Brooklyn Heights and considered sending his twins to PS 307 for pre-K because PS 8 no longer offered it, told me over coffee. "You want it to be multicultural. You know, if you didn't want that, you'd be in private school, or you would be in a different area. So, we're all living in Brooklyn because we want that to be part of the upbringing. But you can understand how a parent might look at it and go, 'While I want diversity, I don't want profound imbalance.'" He thought about what it would have meant for his boys to be among the few middle-class children in PS 307. "We could look at it and see there is probably going to be a clash of some kind," he said. "My kid's not an experiment." In the end, he felt that he could not take a chance on his children's education and sent them to private preschool; they now go to PS 8.

This sense of helplessness in the face of such entrenched segregation is what makes so alluring the notion, embraced by liberals and conservatives, that we can address school inequality not with integration but by giving poor, segregated schools more resources and demanding of them more accountability. True integration, true equality, requires a surrendering of advantage, and when it comes to our own children, that can feel almost unnatural. Najya's first two years in public school helped me understand this better than I ever had before. Even Kenneth Clark, the psychologist whose research showed the debilitating effects of segregation on black children, chose not to enroll his children in the segregated schools he was fighting against. "My children," he said, "only have one life." But so do the children relegated to this city's segregated schools. They have only one life, too.

## New York

FINALIST—REPORTING

*Gabriel Sherman's reporting on the fall of Roger Ailes, the chairman and CEO of Fox News—including more than a dozen articles published online in* New York's *"Daily Intelligencer"— culminated in the cover story of the September 5, 2016, print issue. Headlined "The Revenge of Roger's Angels" (the cover line was the more evocative "Fox and Prey"), the story was, the Ellie judges said, "an astonishing example of what one tenacious reporter can accomplish despite undisguised hostility and attempted intimidation." Sherman knew the subject well—his biography of Ailes,* The Loudest Voice in the Room, *was published in 2014. Less than nine months after this story was published, Ailes was dead, the victim of a brain injury.*

Gabriel Sherman

# The Revenge of
# Roger's Angels

I t took fifteen days to end the mighty twenty-year reign of Roger
Ailes at Fox News, one of the most storied runs in media and
political history. Ailes built not just a conservative cable news
channel but something like a fourth branch of government; a
propaganda arm for the GOP; an organization that determined
Republican presidential candidates, sold wars, and decided the issues of the day for two million viewers. That the place turned out
to be rife with grotesque abuses of power has left even its liberal
critics stunned. More than two dozen women have come forward
to accuse Ailes of sexual harassment, and what they have exposed
is both a culture of misogyny and one of corruption and surveillance, smear campaigns and hush money, with implications reaching far wider than one disturbed man at the top.

It began, of course, with a lawsuit. Of all the people who might
have brought down Ailes, the former *Fox and Friends* anchor
Gretchen Carlson was among the least likely. A fifty-year-old former Miss America, she was the archetypal Fox anchor: blonde,
right-wing, proudly anti-intellectual. A memorable *Daily Show*
clip showed Carlson saying she needed to Google the words *czar*
and *ignoramus*. But television is a deceptive medium. Off-camera,
Carlson is a Stanford- and Oxford-educated feminist who chafed
at the culture of Fox News. When Ailes made harassing comments to her about her legs and suggested she wear tight-fitting

outfits after she joined the network in 2005, she tried to ignore him. But eventually he pushed her too far. When Carlson complained to her supervisor in 2009 about her cohost Steve Doocy, who she said condescended to her on and off the air, Ailes responded that she was "a man hater" and a "killer" who "needed to get along with the boys." After this conversation, Carlson says, her role on the show diminished. In September 2013, Ailes demoted her from the morning show *Fox and Friends* to the lower-rated two p.m. time slot.

Carlson knew her situation was far from unique: It was common knowledge at Fox that Ailes frequently made inappropriate comments to women in private meetings and asked them to twirl around so he could examine their figures, and there were persistent rumors that Ailes propositioned female employees for sexual favors. The culture of fear at Fox was such that no one would dare come forward. Ailes was notoriously paranoid and secretive—he built a multiroom security bunker under his home and kept a gun in his Fox office, according to *Vanity Fair*—and he demanded absolute loyalty from those who worked for him. He was known for monitoring employee e-mails and phone conversations and hiring private investigators. "Watch out for the enemy within," he told Fox's staff during one companywide meeting.

Taking on Ailes was dangerous, but Carlson was determined to fight back. She settled on a simple strategy: She would turn the tables on his surveillance. Beginning in 2014, according to a person familiar with the lawsuit, Carlson brought her iPhone to meetings in Ailes's office and secretly recorded him saying the kinds of things he'd been saying to her all along. "I think you and I should have had a sexual relationship a long time ago, and then you'd be good and better and I'd be good and better. Sometimes problems are easier to solve" that way, he said in one conversation. "I'm sure you can do sweet nothings when you want to," he said another time.

After more than a year of taping, she had captured numerous incidents of sexual harassment. Carlson's husband, sports agent Casey Close, put her in touch with his lawyer Martin Hyman, who introduced her to employment attorney Nancy Erika Smith. Smith had won a sexual-harassment settlement in 2008 for a woman who sued former New Jersey acting governor Donald DiFranceso. "I hate bullies," Smith told me. "I became a lawyer to fight bullies." But this was riskier than any case she'd tried. Carlson's Fox contract had a clause that mandated that employment disputes be resolved in private arbitration—which meant Carlson's case could be thrown out and Smith herself could be sued for millions for filing.

Carlson's team decided to circumvent the clause by suing Ailes personally rather than Fox News. They hoped that with the element of surprise, they would be able to prevent Fox from launching a preemptive suit that forced them into arbitration. The plan was to file in September 2016 in New Jersey Superior Court (Ailes owns a home in Cresskill, New Jersey). But their timetable was pushed up when, on the afternoon of June 23, Carlson was called into a meeting with Fox general counsel Dianne Brandi and senior executive VP Bill Shine, and fired the day her contract expired. Smith, bedridden following surgery for a severed hamstring, raced to get the suit ready. Over the Fourth of July weekend, Smith instructed an IT technician to install software on her firm's network and Carlson's electronic devices to prevent the use of spyware by Fox. "We didn't want to be hacked," Smith said. They filed their lawsuit on July 6.

Carlson and Smith were well aware that suing Ailes for sexual harassment would be big news in a post-Cosby media culture that had become more sensitive to women claiming harassment; still, they were anxious about going up against such a powerful adversary. What they couldn't have known was that Ailes's position at Fox was already much more precarious than ever before.

When Carlson filed her suit, 21st Century Fox executive chairman Rupert Murdoch and his sons, James and Lachlan, were in Sun Valley, Idaho, attending the annual Allen & Company media conference. James and Lachlan, who were not fans of Ailes's, had been taking on bigger and bigger roles in the company in recent years (technically, and much to his irritation, Ailes has reported to them since June 2015), and they were quick to recognize the suit as both a big problem—and an opportunity. Within hours, the Murdoch heirs persuaded their eighty-five-year-old father, who historically has been loath to undercut Ailes publicly, to release a statement saying, "We take these matters seriously." They also persuaded Rupert to hire the law firm Paul, Weiss, Rifkind, Wharton & Garrison to conduct an internal investigation into the matter. Making things look worse for Ailes, three days after Carlson's suit was filed, *New York* published the accounts of six other women who claimed to have been harassed by Ailes over the course of three decades.

A few hours after the *New York* report, Ailes held an emergency meeting with longtime friend Rudy Giuliani and lawyer Marc Mukasey at his home in Garrison, New York, according to a high-level Fox source. Ailes vehemently denied the allegations. The next morning, Ailes and his wife, Elizabeth, turned his second-floor office at Fox News into a war room. "It's all bullshit! We have to get in front of this," he said to executives. "This is not about money. This is about his legacy," said Elizabeth, according to a Fox source. As part of his counteroffensive, Ailes rallied Fox News employees to defend him in the press. *Fox and Friends* host Ainsley Earhardt called Ailes a "family man"; Fox Business anchor Neil Cavuto wrote, reportedly of his own volition, an op-ed labeling Ailes's accusers "sick." Ailes's legal team attempted to intimidate a former Fox correspondent named Rudi Bakhtiar who spoke to *New York* about her harassment.

Ailes told executives that he was being persecuted by the liberal media and by the Murdoch sons. According to a high-level source inside the company, Ailes complained to 21st Century Fox general counsel Gerson Zweifach that James, whose wife had worked for the Clinton Foundation, was trying to get rid of him in order to help elect Hillary Clinton. At one point, Ailes threatened to fly to France, where Rupert was vacationing with his wife, Jerry Hall, in an effort to save his job. Perhaps Murdoch told him not to bother, because the trip never happened.

According to a person close to the Murdochs, Rupert's first instinct was to protect Ailes, who had worked for him for two decades. The elder Murdoch can be extremely loyal to executives who run his companies, even when they cross the line. (The most famous example of this is *Sun* editor Rebekah Brooks, whom he kept in the fold after the UK phone-hacking scandal.) Also, Ailes has made the Murdochs a lot of money—Fox News generates more than $1 billion annually, which accounts for 20 percent of 21st Century Fox's profits—and Rupert worried that perhaps only Ailes could run the network so successfully. "Rupert is in the clouds; he didn't appreciate how toxic an environment it was that Ailes created," a person close to the Murdochs said. "If the money hadn't been so good, then maybe they would have asked questions."

Beyond the James and Lachlan factor, the relationship between Murdoch and Ailes was becoming strained: Murdoch didn't like that Ailes was putting Fox so squarely behind the candidacy of Donald Trump. And he had begun to worry less about whether Fox could endure without its creator. (In recent years, Ailes had taken extended health leaves from Fox and the ratings held.) Now Ailes had made himself a true liability: More than two dozen Fox News women told the Paul, Weiss lawyers about their harassment in graphic terms. The most significant of the accusers was Megyn Kelly, who is in contract negotiations with Fox and is considered by the Murdochs to be the future of the network. So important to Fox is Kelly that Lachlan personally approved her reported $6 million book advance from Murdoch-controlled publisher HarperCollins, according to two sources.

As the inevitability of an ouster became clear, chaos engulfed Ailes's team. After news broke on the afternoon of July 19 that Kelly had come forward, Ailes's lawyer Susan Estrich tried to send Ailes's denial to *Drudge* but mistakenly e-mailed a draft of Ailes's proposed severance deal, which *Drudge*, briefly, published instead. Also that day, Ailes's allies claimed to conservative news site Breitbart that fifty of Fox's biggest personalities were prepared to quit if Ailes was removed, though in reality there was no such pact. That evening, Murdoch used one of his own press organs to fire back, with the *New York Post* tweeting the cover of the next day's paper featuring Ailes's picture and news that "the end is near for Roger Ailes."

Indeed, that evening Ailes was banned from Fox News headquarters, his company e-mail and phone shut off. On the afternoon of July 21, a few hours before Trump was to accept the Republican nomination in Cleveland, Murdoch summoned Ailes to his New York penthouse to work out a severance deal. James had wanted Ailes to be fired for cause, according to a person close to the Murdochs, but after reviewing his contract, Rupert decided to pay him $40 million and retain him as an "adviser." Ailes, in turn, agreed to a multiyear noncompete clause that prevents him from going to a rival network (but, notably, not to a political campaign). Murdoch assured Ailes that, as acting CEO of Fox News, he would protect the channel's conservative voice. "I'm here, and I'm in charge," Murdoch told Fox staffers later that afternoon with Lachlan at his side (James had gone to Europe on a business trip). That night, Rupert and Lachlan discussed the extraordinary turn of events over drinks at Eleven Madison Park.

The Murdochs must have hoped that by acting swiftly to remove Ailes, they had averted a bigger crisis. But over the coming days, harassment allegations from more women would make it clear that the problem was not limited to Ailes but included those who enabled him—both the loyal deputies who surrounded him at Fox News and those at 21st Century Fox who turned a blind eye. "Fox News masquerades as a defender of traditional family values," claimed the lawsuit of Fox anchor Andrea Tantaros, who says she was demoted and smeared in the press after she rebuffed sexual advances from Ailes, "but behind the scenes, it operates like a sex-fueled, Playboy Mansion–like cult, steeped in intimidation, indecency and misogyny."

·　　·　　·

Murdoch knew Ailes was a risky hire when he brought him in to start Fox News in 1996. Ailes had just been forced out as president of CNBC under circumstances that would foreshadow his problems at Fox.

While his volcanic temper, paranoia, and ruthlessness were part of what made Ailes among the best television producers and political operatives of his generation, those same attributes prevented him from functioning in a corporate environment. He hadn't lasted in a job for more than a few years. "I have been through about twelve train wrecks in my career. Somehow, I always walk away," he told an NBC executive.

By all accounts, Ailes had been a management disaster from the moment he arrived at NBC in 1993. But by 1995, things had reached a breaking point. In October of that year, NBC hired the law firm Proskauer Rose to conduct an internal investigation after then–NBC executive David Zaslav told human resources that Ailes had called him a "little fucking Jew prick" in front of a witness.

Zaslav told Proskauer investigators he feared for his safety. "I view Ailes as a very, very dangerous man. I take his threats to do physical harm to me very, very seriously . . . I feel endangered both at work and at home," he said, according to NBC documents, which I first published in my 2014 biography of Ailes. CNBC executive Andy Friendly also filed complaints. "I along with several of my most talented colleagues have and continue to feel emotional and even physical fear dealing with this man every day," he wrote. The Proskauer report chronicled Ailes's "history of abusive, offensive, and intimidating statements/threats and personal attacks." Ailes left NBC less than three months later.

What NBC considered fireable offenses, Murdoch saw as competitive advantages. He hired Ailes to help achieve a goal that had eluded Murdoch for a decade: busting CNN's cable-news monopoly. Back in the midnineties, no one thought it could be done. "I'm looking forward to squishing Rupert like a bug," CNN founder Ted Turner boasted at an industry conference. But Ailes recognized how key wedge issues—race, religion, class—could turn conservative voters into loyal viewers. By January 2002, Fox News had surpassed CNN as the highest-rated cable-news channel. But Ailes's success went beyond ratings: The rise of Fox News provided Murdoch with the political influence in the United States that he already wielded in Australia and the United Kingdom. And by merging news, politics, and entertainment in such an overt way, Ailes was able to personally shape the national conversation and political fortunes as no one ever had before. It is not a stretch to argue that Ailes is largely responsible for, among other things, the selling of the Iraq War, the Swiftboating of John Kerry, the rise of the Tea Party, the sticking power of a host of Clinton scandals, and the purported illegitimacy of Barack Obama's presidency.

Ailes became untouchable. At News Corp., he behaved just as he had at NBC, but Murdoch tolerated Ailes's abusiveness because he was pleased with the results.

Ailes used Fox's payroll as a patronage tool, doling out jobs to Republican politicians, friends, and political operatives. He made his personal lawyer, Peter Johnson Jr., a regular guest on Fox shows, despite producers' misgivings about Johnson's on-air performance. (They nicknamed Johnson "The Must-Do.") Manny

Alvarez, whose daughter went to school with Ailes's son, became a medical commentator.

Ailes also positioned his former secretaries in key departments where he could make use of their loyalty to him. One, Nikole King, went to the finance department, where she handled Ailes's personal expenses, a Fox executive said. Another, Brigette Boyle, went to human resources, where she was "tasked with hiring the 'right' people," a former executive recalled.

But most striking is the extent to which Ailes ruled Fox News like a surveillance state. According to executives, he instructed Fox's head of engineering, Warren Vandeveer, to install a CCTV system that allowed Ailes to monitor Fox offices, studios, greenrooms, the back entrance, and his homes. When Ailes spotted James Murdoch on the monitor smoking a cigarette outside the office, he remarked to his deputy Bill Shine, "Tell me that mouth hasn't sucked a cock," according to an executive who was in the room; Shine laughed. (A Fox spokesperson said Shine did not recall this.) Fox's IT department also monitored employee e-mail, according to sources. When I asked Fox's director of IT, Deborah Sadusingh, about e-mail searches, she said, "I can't remember all the searches I've done."

When Ailes uncovered something he didn't like, he had various means of retaliation and increased surveillance. Fox's notorious PR department, which for years was directed by Brian Lewis and is now overseen by Irena Briganti, was known for leaking negative stories about errant employees to journalists. Fox contributor Jim Pinkerton wrote an anonymous blog called *The Cable Game* that attacked Ailes-selected targets, two Fox executives confirmed. Fox contributor Bo Dietl did private-investigation work for Ailes, including following former Fox producer Andrea Mackris after she sued Bill O'Reilly for sexual harassment, a Fox source said. Ailes turned these same tactics on his enemies outside the company, including journalists. CNN's

Brian Stelter recently reported on Fox's 400-page opposition-research file on me.

Fox News also obtained the phone records of journalists, by legally questionable means. According to two sources with direct knowledge of the incident, Brandi, Fox's general counsel, hired a private investigator in late 2010 to obtain the personal home- and cell-phone records of Joe Strupp, a reporter for the liberal watch-dog group Media Matters. (Through a spokesperson, Brandi denied this.) In the fall of that year, Strupp had written several articles quoting anonymous Fox sources, and the network wanted to determine who was talking to him. "This was the culture. Getting phone records doesn't make anybody blink," one Fox executive told me.

What makes this practice all the more brazen is that the *Guardian* was already publishing articles about phone hacking at Murdoch's British newspaper division. About that scandal, Murdoch said, "I do not accept ultimate responsibility. I hold responsible the people that I trusted to run it and the people they trusted." In this case, of course, the person he trusted, inexplicably, was Ailes, and Murdoch does not seem to have wanted to know how Ailes chose to spend company funds. Every year, Murdoch approved Ailes's budgets without question. "When you have an organization making that much money, we didn't go line by line through people's budgets," a former News Corp. executive said.

. . .

Ailes was born in May 1940 in Warren, Ohio, then a booming industrial town. His father, a factory foreman, abused his wife and two sons. "He did like to beat the shit out of you with that belt . . . It was a pretty routine fixture of childhood," Ailes's brother Robert told me when I was reporting my book. His parents divorced in 1960. In court papers, Ailes's mother alleged that her husband "threatened her life and to do her physical harm."

Perhaps as an escape, Ailes lost himself in television. He suffered from hemophilia and was often homebound from school, so he spent hours on the living-room couch watching variety shows and westerns. "He analyzed it, and he figured it out," his brother told me of Ailes's fascination with TV.

After graduating from Ohio University in 1962, Ailes landed a job as a gofer on *The Mike Douglas Show*, a daytime variety program that at the time was broadcast from Cleveland. Within four years, he had muscled aside the show's creator and more seasoned colleagues to become the executive producer. Ailes's mentor at *The Mike Douglas Show*, Chet Collier, who would later serve as his deputy at Fox, drilled into him the notion that television is a visual medium. "I'm not hiring talent for their brainpower," Collier would say.

Though Ailes had married his college girlfriend, he used his growing power to take advantage of the parade of beautiful women coming through his office hoping to be cast on the show. Over the past two months, I interviewed eighteen women who shared accounts of Ailes's offering them job opportunities if they would agree to perform sexual favors for him and for his friends. In some cases, he threatened to release tapes of the encounters to prevent the women from reporting him. "The feeling I got in the interview was repulsion, power-hungriness, contempt, violence, and the need to subjugate and humiliate," says a woman who auditioned for Ailes in 1968 when she was a college student.

In August 1968, Ailes left *The Mike Douglas Show* to join Richard Nixon's presidential campaign as a media strategist. Ailes's success in reinventing the candidate for television helped propel Nixon to the White House and made Ailes a media star (he was the antihero of Joe McGinniss's landmark book *The Selling of the President*). But even back then, Ailes's recklessness put his thriving career at risk. A former model told me that her parents called the police on Ailes after she told them he assaulted her in a Cincinnati hotel room in 1969. "I remember Ailes sweet-talking my parents out of pressing charges," she says.

One prominent Republican told me that it was Ailes's well-known reputation for awful behavior toward women that prevented him from being invited to work in the Nixon White House (or, later, in the administration of Bush 41). So after the '68 election, he moved to New York, where he continued to use his power to demand sex from women seeking career opportunities. During this time Ailes divorced, remarried, and divorced again. A former television producer described an interview with Ailes in 1975, in which he said: "If you want to make it in New York City in the TV business, you're going to have to fuck me, and you're going to do that with anyone I tell you to." While running media strategy on Rudy Giuliani's 1989 mayoral campaign, Ailes propositioned an employee of his political-consulting firm: He name-dropped his friend Barry Diller and said that if she'd have sex with him he'd ask Diller to get her a part on *Beverly Hills 90210.* (Diller said he never received such a request.)

In 1998, two years after launching Fox, Ailes got married for the third time, to a woman named Elizabeth Tilson, a thirty-seven-year-old producer who had worked for him at CNBC. Two years later, when Ailes was fifty-nine, the couple had a son. But neither a new marriage nor parenthood changed his predatory behavior toward the women who worked for him.

According to interviews with Fox News women, Ailes would often begin by offering to mentor a young employee. He then asked a series of personal questions to expose potential vulnerabilities. "He asked, 'Am I in a relationship? What are my familial ties?' It was all to see how stable or unstable I was," said a former employee. Megyn Kelly told lawyers at Paul, Weiss that Ailes made an unwanted sexual advance toward her in 2006 when she was going through a divorce. A lawyer for former anchor Laurie Dhue told me that Ailes harassed her around 2006; at the time, she was struggling with alcoholism.

Ailes's longtime executive assistant Judy Laterza—who became one of his top lieutenants, earning more than $2 million a year, according to a Fox executive—seemed to function as a recruiter of sorts. According to Carlson's attorney, in 2002, Laterza remarked to a college intern she saw on the elevator about how pretty she was and invited her to meet Ailes. After that meeting, Ailes arranged for the young woman to transfer to his staff. Her first assignment was to go down to the newsstand and fetch him the latest issue of *Maxim*. When she returned with the magazine, Ailes asked her to stay with him in his office. He flipped through the pages. The woman told the *Washington Post* that Ailes said, "You look like the women in here. You have great legs. If you sleep with me, you could be a model or a newscaster." She cut short her internship. (Laterza did not respond to a request for comment.)

I spoke with another Fox News administrative assistant who said Laterza invited her to meet Ailes in 2004. The woman, then twenty-five, told Ailes that her ambition was to do commercials. Ailes offered to pay for voice lessons (she declined) and helped her land an agent at William Morris. A few months later, Ailes summoned her to his office for an update. She told him how excited she was about the opportunities, and Ailes invited her for a drink. She suggested happy hour, but he demurred. "For a man in my position, it would have to be alone at a hotel," she recalls him saying. "Do you know how to play the game?" She tried to get out of the situation as tactfully as possible. "I don't feel comfortable doing this," she said. "I respect your family; what about your son?" She remembers Ailes's reply: "I'm a multifaceted man. That's one side of me." As she left the office, she says, Ailes tried to kiss her. "I was holding a binder full of voice-over auditions that I put between us. I was terrified." She says she never heard from the William Morris agent again.

The fact that these incidents of harassment were so common may have contributed to why no one at Fox came forward or filed a lawsuit until now. Ailes's attitudes about women permeated the very air of the network, from the exclusive hiring of attractive women to the strictly enforced skirts-and-heels dress code to the "leg cam" that lingers on female panelists' crossed legs on air. It was hard to complain about something that was so normalized. Other senior executives harassed women, too. "Anyone who claimed there was a hostile work environment was seen as a complainer," says a former Fox employee who says Ailes harassed her. "Or that they can't take a joke."

.    .    .

It is unfathomable to think, given Ailes's reputation, given the number of women he propositioned and harassed and assaulted over decades, that senior management at Fox News was unaware of what was happening. What is more likely is that their very jobs included enabling, abetting, protecting, and covering up for their boss. "No one said no to Roger," a Fox executive said.

The story of Laurie Luhn, which I reported in July, is an example of how Ailes used Fox's public-relations, legal, and finance departments to facilitate his behavior. Ailes met Luhn on the 1988 George H. W. Bush campaign, and soon thereafter he put her on a $500 monthly retainer with his political-consulting firm to be his "spy" in Washington, though really her job was to meet him in hotel rooms. (During their first encounter, Luhn says, Ailes videotaped her in a garter belt and told her: "I am going to put [the tape] in a safe-deposit box just so we understand each other.") Ailes recruited Luhn to Fox in 1996, before the network even launched. Collier, then his deputy, offered her a job in guest relations in the Washington bureau.

Laterza, Shine, and Shine's deputy Suzanne Scott would take turns summoning Luhn for "meetings" in New York. (A Fox spokesperson said executives were not aware Ailes was sexually involved with Luhn.) Ailes and Luhn would meet in the afternoons, Luhn said, at hotels near Times Square, and Ailes paid her cash for sexual favors. She was also on the payroll at Fox—at her peak, she earned $250,000 a year as an event planner for the channel; multiple sources confirmed that she was a "Friend of Roger," with special protection within the company. But the arrangement required her to do many things that now cause her anguish, including luring young female Fox employees into one-on-one meetings with Ailes that Luhn knew would likely result in harassment. "You're going to find me 'Roger's Angels,'" he reportedly told her. One of Luhn's employees received a six-figure settlement after filing a harassment claim against Ailes.

By the fall of 2006, Luhn says, Ailes was worried that she might go public with her story or cause a scene of some kind. That's when the Fox machine really kicked into gear. According to Luhn, Fox PR tried to spread a rumor to the *New York Daily News* that Luhn had had an affair with Lee Atwater (which she denies), a story designed to make Luhn seem promiscuous so that her credibility would be damaged. When Luhn had an emotional breakdown en route to a vacation in Mexico, it was Shine's job to arrange to bring her home. Scott picked her up at the airport and drove her to the Warwick Hotel on Sixth Avenue, where Luhn recalls that Scott checked her in under Scott's name. (Scott denies this.)

Luhn later moved into a Fox corporate apartment in Chelsea, during which time, she says, Laterza and Shine monitored her e-mail. (Shine denies this.) Luhn's father says that Shine called him several times to check up on Luhn after she moved to California while still on the Fox payroll. Eventually, Shine even recommended a psychiatrist, who medicated and hospitalized her. At one point, Luhn attempted suicide. Through a spokesperson, Shine says he "was only trying to help."

In late 2010 or early 2011, Luhn wrote a letter to Brandi, the Fox lawyer, saying she had been sexually harassed by Ailes for twenty years. According to a source, Brandi asked Ailes about the allegations, which he denied. Brandi then worked out a settlement at Ailes's request. On June 15, 2011, Luhn signed a $3.15 million settlement agreement with extensive nondisclosure provisions. The payment was approved by Fox News CFO Mark Kranz. The check, which I viewed, was signed by David E. Miller, a treasurer for Fox Television Stations, Inc., a division run by current Fox copresident Jack Abernethy. "I have no idea how my name ended up on the check," says Miller, citing standard company practice of signing checks and not asking questions. The settlement documents, which Luhn also showed me, were signed by Ailes, Brandi, and Shine.

After Luhn left Fox, Ailes took additional measures to conceal his harassment of employees. In 2011, he installed a floor-to-ceiling wooden door outside his executive suite. Only his assistants could see who entered his office. According to a former Fox producer, Laterza entered fake names into Ailes's date book when women went into his office: "If you got ahold of his ledger, you would not know who visited him."

Still, the whispers about Ailes and women were growing louder. Karem Alsina, a former Fox makeup artist, told me she grew suspicious when Fox anchors came to see her before private meetings with Ailes to have their makeup done. "They would say, 'I'm going to see Roger, gotta look beautiful!'" she recalled. "One of them came back down after a meeting, and the makeup on her nose and chin was gone."

In 2012, after I had been reporting my Ailes biography for a year, Megyn Kelly became so concerned about the rumors that she went to Ailes's then–PR chief, Brian Lewis, and attempted an intervention, according to a person close to Kelly. She told Lewis that Ailes was being reckless and that I might include his behavior in my book. (I did report the stories of two women who claimed Ailes had harassed them earlier in his career, and though I heard rumors of Ailes and Fox News women, I could not confirm them at the time.) Lewis, according to the source, asked Laterza to tell Ailes to stop because he thought Ailes might listen to his longtime assistant. Instead, according to the source, Laterza told Ailes that his PR chief was being disloyal. Less than a year later, Ailes fired Lewis.

.    .    .

Megyn Kelly was not a household name when she started at Fox News in 2004. A former corporate lawyer, she landed at Fox when former *Special Report* anchor Brit Hume recommended her to Ailes. She still wasn't well known in 2006, when she got divorced and Ailes tried to take advantage of her perceived vulnerability. She may not have been any more powerful, at the time, than the other women he preyed on, but she was one of the lucky ones: She managed to rebuff his sexual overtures in a way that didn't alienate her boss. "She was able to navigate the relationship to a professional place," a person close to Kelly told me. In fact, Kelly's career flourished after this. In 2010, Ailes gave her a two-hour midday show, on which she enthusiastically fanned his right-wing agenda—for instance, hyping stories about the New Black Panthers that many thought were racist. In October 2013, Ailes promoted Kelly to Sean Hannity's nine p.m. prime-time slot, where she memorably declared that Jesus and Santa are "white." When asked by a fan on Twitter to name her biggest influence, she responded, "Roger Ailes."

By 2015, although her show was still reliably right-wing, Kelly's brand was evolving. After several high-profile clashes with Republican men, including Dick Cheney, she was developing something of a reputation as a feminist. As she entered the final two years of her contract, she started to think about a future outside of Fox, meeting with CNN chief Jeff Zucker in 2013.

Then came Donald Trump. Kelly's feud with the GOP nominee was one of the dominant story lines of the presidential election; it also exploded the fragile balance of relationships at the top of Fox News.

According to Fox sources, Murdoch blamed Ailes for laying the groundwork for Trump's candidacy. Ailes had given Trump, his longtime friend, a weekly call-in segment on *Fox and Friends* to sound off on political issues. (Trump used Fox News to mainstream the birther conspiracy theory.) Ailes also had lunch with Trump days before he launched his presidential campaign and continued to feed him political advice throughout the primaries, according to sources close to Trump and Ailes. (And in the days after Carlson filed her lawsuit, Trump advised Ailes on navigating the crisis, even recommending a lawyer.)

Murdoch was not a fan of Trump's and especially did not like his stance on immigration. (The antipathy was mutual: "Murdoch's been very bad to me," Trump told me in March.) A few days before the first GOP debate on Fox in August 2015, Murdoch called Ailes at home. "This has gone on long enough," Murdoch said, according to a person briefed on the conversation. Murdoch told Ailes he wanted Fox's debate moderators—Kelly, Bret Baier, and Chris Wallace—to hammer Trump on a variety of issues. Ailes, understanding the GOP electorate better than most at that point, likely thought it was a bad idea. "Donald Trump is going to be the Republican nominee," Ailes told a colleague around this time. But he didn't fight Murdoch on the debate directive.

On the night of August 6, in front of twenty-four million people, the Fox moderators peppered Trump with harder-hitting questions. But it was Kelly's question regarding Trump's history of crude comments about women that created a media sensation. He seemed personally wounded by her suggestion that this spoke to a temperament that might not be suited for the presidency. "I've been very nice to you, though I could probably maybe not be based on the way you have treated me," he said pointedly.

After the debate, Trump called Ailes and screamed about Kelly. "How could you do this?" he said, according to a person briefed on the call. Ailes was caught between his friend Trump, his boss Murdoch, and his star Kelly. "Roger lost control of Megyn and Trump," a Fox anchor said.

The parties only became more entrenched when Trump launched a series of attacks against Kelly, including suggesting that her menstrual cycle had influenced her debate question. Problematically for Ailes, Fox's audience took Trump's side in the fight; Kelly received death threats from viewers, according to a person close to her. Kelly had even begun to speculate, according to one Fox source, that Trump might have been responsible for her getting violently ill before the debate last summer. Could he have paid someone to slip something into her coffee that morning in Cleveland? she wondered to colleagues.

While Ailes released a statement defending Kelly, he privately blamed her for creating the crisis. "It was an unfair question," he told a Fox anchor. Kelly felt betrayed, both by Ailes and by colleagues like O'Reilly and Baier when they didn't defend her, sources who spoke with her said. "She felt she put herself out there," a colleague said.

Frustrated at Fox, Kelly hired a powerhouse agent at CAA and began auditioning in earnest, and in public, for a job at another network. In interviews, she said her ambition was to become the next Barbara Walters and to host prime-time specials. She wanted to prove to the industry she could land a "big get"—and the biggest get of all was Trump. So Kelly went to Trump Tower to lobby the candidate for an interview. It worked—even Trump couldn't resist the spectacle of a rematch—but in the end the show failed: The ratings were terrible and reviewers panned her generally sycophantic questions. Worse for Kelly, it eroded her burgeoning status as a tough journalist who stood up to Trump. Afterward, her relationship with Ailes further deteriorated. According to Fox sources, they barely spoke in recent months.

Kelly and Gretchen Carlson were not friends or allies, but Carlson's lawsuit presented an opportunity. Kelly could bust up the boys' club at Fox, put herself on the right side of a snowballing media story, and rid herself of a boss who was no longer supportive of her—all while maximizing her leverage in a contract negotiation. She also had allies in the Murdoch sons. According to a source, Kelly told James Murdoch that Ailes had made harassing comments and inappropriately hugged her in his office. James and Lachlan both encouraged her to speak to the Paul, Weiss lawyers about it. Kelly was only the third or fourth woman to speak to the lawyers, according to a source briefed on the inquiry, but she was by far the most important. After she spoke with investigators, and made calls to current and former Fox colleagues to encourage them to speak to Paul, Weiss as well, many more women came forward.

Ailes was furious with Kelly for not defending him publicly. According to a Fox source, Ailes's wife Elizabeth wanted Fox PR to release racy photos of Kelly published years ago in *GQ* as a way of discrediting her. The PR department, in this instance, refused. (Elizabeth is said to be taking all of the revelations especially hard, according to four sources close to the family. Giuliani, who officiated their wedding, told Murdoch she would likely divorce Ailes, according to two sources: "This marriage won't last," he said.)

Two days after *New York* reported that Kelly had told her story to Paul, Weiss attorneys, Ailes was gone. And Kelly had made herself more important to the network than ever.

.     .     .

Ailes's ouster has created a leadership vacuum at Fox News. Several staffers have described feeling like being part of a totalitarian regime whose dictator has just been toppled. "No one knows what to do. No one knows who to report to. It's just mayhem," said a Fox host. As details of the Paul, Weiss investigation have filtered through the offices, staffers are expressing a mixture of shock and disgust. The scope of Ailes's alleged abuse far exceeds what employees could have imagined. "People are so devastated," one senior executive said. Those I spoke with have also been unnerved by Shine and Brandi's roles in covering up Ailes's behavior.

Despite revelations of how Ailes's management team enabled his harassment, Murdoch has so far rejected calls—including from James, according to sources—to conduct a wholesale housecleaning. On August 12, Murdoch promoted Shine and another Ailes loyalist, Jack Abernethy, to become copresidents of Fox News. He named Scott executive vice president and kept Brandi and Briganti in their jobs. Fox News's chief financial officer, Mark Kranz, is the only senior executive to have been pushed out (officially he retired), along with Laterza and a handful of assistants, contributors, and consultants. "Of course, they are trying to isolate this to just a few bad actors," a 21st Century Fox executive told me.

Many people I spoke with believe that the current management arrangement is just a stopgap until the election. "As of November 9, there will be a bloodbath at Fox," predicts one host. "After the election, the prime-time lineup could be eviscerated. O'Reilly's been talking about retirement. Megyn could go to another network. And Hannity will go to Trump TV."

The prospect of Trump TV is a source of real anxiety for some inside Fox. The candidate took the wedge issues that Ailes used to build a loyal audience at Fox News—especially race and class—and used them to stoke barely containable outrage among a downtrodden faction of conservatives. Where that outrage is channeled after the election—assuming, as polls now suggest, Trump doesn't make it to the White House—is a big question for the Republican Party and for Fox News. Trump had a complicated relationship with Fox even when his good friend Ailes was in charge; without Ailes, it's plausible that he will try to monetize the movement he has galvanized in competition with the network rather than in concert with it. Trump's appointment of Steve Bannon, chairman of Breitbart, the digital-media upstart that has by some measures already surpassed Fox News as the locus of conservative energy, to run his campaign suggests a new right-wing news network of some kind is a real possibility. One prominent media executive told me that if Trump loses, Fox will need to try to damage him in the eyes of its viewers by blaming him for the defeat.

Meanwhile, the Murdochs are looking for a permanent CEO to navigate these post-Ailes, Trump-roiled waters. According to sources, James's preferred candidates include CBS president David Rhodes (though he is under contract with CBS through 2019); Jesse Angelo, the *New York Post* publisher and James's Harvard roommate; and perhaps a television executive from London. Sources say Lachlan, who politically is more conservative than James, wants to bring in an outsider. Rupert was seen giving Rebekah Brooks a tour of the Fox offices several months ago, creating speculation that she could be brought in to run Fox. Another contender is Newsmax CEO Chris Ruddy.

As for the women who collectively brought an end to the era of Roger Ailes, their fortunes are mixed. Megyn Kelly is in a strong position in her contract talks, and sources say Gretchen Carlson will soon announce an eight-figure settlement. But because New York has a three-year statute of limitations on sexual harassment, so far just two women in addition to Carlson are said to be receiving settlements from 21st Century Fox. The many others who left or were forced out of the company before the investigation came away with far less—in some cases nothing at all.

It's hard to say that justice has been served. But the story isn't over: Last week, the shareholder law firm Scott & Scott announced it was investigating 21st Century Fox to "determine whether Fox's Officers and Directors have breached their fiduciary duties." Meanwhile, Ailes is walking away from his biggest career train wreck yet, seeking relevance and renewed power through the one person in the country who doesn't see him as political kryptonite, the candidate he created: Donald J. Trump. Ailes may be trying to sell us another president, but now we know the truth about the salesman.

## The New Yorker

FINALIST—PUBLIC
INTEREST

*Sarah Stillman is no stranger to readers of previous* Best American Magazine Writing *anthologies. Her story "The Invisible Army," about the abuse of foreign workers on American bases in Iraq and Afghanistan, won the Ellie for Public Interest in 2012 when she was still in her twenties. She was nominated in the same category the following two years, first for "The Throwaways," about young offenders working as confidential informants, and then for "Taken," on the questionable use of civil forfeiture. "The List" explores another controversial practice— the placement of juveniles on sex-offender registries. The Ellie judges praised Stillman's reporting, of course, but also said she was "a genius at narrative pacing."*

Sarah Stillman

# **The List**

One morning in 2007, Leah DuBuc, a twenty-two-year-old college student in Kalamazoo, began writing an essay for English class that she hoped would save her life. She knew that people like her had been beaten, bombed, shot at, killed. The essay aired details about her past that she'd long tried to suppress; by posting it on her class's server, where anyone who Googled her name could find it, she thought she might be able to quiet the whispers, the threats, and possibly make it easier to find a job. Her story, she warned, "is not a nice one, but hopefully it will have a happy ending."

DuBuc had grown up in Howell, Michigan, a small town of berry and melon farmers. In high school, she had thrived. She had earned straight A's, written for the school newspaper, led Students Against Driving Drunk (she voted to change the name to Students Against Destructive Decisions, she says, to stress that "there are lots of bad decisions that can get you killed"), and performed in *Grease* and *Once Upon a Mattress*, while working part time as a cashier at Mary's Fabulous Chicken & Fish. "High school was bliss for me," DuBuc said recently. "I tried not to dwell on the stuff that wasn't good." But, as she was about to start her freshman year at Western Michigan University, she got a call from a close childhood friend, Victoria, who asked, "Did you know you're on the public sex-offender registry?"

Her friend, who had just given birth to a baby girl, had logged on to the Michigan Public Sex Offender Registry website to search for local predators. She had entered her zip code, and there was Leah's face—her copper bangs, her wide cheeks, her brown eyes staring blankly from the photograph. Her name, weight, and height were listed; so was the address where she'd grown up, playing beneath tall pines and selling five-cent rocks that she'd painted with nail polish. Something DuBuc had done at the age of ten had caught up with her. Victoria knew the story, which DuBuc described as "play-acting sex," in elementary school, with her younger step-siblings. Online browsers would see only the words on the page: "CRIMINAL SEXUAL CONDUCT."

A senior in college now, DuBuc was tired of hiding. She wanted everyone to know what it was like to join the many thousands of people across the country who are on the registry—often decades into adulthood—for crimes they committed as children. "After reading my very condensed life story," she wrote, "I am convinced you will agree that I am a strong, determined young woman, who has risen above the obstacles which have been set in my path." On an April morning, she published the essay, titled "So, Who Is Leah DuBuc Anyway?," and prayed for relief.

·     ·     ·

When I visited DuBuc in Howell last summer, I had already spoken to a number of people who had been accused of sex offenses as juveniles and ended up on a public registry. Some, like DuBuc, had been placed on the registry for things they'd done before they reached their teens.

In Charla Roberts's living room, not far from Paris, Texas, I learned how, at the age of ten, Roberts had pulled down the pants of a male classmate at her public elementary school. She was prosecuted for "indecency with a child," and added to the state's online offender database for the next ten years. The terms of her probation barred her from leaving her mother's house after six in the evening, leaving the county, or living in proximity to "minor children," which ruled out most apartments. When I spoke to the victim, he was shocked to learn of Roberts's fate. He described the playground offense as an act of "public humiliation, instead of a sexual act"—a hurtful prank, but hardly a sex crime. Roberts can still be found on a commercial database online, her photo featured below a banner that reads, "PROTECT YOUR CHILD FROM SEX OFFENDERS."

New technologies in the hands of teens are another route to the registry. In Prince William County, Virginia, two years ago, a seventeen-year-old high-school junior sent a sexual video to his teenage girlfriend, and found himself charged with manufacturing and distributing child pornography. The county prosecutor obtained a search warrant to photograph "the erect penis of the defendant." (Pursuit of the photo was abandoned only after there was a public outcry.) In Fayetteville, North Carolina, a sixteen-year-old girl faced multiple felony charges for "sexting" a picture of herself to her boyfriend. According to the county sheriff's warrant, she was both the adult perpetrator of the crime at hand—"sexual exploitation of a minor"—and its child victim. Her boyfriend faced similar charges.

Most juveniles on the sex-offender registry pose a more daunting public-policy challenge: they have caused sexual harm to other children, through nonconsensual touch and other abusive behaviors. Childhood sexual abuse is troublingly widespread. According to the Centers for Disease Control, as many as one out of every four girls and one out of every six boys have experienced some form of sexual abuse before the age of eighteen, and in a third of such cases, the National Center on the Sexual Behavior of Youth says, the offenses were committed by other juveniles. "The single age with the greatest number of offenders from the perspective of law enforcement was age 14," a study sponsored by the Department of Justice notes.

Often, these incidents go unreported. But the devastation that may result from childhood sexual assault can last a lifetime, fueling depression, addiction, suicidal thoughts, and other signs of post-traumatic stress. Compounding the original trauma is the fact that victims' voices are often silenced, sometimes by those in positions of trust or power.

Kids who sexually harm other kids seldom target strangers. A very small number have committed violent rapes. More typical is the crime for which Josh Gravens, of Abilene, Texas, was sent away, more than a decade ago, at the age of thirteen. Gravens was twelve when his mother learned that he had inappropriately touched his eight-year-old sister on two occasions; she sought help from a Christian counseling center, and a staffer there was legally obliged to inform the police. Gravens was arrested, placed on the public registry, and sent to juvenile detention for nearly four years. Now, at twenty-nine, he's become a leading figure in the movement to strike juveniles from the registry and to challenge broader restrictions that he believes are ineffectual. He has counseled more than a hundred youths who are on public registries, some as young as nine. He says that their experiences routinely mirror his own: "Homelessness; getting fired from jobs; taking jobs below minimum wage, with predatory employers; not being able to provide for your kids; losing your kids; relationship problems; deep inner problems connecting with people; deep depression and hopelessness; this fear of your own name; the terror of being Googled."

Often, juvenile defendants aren't seen as juveniles before the law. At the age of thirteen, Moroni Nuttall was charged as an adult, in Montana, for sexual misconduct with relatives; after pleading guilty, he was sentenced to forty years in prison, thirty-six of which were suspended, and placed on a lifetime sex-offender registry. In detention, the teenager was sexually assaulted and physically abused. Upon his release, his mother, Heidi, went online in search of guidance. "I'm trying to be hopeful," she wrote on an online bulletin board, but "I wonder if he even stands a chance."

Last fall, she contacted a national group called Women Against Registry, joining the ranks of mothers who are calling into question what a previous group of parents, those of victimized children, fought hard to achieve. Recently, common ground between the two groups has emerged. Many politicians still won't go near the issue, but a growing number of parents—along with legal advocates, scholars, and even law-enforcement officials—are beginning to ask whether the registry is truly serving the children whom it was designed to protect.

·    ·    ·

If the sex-offender registry is a modern development, the impulse behind it—to prevent crimes by keeping tabs on "bad actors"—is not. In 1937, after the sexualized murders of several young girls in New York, Mayor Fiorello LaGuardia called for the police to keep a secret list of "all known degenerates." A decade later, California built the first database of sex offenders, for private use by the police. But the practice of regulation took off only in the 1990s, when a tragedy changed the public's sense of the stakes involved.

One evening in 1989, in the quiet town of St. Joseph, Minnesota, Patty and Jerry Wetterling set out for dinner at a friend's house, leaving their eleven-year-old son, Jacob, at home with two of his siblings and a friend. Just after sundown, three of them left on their bikes and scooters to rent movies. Returning home, the kids came upon a masked gunman, who grabbed Jacob and chased off the others with death threats. Frantic searches followed, to no avail. Investigators didn't know the abductor's motivation, but feared that it was sexual. Afterward, Patty Wetterling kept returning to the question of what might have helped the police find her son's abductor during those critical early hours. Officials told her that what they needed was a unified database of local residents who had sex-crime convictions. Wetterling went on to fight for such a registry—first in Minnesota, and then nationally. In 1994, she helped win the first federal mandate that all states create a database of people convicted of violent sex crimes or crimes against children. It was known as the Jacob Wetterling Act. "Initially, this was supposed to be a private law-enforcement tool," Patty Wetterling told me. "I was one of those people who thought, Once a sex offender, always a sex offender, and my view was: Lock 'em up and send 'em away, forever and ever."

The act marked the first in a series of sex-registry laws, mostly named after nightmarish "stranger-danger" cases. Megan's Law, passed in 1996, required that states make their registries accessible to the public. Jessica's Law, and its variants, established long mandatory minimum sentences for first-time offenders convicted of sex crimes against children and stipulated that certain offenders be subject to lifetime electronic monitoring after their release. Particularly consequential was the crusade of John Walsh, the host of *America's Most Wanted* and the father of a six-year-old boy who, in 1981, was abducted inside a shopping mall and beheaded. Walsh lobbied for the most sweeping set of changes to date: the Adam Walsh Act. It broadened the scope of the sex-offender registry, mandating the full disclosure of a former offender's address, along with a photograph, and more; promulgated a form of indefinite detention, known as "civil commitment"; and, in a late addition to the bill, required that children as young as fourteen who had committed certain sex offenses be placed on the public registry. Jurisdictions that refused to comply would lose federal funds.

In 2005, Patty Wetterling traveled to Washington, D.C., with other grieving parents, to support an early version of the bill. "We will not tolerate sexual violence against our children," she said at a press conference. An amendment adding certain juvenile offenders to the federal bill had been spurred by the devastating testimony of a teenager named Amie Zyla; at the age of eight, Zyla had been sexually abused by another youth, who had gone on to reoffend years later. "We cannot sit back and allow kids to continue to be hurt," Zyla told Congress. "The simple truth is that juvenile sex offenders turn into adult predators." On July 27, 2006, George W. Bush signed the Adam Walsh Act into law.

.     .     .

Leah DuBuc was a gregarious child. Plump and pleasant-looking, with ginger hair and freckles, she took the crown at the Little Miss Summer pageant, in lakeside Pentwater, Michigan, belting out "You Are My Sunshine"; she brought the same gusto to gardening and tap-dance recitals. Leah's troubles began when she was eight and her parents got divorced. Her father remarried and won custody of her and her little sister; her mom, mired in personal issues, was granted supervised visits with the girls at the local Dairy Queen. DuBuc was now sharing her old home with her stepmother and her four children—three boys and a girl.

"I'd never had brothers before, and I was curious," DuBuc told me. One afternoon, after watching movies with her new step-siblings, ten-year-old Leah mimicked having sex with them— "like we'd seen in the movies," she says—and then, by her account, exposed herself to the younger kids. It happened several more times, she said.

Later that year, DuBuc recounts, a law-enforcement officer visited her elementary-school class and told the students to inform a trusted adult if they had been subject to abuse. DuBuc remembers complaining to him about mistreatment at home; when authorities arrived to investigate, she says, they learned of her sexual misbehavior. According to another family member, however, one of DuBuc's step-siblings talked about her actions to a therapist, who then alerted the authorities. (As is often true in such cases, the details may be impossible to establish definitively.)

Amid extensive therapeutic interventions, DuBuc was charged with eight counts of criminal sexual conduct, in the first and second degree. The prosecutor, Marilyn Bradford, insists, "There were a lot of scary things that happened to the victims in the case—ongoing things that happened to the little siblings." But DuBuc's court-appointed clinical social worker, Wendy Kunce, noted that at the time "there was a history of 'charging large.'"

At the age of twelve, DuBuc arrived in juvenile court for a series of hearings. Her father, a mechanic, drove her to the courthouse, but he didn't fully grasp the implication of the charges. (DuBuc's interviews with authorities often occurred without the presence of a parent or a guardian.) Moments before stepping in front of a judge, DuBuc met with her court-appointed attorney, alone. She remembers giggling when she had to say the words "penis" and "vagina," and when her fingerprints were taken, she told me, "I felt like I was in a movie."

DuBuc recalls the court-appointed attorney explaining that if she pleaded guilty to two counts of criminal sexual conduct—a graver crime than the one that she says she committed, because it involved penetration—she'd be taken from her home. Given that she wanted to escape the difficult conditions there, she agreed. DuBuc's investigating officer, Deputy Sheriff Mike Capra, told me, "I think she was hoping to make it easier on everybody by avoiding a long, drawn-out process and saying, 'OK, I goofed up, I'm a kid, I'll learn from it and move on.'"

In April, 1997, the judge ordered that DuBuc be sent to a residential juvenile-sex-offender treatment facility in Manteno, Illinois, called Indian Oaks Academy, where she stayed for nearly two years. An adult could have gone to prison for life, the judge warned, and, as she recalls it, proclaimed her a "lucky girl."

•　　　•　　　•

She was the youngest child in her program at Indian Oaks, a facility surrounded by cornfields and a golf course. Many of the girls there were sixteen or seventeen, with histories of trauma that surfaced as rage. The older girls—Leah roomed with three others—verbally and physically abused one another, and occasionally her. A staffer sometimes sat on top of girls to restrain them, DuBuc recalls. "There was this padded room, and I'd take a book in there and read," she told me. "I felt safe there."

Five days a week, she went to sex-offender treatment with the girls from her unit. The program borrowed heavily from addiction theory. "Your identity is you're a sex offender," DuBuc recalls the girls being told. They'd never be cured, but they could learn to refrain from harming people in the future. To graduate, DuBuc would have to admit to acts that she says she never committed (such as the contested claims of penetration) but to which she'd pleaded guilty, under conditions that she has come to view as coercion. The daily treatment was exhausting, though she did have one therapist who seemed to believe in her. She was grateful, too, for a pastor who arrived one day, teaching the Gospel, and gave her a Bible. "From that point forward," she recalls, "I had hope."

What *is* available, too often, is a form of commercial treatment that can be abusive in its own right. In my interviews with registrants and their families, one question came up repeatedly: "Have you looked into the therapy industry?" Many treatment programs have dedicated, well-trained staff members who engage with families and seem to help children thrive. But some providers lack the resources that would allow them to separate offenders of various risk levels. And, in some parts of the country, I found a cottage industry of court-authorized but poorly regulated therapy providers subjecting kids and teens to widely debunked interventions or controversial invasive technologies. Juveniles undergoing treatment for sex offenses have been exposed to severe verbal abuse, beatings, and even sexual predation at residential facilities. Not a few people have been placed in dubious but costly treatment programs for actions that many believe should never have been criminalized in the first place. These experiences are hardly exclusive to juveniles; they extend to many youths over eighteen, whose journeys through the justice system can be equally alarming. The most surprising instances are known as the "Romeo and Juliet" cases, involving consensual sex between teens.

.        .        .

In July of 2003, not long after his senior year of high school, Anthony Metts got a summer job at the lakeside camp where he'd once been a camper. Metts, who grew up in Midland, Texas, was adopted; at school, where he was one of its few Mexican Americans, he'd been taunted for being a "wetback." But things were different at the camp, and as a counselor he was in heaven. He ran archery sessions and visits to the Blob, the camp's famous floating trampoline. Then, one afternoon, a Texas Ranger and a Midland cop arrived at the camp and asked to speak with him. After driving him to a local police station, the officers told him that they were investigating the illegal sale of items from a Midland Police Department evidence room, and an informant had tossed out his name as a potential source of information.

Officers noted that Metts had been keenly cooperative. But he knew nothing about the theft, which, it later emerged, had been perpetrated by a rogue employee of the police department. Eager to get a confession, and seemingly convinced of his association with the crime, the officers pressed him on another tip they'd heard: Hadn't Metts been hanging out with younger girls the previous year? Was it possible that he'd had sex with them?

Metts told them that when he was eighteen he dated a girl who was three years younger. And he'd also had a brief sexual relationship with a girl more than three years younger, whom he met during his junior year of high school, when she was a freshman.

Metts helped the officers proofread his statement, oblivious of its significance. When the officers turned the information over to the Midland District Attorney's Office, the DA filed two felony indictments for sexual assault of a child, based on the age-of-consent laws in Texas at the time. (A third charge of sexual assault of a child was raised, then dropped.)

Consent was irrelevant—in fact, impossible—before the law. Not too far away, in the town of Caldwell, a young man had been convicted, at nineteen, for a consensual relationship with a girl who was four years younger, and who later became his wife. Metts's case was messier; it involved more than one relationship, and he'd left a trail of adolescent misbehavior—speeding tickets, pot, and pranks. His lawyer told him that he would face life in prison if the case went to trial. He decided to take a plea deal: a suspended sentence and ten years of probation.

Metts, who was twenty-one by then, read the terms of his postplea life. For the next decade, he'd be barred from alcohol and the Internet; from entering the vicinity of schools, parks, bus stops, malls, and movie theatres; and from living within a thousand feet of a "child-safety zone." A mugshot of his curly-haired, round-cheeked face would appear for life on the Texas sex-offender registry, beside the phrase "Sexual Assault of a Child." And he would have to start sex-offender treatment.

The treatment plan was extensive. He was told to write up a detailed sexual history and then to discuss it with a room full of adults, some of whom had repeatedly committed child assaults. On his first day of class, he recalls, he entered a group circle beside a dentist who had violated several patients while they were under anesthesia. To graduate, he would have to narrate his "assaults" in detail: "How many buttons on her shirt did you unbutton?"

The plan also included a monthly polygraph ($150) and a computerized test that measured how long his eyes lingered on deviant imagery ($325). He would also have to submit to a "penile plethysmograph," or PPG. According to documents produced by the state of Texas, the PPG—known jokingly to some patients as a "peter meter"—is "a sophisticated computerized instrument capable of measuring slight changes in the circumference of the penis." A gauge is wrapped around the shaft of the penis, with wires hooked up to a laptop, while a client is presented with "sexually inappropriate" imagery and, often, "deviant" sexual audio. Metts would be billed around $200 per test.

In parts of the country, including New York, judges have banned the PPG; one federal ruling noted "the obviously substantial humiliation of having the size and rigidity of one's penis measured and monitored by the government." (The PPG was invented in the 1950s by a sexologist from Czechoslovakia and used by the Czech military to expose soldiers suspected of pretending to be gay in order to avoid service.) But Texas's Council on Sex Offender Treatment says that the test is capable of "breaking through the offender's denial," helping to tailor treatments that can "address all of the offender's sexual interests."

When Metts balked at what felt to him like technological invasions—not least the prospect of having a stranger measure his penis—he was jailed for ten days. A new round of weekly therapy sessions (thirty dollars for group, and fifty dollars for one-on-one) then commenced.

When I reviewed half a dozen sex-offender-treatment workbooks, I found that most elicit a thorough sexual history. ("Describe and discuss, in detail, a repeated masturbatory fantasy.") Then come the exercises. One workbook instructs patients to masturbate to an illicit scene then sniff an "ammonia inhalant" until their "state of sexual arousal is completely removed." Another manual introduces children and teens to the practice of "aversive scenes." Youths must masturbate to a deviant thought, then, at peak arousal, switch to an image of "something that you find disgusting . . . e.g. Brussels sprouts." A third requires patients to imagine a "punishment scene," conjuring up unbearable shame as a prophylactic, much as gay youths were once taught, in conversion therapy, to use the fear of familial judgment as a corrective.

Several scholars told me that the notion of shaming youths into compliance is itself a fantasy. In the journal *Child Maltreatment*, the pediatric psychologist Mark Chaffin describes polygraphs, masturbation logs, and other such methods as "coercive techniques of doubtful accuracy, untested benefit, and considerable potential for harm." But therapeutic failures can be lucrative for providers: the longer someone stays in treatment, the longer the person provides a steady income.

"There's an awful lot of money involved in prosecuting, locking up, treating, and registering these folks," Phil Taylor, a former therapist for men convicted of sex offenses in Texas, told me. Under contract with the state, he spent some ten years treating hundreds of adults convicted of violent sex crimes, along with young adults who had had consensual relationships with other teens. A decade ago, in 2006, Taylor's faith in the treatment protocols was shaken by new research. He renounced the field and began working for legislative reform of the registry. "It's hard for people to change their minds when their livelihood depends upon this money stream," he told me.

In Midland, Anthony Metts continued to struggle with treatment. He acknowledged that his behavior as a teen had been reckless. He told me, "Do I think I needed some sort of therapy? Yes. But do I think I needed sex-offender therapy? Hell, no." Still, the rules left few options. Eventually, he agreed to acknowledge how he'd "groomed" his "victims": in one case, they'd gone to dinner, a movie, and—for a Halloween date—to a local haunted house.

His life, meanwhile, increasingly felt like a series of derailments. He had been fired from a job he loved at a local radio station when an advertiser learned of his status on the registry and protested. The best gig he could find was in Midland's oil fields, working dispatch. His mother began to worry about whether he'd make it through a decade of probation. She recalled the judge's warning, on the day that Metts took the plea: "It's a good deal if you make it, or else it's a pretty lousy deal if you don't."

.    .    .

At Indian Oaks, Leah DuBuc told me, "I did what I had to do to save my own skin." She was released on a summer morning, and her father, who had divorced her stepmother, drove her to a campsite, where three of her childhood friends celebrated her return from "boarding school." DuBuc flourished in high school. Her occasional check-ins with her probation officer weren't onerous. Victoria was one of the few classmates who knew about her secret.

But, not long after DuBuc's time at Indian Oaks, the Michigan legislature passed a new sex-offender law creating an online registry that was available to anyone with an Internet connection. DuBuc was required to register privately with the local authorities; when she was eighteen, her name and personal information would be made public online. The law set a mandatory minimum of twenty-five years on the registry—based on a template that was spreading across the country.

At first, the requirements were easily met. Each year, DuBuc's dad would send in her latest weight, height, and address. In school, meanwhile, DuBuc earned a reputation as Little Miss Civics; she ran the Diversity Club and, after graduation, went to Guatemala with church friends to build an orphanage. But when she got Victoria's call she learned that strangers could now map an easy route to her childhood home, using the state's online sex-offender database. "This is where my life became a living hell all over again," she later wrote.

Throughout her first semester in college, she was dogged by fears of being outed. During winter break, her boyfriend invited her home to Brighton, Michigan. DuBuc agreed, but sheepishly explained that their first stop in town would have to be the police station. Her understanding was that she had to check in with local cops within forty-eight hours of arriving in a new town or face a felony charge.

Her boyfriend parked in the lot of the Brighton Police Post. "I'm here to fill out the paperwork," DuBuc told the trooper at the front desk. "I'm a registered sex offender."

"We don't serve your kind here," he replied. "You better leave before I take you out back and shoot you myself."

Back at the car, DuBuc wept. Her boyfriend filed a formal complaint, and eventually a letter arrived from the station's lieutenant, apologizing for the trooper's "unacceptable" behavior.

DuBuc felt increasingly unsettled. "I didn't really have people I could talk to who understood my situation," she recalls. "I couldn't talk to my mom—she was going through her own issues—and my dad would feel too guilty. I fell into a deep depression." She made an effort to stay engaged in the world she still hoped to build, marching with the local living-wage campaign, travelling with her church group to Japan for the summer. At college, where she pursued a double major in comparative religion and social work, she racked up accolades: a Presidential Scholar award, a steady spot on the dean's list. But, outside of her academics, things seemed only to get worse. As shows like *To Catch a Predator* debuted and awareness grew, registrant shaming became a popular pastime. Soon, the state legislature voted to require registrants to report their place of work, volunteer activity, and education; new "Predator-Free Zones" were also introduced, prohibiting convicted sex offenders from going within a thousand feet of a school. Many such laws were applied retroactively, lumping juvenile offenses with those of adults.

One morning during her junior year, DuBuc returned to her room from psychology class to find a yellow Post-it on her door: "We know you're a sex offender. GET OUT OF OUR DORM. You're not wanted here." She tore it up, and told no one. A few days later, as she sat in her room working on a paper for class, she heard a *ping* from her AOL Instant Messenger account. The sender was anonymous. "We know you're a sex offender," DuBuc read. "Get out."

She no longer felt safe in the dorm. But in order to rent her own apartment she'd need a decent income. She applied for jobs that interested her—working with the homeless, helping out an urban ministry—without success. Then McDonald's, Burger King, and Subway turned her down because of her offender status. For a while, she dropped out of school, returning to Howell and working as a home-health-care aide. But she knew that her best chance of becoming independent was to complete her education. She moved into a homeless shelter in Kalamazoo and returned to class. Eventually, a church friend with whom she'd gone on a mission trip to Japan took her in, letting her sleep on the sofa.

Unable to escape the public registry, DuBuc decided to study it and then take it on. She bought a thick green binder and began to compile research: notes on the historical development of the juvenile-justice system and studies of the registry's impact on public safety. Finally, she began to write her story. "I'm a loving sister. . . . I'm an intern for the Kalamazoo City Commission," she wrote in "So, Who Is Leah DuBuc Anyway?" uploading the essay, along with friendly photographs (Leah with a campus Christian group, Leah arm in arm with her siblings). "I'm an advocate for the homeless, and disenfranchised. . . . Do I sound like a violent, predatory sex offender to you?"

But vigilantism, too, has found opportunity in transparency. Most state registries publish an explicit warning against using the database for so-called citizen justice. To judge from my conversations with more than forty youth registrants and their families, however, these warnings have done little to prevent threats and violent attacks. Mike Grottalio, in Weatherford, Texas, told me how his daughter, who was sexually abused by her brothers when they were ten and twelve (and she was seven), had suffered

further because of her siblings' registration. After the boys returned from two years of detention, the family dog was shot to
death by a neighbor. Then the local paper ran their names and
address under the headlines "County Sex-Offender Roundup"
and, later, for Halloween, "Know Where the Monsters Are." More
recently, a Molotov cocktail spilled flames across the family's
driveway, and BB-gun pellets were fired at their home's vinyl sid-
ing after a neighbor passed out warning flyers. "It's made out-
casts of our whole family," Grottalio said of the registry. "The
damage has been done. There's no repairing it."

In a small, religious neighborhood of Pinesdale, Montana,
Heidi Nuttall described how locals held a meeting about her
son—a registrant since the age of fourteen—that amounted to
something "just short of a lynch mob." Soon afterward, someone
fired a BB gun at the door of the home where her son slept. A
third mother, from Missouri, showed me photographs sent to her
by local registrants who had apparently been singled out for retribution. She'd blown the pictures up to poster size, showing
them to anyone who would look. One featured a registrant's face
that resembled a smashed tomato: two men had broken into his
home and bashed him with a tire iron.

In recent years, mothers like these have come together in
groups like Women Against Registry, and they've begun showing
up at the same events as Stacie Rumenap's Stop Child Predators,
sharing their own stories. Rumenap, for one, has little sympathy
for those in the group advocating for husbands or adult sons
who have been convicted of harming children; she isn't convinced that most convicted adults should get a second chance.
But the stories of juveniles on the registry have increasingly
swayed her. "Never in our wildest dreams were we going state by
state asking lawmakers to punish juveniles," she told me, of her
early years of lobbying for registry laws. "You can't handle these
types of kids—and they're kids—in the same way you handle an
adult and expect them to be rehabilitated."

Back in 2006, she helped bring a Florida father, Mark Lunsford, to Capitol Hill, to tell the story of how his daughter, Jessica, had been kidnapped, raped, killed, and buried by a man with a long history of abusing children. Together, they lobbied for the passage of Jessica's Law, in Florida and beyond. But, soon afterward, Rumenap learned that Lunsford's eighteen-year-old son had been arrested in Ohio, for heavy petting with a fourteen-year-old. Now the teen faced inclusion on the very registry that his father had fought to bolster in his murdered sister's name. "When these laws started getting implemented and enforced, we didn't realize what would happen," Rumenap told me. "Now here we are, stuck asking, How do we solve this problem?"

·   ·   ·

Leah DuBuc's study of the registry evolved into an encyclopedia on juvenile registration. Under the tab "Definitions, History, and Origins," she charted the creation of the Adam Walsh Act and how use of the registry varied from state to state. In South Carolina, she noted, a nine-year-old could be placed on the registry for life. Other states, including New York and Georgia, defied the act's requirements and declined to place children in their online databases, at the risk of losing funds.

DuBuc had come from a tight-lipped family—even today, some of her relatives have no idea why she was suddenly whisked away from home in sixth grade. But she began writing letters to every local power broker she could think of, asking for a second chance and pleading for the same consideration to be extended to others who faced charges as juveniles. She took her story to the state legislature and urged legal reform, calling for juveniles to be removed from public registries. "I am not alone," she testified. At the very least, she told the state senate, youthful offenders deserved a chance to have their cases reviewed for risk and fairness.

Then she waited. In Lansing, a reform bill stalled, then failed. A letter came from a judge, apologizing that her record couldn't be expunged under current law. In 2008, when DuBuc graduated with a master's degree in social work, she had earned academic honors but her efforts to either clear or seal her juvenile record had gone nowhere, and she could find few decent prospects for employment.

So DuBuc left her green binder at her father's house, gave away much of what she owned, and stuffed her favorite sweaters, a Bible, and her CD collection into two duffel bags. America no longer had a place for her, she decided. And, although she didn't want to separate herself from her friends and her family, she felt that she had no choice but to leave the country.

·   ·   ·

In rural Minnesota, Patty Wetterling had, by the late 2000s, devoted more than two decades of her life to keeping young people safe. First, she and her husband established a child-advocacy group, the Jacob Wetterling Resource Center. Then came a brief foray into politics—she ran for Congress in 2006, as a Democrat against Michele Bachmann, touting her years of fighting for "tough penalties for those who harm children"—and a long period of service as the chair of the National Center for Missing and Exploited Children.

With each passing year, Wetterling learned more about the costs and the causes of sexual harm. She studied the prevalence of the problem (vast), its perpetrators (trusted familiars far more often than strangers), and its most effective remedies (programs centered on open lines of communication in households, schools, and communities). Her first major clue that juvenile registration might demand closer scrutiny came in the 1990s. She had been touring the country, speaking out against the sexual exploitation of children, when she got an invitation to visit a juvenile-sex-offender treatment facility in Alabama. There she met a child who had just spent his tenth birthday at the institution. "He was nine when he first went into treatment," she told me. "I was overwhelmed by that. I kept thinking about this kid, who goes away, gets sex-offender treatment, then goes back to his junior high school, and is on the public registry—this young person who really wants to return to school, to learn, to make friends, but can't have a second chance. That's a life sentence for this kid." Still, she focused on child sex-crime victims, and it was easy to understand the common thirst for retribution among fellow parents: "You can see the fear and anger, as a parent. I get that."

In 2007, Wetterling took a job with the Sexual Violence Prevention Program at the Minnesota Department of Health. She received a call from a Minneapolis mother who wanted to tell the story of her son, and soon followed up with a letter from him. "My name is Ricky," it began, "and I'm a 19-year-old Registered Sex Offender." The letter described how, at sixteen, Ricky had met a girl at a teen club who said she was nearly sixteen. They'd had consensual sex on two occasions, according to the note. Later, Ricky wrote, it came out that the girl was thirteen, and he was prosecuted for "Sexual Abuse, 3rd degree," and placed on the public sex-offender registry; it left him and his family "shattered."

By then, Wetterling had watched the registry evolve into something very different from what she'd fought to create. The database was no longer for the private use of law enforcement. Nor was it confined to high-risk offenders or adults who targeted kids. (In some states, the registry pooled juveniles and those charged with public urination together with adults who had repeatedly raped children.) It also imposed a costly burden on law enforcement—time and money that might have gone for supervision of the highest-risk offenders and the training of officers in preventive measures.

Wetterling began to talk to Ricky. He was "a young man with so much to contribute to the world," she told me, but his attempts to lead a better life had time and again been thwarted by registration. Ricky's letter also raised questions, for Wetterling, about the "Romeo and Juliet" problem—consensual teen-sex prosecutions. These included not just juveniles but also young adults, eighteen and older, who could be tried and sentenced accordingly. In at least twenty-nine states, Human Rights Watch reports, consensual sex between teenagers can trigger registration. There have been scattered efforts at reform, including in Texas. But for many people found guilty of sex offenses, including Anthony Metts, in Midland, they came too late.

• • •

Metts settled into his new life in the oil fields, reluctantly accommodating an array of strictures that he regarded as pointless. Each Halloween, for instance, he reported to the county probation office with dozens of other local sex offenders, and was held from six to ten p.m. and shown movies like *Iron Man 2*, until trick-or-treating was over. "If someone's that dangerous that they need to be locked up, what about all of the other three hundred and sixty-four days of the year?" he asked me.

In 2006, he fell in love with a deputy sheriff's daughter. One night, he took her out to his favorite Italian place in Odessa, ordered two steaks with risotto, and arranged for the waiter to bring out a dessert menu that read, among the à la carte selections, "Will you marry me?" She said yes, and a baby girl soon followed. "My daughter was a blessing and a miracle to me," Metts told me. But it also introduced him to a troubling new aspect of his life on the registry.

Metts, then twenty-four, learned that he wouldn't be allowed to see his daughter. His status banned him from living with her and thus with his wife. Still, Metts sneaked visits, breaking the rules. His mother, Mary Helen, obtained formal certification as a chaperon so that he could see his daughter in her presence, spending Saturday mornings by the duck pond or having brunch at Fuddruckers. Eventually, as his daughter grew, Metts says that his probation officer granted him approval for simple, unchaperoned outings, like crafting trips to Hobby Lobby, with a stop for doughnuts.

One night, a former classmate saw Metts buying a sandwich at Walmart and shouted a slur at him; she'd seen his face on the registry for "Sexual Assault of a Child." Rattled, he went to Buffalo Wild Wings to down a beer and got busted. Metts had a record of technical violations, so a judge ordered him to wear an electronic ankle bracelet, administered by a private monitoring company that charged several hundred dollars a month. The device would notify the authorities of any infractions—stepping too close to a mall, park, bar, or church, or leaving the county without permission.

The circumference of permissible life kept shrinking. "A flame inside of me just went out," Metts told me. In the darkness that followed, he recalls, "I hermited myself." He moved back in with his parents, to save money for his child and for his electronic-monitoring bills. Most days, he'd drive straight home from work to play Grand Theft Auto: San Andreas on his Xbox. Within a year and a half, he had gained a hundred pounds. He didn't want his scarlet letter to further affect his wife and child; the couple got divorced.

In the eighth year of his ten-year probation term, Metts decided to reenter the world. He returned to college, began to party, and made friends for the first time in years. On a warm afternoon in May during his final year of probation, he invited some of those new friends over to his parents' swimming pool. He tossed back several beers and took a dip. He'd failed to charge his ankle bracelet properly, and the battery died at around 5 PM.

Shortly before midnight, his probation officer arrived at his door: she'd be filing to revoke his probation. A few weeks later, Metts was led into a courtroom in handcuffs, leg cuffs, and a chain around his waist connecting them. "I looked like Hannibal Lecter without the mask," he told me. The judge's name sounded familiar: she had helped prosecute his original case. (The Texas Court of Criminal Appeals has since agreed to consider whether her involvement in the earlier proceedings disqualified her from presiding over Metts's fate.)

The prosecutor pushed for two years in prison, arguing that the long list of Metts's technical infractions was "not just a fluke . . . not just 'Oops, I messed up.'" Metts's attorney urged alternatives that would be less costly for taxpayers. None of Metts's violations, he noted, had any connection to the original charges of sexual assault of a child. A typical mistake was failing to charge his ankle bracelet's battery. The judge took some time to think it over. The next morning, she sentenced Metts to ten years in prison.

.     .     .

In many states, compliance with the registry can prove to be a Sisyphean task. In McMinnville, Oregon, I met with Catherine Barnes, whose son, Christian, had been placed on a sex-offender registry for life after a sexual encounter, at the age of seventeen, with a thirteen-year-old girl. (In Oregon, the age of consent is eighteen.) Barnes told me that years of treatment, documenting "his masturbation and all that jazz," and a life confined by the registry's restrictions had changed him "one hundred percent."

McMinnville is a town built on second chances. In the past few decades, it had lost its Hewlett-Packard and Pillsbury plants. But, as domestic-wine prices have surged in recent years, tasting bars have cropped up in the wine-country town, filled with tea lights and tourists. At a bright new bistro, Barnes showed me a video on her iPhone. "This was the happiest I've ever seen him," she said. Christian, in his late twenties, was rapping the lyrics to Vanilla Ice's "Ice Ice Baby" while seated in class at a windmill-repair school; he was physically hulking, but he shared his mother's blond hair and high cheekbones.

"A lot of doors would have opened for Christian if we could have gotten him off the registry," his attorney, Claire Brown, had told me at her Portland office. (Brown represented Christian through the CLiF Project, which helps provide legal aid to people placed on Oregon's sex-offender registry for juvenile adjudications.)

After our meal, Barnes took me to her house, where Christian had lived with her. "I'll show you where it happened," she told me, leading me by the arm to a small mauve bedroom, where a decade-long registration story had, not long ago, come to an end.

In the winter of 2013, after years of being turned down for employment, Christian, then twenty-eight, was offered a job in Idaho as a clean-energy repairman for a well-known company. Giddy, he packed his suitcase and said his good-byes. The night before his departure, he got a call. "Something's come up," a woman from the company told him; the company had run a criminal-background check and learned of his sex offense, and she had to let him know the bad news. "I heard the call," Barnes said. "He was absolutely destroyed."

One afternoon the following spring, Christian called his mother, sounding frantic: "Mom, did you know I can't even come into the school and pick up my own kid?" His daughter was entering preschool. Christian hadn't realized that his registrant status barred him from things like school visits and dance recitals. His mental health deteriorated, and within weeks he was facing a possible felony charge for falling behind on his annual registration at the police station.

On a Friday in April, Barnes called Christian from the grocery store in the early afternoon to see if he wanted anything; there was no answer. "Then I came in with my groceries, and I saw him lying there on the floor." She pointed to the carpet, where she'd since placed an Autumn Cedar candle. "And I saw the gun three feet from his body."

Christian had long struggled with depression, debt, and other pressures, and his former probation officer cautioned me against overly tidy explanations for suicide: "Who can know the hearts of men?" But Barnes remembers him as a fearless kid, swinging from ropes and snatching lizards from the woods. As Christian's teenage mistake trailed him into adulthood, Barnes believes, his resilience proved unequal to the burden. She has since learned that suicide is not uncommon among registrants. Her son, who left no note, sent his girlfriend a goodbye text. "I shot myself," it read.

      •      •      •

Often, parents are the ones who carry the weight of the registry. In her grief, Catherine Barnes contacted Oregon Voices, an advocacy group that has the stated goal of achieving "justice and rationality in policies regarding sex offenses." It was run by a professor whose son was arrested, several years ago, for an Internet sex crime and who had since become exercised by what he considered to be the evidence-blind nature of much sex-offense law. (In a study of more than a thousand male juveniles with sex-crime convictions, Elizabeth Letourneau and her colleagues found that public registration did not reduce repeat-offense rates.) Similar groups had emerged around the country, consisting mostly of parents whose children were on the registry or in detention. In the Midwest, there were the mothers who had formed Women Against Registry, seeking to educate the public about the effects of registration on families. In Maryland, another mother led parents in lobbying against strict residency restrictions. One of the largest and most effective advocacy groups was Texas Voices for Reason and Justice; its members include Mary Helen Metts, Anthony's mother.

"People would rather have a murderer next door, especially here in the Bible Belt," Metts, a Catholic hospice worker with a Southern-belle bearing, told me. When her son first appeared on the Texas registry, some friends and relatives stopped speaking to her. Then she got a letter from Mary Sue Molnar, a San Antonio mother whose son was in detention for a sex offense. The founder of Texas Voices, Molnar had contacted the families of thousands of registrants in the state. At first, Mary Helen Metts didn't see the point of participating in the group. But after her son was sent to prison she agreed to start a local chapter of the organization in Midland. Soon she was hosting Texas Voices meetings at her husband's oil-company office after hours. "We don't feel like lepers anymore," she told me.

This past June, Texas Voices hosted a gathering for a national umbrella advocacy organization called Reform Sex Offender Laws, at a church in Dallas. As many as 200 registrants and their loved ones traveled across the country to attend. Around big circular tables, parents shared stories about vigilantism and therapy troubles, as well as tips on navigating the demands of compliance. In the church's dining hall, the group held a humble auction ("Antique cookie jar, anyone? Eighteen dollars? Twelve dollars?") to raise lobbying funds. Among the parents whose children were charged with sex crimes, discussion revolved around how to change registry laws. Josh Gravens, the young man from Abilene who had been placed on the registry at thirteen, stood at the microphone and said that, if parents didn't tell their kids' stories, no one else would. "It takes a lot for a legislator to stick their neck out on this issue," he said. "So it's vitally important that you speak up."

•　　　•　　　•

After packing up her life in Howell, Leah DuBuc boarded a plane for Tokyo. Her visit to Japan during college had filled her with a rush of big-city anonymity. Now she was determined to seek her second chance abroad.

"It was such a relief to have a fresh start," DuBuc told me. Like nearly every other country, Japan has no public sex-offender registry. DuBuc taught English and fell in love with a Filipino man from her church named Kimo, a surfer and a karaoke enthusiast who worked at a Disney resort. She had dreamed of volunteering in India, and with Kimo's encouragement she spent six months working in orphanages from New Delhi to Kolkata. Along the way, Kimo joined her and proposed. In 2010, they married over doughnuts in Bangalore, and soon returned to Tokyo, where their son was born.

To show the baby off, they planned to travel to Fukushima, where Kimo had spent much of his childhood and where his family still lived. But, three days after the birth, the earthquake hit, followed by the tsunami, which killed Kimo's mother and his twelve-year-old sister.

DuBuc planned to stay in Japan, despite the devastation; she felt that God had called on her to help rebuild. Then, after a trip to obtain her in-laws' remains, she received a flurry of Facebook messages from Sharon Denniston, her juvenile advocate in Michigan. Denniston had been pushing the legislative reforms that DuBuc had helped promote. "Be sure you are sitting down," she wrote. "Juveniles that were less than 14 at the time of their offense will be straight out removed from the registry: no hearing, no court visit, no paperwork to fill out!"

DuBuc asked Denniston for updates as the bill was implemented.

"Sweet child of God, Leah," Denniston wrote one evening. "Your name no longer appears on the public registry."

DuBuc decided to take her family home. Her father now had a girlfriend who owned a horse-rescue farm, where Leah and Kimo could work while they looked for steady employment. Even without a high-school diploma, Kimo quickly found a factory job making plastic car parts. Leah's search proved harder, despite her master's degree. Her fingerprints and her record still popped up in certain criminal-background checks. She spent months with the baby on her back, shoveling snow from horse stalls and tending to the hogs and cows before dawn, continuing her job search when the sun came up.

She found work at the Salvation Army, helping families in search of housing, but she was let go after several months without an explanation. The pattern persisted through jobs at a bookstore, a gas station, and a fry house—the same place she'd worked as a teen, when she was certain that her adult life was destined for public service.

As DuBuc discovered, getting off a state's online database doesn't mean the end of online notoriety. Some companies have programs that retain information that was expunged from registries, which they publish online, demanding that offenders pay steep fees in order to have the damaging data removed. Charla Roberts, who had "pantsed" her classmate in Paris, Texas, when she was ten, was removed from the registry in her early twenties, with the help of Lone Star Legal Aid. But the Internet refused to forget. Not long ago, she learned that her ex-boyfriend's new girlfriend was circulating a link to a commercial website called SexOffenderRecord.com. The site featured Charla's photograph along with her race (black), age (twenty-five), and home address, as well as the message: "To alert others about Charla Lee Roberts's Sex Offender Record . . . Just Click the Facebook Icon."

With each rebuff, DuBuc tried to motivate herself afresh. By her bed, she stuck a NASA bumper sticker that Kimo had given her, which read, "Failure is not an option." And Sharon Denniston had made a present of DuBuc's favorite prayer, from Jeremiah, in a gilt frame: " 'For I know the plans I have for you,' declares the Lord. 'Plans to prosper you and not to harm you, plans to give you hope and a future.' "

•     •     •

The reform movement's efforts have started to see gains. In recent years, many institutions—from district attorneys' offices to detention facilities—have improved the way they deal with youths who have committed sexual offenses. The broader justice system, too, has shifted, acknowledging that juveniles aren't just mini-adults; not long ago, the Supreme Court affirmed that "children who commit even heinous crimes are capable of change." The current executive director of Indian Oaks Academy, Mike Chavers, says that the institution has advanced considerably since the era of DuBuc's treatment. "Today, while there are some children who need treatment in a more controlled setting, we know that the vast majority of individuals are better off in their own communities, closer to their families, and that's what we're pushing to have done," he told me. Chavers has also recently joined the fight to reform Illinois's juvenile-registry laws. "To write a kid off at an early age and to label them like that is just unconscionable," he says.

In Pennsylvania, in 2014, the state Supreme Court ruled that mandatory lifetime sex-offender registration for juveniles was unconstitutional, after the Philadelphia-based Juvenile Law Center led a legal challenge. And in Texas an official task force has formed to assess ways of improving outcomes for juveniles charged with sex offenses; Josh Gravens was invited to testify at one of its hearings this month. But the legislative provisions have proved far more recalcitrant.

One of the movement's best hopes for advancing legislative change is an attorney named Nicole Pittman. In the early 2000s, Pittman worked as a public defender on the juvenile docket in New Orleans, where she first noticed the long-term toll that the registry took on convicted offenders. (In Louisiana, teenagers' licenses are stamped in red with "SEX OFFENDER.") In 2011, she embarked on a cross-country trek to interview youth registrants and their families. Her findings were released in a hundred-plus-page Human Rights Watch report, which she was sure would inspire changes in policy. On the road, Pittman met with members of local government to present her findings, and most politicians listened politely. But few, if any, were moved to action.

"The biggest barrier in this work is: 'If I act, I'm going to lose the next election,'" she says. She was dejected and weighed giving up, but when she won last-minute funding from the Stoneleigh Foundation she moved her operations to Oakland, California, and launched a program called the Center on Youth Registration Reform, with a new criminal-justice-advocacy group known as Impact Justice. Then she forged a surprising alliance with Eli Lehrer, the president of the R Street Institute, a conservative think tank in Washington, D.C.

It was a curious pairing. Pittman favors funky red Converse sneakers, a silver nose ring, and a punk-rock-meets-courtroom aesthetic; Lehrer, a navy-blazer type, had a life-sized cutout of President Reagan in his office. Yet they both deplored juvenile registration; he saw it as a costly and invasive problem of big government, and one that flew in the face of the prevailing evidence about kids who offend against other kids. Pittman observed that some conservatives were willing to take risks that their progressive counterparts wouldn't, to defend second chances for juvenile offenders. The religious right, for instance, shared a ready-made language of redemption.

Last summer, Pittman and Lehrer drafted a plan of action that focused on revising a single clause of the Adam Walsh Act. Instead of mandating that states include certain kids on the public registry, they proposed that the law stipulate the opposite: that states failing to eliminate the practice of juvenile registration would fall afoul of federal law and lose funds. Any savings could be put toward programs that took a preventive approach to childhood sexual assault. Pittman and Lehrer contacted Stacie Rumenap, the head of Stop Child Predators, who agreed to help push the proposal nationwide and to work with them on state-level reforms. "Over the years," Rumenap told me, "I've become more sympathetic and more aware that, as we draft our sex-offender laws, we need to be very careful about how we insure young kids' lives aren't being ruined."

.     .     .

This past July, I drove around Midland, Texas, trying to find the girls—now women—who were involved in Anthony Metts's case. Having no luck with doorbells, I left notes, and two days later I got a call from one of them. "I never wanted Anthony to be prosecuted," she told me. "It was a consensual relationship—the kind when you're young and you're stupid. My mom knew about it. We'd go on dates, drive around, hang out." She was shocked to learn of Metts's fate: his nine-plus years of probation, his current decade of incarceration. "I told [law enforcement] that I didn't feel like he should have to be prosecuted," she said.

That same month, I made plans to visit Metts in prison, at Fort Stockton. For nearly two years, I'd routinely spoken with him by phone. But now Anthony's calls had mysteriously stopped. His mother told me that he had been assaulted by two inmates after they took his ID number and found out that he was a sex offender. He was hospitalized and then moved to solitary confinement.

Several weeks later, he was transferred to a remote penitentiary in deep East Texas, eight hours away, built on farmland cleared by former slaves and now maintained by prison labor. When I drove there for an interview, guards shuffled Metts, tall and monkish in his prison whites, into a small booth with a partition between us. The night before, he learned that he'd lost a pending appeal in his case. His eyes were puffy from tears and sleeplessness.

"I thought, by the time we finally met, we'd be on the rooftop at the Hilton," he said, laughing halfheartedly. For most of the next four hours, he spoke of how he planned to get through the coming decade. "In my mind, I don't live here," he told me.

He spends his days reading business and life-style magazines and making plans to return to his daughter, who is now eight. "I look forward to being the dad she deserves, the dad I feel I am," he said. "I miss reading her stories. Getting doughnuts with her, helping her with her homework, brushing her hair. Everything. Everything."

He began to sob. "It's a son of a bitch," he said. Eventually, guards came over and recuffed his hands. After he'd been shuffled back to segregation, it occurred to me that if Anthony Metts serves out his full sentence he will have spent more than twenty years—nearly half his life—under state supervision.

. . .

Last October, Patty Wetterling got a startling piece of news at home, in St. Joseph, Minnesota. Twenty-six years after Jacob's unsolved disappearance, the police had identified a "person of interest" in the case: Daniel James Heinrich, a man whose DNA allegedly matched that found in another unsolved case involving child kidnapping and sexual assault from 1989, in a nearby town. Heinrich was subsequently arrested on five counts of child pornography, unrelated to Jacob; he has pleaded not guilty and is currently awaiting trial. He appeared to be the sort of figure for whom Patty Wetterling first envisaged a private law-enforcement registry.

On a Tuesday afternoon a few days later, Wetterling and her husband walked to the end of their driveway in St. Joseph and stood before a group of reporters. "We still don't know who took Jacob—we have as many questions, or more, as all of you," she said, according to local newspapers. "Child sexual abuse and abduction is something we cannot tolerate. I refuse to be silent."

The discovery of Heinrich took place a few months after Wetterling's retirement as the director of Minnesota's Sexual Violence Prevention Program. Just before stepping down, Wetterling had overseen the publication of a remarkable legislative report, titled "Sexual Violence Prevention," which maps out a public-health response to rape, incest, and childhood sexual assault. It calls for "taking on the root causes like alcohol and drug use, emotionally unsupportive family environments, and societal norms that support male superiority and sexual entitlement."

The report was an apt summary of Wetterling's work, and—with its emphasis on prevention—belonged to a maturing vision that began, years before, with the open-ended pain of losing a child. That pain had helped her craft an early model of the sex-offender registry and, later, a nuanced critique of what it had become. But Wetterling's grief had never abated into abstraction. And so, on that Tuesday afternoon in November, flanked by her husband, she returned to a touchstone. "The one question that we have said for twenty-six years is, Where is Jacob? Where is Jacob?" she said. "I will still always, always hope."

·　　　·　　　·

In Howell, Leah DuBuc has grown largely reconciled to her circumstances. On occasion, though, her fear resurges; when I first visited her at her home, she'd spent the previous night in her rocking chair, keeping watch, having been alerted by a noise that stirred thoughts of vigilantes. She still tracks news of registrant attacks across the country. Last year, a neo-Nazi couple were convicted of murdering a man on the registry and his wife, with plans to take down others. "Child molesters don't deserve to live," the man told reporters, adding that if he "had to do it over again, I'd kill more."

DuBuc and I spent part of the day in her garden, with the tomatoes and the strawberries that her four-year-old son had helped plant. Her two-year-old daughter played in a sandbox nearby. DuBuc spoke of her efforts to find a job. She's been working for a company called Life Leadership, which does "financial fitness" coaching; at night, she sells the company's self-help books,

CDs, and videos from her car. She believes that self-employment is the best option for current and former registrants. She also holds regular yard sales, selling old baby clothes and toys, and makes her own home decor, including a wreath on the front door which lists, in bright colors, the things the family is grateful for: "Food," "Our health," "Daddy's Job," "Mommy's Hope."

DuBuc has worked hard to protect her kids from the experiences that defined her childhood: the chaotic home life, most of all, and the lack of supervision that she believes got her into trouble. "That's my number-one life mission," she told me. "Raising my kids to be empathetic, good citizens." As DuBuc recounted her memories of Indian Oaks Academy—the assaults she witnessed as a girl, the grueling therapies—her son raced over, wearing a pirate's eye patch and a sword at his hip.

As the kids settled down to watch *Shrek*, Leah rummaged in the basement for her old green binder. Inside was the apologetic letter from the Brighton Police lieutenant and the countless appeals she'd written to politicians, judges, and journalists, hoping for a break. She peeled open the sticky pages of her photo album, which chronicled her travels to Japan and India and her lobbying in Lansing.

Together, we flipped from back to front, pausing often to talk. By the time we reached the opening pages, it was nearly midnight. We'd landed on a photograph of a ten-year-old DuBuc at a dance recital, her emerald-green tank top contrasting with her flaming-red hair. She was holding a carnation. In a moment, DuBuc would get up to look in on her sleeping son and daughter, wishing for them what Jeremiah 29:11 had spoken of—"hope, and a future"—before double-checking the deadbolts. But for now she sat in silence. "That's me," she finally said. "A kid."

**New York Times Magazine**

FINALIST—REPORTING

*Born in New Delhi in 1970, Siddhartha Mukherjee studied at Stanford and Oxford universities before attending medical school at Harvard. He now works at the Columbia University Medical Center. His first book,* The Emperor of All Maladies: A Biography of Cancer, *won the Pulitzer Prize for General Nonfiction in 2011. This piece, from "The Improvisational Oncologist," was published as part of a six-part package called "The New Anatomy of Cancer" in the annual Health Issue of the* New York Times Magazine. *The Ellies judges described "The Improvisational Oncologist" as "a lucid, beautifully written introduction to the latest treatments"—what Mukherjee calls an "artisanal approach in oncology."*

Siddhartha Mukherjee

# The Improvisational Oncologist

The bone-marrow biopsy took about twenty minutes. It was ten o'clock on an unusually chilly morning in New York in April, and Donna M., a self-possessed seventy-eight-year-old woman, had flown in from Chicago to see me in my office at Columbia University Medical Center. She had treated herself to orchestra seats for *The Humans* the night before and was now waiting in the room as no one should be asked to wait: pants down, spine curled, knees lifted to her chest—a grown woman curled like a fetus. I snapped on sterile gloves while the nurse pulled out a bar cart containing a steel needle the length of an index finger. The rim of Donna's pelvic bone was numbed with a pulse of anesthetic, and I drove the needle, as gently as I could, into the outer furl of bone. A corkscrew of pain spiraled through her body as the marrow was pulled, and then a few milliliters of red, bone-flecked sludge filled the syringe. It was slightly viscous, halfway between liquid and gel, like the crushed pulp of an overripe strawberry.

I had been treating Donna in collaboration with my colleague Azra Raza for six years. Donna has a preleukemic syndrome called myelodysplastic syndrome, or MDS, which affects the bone marrow and blood. It is a mysterious disease with few known treatments. Human bone marrow is normally a site for the genesis of most of our blood cells—a white-walled nursery for young blood. In MDS, the bone-marrow cells acquire genetic mutations, which force them to grow uncontrollably—but the cells also fail to mature into blood, instead dying in droves. It is a dual curse. In most cancers, the main problem is cells that refuse to stop growing. In Donna's marrow, this problem is compounded by cells that refuse to grow up.

Though there are commonalities among cancers, of course, every tumor behaves and moves—"thinks," even—differently. Trying to find a drug that fits Donna's cancer, Raza and I have administered a gamut of medicines. Throughout all this, Donna has been a formidable patient: perennially resourceful, optimistic, and willing to try anything. (Every time I encounter her in the clinic, awaiting her biopsy with her characteristic fortitude, it is the doctor, not the patient, who feels curled and small.) She has moved nomadically from one trial to another, shuttling from city to city and from one drug to the next, through a landscape more desolate and exhilarating than most of us can imagine; Donna calls it her "serial monogamy" with different medicines. Some of these drugs have worked for weeks, some for months—but the transient responses have given way to inevitable relapses. Donna is getting exhausted.

Her biopsy that morning was thus part routine and part experiment. Minutes after the marrow was drawn into the syringe, a technician rushed the specimen to the lab. There he extracted the cells from the mixture and pipetted them into tiny grain-size wells, 500 cells to a well. To each well—about 1,000 in total—he will add a tiny dab of an individual drug: prednisone, say, to one well, procarbazine to the next and so forth. The experiment will test about 300 medicines (many not even meant for cancer) at three different doses to assess the effects of the drugs on Donna's cells.

Bathed in a nutrient-rich broth suffused with growth factors, the cells will double and redouble in an incubator over the course of the following two weeks, forming a lush outgrowth of malignant cells—cancer abstracted in a dish. A computer, taught to count and evaluate cells, will then determine whether any of the drugs killed the cancerous cells or forced them to mature into nearly normal blood. Far from relying on data from other trials, or patients, the experiment will test Donna's own cancer for its reactivity against a panel of medicines. Cells, not bodies, entered this preclinical trial, and the results will guide her future treatment.

I explained all this to Donna. Still, she had a question: What would happen if the drug that appeared to be the most promising proved unsuccessful?

"Then we'll try the next one," I told her. "The experiment, hopefully, will yield more than one candidate, and we'll go down the list."

"Will the medicine be like chemotherapy?"

"It might, or it might not. The drug that we end up using might be borrowed from some other disease. It might be an anti-inflammatory pill, or an asthma drug. It might be aspirin, for all we know."

My conversation with Donna reflected how much cancer treatment has changed in the last decade. I grew up as an oncologist in an era of standardized protocols. Cancers were lumped into categories based on their anatomical site of origin (breast cancer, lung cancer, lymphoma, leukemia), and chemotherapy treatment, often a combination of toxic drugs, was dictated by those anatomical classifications. The combinations—Adriamycin, bleomycin, vinblastine, and dacarbazine, for instance, to treat Hodgkin's disease—were rarely changed for individual patients. The prospect of personalizing therapy was frowned upon: The more you departed from the standard, the theory ran, the more likely the patient would end up being undertreated or improperly managed, risking recurrence. In hospitals and clinics, computerized systems were set up to monitor an oncologist's compliance with standard therapy. If you chose to make an exception for a particular patient, you had to justify the choice with an adequate excuse. Big Chemo was watching you.

I memorized the abbreviated names of combination chemo—the first letter of each drug—for my board exams, and I spouted them back to my patients during my clinic hours. There was something magical and shamanic about the multiletter contractions. They were mantras imbued with promise and peril: ABVD for Hodgkin's, CMF for breast cancer, BEP for testicular cancer. The lingo of chemotherapists was like a secret code or handshake; even the capacity to call such baleful poisons by name made me feel powerful. When my patients asked me for statistical data, I had numbers at my fingertips. I could summon the precise chance of survival, the probability of relapse, the chance that the chemo would make them infertile or cause them to lose their hair. I felt omniscient.

Yet as I spoke to Donna that morning, I realized how much that omniscience has begun to wane—unleashing a more experimental or even artisanal approach in oncology. Most cancer patients are still treated with those hoary standardized protocols, still governed by the anatomical lumping of cancer. But for patients like Donna, for whom the usual treatments fail to work, oncologists must use their knowledge, wit, and imagination to devise individualized therapies. Increasingly, we are approaching each patient as a unique problem to solve. Toxic, indiscriminate, cell-killing drugs have given way to nimbler, finer-fingered molecules that can activate or deactivate complex pathways in cells, cut off growth factors, accelerate or decelerate the immune response or choke the supply of nutrients and oxygen. More and more, we must come up with ways to use drugs as precision tools to jam cogs and turn off selective switches in particular cancer cells. Trained to follow rules, oncologists are now being asked to reinvent them.

The thought that every individual cancer might require a specific individualized treatment can be profoundly unsettling. Michael Lerner, a writer who worked with cancer patients, once likened the experience of being diagnosed with cancer to being parachuted out of a plane without a map or compass; now it is the oncologist who feels parachuted onto a strange landscape, with no idea which way to go. There are often no previous probabilities and even fewer certainties. The stakes feel higher, the successes more surprising and the failures more personal. Earlier, I could draw curtain upon curtain of blame around a patient. When she did not respond to chemotherapy, it was her fault: She failed. Now if I cannot find a tool in the growing kit of drugs to target a cancer's vulnerabilities, the vector feels reversed: It is the doctor who has failed.

Yet the mapless moment that we are now in may also hold more promise for patients than any that has come before—even if we find the known world shifting under our feet. We no longer have to treat cancer only with the blunt response of standard protocols, in which the disease is imagined as a uniform, if faceless, opponent. Instead we are trying to assess the particular personality and temperament of an individual illness so that we can tailor a response with extreme precision. It's the idiosyncratic *mind* of each cancer that we are so desperately trying to capture.

.   .   .

Cancer—and its treatment—once seemed simpler. In December 1969, a group of cancer advocates led by the philanthropist Mary Lasker splashed their demand for a national war on cancer in a full-page ad in the *New York Times*: "Mr. Nixon: You Can Cure Cancer." This epitomized the fantasy of a single solution to a single monumental illness. For a while, the centerpiece of that solution was thought to be surgery, radiation, and chemotherapy, a strategy colloquially known as "slash and burn." Using combination chemotherapy, men and women were dragged to the very brink of physiological tolerability but then pulled back just in time to send the cancer, but not its host, careering off the edge.

Throughout the 1980s and 1990s, tens of thousands of people took part in clinical trials, which compared subjects on standard chemo combinations with others administered slightly different combinations of those drugs. Some responded well, but for many others, relapses and recurrences were routine—and gains were small and incremental for most cancers. Few efforts were made to distinguish the patients; instead, when the promised cures for most advanced malignancies failed to appear, the doses were intensified and doubled. In the Margaret Edson play *Wit*, an English professor who had ovarian cancer recalled the bewildering language of those trials by making up nonsensical names for chemotherapy drugs that had been pumped into her body: "I have survived eight treatments of hexamethophosphacil and vinplatin at the full dose, ladies and gentlemen. I have broken the record."

To be fair, important lessons were garnered from the trials. Using combinations of chemotherapy, we learned to treat particular cancers: aggressive lymphomas and some variants of breast, testicular, and colon cancers. But for most men and women with cancer, the clinical achievements were abysmal disappointments. Records were not broken—but *patients* were.

A breakthrough came in the 2000s, soon after the Human Genome Project, when scientists learned to sequence the genomes of cancer cells. Cancer is, of course, a genetic disease at its core. In cancer cells, mutated genes corrupt the normal physiology of growth and ultimately set loose malignant proliferation. This characteristic sits at the heart of all forms of cancer: Unlike normal cells, cancer cells have forgotten how to stop dividing (or occasionally, have forgotten how to die). But once we could sequence tens of thousands of genes in individual cancer specimens, it became clear that uniqueness dominates. Say two identical-looking breast cancers arise at the same moment in identical twins; are the mutations themselves in the two cancers identical? It's unlikely: By sequencing the mutations in one twin's breast cancer, we might find, say, 74 mutated genes (of the roughly 22,000 total genes in humans). In her sister's, we might find 42 mutations, and if we looked at a third, unrelated woman with breast cancer, we might find 18. Among the three cases, there might be a mere five genes that overlap. The rest are mutations particular to each woman's cancer.

No other human disease is known to possess this degree of genetic heterogeneity. Adult-onset diabetes, for example, is a complex genetic disease, but it appears to be dominated by variations in only about a dozen genes. Cancer, by contrast, has potentially unlimited variations. Like faces, like fingerprints—like selves— every cancer is characterized by its distinctive marks: a set of individual scars stamped on an individual genome. The iconic illness of the twentieth century seems to reflect our culture's obsession with individuality.

If each individual cancer has an individual combination of gene mutations, perhaps this variability explains the extraordinary divergences in responses to treatment. Gene sequencing allows us to identify the genetic changes that are particular to a given cancer. We can use that information to guide cancer treatment—in effect, matching the treatment to an individual patient's cancer.

Many of the remarkable successes of cancer treatments of the last decades are instances of drugs that were matched to the singular vulnerabilities of individual cancers. The drug Gleevec, for instance, can kill leukemia cells—but only if the patient's cancer cells happen to carry a gene mutation called BCR-ABL. Tarceva, a targeted therapy for lung cancer, works powerfully if the patient's cancer cells happen to possess a particular mutant form of a gene; for lung-cancer patients lacking that mutation, it may be no different from taking a placebo. Because the medicines target mutations or behaviors that are specific to cancer cells (but not normal cells), many of these drugs have surprisingly minimal toxicities—a far cry from combination chemotherapies of the past.

A few days after Donna's visit to the clinic, I went to my weekly meeting with Raza on the ninth floor of the hospital. The patient that morning was K.C., a seventy-nine-year-old woman with blood cancer. Raza has been following her disease—and keeping her alive—for a decade.

"Her tumor is evolving into acute leukemia," Raza said. This, too, is a distinctive behavior of some cancers that we can now witness using biopsies, CT scans, and powerful new techniques like gene sequencing: We can see the cancers morphing from smoldering variants into more aggressive types before our eyes.

"Was the tumor sequenced?" I asked.

"Yes, there's a sequence," Raza said, as we leaned toward a screen to examine it. "P53, DNMT3a and Tet2," she read from the list of mutant genes. "And a deletion in Chromosome 5." In K.C.'s cancer, an entire segment of the genome had been lopped off and gone missing—one of the crudest mutations that a tumor can acquire.

"How about ATRA?" I asked. We had treated a few patients carrying some of K.C.'s mutations with this drug and noted a few striking responses.

"No. I'd rather try Revlimid, but at a higher dose. She's responded to it in the past, and the mutations remain the same. I have a hunch that it might work."

As Raza and I returned to K.C.'s room to inform her of the plan, I couldn't help thinking that this is what it had come down to: inklings, observations, instincts. Medicine based on premonitions. Chemo by hunch. The discussion might have sounded ad hoc to an outsider, but there was nothing cavalier about it. We parsed these possibilities with utmost seriousness. We studied sequences, considered past responses, a patient's recent history—and then charged forward with our best guess. Our decisions were spurred by science, yes, but also a sense for the art of medicine.

Oncologists are also practicing this art in areas that rely less on genes and mutations. A week after Donna's biopsy, I went to see Owen O'Connor, an oncologist who directs Columbia's lymphoma center. O'Connor, in his fifties, reminds me of an amphibious all-terrain vehicle—capable of navigating across any ground. We sat in his office, with large, sunlit windows overlooking Rockefeller Plaza. For decades, he explained, oncologists had treated relapsed Hodgkin's lymphoma in a standard manner. "There were limited options," O'Connor said. "We gave some patients more chemotherapy, with higher doses and more toxic drugs, hoping for a response. For some, we tried to cure the disease using bone-marrow transplantation." But the failure rate was high: About thirty percent of patients didn't respond, and half of them died.

Then a year or two ago, he tried something new. He began to use immunological therapy to treat relapsed, refractory Hodgkin's lymphoma. Immunological therapies come in various forms. There are antibodies: missile-like proteins, made by our own immune systems, that are designed to attack and destroy foreign microbes (antibodies can also be made artificially through genetic engineering, armed with toxins and used as "drugs" to kill cancer cells). And there are drugs that incite a patient's own immune system to recognize and kill tumor cells, a mode of treatment that lay fallow for decades before being revived. O'Connor used both therapies and found that they worked in patients with Hodgkin's disease. "We began to see spectacular responses," he said.

Yet even though many men and women with relapsed Hodgkin's lymphoma responded to immunological treatments, there were some who remained deeply resistant. "These patients were the hardest to treat," O'Connor continued. "Their tumors seemed to be unique—a category of their own."

Lorenzo Falchi, a fellow training with O'Connor and me, was intrigued by these resistant patients. Falchi came to our hospital from Italy, where he specialized in treating leukemias and lymphomas; his particular skill, gleaned from his experience with thousands of patients, is to look for patterns behind seemingly random bits of data. Rooting about in Columbia's medical databases, Falchi made an astonishing discovery: The men and women who responded most powerfully to the immune-boosting therapies had invariably been pretreated with another drug called azacitidine, rarely used in lymphoma patients. A thirty-five-year-old woman from New York with relapsed lymphoma saw her bulky nodes melt away. She had received azacitidine as part of another trial before moving on to the immunotherapy. A man, with a similar stage of cancer, had not been pretreated. He had only a partial response, and his disease grew back shortly thereafter.

Falchi and O'Connor will use this small "training set" to begin a miniature trial of patients with relapsed Hodgkin's disease. "We will try it on just two or three patients," Falchi told me. "We'll first use azacitidine—intentionally, this time—and then chase it with the immune activators. I suspect that we'll reproduce the responses that we've seen in our retrospective studies." In lung cancer too, doctors have noted that pretreating patients with azacitidine can make them more responsive to immunological therapy. Falchi and O'Connor are trying to figure out why patients respond if they are pretreated with a drug that seems, at face value, to have nothing to do with the immune system. Perhaps azacitidine makes the cancer cells more recognizably foreign, or perhaps it forces immune cells to become more aggressive hunters.

Falchi and O'Connor are mixing and matching unexpected combinations of medicines based on previous responses—departing from the known world of chemotherapy. Even with the new combination, Falchi suspects, there will be resistant patients, and so he will divide these into subsets, and root through their previous responses, to determine what might make these patients resistant—grinding the data into finer and finer grains until he's down to individualized therapy for every variant of lymphoma.

. . .

Suppose every cancer is, indeed, unique, with its own permutation of genes and vulnerabilities—a sole, idiosyncratic "mind." It's obviously absurd to imagine that we'll find an individual medicine to treat each one: There are fourteen million new cases of cancer in the world every year, and several million of those patients will present with advanced disease, requiring more than local or surgical treatment. Trying to individualize treatment for those cases would shatter every ceiling of cost.

But while the medical costs of personalized therapy are being debated in national forums in Washington, the patients in my modest waiting room in New York are focused on its personal costs. Insurance will not pay for "off-label" uses of medicines: It isn't easy to convince an insurance company that you intend to use Lipitor to treat a woman with pre-leukemia—not because she has high cholesterol but because the cancer cells depend on cholesterol metabolism for their growth (in one study of a leukemia subtype, the increasing cells were highly dependent on cholesterol, suggesting that high doses of Lipitor-like drugs might be an effective treatment).

In exceptional cases, doctors can requisition pharmaceutical companies to provide the medicines free—for "compassionate use," to use the language of the pharma world—but this process is unpredictable and time-consuming. I used to fill out such requests once every few months. Now it seems I ask for such exceptions on a weekly basis. Some are approved. A majority, unfortunately, are denied.

So doctors like Falchi and O'Connor do what they can—using their wiles not just against cancer but against a system that can resist innovation. They create minuscule, original clinical trials involving just ten or twenty patients, a far cry from the hundred-thousand-patient trials of the eighties and nineties. They study these patients with monastic concentration, drawing out a cosmos of precious data from just that small group. Occasionally, a patient may choose to pay for the drugs out of his or her own pockets—but it's a rare patient who can afford the tens of thousands of dollars that the drugs cost.

But could there be some minimal number of treatments that could be deployed to treat a majority of these cancers effectively and less expensively? More than any other scientist, perhaps, Bert Vogelstein, a cancer geneticist at Johns Hopkins University, has tackled that conundrum. The combination of genetic mutations in any individual cancer is singular, Vogelstein acknowledges. But these genetic mutations can still act through common pathways. Targeting pathways, rather than individual genes, might reorganize the way we perceive and treat cancer.

Imagine, again, the cell as a complex machine, with thousands of wheels, levers, and pulleys organized into systems. The machine malfunctions in the cancer: Some set of levers and pulleys gets jammed or broken, resulting in a cell that continues to divide without control. If we focus on the individual parts that are jammed and snapped, the permutations are seemingly infinite: Every instance of a broken machine seems to have a distinct fingerprint of broken cogs. But if we focus, instead, on *systems* that malfunction, then the seeming diversity begins to collapse into patterns of unity. Ten components function, say, in an interconnected loop to keep the machine from tipping over on its side. Snap any part of this loop, and the end result is the same: a tipped-over machine. Another twenty components control the machine's internal thermostat. Break any of these twenty components, and the system overheats. The number of components—ten and twenty—are deceptive in their complexity and can have endless permutations. But viewed from afar, only two systems in this machine are affected: stability and temperature.

Cancer, Vogelstein argues, is analogous. Most of the genes that are mutated in cancer also function in loops and circuits—pathways. Superficially, the permutations of genetic flaws might be boundless, but lumped into pathways, the complexity can be organized along the archetypal, core flaws. Perhaps these cancer pathways are like Hollywood movies; at first glance, there seems to be an infinite array of plot lines in an infinite array of settings—gold-rush California, the Upper West Side, a galaxy far, far away. But closer examination yields only a handful of archetypal narratives: boy meets girl, stranger comes to town, son searches for father.

How many such pathways, or systems, operate across a subtype of cancer? Looking at one cancer, pancreatic, and mapping the variations in mutated genes across hundreds of specimens, Vogelstein's team proposed a staggeringly simple answer: twelve. (One such "core pathway," for instance, involves genes that enable cells to invade other tissues. These genes normally allow cells to migrate through parts of the body—but in cancer, migration becomes distorted into invasion.) If we could find medicines that could target these twelve core pathways, we might be able to attack most pancreatic cancers, despite their genetic diversity. But that means inventing twelve potential ways to block these core paths—an immense creative challenge for scientists, considering that they haven't yet figured out how to target more than, at best, one or two.

Immunological therapies provide a second solution to the impasse of unlimited diversity. One advantage of deploying a patient's own immune system against cancer is that immunological cells are generally agnostic to the mutations that cause a particular cancer's growth. The immune system was designed to spot differences in the superficial features of a diseased or foreign cell, thereby identifying and killing it. It cares as little about genes as an intercontinental ballistic missile cares about the e-mail addresses or dietary preferences of the population that it has been sent to destroy.

·    ·    ·

A few years ago, in writing a history of cancer, I interviewed Emil Freireich. Freireich, working with Emil Frei at the National Cancer Institute in the 1960s and 1970s, stumbled on the idea of deploying multiple toxic drugs simultaneously to treat cancer—combination chemotherapy. They devised one of the first standard protocols—vincristine, Adriamycin, methotrexate, and prednisone, known as VAMP—to treat pediatric leukemias. Virtually nothing about the VAMP protocol was individualized (although doses could be reduced if needed). In fact, doctors were discouraged from trying alternatives to the formula.

Yet as Freireich recalled, long before they came up with the idea for a protocol, there were small, brave experiments; before trials, there was trial and error. VAMP was brought into existence through grit, instinct, and inspired lunges into the unknown. Vincent T. DeVita Jr., who worked with Freireich in the 1960s, wrote a book, *The Death of Cancer*, with his daughter, Elizabeth DeVita-Raeburn. In it, he recalled a time when the leukemic children in Freireich's trial were dying of bacterial meningitis during treatment. The deaths threatened the entire trial: If Freireich couldn't keep the children alive during the therapy, there would be no possibility of remission. They had an antibiotic that could kill the microbe, but the medicine wouldn't penetrate the blood-brain barrier. So Freireich decided to try something that pushed the bounds of standard practice. He ordered DeVita, his junior, to inject it directly into the spinal cords of his patients. It was an extreme example of off-label use of the drug: The medicine was not meant for use in the cord. DeVita writes:

> The first time Freireich told me to do it, I held up the vial and showed him the label, thinking that he'd possibly missed something. "It says right on there, 'Do not use intrathecally,'" I said. Freireich glowered at me and pointed a long, bony finger in my face. "Do it!" he barked. I did it, though I was terrified. But it worked every time.

When I asked Freireich about that episode and about what he would change in the current landscape of cancer therapy, he pointed to its extreme cautiousness. "We would never have achieved anything in this atmosphere," he said. The pioneer of protocols pined for a time before there were any protocols.

Medicine needs standards, of course; otherwise it can ramble into dangerous realms, compromising safety and reliability. But cancer medicine also needs a healthy dose of Freireich: the desire to read between the (guide)lines, to reimagine the outer boundaries, to perform the experiments that become the standards of the future. In January, President Obama introduced an enormous campaign for precision medicine. Cancer is its molten centerpiece: Using huge troves of data, including gene sequences of hundreds of thousands of specimens and experiments performed in laboratories nationwide, the project's goal is to find individualized medicines for every patient's cancer. But as we wait for that decades-long project to be completed, oncologists still have to treat patients *now*. To understand the minds of individual cancers, we are learning to mix and match these two kinds of learning—the standard and the idiosyncratic—in unusual and creative ways. It's the kind of medicine that so many of us went to medical school to learn, the kind that we'd almost forgotten how to practice.

## The New Yorker

FINALIST—FEATURE
WRITING

"Nothing embodied the manic, angry spirit of the phenomenon known as Donald Trump more than his campaign rallies," said the Ellie judges. "And no one was better suited to capture that reality than George Saunders." Trump, Saunders wrote during the summer before the election, "was not trying to persuade, detail, or prove: he [was] trying to thrill, agitate, be liked, be loved." The nomination of "Trump Days" was the seventh for Saunders's work but his first in the Feature Writing category. His short stories won Ellies for Fiction in 1994, 1996, 2000, and 2004 and were also nominated for the Fiction award in 1999 and 2010. "Trump Days" was soon followed by the publication of Saunders's first novel, the widely acclaimed Lincoln in the Bardo.

George Saunders

# Trump Days

## He Appears

Trump is wearing the red baseball cap, or not. From this distance, he is strangely handsome, well proportioned, puts you in mind of a sea captain: Alan Hale from *Gilligan's Island*, say, had Hale been slimmer, richer, more self-confident. We are afforded a side view of a head of silver-yellow hair and a hawklike orange-red face, the cheeks of which, if stared at steadily enough, will seem, through some optical illusion, to glow orange-redder at moments when the crowd is especially pleased. If you've ever, watching *The Apprentice*, entertained fantasies of how you might fare in the boardroom (the Donald, recognizing your excellent qualities with his professional businessman's acumen, does not fire you but, on the contrary, pulls you aside to assign you some important non-TV, real-world mission), you may, for a brief, embarrassing instant, as he scans the crowd, expect him to recognize you.

He is blessing us here in San Jose, California, with his celebrity, promising never to disappoint us, letting us in on the latest bit of inside-baseball campaign strategy: "Lyin' Ted" is no longer to be Lyin' Ted; henceforth he will be just "Ted." Hillary, however, shall be "Lyin' Crooked." And, by the way, Hillary has to go to jail. The statute of limitations is five years, and if he gets elected in November, well . . . The crowd sends forth a coarse blood roar. "She's guilty as hell," he snarls.

He growls, rants, shouts, digresses, careens from shtick nugget to shtick nugget, rhapsodizes over past landslides, name-drops Ivanka, Melania, Mike Tyson, Newt Gingrich, Bobby Knight, Bill O'Reilly. His right shoulder thrusts out as he makes the pinched-finger mudra with down-swinging arm. His trademark double-eye squint evokes that group of beanie-hatted street-tough Munchkin kids; you expect him to kick gruffly at an imaginary stone. In person, his autocratic streak is presentationally complicated by a Ralph Kramdenesque vulnerability. He's a man who has just dropped a can opener into his wife's freshly baked pie. He's not about to start groveling about it, and yet he's sorry—but, come on, it was an *accident*. He's sorry, he's sorry, OK, but do you expect him to *say it*? He's a good guy. Anyway, he didn't do it.

Once, Jack Benny, whose character was known for frugality and selfishness, got a huge laugh by glancing down at the baseball he was supposed to be first-pitching, pocketing it, and walking off the field. Trump, similarly, knows how well we know him from TV. He is who he is. So sue me, OK? I probably shouldn't say this, but oops—just did. (Hillary's attack ads? "*So* false. Ah, some of them aren't that false, actually.") It's oddly riveting, watching someone take such pleasure in going so much farther out on thin ice than anyone else as famous would dare to go. His crowds are ever hopeful for the next thrilling rude swerve. "There could be no politics which gave warmth to one's body until the country had recovered its imagination, its pioneer lust for the unexpected and incalculable," Norman Mailer wrote in 1960.

The speeches themselves are nearly all empty assertion. Assertion and bragging. Assertion, bragging, and defensiveness. He is always boasting about the size of this crowd or that crowd, refuting some slight from someone who has treated him "very unfairly," underscoring his sincerity via adjectival pile-on (he's "going to appoint beautiful, incredible, unbelievable Supreme Court

Justices"). He lies, bullies, menaces, dishes it out but can't seem to take it, exhibits such a muddy understanding of certain American principles (the press is free, torture illegal, criticism and libel two different things) that he might be a seventeenth-century Austrian prince time-transported here to mess with us. Sometimes it seems that he truly does not give a shit, and you imagine his minders cringing backstage. Other times you imagine them bored, checking their phones, convinced that nothing will ever touch him. Increasingly, his wild veering seems to occur against his will, as if he were not the great, sly strategist we have taken him for but, rather, someone compelled by an inner music that sometimes produces good dancing and sometimes causes him to bring a bookshelf crashing down on an old Mexican lady. *Get more*, that inner music seems to be telling him. *Get, finally, enough. Refute a lifetime of critics. Create a pile of unprecedented testimonials, attendance receipts, polling numbers, and pundit gasps that will, once and for all, prove—what?*

Apply Occam's razor: if someone brags this much, bending every ray of light back to himself, what's the simplest explanation?

"We're on the cover of every newspaper, every magazine," he says in San Jose in early June. "*Time* magazine many times. I just learned they're doing yet another cover on Trump—I love that. You know, *Time* magazine's a good magazine. You grow up reading *Time* magazine—who ever thought you'd be on the cover of *Time* magazine? Especially so much?"

It's considered an indication of authenticity that he doesn't generally speak from a teleprompter but just wings it. (In fact, he brings to the podium a few pages of handwritten bullet points, to which he periodically refers as he, mostly, wings it.) He wings it because winging it serves his purpose. He is not trying to persuade, detail, or prove: he is trying to thrill, agitate, be liked, be loved, here and now. He is trying to make energy. (At one point in his San Jose speech, he endearingly fumbles with a sheaf of "statistics," reads a few, fondly but slightingly mentions the loyal, hapless statistician who compiled them, then seems unable to go on, afraid he might be boring us.)

And make energy he does. It flows out of him, as if channeled in thousands of micro wires, enters the minds of his followers: their cheers go ragged and hoarse, chanting erupts, a look of religious zeal may flash across the face of some nonchanter, who is finally getting, in response to a question long nursed in private, exactly the answer he's been craving. One such person stays in my memory from a rally in Fountain Hills, Arizona, in March: a solidly built man in his midforties, wearing, in the crazy heat, a long-sleeved black shirt, who, as Trump spoke, worked himself into a state of riveted, silent concentration-fury, the rally equivalent of someone at church gazing fixedly down at the pew before him, nodding, Yes, yes, yes.

## A Tiny Pissed Voice Rings Out

"Wow, what a crowd this is," he begins at Fountain Hills. "What a great honor! . . . You have some sheriff—there's no games with your sheriff, that's for sure. . . . We have a movement going on, folks. . . . I will never let you down! Remember. And I want to tell you, you know, it's so much about illegal immigration and so much has been mentioned about it and talked about it, and these politicians are all talk, no action. They're never going to do anything—they only picked it up because when I went, and when I announced, that I'm running for president, I said, 'You know, this country has a big, big problem with illegal immigration,' and all of a sudden we started talking about it. . . . And there was crime and you had so many killings and so much crime, drugs were pouring through the border." ("STOP IT!" someone pleads from the crowd.) "People are now seeing it. And you know what? We're going to build a wall and we are going to stop it!"

Mayhem. The Wall is their favorite. (Earlier in the afternoon, Jan Brewer, the former governor of Arizona and legislative mother of that state's draconian immigration policies, nearly undoes all the good right-wing work of her career by affirming that, yes, Trump is "going to build *the Fence*." Like new Americans who have just been told that Hulk Hogan was the first president, the crowd rises up in happy outrage to correct her.)

"THANK YOU, TRUMP!" bellows a kid in front of me, who, later in the speech, will briefly turn his back on Trump to take a Trump-including selfie, his smile taut, braces-revealing, grimace-like yet celebratory, evoking that circa-1950 photograph of a man in a high-velocity wind tunnel.

"I only wish these cameras—because there's nothing as dishonest as the media, that I can tell you." ("THEY SUCK!") "I only wish these cameramen would spin around and show the kind of people that we have, the numbers of people that we have here. I just wish they'd for once do it, because you know what?" ("PAN THE CAMERAS!") "We have a silent majority that's no longer so silent. It's now the loud, noisy majority, and we're going to be heard. . . . They're chipping away at the Second Amendment, they're chipping away at Christianity. . . . We're not going to have it anymore. It comes Christmas time, we're going to see signs up that say 'Merry Merry Merry Christmas!' OK? Remember it, remember it. We have become so politically correct that we're totally impotent as a country—"

Somewhere in the crowd, a woman is shouting "Fuck you, Trump!" in a voice so thin it seems to be emanating from some distant neighborhood, where a girl is calling home her brother, Fuckhugh Trump.

The shouter is Esperanza Matamoros, tiny, seventeen years old. The crowd now halts her forward progress, so she judiciously spins and, still shouting, heads toward the exit. As she passes a tall, white-haired, professorial-looking old man, he gives her a little shove. He towers over her, the top of her head falling below his armpit. She could be his daughter, his granddaughter, his favorite student. Another man steps in front of her to deliver an impromptu manners lesson; apparently, she bumped him on her way up. "*Excuse me*," he says heatedly. "Around here, we say *excuse me*."

An ungentleness gets into the air when Trump speaks, prompting the abandonment of certain social norms (e.g., an old man should show forbearance and physical respect for a young woman, even—especially—an angry young woman, and might even think to wonder what is making her so angry), norms that, to fired-up Trump supporters, must feel antiquated in this brave new moment of ideological foment. They have thought and thought, in projective terms, about theoretical protesters, and now here are some real ones.

This ungentleness ripples out through the crowd and into the area beyond the fence where the protesters have set up shop. One of them, Sandra Borchers, tells me that out there all was calm (she was "actually having dialogues" with Trump supporters, "back-and-forth conversations, at about this talking level") until Trump started speaking. Then things got "violent and aggressive." Someone threw a rock at her head. A female Trump supporter "in a pink-peachy-color T-shirt" attacked a protester, kicking and punching him. Rebecca LaStrap, an African American woman, twenty years old, wearing a "FUCK TRUMP" T-shirt, was grabbed by the breast, thrown to the ground, slapped in the face. (She was also told to "go back on the boat," a perplexing instruction, given that she was born and raised in Mesa.) Later that day, in Tucson, two young Hispanic women, quietly watching the rally there, are thrown out of the venue, and one (as a member of Trump's security staff bellows, "Out! Out! Out!") is roughly shoved through a revolving door by a Trump supporter who looks to be in his seventies and who then performs a strange little quasi-karate move, as if he expects her to fly back in and counterattack. A pro-immigration protester named George Clifton, who is wearing a sign that says "Veteran: U.S.M.C. *and* C.I.A.," tells me that two Trump supporters came up to him separately after the Fountain Hills rally and whispered "almost verbatim the same thing, not quite, but in a nutshell": that they'd like to shoot him in the back of the head.

## I'm Here for an Argument

In Tucson, Trump supporters flow out of the Convention Center like a red-white-and-blue river, along hostile riverbanks made of protesters, who have situated themselves so as to be maximally irritating. When a confrontation occurs, people rush toward it, to film it and stoke it, in the hope that someone on the other side will fly off the handle and do something extreme, and thereby incontrovertibly discredit his side of the argument. This river-and-shore arrangement advantages the Trump supporters: they can walk coolly past, playing the offended party, refusing to engage.

Most do, but some don't.

"Trump is racist, so are YOU!" the protesters chant, maximizing the provocation. A South Asian–looking youth of uncertain political affiliation does a crazy Borat dance in front of the line as a friend films him. An aging blond bombshell strolls by in a low-cut blouse, giving the protesters a leisurely finger, blowing them kisses, patting one of her large breasts. A matronly Hispanic protester says that the woman has a right to do what she likes with her breasts since, after all, "she paid for them." A grandmotherly white woman tucks a strand of graying hair behind her ear, walks resolutely over, and delicately lifts a Mexican flag from where it lies shawl-like across the shoulders of a young, distractedly dancing Hispanic girl, as if the flag had fallen across the girl's shoulders from some imaginary shelf and the grandmother were considerately removing it before it got too heavy. The girl, offended, pulls away. But wait: the woman shows her anti-Trump sign: they're on the same side. The girl remains unconvinced; she'll keep the flag to herself, thanks. "So *sorry*," the white woman says and rejoins a friend, to commiserate over the girl's response, which strikes her, maybe, as a form of racial profiling.

Two tall Trump supporters tower over a small liberal in a green T-shirt.

"Stupid! Uneducated!" Trumpie A shouts. "Do you know anything that goes *on* in the world?"

"Articulate a little more," the guy in the green shirt says.

"I don't want to live in a fascist country!" Trumpie B says.

"You don't know what fascism *is*," Green Shirt says.

"Oh, I'm getting there, man!" Trumpie B says. "Obama's teaching me!"

"Go back to California," Trumpie A shouts at Green Shirt. "Bitch!"

The four of us stand in a tight little circle, Trumpie A shouting insults at Green Shirt while filming Green Shirt's reaction, me filming Trumpie A filming Green Shirt. The bulk and intensity of the Trumpies, plus the fact that Green Shirt seems to be serving as designated spokesperson for a group of protesters now gathering around, appears to be making Green Shirt nervous.

"Obama's teaching you what fascism is?" he sputters. "Obama's a fascist? The left is the fascists? This is so rich! So, like, the people who are being oppressed are the oppressors?"

"Do you know what's going on in the world, man?" Trumpie A says. "You're not fucking *educated*."

This stings.

"I am very educated," Green Shirt says.

"You have no *idea* what's going on," Trumpie B says.

"I am very educated," Green Shirt says.

"You've got no idea, bro," Trumpie A says sadly.

"Ask me a question, ask me a question," Green Shirt says.

The Tall Trumpies, bored, wander away.

Green Shirt turns to one of his friends. "Am I educated?"

"You're fucking educated," the friend says.

Green Shirt shouts at the Tall Trumpies (who, fortunately for him, are now safely out of earshot), "And I'll stomp the fucking *shit* out of you!"

Spotting a round-faced, brown-skinned youth in a "Make America Great Again" T-shirt, who's been quietly listening nearby, Green Shirt snarls, "And *you* can get your fat fucking Chinese face out of here."

The kid seems more quizzical than hurt.

I ask Green Shirt for clarification: did he just tell that guy to get his Chinese face out of here?

"No, I was calling his *shirt* Chinese," he clarifies. "I told him to get his Chinese *shirt* out of here. The Trump campaign gets those shirts from China."

I'm relieved. My liberal comrade did not commit a racial slur.

"I did call him fat, though," he admits, then dashes back over to the kid, hisses, "Why don't you make your *waistline* great again?" and slips away into the crowd.

"This is America!" a Trump supporter rages desperately into the line of protesters, after one of them forces his phone camera down. "I'm American! I'm Mexican American! Are you a marine?" he demands of an elderly protester in a floppy fatigue hat. "I'm a veteran. I'm a *veteran*. You're idiots. You're *idiots*. I'm a navy corpsman! I saved marines' *asses*. Mexican, white, and black. We're red, white, and blue!" The guy in the floppy hat answers, in heavily accented English, that, yes, he was a marine. This conflict rapidly devolves into a bitter veteran-off: two old guys, who've presumably seen some things in their time, barking hatefully at each other. I know (or *feel* I know) that, on another day, these two guys might have grabbed a beer together, jump-started each other's cars, whatever—but they're not doing that today.

"What are you *doing* here?" a girl shouts at the Trump-supporting Mexican American former corpsman. "You should be ashamed!"

"What am I doing?" he shouts back. "I'm supporting a man who's going to clean up Mexico, build a wall, fix the economy!"

"*Puto!*" a protester snaps, as the corpsman storms off, to go home and, I'm guessing, feel like crap the rest of the day.

If you are, as I am, a sentimental middle-aged person who cherishes certain Coplandian notions about the essential goodness of the nation, seeing this kind of thing in person—adults shouting wrathfully at one another with no intention of persuasion, invested only in escalating spite—will inject a palpable sadness into your thinning, under-exercised legs, and you may find yourself collapsing, post-rally, against a tree in a public park, feeling hopeless. Craving something positive (no more fighting, no more invective, please, please), forcing yourself to your feet, you may cross a busy avenue and find, in a mini-mall themed like Old Mexico, a wedding about to begin. Up will walk the bridesmaids, each leading, surprisingly, a dog on a leash, and each dog is wearing a tutu, and one, a puppy too small to be trusted in a procession, is being carried, in its tutu, in the arms of its bridesmaid.

And this will somehow come as an unbelievable relief.

### Let's Call the Whole Thing Off

Where is all this anger coming from? It's viral, and Trump is Typhoid Mary. Intellectually and emotionally weakened by years of steadily degraded public discourse, we are now two separate ideological countries, LeftLand and RightLand, speaking different languages, the lines between us down. Not only do our two subcountries reason differently; they draw upon nonintersecting data sets and access entirely different mythological systems. You and I approach a castle. One of us has watched only *Monty Python and the Holy Grail*, the other only *Game of Thrones*. What is the meaning, to the collective "we," of yon castle? We have no common basis from which to discuss it. You, the other knight, strike me as bafflingly ignorant, a little unmoored. In the old days, a liberal and a conservative (a "dove" and a "hawk," say) got their data from one of three nightly news programs, a local paper, and a handful of national magazines, and were thus starting with the same basic facts (even if those facts were questionable, limited, or erroneous). Now each of us constructs a custom informational universe, wittingly (we choose to go to the sources that uphold our existing beliefs and thus flatter us) or unwittingly (our app algorithms do the driving for us). The data we get this way, preimprinted with spin and mythos, are intensely one-dimensional. (As a proud knight of LeftLand, I was interested to find that, in RightLand, Vince Foster has still been murdered, Dick Morris is a reliable source, kids are brainwashed "way to the left" by going to college, and Obama may yet be Muslim. I expect that my interviewees found some of my core beliefs equally jaw-dropping.)

A Trump supporter in Fountain Hills asks me, "If you're a liberal, do you believe in the government controlling everything? Because that's what Barry wants to do, and what he's pretty much accomplished." She then makes the (to me, irrational and irritating) claim that more people are on welfare under Obama than ever were under Bush.

"Almost fifty million people," her husband says. "Up 30 percent."

I make a certain sound I make when I disagree with something but have no facts at my disposal.

Back at the hotel, I Google it.

Damn it, they're right. Rightish.

What I find over the next hour or so, from a collection of websites, left, right, and fact-based:

Yes, true: there are approximately seven million more Americans in poverty now than when Obama was elected. On the other hand, the economy under Obama has gained about seven times as many jobs as it did under Bush; even given the financial meltdown, the unemployment rate has dropped to just below the historical average. But, yes: the poverty *rate* is up by 1.6 percentage points since 2008. Then again the *number* of Americans in poverty fell by nearly 1.2 million between 2012 and 2013. However, true: the proportion of people who depend on welfare for the majority of their income *has* increased (although it was also increasing under Bush). And under Obama unemployment has dropped, GDP growth has been "robust," and there have been close to seventy straight months of job growth. But, OK: there has indeed been a "skyrocketing" in the number of Americans needing some form of means-tested federal aid, although Obama's initiatives kept some six million people out of poverty in 2009, including more than two million children.

So the couple's assertion was true but not *complexly* true. It was a nice hammer with which to pop the enemy, i.e., me. Its intent: discredit Obama and the liberal mind-set. What was my intent as I Googled? Get a hammer of my own, discredit Bush and the conservative mind-set.

Meanwhile, there sat reality: huge, ambiguous, too complicated to be usefully assessed by our prevailing mutual ambition— to fight and win, via delivery of the partisan zinger.

LeftLand and RightLand are housemates who are no longer on speaking terms. And then the house is set on fire. By Donald Trump. Good people from both subnations gape at one another through the smoke.

## Who Are They? (Part I)

It's clear enough to those of us who don't like Trump why we don't like him. What isn't clear is why it isn't clear to those who like him. The Trump supporter is your brother who has just brought home a wildly inappropriate fiancée. Well, inappropriate to *you*. Trump support, nationwide, stands at around 40 percent. If you had ten siblings and four of them brought home wildly inappropriate fiancées, you might feel inclined to ask yourself what was going on in your family to make your judgment and that of your siblings so divergent.

It seems futile to try to generalize about a group as large and disparate as "Trump supporters"—like generalizing, say, "people who own riding lawnmowers," who, of course, tend to be, but are not exclusively limited to, people with large or largish lawns but can also include people with small yards who, for whatever reason, can't manage a push mower, and/or people (both large- and small-yarded) who may have received a riding mower from a father-in-law or an uncle and don't want to rock the boat. But sometimes, standing at a rally among several thousand madly cheering Trump supporters, I'd think, All these people have *something* in common. What is it?

I didn't meet many people who were unreservedly for Trump. There is, in the quiver containing his ideas, something for nearly everyone to dislike. But there is also something for nearly everyone to *like*. What allows a person not crazy about Trump to vote for him is a certain prioritization: a person might, for example, like Trump's ideas about trade or his immigration policies or the fact that Trump is, as one supporter told me, "a successful businessman," who has "actually done something," unlike Obama, who has "never done anything his entire life."

The Trump supporters I spoke with were friendly, generous with their time, flattered to be asked their opinion, willing to give it, even when they knew I was a liberal writer likely to throw them under the bus. They loved their country, seemed genuinely panicked at its perceived demise, felt urgently that we were, right now, in the process of losing something precious. They were, generally, in favor of *order* and had a propensity toward the broadly normative, a certain squareness. They leaned toward skepticism (they'd believe it when they saw it, "it" being anything feelings-based, gauzy, liberal, or European, i.e., "socialist"). Some (far from all) had been touched by financial hardship—a layoff was common in many stories—and (paradoxically, given their feelings about socialism) felt that, while in that vulnerable state, they'd been let down by their government. They were antiregulation, pro–small business, pro–Second Amendment, suspicious of people on welfare, sensitive (in a "Don't tread on me" way) about any infringement whatsoever on their freedom. Alert to charges of racism, they would precounter these by pointing out that they had friends of all colors. They were adamantly for law enforcement and veterans' rights, in a manner that presupposed that the rest of us were adamantly against these things. It seemed self-evident to them that a businessman could and should lead the country. "You run your family like a business, don't you?" I was asked more than once, although, of course, I don't, and none of us do.

The Trump supporter comes out of the conservative tradition but is not a traditional conservative. He is less patient: something is bothering him and he wants it stopped *now*, by any means necessary. He seems less influenced by Goldwater and Reagan than by Fox News and reality TV, his understanding of history recent and selective; he is less religiously grounded and more willing, in his acceptance of Trump's racist and misogynist excesses, to (let's say) forgo the niceties.

As for Trump's uncivil speech—the insults, the petty meanness, the crudeness, the talk about hand size, the assurance, on national TV, that his would-be presidential dick is up to the job, his mastery of the jaw-droppingly untrue personal smear (Obama is Kenyan, Ted Cruz's dad was in cahoots with Lee Harvey Oswald, U.S. Muslims knew what was "going on" pre-Orlando), which he often dishonorably eases into the world by attaching some form of the phrase "many people have said this" (*The world is flat; many people have said this. People are saying that birds can play the cello: we need to look into that*)—his supporters seem constitutionally reluctant to object, as if the act of objecting would mark them as fatally delicate. Objecting to this sort of thing is for the coddled, the liberal, the elite. "Yeah, he can really improve, in the way he says things," one woman in Fountain Hills tells me. "But who gives a shit? Because if he's going to get the job done? I'm just saying. You can't let your feelings get hurt. It's kind of like, get over it, you know what I mean? What's the big picture here? The big picture is we've got to get America back on track."

The ability to shrug off the mean crack, the sexist joke, the gratuitous jab at the weak is, in some quarters, seen as a form of strength, of "being flexible," of "not taking shit serious." A woman who wilts at a sexist joke won't last long in certain work-places. A guy who prioritizes the sensitive side of his nature will, trust me, not thrive in the slaughterhouse. This willingness to gloss over crudeness becomes, then, an encoded sign of competence, strength, and reliability.

Above all, Trump supporters are "not politically correct," which, as far as I can tell, means that they have a particular aversion to that psychological moment when, having thought something, you decide that it is not a good thought, and might pointlessly hurt someone's feelings, and therefore decline to say it.

## Who Are They? (Part II)

I observed, in Trump supporters' storytelling, a tendency to conflate things that, to a non–Trump supporter, might seem un-related. For example, in 2014, Mary Ann Mendoza's son, Bran-don, an openly gay policeman in Mesa, who volunteered at the local Boys and Girls Club, was killed in a car accident caused by an intoxicated, undocumented Mexican man who had spent at least twenty years drifting in and out of the United States and had been charged with a number of crimes, including assaulting a police officer, and was convicted of criminal conspiracy, but was free at the time of the crash, having been shown leniency by a Colorado court. At the rally in Fountain Hills, Ms. Mendoza gave a moving speech about her son, which she concluded this way: "This was the kind of man my son was. . . . *Was*. Not is. *Was*. Because of the lack of concern that this administration has for American citizens. . . . Brandon's. Life. Matters." The crowd roared. Something key lay in that juxtaposition and that roar. What was the connection between her son's death and the Black Lives Matter movement? Couldn't a person be against the killing of innocent black men *and* against illegal immigration (or drunk driving, or the lax enforcement of existing laws, etc.)?

A man comes to Arizona from Vermont and finds that "the illegals" are getting all the kitchen jobs for which he's qualified. "So once Trump started talking about the Wall," he says, "I was like, all right, now I think I've got to start paying attention to this." How does he know those workers were undocumented? He doesn't; there's no way, situationally, that he could. Stephanie, an executive administrator for a finance group in Minnesota, gets laid off, and the only benefit she qualifies for is "a measly little unemployment check." Standing next to her at the government office are "these people, that are from other countries, nonspeaking— I'm not biased, I have no reason to be—but . . . I'm seeing them getting cash, getting their bills paid, and, as a taxpaying citizen, I don't get anything. And so the border thing really resonated with me." Does she know for a fact that these were illegal immigrants? "That's a good question, and I don't know the answer," she says. "I'm not a hundred percent on it."

Bill Davis, a funny, genial sales rep in the packaging industry, has nothing against legal immigration but feels that illegal immigration is "killing" the area in Southern California where he lives. How, specifically, is it doing this? He mentions a neighbor of his who speaks no English, has two hundred chickens running around his yard, goats everywhere, doesn't "play by the rules"— and hence Bill's property values are going down. Is his neighbor undocumented? It doesn't matter, he says. He's "not assimilated." Growing up, Davis says, he had a lot of first-generation Hispanic friends. These people took pride in assimilating. "Those days are over," he explains. "So Trump is onto something about that. We don't want you guys throwing your fast-food wrappers out your windows when you're driving down the freeway. Take some pride in what you do. And learn to work in this country by the rules and regulations that we've developed over two hundred and fifty years. I'm not opposed to immigration, by any means. Come here, but when you leave Mexico—when you leave Germany, when you leave Russia, wherever—you've left that culture for a reason. It's America now. So you can have your parties and your stuff at your house, but don't expect us to cater to your culture."

"Thousands of Cubans coming in," Kathryn Kobor, a Trump supporter and animal-rights activist in her seventies, tells me in Phoenix, as she sits in protest of the Hillary Clinton rally across the street, beneath an umbrella provided by a Clinton supporter. "Three hundred sixty thousand Guatemalan kids and mothers standing at the border, they have to be taken in. We're going to be taking in thousands of Syrians, whom we cannot vet." I tell her that the thought of deporting and dividing families breaks my heart. "Of course it does—you're a human, you care about people. That's not the question. The question is, Do you want to live like India? Sewage running in the streets? . . . The infrastructure is crumbling. . . . I'm not speaking for tomorrow. I'm not speaking for a year, two years from now. I'll be gone. I'm speaking for my descendants. I have a granddaughter. I have a son. I want them to live a decent, clean life. . . . Trump just wants the laws enforced. . . . He's not a mean-spirited person."

A former marine in line for a Trump rally in Rothschild, Wisconsin, tells me that, returning to the United States from a deployment overseas, he found himself wondering, "Where did my country go?" To clarify, he tells me that he was in Qatar on the day that Obama was first elected. "I was actually sitting in the chow hall when they announced the results and he gave his speech," he says. "I saw such a division at that time. Every black member of the military was cheering. Everybody else was sitting there mute. Like stunned."

What unites these stories is what I came to think of as usurpation-anxiety syndrome—the feeling that one is, or is about to be, scooped, overrun, or taken advantage of by some Other with questionable intentions. In some cases, this has a racial basis, and usurpation anxiety grades into racial nostalgia, which can grade into outright racism, albeit cloaked in disclaimer.

In the broadest sense, the Trump supporter might be best understood as a guy who wakes up one day in a lively, crowded house full of people, from a dream in which he was the only one living there, and then mistakes the dream for the past: a better time, manageable and orderly, during which privilege and respect came to him naturally, and he had the whole place to himself.

## How Do You Solve a Problem Like Noemi?

Talking to a Trump supporter about Trump's deportation policy, I'd sometimes bring up Noemi Romero, a sweet, soft-spoken young woman I met in Phoenix. Noemi was brought to the United States when she was three, by undocumented parents. A few years ago, she had the idea of applying for legal status through the Deferred Action for Childhood Arrivals (DACA) program. But the application costs $465, money her family didn't have. Hearing that a local Vietnamese grocery was hiring, she borrowed her mother's Social Security card and got the job. A few months later, the store was raided. Noemi was arrested, charged with aggravated identity theft and forgery, and taken to jail and held there, within the general prison population, for two months. She was given spoiled milk and food that, she said, had tiny worms in it. Her lawyer arranged a plea bargain; the charges were reduced to criminal impersonation. This was a good deal, he told her, the best she could hope for. She accepted, not realizing that, as a convicted felon, she would be permanently ineligible for

DACA. Puente, a local grassroots organization, intervened and saved her from deportation, but she is essentially doomed to a kind of frozen life: can't work and can't go to college, although she has lived virtually her whole life in the United States and has no reason to go back to Mexico and nowhere to live if she's sent there.

I'd ask the Trump supporter, "What do we do about Noemi?" I always found the next moment in our exchange hopeful.

Is she a good person? the Trump supporter might ask. I couldn't feel more sorry for her, he might say. That kid is no better or worse than I am and deserves the best God can give her. Or he might say that deportation would have to be done on a case-by-case basis. Or propose some sort of registry—Noemi, having registered, would go back to Mexico and, if all checked out, come right back in. There had to be some kind of rule of law, didn't there? Tellingly, the Trump supporter might confess that she didn't think Trump really intended to do this mass-deportation thing anyway—it was all just campaign talk. The most extreme supporter might say that, yes, Noemi had to go—he didn't like it, but ultimately the fault lay with her parents.

Sometimes I'd mention a Central American family I met in Texas, while reporting another story. In that case, the father and son were documented but the mother and daughters weren't. Would you, I'd ask, split that family up? Send those girls to a country in which they'd never spent a single day? Well, my Trump-supporting friend might answer, it was complicated, wasn't it? Were they good people? Yes, I'd say. The father, in spare moments between his three jobs, built a four-bedroom house out of cinder blocks he acquired two or three at a time from Home Depot, working sometimes late into the night. The Trump supporter might, at this point, fall silent, and so might I.

In the face of specificity, my interviewees began trying, really trying, to think of what would be fairest and most humane for this real person we had imaginatively conjured up. It wasn't that we suddenly agreed, but the tone changed. We popped briefly out of zinger mode and began to have some faith in one another, a shared confidence that if we talked long enough, respectfully enough, a solution could be found that might satisfy our respective best notions of who we were.

Well, let's not get too dreamy about it. We'd stay in that mode for a minute or two, then be off again to some new topic, rewrapped in our respective Left and Right national flags. Once, after what felt like a transcendent and wide-ranging conversation with a Trump supporter named Danny (a former railroad worker, now on disability), I said a fond goodbye and went to interview some Hillary supporters across the street. A few minutes later, I looked over to find Danny shouting at us that Hillary was going to prison, not the White House. I waved to him, but he didn't seem to see me, hidden there in the crowd of his adversaries.

## The Elephant in the Room

The average Trump supporter is not the rally pugilist, the white supremacist, the bitter conspiracy theorist, though these exist and are drawn to Trump (see: *the Internet*)—and, at times, the first flowerings of these tendencies were present among some of the rank-and-file supporters I met. A certain barely suppressed rage, for example, is evident in the guy in Phoenix who wears his gun to a protest against Hillary ("I'm out here with two friends, Smith and Wesson"). One of his fellow protesters tells me that Hillary has had oral sex with many female world leaders ("She's munched with a lot of our enemies, man").

After a rally in Eau Claire, a handful of Trump protesters stand silently in the Wisconsin cold as the Trump supporters file out—a spontaneous little lab experiment investigating the Trumpies' response to silent rebuke. "I guess you guys don't read too much," someone shouts at the protesters. "Or watch the news. *Fox News!* Watch that once in a while!" Other Trump supporters yell over incredulously, "Fifteen bucks an hour?" And "Go to socialist Europe! Save your checks and move to a socialist country!"

But the line I won't forget comes from a guy leaving the rally, alone, who shout-mutters, if such a thing is possible, "Hey, I'm not paying for your shit, I'm not paying for your college, so you go to hell, go to work, go to hell, suck a dick."

Not far away, a group of enterprising Girl Scouts is out late, selling cookies under a winter-leafless tree. "Cookies for sale, last time this season," they seem to sing. "Girl Scout cookies, last weekend to get them."

So, yes, there are bigots in the Trump movement, and wackos, and dummies, and sometimes I had to remind myself that the important constituency is the persuadable middle segment of his supporters, who are not finding in Trump a suitable vessel for their hate but are misunderstanding him or overestimating him, and moving in his direction out of a misplaced form of hope.

### Who Are They? (Part III)

Sometimes it seemed that they were, like me, just slightly spoiled Americans, imbued with unreasonable boomer expectations for autonomy, glory, and ascension, and that their grievances were more theoretical than actual, more media-induced than experience-related.

Before the rally in San Jose on June 2, I talk to a group of construction workers, each of whom is in some state of layoff: current, recent, chronic. One, who's hoping to get a job working construction on the Wall, rails against millennials, the unions, a minimum-wage hike for fast-food workers, and "these people" who get fired, then turn around and sue. I ask for examples. He says he isn't going to give me any names. I say forget the names, just tell me a particular story. A guy got fired from his workplace just last week, he says. "Is he suing?" I ask. "Well, probably," he says.

I ask one of his friends, a thoughtful Chinese American guy, how his life has been made worse over the past eight years. He comes up with this: he pays more for his insurance because of Obamacare. Anything else? Not really. How has he personally been affected by illegal immigration? He hasn't, he tells me, but he's been fortunate enough to have the resources to keep his family away from the danger.

At one point, in line at the Fountain Hills rally, frustrated by a litany of anti-Obama grievances being delivered by the woman in front of me, I say that I think life is good, pretty good, you know?

"You think this is *good*?" she says.

"I do, yeah," I say. "We're out here on a nice day, having a beautiful talk—"

She groans, meaning, You know that's not what I mean.

But I don't, really, so I ask her what, in terms of her day-to-day life, she thinks is wrong with America.

"I don't like people shoving Obamacare down my throat, OK?" she says. "And then getting penalized if I don't have insurance."

Is she covered through Obamacare?

No. She has insurance through her work, thank God, but "every day my rights are being taken away from me, you know?" she says. "I mean—this is America. In the U.S., we have a lot of freedoms and things like that, but we're not going to have all that if we have all these people coming in, that are taking our—"

"We have our own people to take care of, I'm sorry," interjects a seventeen-year-old girl who is standing nearby, holding up a sign that says "Marry Me Don."

## Who Are They? (Part IV)

American presidential campaigns are not about ideas; they are about the selection of a hero to embody the prevailing national ethos. "Only a hero," Mailer wrote, "can capture the secret imagination of a people, and so be good for the vitality of his nation;

a hero embodies the fantasy and so allows each private mind the liberty to consider its fantasy and find a way to grow. Each mind can become more conscious of its desire and waste less strength in hiding from itself." What fantasy is Trump giving his supporters the liberty to consider? What secret have they been hiding from themselves?

Trump seems to awaken something in them that they feel they have, until now, needed to suppress. What is that thing? It is not just (as I'm getting a bit tired of hearing) that they've been *left behind economically*. (Many haven't, and au contraire.) They've been left behind in other ways, too, or feel that they have. To them, this is attributable to a country that has moved away from them, has been *taken away* from them—by Obama, the Clintons, the "lamestream" media, the "elites," the business-as-usual politicians. They are stricken by a sense that things are not as they should be and that, finally, someone sees it their way. They have a case of Grievance Mind, and Trump is their head kvetcher.

In college, I was a budding Republican, an Ayn Rand acolyte. I voted for Reagan. I'd been a bad student in high school and now, in engineering school, felt (and was) academically outgunned, way behind the curve. In that state, I constructed a worldview in which I was not behind the curve but ahead of it. I conjured up a set of hazy villains, who were, I can see now, externalized manifestations, imaginary versions of those who were leaving me behind; i.e., my better-prepared, more sophisticated fellow students. They were, yes, smarter and sharper than I was (as indicated by the tests on which they were always creaming me), but I was . . . what was I? Uh, tougher, more resilient, more able to get down and dirty as needed. I distinctly remember the feeling of casting about for some worldview in which my shortfall somehow constituted a hidden noble advantage.

While reporting this story, I drove from New York to California. During all those days on the highway, with lots of time on my hands for theorizing, generalizing, and speaking my generalized theories into my iPhone while swerving off into the spacious landscape, I thought about this idea of grievance, of feeling left behind. All along the fertile interstate-highway corridor, our corporations, those new and powerful nation-states, had set up shop parasitically, so as to skim off the drive-past money, and what those outposts had to offer was a blur of sugar, bright color, and crassness that seemed causally related to more serious addictions. Standing in line at the pharmacy in an Amarillo Walmart superstore, I imagined some kid who had moved only, or mostly, through such bland, bright spaces, spaces constructed to suit the purposes of distant profit, and it occurred to me how easy it would be, in that life, to feel powerless, to feel that the local was lame, the abstract extraneous, to feel that the only valid words were those of materialism ("get" and "rise")—words that are perfectly embodied by the candidate of the moment.

Something is wrong, the common person feels, correctly: she works too hard and gets too little; a dulling disconnect exists between her actual day-to-day interests and (1) the way her leaders act and speak and (2) the way our mass media mistell or fail entirely to tell her story. What does she want? Someone to notice her over here, having her troubles.

## But, Then Again, Come On

A bully shows up, is hateful, says things so crude we liberals are taken aback. We respond moderately. We keep waiting for his supporters, helped along by how compassionately and measuredly we are responding, to be persuaded. For the bully, this is perfect. Every fresh outrage pulls the camera back to him, and meanwhile those of us moderately decrying his immoderation are a little boring and tepid, and he keeps getting out ahead of us. He has Trumpmunity: his notions are so low and have been so many times decried, and yet they keep arriving, in new and escalating varieties, and the liberal imagination wilts.

I have been mentally gathering all those nice, friendly Trump supporters I met and asking them, Still? Even after the Curiel fiasco and the post-Orlando self-congrat fest, and Trump's insinuation that President Obama was in cahoots with the terrorists? Guys, still, really? The tragedy of the Trump movement is that one set of struggling people has been pitted against other groups of struggling people by someone who has known little struggle, at least in the material sense, and hence seems to have little empathy for anyone struggling, and even to consider struggling a symptom of weakness. "I will never let you down," he has told his supporters, again and again, but he will, and in fact already has, by indulging the fearful, xenophobic, Other-averse parts of their psychology and reinforcing the notion that their sense of being left behind has no source in themselves.

## All That Bad Energy Comes Home to Roost

Ah, how fondly I now recall those idyllic rally days in Fountain Hills, Tucson, Rothschild, and Eau Claire, back in March and early April, when the punching was being done by Trump supporters.

After the San Jose rally in early June, protesters bullied and spat on straggling Trump supporters. Sucker punchers lurched up, punched hard, darted away, hands raised in victory. A strange little protester, mask around his neck, mumbled, as he scuttled past a female reporter conducting an interview, "Fuck you in the pussy." Some sick genie, it seemed, had been let out of the bottle. I had to pull an older white woman out of a moblet of slapping young women of color, after she'd been driven down to one knee and had her glasses knocked off. When I told the young African American woman who'd given the first slap that this was exactly the kind of thing the Trump movement loved to see and would be happy to use, she seemed to suddenly come back to herself and nearly burst into tears. The slapped woman was around sixty, tall, lean, sun-reddened, scrappy, a rancher, maybe, and we stood there a few minutes, recovering ourselves. Seeing something unsteady behind her eyes, I suggested that she be sure to take a few deep breaths before driving home. She said she would, but a few minutes later I saw her again, at the edge of the crowd, watching the protesters in fascination, as if what had just happened to her made it impossible for her to leave.

The order to disperse was given, first from a helicopter circling above, then barked out repeatedly on the ground, through megaphones. Police, in riot gear, stepped forward, shoulder to shoulder, chanting, "MOVE MOVE MOVE!" and the kids played at revolution, chanting back, "HANDS UP! DON'T SHOOT!" and "FUCK TRUMP!" and "FUCK THE SYSTEM!" and "FUCK THE POLICE!" occasionally dashing ahead of the advancing line to gain a few minutes to call home on their cells to reassure their worried parents. The police line formed a human wiper blade that, over the next couple of hours, drove the protesters around and around the downtown area. It was like some large-form board game: the longer the blue wiper blade pushed forward, the more protesters fell off the game board and went home, until, finally, only a handful remained, regrouping in the dark under the freeway.

Up on grassless viaduct slopes, whippet-thin young men of color gathered stones, carried them down furtively in clenched fists. When asked not to throw them, they averted their eyes guiltily, the way a busted third grader might. Some dropped their rocks; others just slipped away into the crowd. I saw two friends hurl their rocks at once, high, weak, arcing throws that burst up through street-light-yellow, low-hanging branches. I told an African American kid wearing an elaborate Darth Vaderish multimask arrangement that this made him look like he was up to no good and aggravated the ambient white-privileged notion of the protesters as thugs out to make trouble. He sweetly agreed but then (dashing off) said that, still, the protesters "have to do what we have to do."

They were so young, mostly peaceful, but angered by the hateful rhetoric addressed at their communities, and their disdain for Trump morphed too easily into disrespect for the police, a group of whom, when all was over, huddled in a bank doorway, bathed in sweat, a couple of them taking a knee, football style, and when their helmets came off it was clear that they'd been scared, too, and I imagined them later that night, in darkened living rooms, reviewing the night, assessing how they'd done.

Early in the evening, a protester about my age asked me, "Where's your sheet?" Seeing my confusion, he regrouped. "If you're a Trump supporter, I mean." Later, I saw him again, shouting to the police that they were all "pigs." Still smarting over his Klan crack, I asked how he could hold a sign claiming that hate doesn't work while calling a group of people he didn't know "pigs." "They *are* pigs," he said. "Every one of them." His wife was murdered a few years ago, he added, and they did nothing about it.

So there you go. Welcome to America.

The night was sad. The center failed to hold. Did I blame the rioting kids? I did. Did I blame Trump? I did. This, Mr. Trump, I thought, is why we practice civility. This is why, before we say exactly what is on our minds, we run it past ourselves, to see if it makes sense, is true, is fair, has a flavor of kindness, and won't hurt someone or make someone's difficult life more difficult. Because there are, among us, in every political camp, limited, angry, violent, and/or damaged people, waiting for any excuse to throw off the tethers of restraint and get after it. After which it falls to the rest of us, right and left, to clean up the mess.

## The Somewhat Better Angels of Our Nature

Well, it wasn't all doom and gloom. Who could fail to be cheered by the sight of a self-described "street preacher" named Dean, whose massive laminated sign read "Muhammad Is a Liar, False Prophet, Child Raping Pervert! (see history for details)" and, on the flip side, "Homo Sex Is Sin—Romans 1," being verbally taken down by an inspiring consortium consisting of a gay white agnostic for Trump, a straight Christian girl for Trump, and a lesbian Latina agnostic for Bernie? Who could resist the raw wonder in the voice of a rangy young Trump supporter who reminded me of a gentler version of Sid Phillips, the bad neighbor boy in *Toy Story*, as he said, rather dreamily, "I love that everything in Trump's house is gold. That's like real-life Batman. That's some real Bruce Wayne shit." A group of anti-Trump college students in Eau Claire concocted the perfect Zen protest: singing and dancing en masse to Queen's "Bohemian Rhapsody." If there's anything common across the left-right divide, it's the desire not to come off as tight-assed or anti–rock and roll, and what could the passing Trump supporters do but dance and sing along, a few holdouts scowling at the unfairness of the method?

Outside a Clinton rally in Phoenix, a Native American–looking man in an Aztec-patterned shirt joined the line of Trump supporters, with his megaphone, through which he slowly said, one word at a time, "Make. America. White. Again." Once the Trump supporters caught on to the joke, they moved away, but he was a good sport and scooted down to join them.

"Make. America. White. Again," he said, in the calmest voice.

"We don't want you," one of the Trumpies said. "We don't want your racism!"

And civility is still alive and well, if you know where to look for it. Outside a Lutheran church meeting hall in Mesa that is being used as a polling place on primary day, for example, where an eighty-eight-year-old woman sits, beautifully dressed for the occasion. "Oh, my goodness," she says. "I've never seen anything like this."

Hundreds of voters are waiting in a line that runs around the parking lot and down the street. She came earlier, she says, and thought she might just forget it. "But then," she says, "I thought,

I'm getting up there in years—not going to have that many more chances to vote. I don't want to skip it. Because I always vote."

The voters move slowly, under crossed palm fronds, up for Palm Sunday, past a grapefruit tree in a graveled breezeway: its three trunks have been whitewashed, and it looks like a three-legged creature in white pants, standing on its head.

For the next five hours, America passes by, wearing work badges, fanny packs, surgical scrubs, sparkly dance-short-leotards, suspenders, wool caps, head scarves, dreadlocks; pushing walkers, baby strollers, a fat-wheeled trail bike, a shopping cart (containing a bamboo cane and a Burger King crown); carrying walkie-talkies, books, a man-purse shaped like a gigantic tennis shoe, squirming babies, portable fold-up seats that never get used.

Someone says that in twenty-nine years she's never seen this level of excitement. Someone says that it takes all kinds. Someone says that this is what makes the United States great: so much difference, and everyone gets a chance. Someone says that there are so many extremes at play in this election, people are coming out just to resist the extreme they're most against.

A man says, "I'm a good guy, I hope," and his wife nods.

A hipster dad picks up a bit of cookie his kid has dropped on the sidewalk and eats it.

A college-age kid in a "Captain America" shirt demonstrates that there is a certain portion of one's elbow flesh that will never hurt, no matter how hard one pinches it.

At seven, the polls are supposed to close, but the line is the longest it's been all day.

No one seems angry. There isn't much political talk, and what there is is restrained, chatty. They are here to vote, and that is a privilege and a private matter.

How fragile this mind-set is, I think. It could be lost in a single generation.

By 8:18 p.m., per the Internet, with only 1 percent of precincts reporting, it's over: Trump wins, Clinton wins.

Even though their votes now seem technically meaningless, there is no mass exodus. The people just keep coming. They've raced over from work, weary kids trudging along beside them. They are fantastically old people; people in terrible health, in wheelchairs or hobbling along on walkers, or joining me on my bench to stretch out a stiff leg or adjust a bad back. What makes them do it? Keep standing in line, after dark, at the end of a long day, to vote in an election that is already over?

A young woman says, cheerfully, to her toddler, "Don't hit yourself. You only have one face, one head. That carries your brain. Which is very important."

"After all these many years, in the back of my head," a man says thoughtfully, "I still hear this voice: 'Wait until your father gets home.' And that's my mom's voice."

At 9:50 p.m., the last person in line disappears inside.

I am joined by a trans woman about my age. People get afraid, she tells me, and nobody wants to feel afraid. But if you get angry, you feel empowered. Trump is playing on people's fears, to get them angry, which in turn makes *us*, on the other side, feel fearful. It's a domino effect. And, she says, it will continue even if Trump is out of the equation.

Another trans woman, apparently a stranger to the first, comes out of the church, holding a journal.

"All I have to write in here," she says, "is: I voted from hell."

The last fifty or so voters are still visible inside: patient, calm, plodding forward a few steps at a time.

Mailer described what he called democracy's "terrifying premise" this way: "Let the passions and cupidities and dreams and kinks and ideals and greed and hopes and foul corruptions of all men and women have their day and the world will still be better off, for there is more good than bad in the sum of us and our workings."

Well, we'll see.

From the beginning, America has been of two minds about the Other. One mind says, Be suspicious of it, dominate it, deport it, exploit it, enslave it, kill it as needed. The other mind denies that there can be any such thing as the Other, in the face of the claim that all are created equal.

The first mind has always held violence nearby, to use as needed, and that violence has infused everything we do—our entertainments, our sex, our schools, our ads, our jokes, our view of the earth itself, somehow even our food. It sends our young people abroad in heavy armor, fills public spaces with gunshots, drives people quietly insane in their homes.

And here it comes again, that brittle frontier spirit, that lone lean guy in our heads, with a gun and a fear of encroachment. But he's picked up a few tricks along the way, has learned to come at us in a form we know and have forgotten to be suspicious of, from TV: famous, likeably cranky, a fan of winning by any means necessary, exploiting our recent dullness and our aversion to calling stupidity stupidity, lest we seem too precious.

"Donald J Trump a Guardian Angel from Heaven," reads a poster I retrieved from the floor of the Rothschild rally. "His Spirit and Hard Work as President Will Make the People and America Great Again!!!"

Although, to me, Trump seems the very opposite of a guardian angel, I thank him for this: I've never before imagined America as fragile, as an experiment that could, within my very lifetime, fail.

But I imagine it that way now.

## Rolling Stone

FINALIST—COLUMNS AND COMMENTARY

*Matt Taibbi was wrong. Trump won (Taibbi thought he wouldn't). But the true subject of these columns is not Trump the man, Trump the candidate, or even Trump the specter of liberal nightmares but, like nearly everything Taibbi has written, the corruption of the American spirit. Or as Taibbi put it in February 2016: "It turns out we let our electoral process devolve into something so fake and dysfunctional that any half-bright con man with the stones to try it could walk right through the front door and tear it to shreds on the first go." Taibbi's earlier work for* Rolling Stone *won the Ellie for Columns and Commentary in 2008 and includes "The Great American Bubble Machine," in which he famously likened Goldman Sachs to a "vampire squid."*

Matt Taibbi

# President Trump, Seriously *and* "Appetite for Destruction" *and* The Fury and Failure of Donald Trump

## President Trump, Seriously

February 24, 2016

The first thing you notice at Donald Trump's rallies is the confidence. Amateur psychologists have wishfully diagnosed him from afar as insecure, but in person the notion seems absurd.

Donald Trump, insecure? We should all have such problems.

At the Verizon Giganto-Center in Manchester the night before the New Hampshire primary, Trump bounds onstage to raucous applause and the booming riffs of the Lennon-McCartney anthem "Revolution." The song is, hilariously, a cautionary tale about the perils of false prophets peddling mindless revolts, but Trump floats in on its grooves like it means the opposite. When you win as much as he does, who the hell cares what anything means?

He steps to the lectern and does his Mussolini routine, which he's perfected over the past months. It's a nodding wave, a grin, a half-sneer, and a little U.S. Open–style applause back in the direction of the audience, his face the whole time a mask of pure self-satisfaction.

"This is unbelievable, unbelievable!" he says, staring out at a crowd of about 4,000 whooping New Englanders with snow hats, fleece, and beer guts. There's a snowstorm outside and cars are flying off the road, but it's a packed house.

He flashes a thumbs-up. "So everybody's talking about the cover of *Time* magazine last week. They have a picture of me from behind, I was extremely careful with my hair . . ."

He strokes his famous flying fuzz-mane. It looks gorgeous, like it's been recently fed. The crowd goes wild. *Whoooo! Trump!*

It's pure camp, a variety show. He singles out a Trump impersonator in the crowd, tells him he hopes the guy is making a lot of money. "Melania, would you marry that guy?" he says. The future first lady is a Slovenian model who, apart from Trump, was most famous for a TV ad in which she engaged in a Frankenstein-style body transfer with the Aflac duck, voiced by Gilbert Gottfried.

She had one line in that ad. Tonight, it's two lines:

"Ve love you, New Hampshire," she says, in a thick vampire accent. "Ve, together, ve vill make America great again!"

As reactionary patriotic theater goes, this scene is bizarre—Melania Knauss didn't even arrive in America until 1996, when she was all of twenty-six—but the crowd goes nuts anyway. Everything Trump does works these days. He steps to the mic.

"She's beautiful, but she's more beautiful even on the inside," he says, raising a finger to the heavens. "And, boy, is she smart!"

Before the speech, the PA announcer had told us not to "touch or harm" any protesters, but to instead just surround them and chant, "Trump! Trump! Trump!" until security can arrive (and presumably do the touching and/or harming).

I'd seen this ritual several times, and the crowd always loves it. At one event, a dead ringer for John Oliver ripped off his shirt in the middle of a Trump speech to reveal body paint that read "Eminent Domain This!" on his thorax. The man shouted, "Trump is a racist!" and was immediately set upon by Trump supporters, who yelled "Trump! Trump! Trump!" at him until security arrived and dragged him out the door to cheers. The whole Trump run is like a *Jerry Springer* episode, where even the losers seem in on the gags.

In Manchester, a protester barely even manages to say a word before disappearing under a blanket of angry boos: "Trump! Trump! Trump!" It's a scene straight out of *Freaks*. In a Trump presidency, there will be free tar and feathers provided at the executive's every public address.

It's a few minutes after that when a woman in the crowd shouts that Ted Cruz is a pussy. She will later tell a journalist she supports Trump because his balls are the size of "watermelons" while his opponents' balls are more like "grapes" or "raisins."

Trump's balls are unaware of this, but he instinctively likes her comment and decides to go into headline-making mode. "I never expect to hear that from you again!" he says, grinning. "She said he's a pussy. That's terrible." Then, theatrically, he turns his back to the crowd. As the 500 or so reporters in attendance scramble to instantly make this the most important piece of news in the world—in less than a year Trump has succeeded in turning the USA into a massive high school—the candidate beams.

What's he got to be insecure about? The American electoral system is opening before him like a flower.

In person, you can't miss it: The same way Sarah Palin can see Russia from her house, Donald on the stump can see his future. The pundits don't want to admit it, but it's sitting there in plain view, twelve moves ahead, like a chess game already won:

President Donald Trump.

A thousand ridiculous accidents needed to happen in the unlikeliest of sequences for it to be possible, but absent a dramatic turn of events—an early primary catastrophe, Mike Bloomberg ego-crashing the race, etc.—this boorish, monosyllabic TV tyrant with the attention span of an Xbox-playing eleven-year-old really is set to lay waste to the most impenetrable oligarchy the Western world ever devised.

It turns out we let our electoral process devolve into something so fake and dysfunctional that any half-bright con man with the stones to try it could walk right through the front door and tear it to shreds on the first go.

And Trump is no half-bright con man, either. He's way better than average.

It's been well-documented that Trump surged last summer when he openly embraced the ugly race politics that, according to the Beltway custom of fifty-plus years, is supposed to stay at the dog-whistle level. No doubt, that's been a huge factor in his rise. But racism isn't the only ugly thing he's dragged out into the open.

Trump is no intellectual. He's not bringing *Middlemarch* to the toilet. If he had to jail with Stephen Hawking for a year, he wouldn't learn a thing about physics. Hawking would come out on day 365 talking about models and football.

But, in an insane twist of fate, this bloated billionaire scion has hobbies that have given him insight into the presidential electoral process. He likes women, which got him into beauty pageants. And he likes being famous, which got him into reality TV. He knows show business.

That put him in position to understand that the presidential election campaign is really just a badly acted, billion-dollar TV show whose production costs ludicrously include the political disenfranchisement of its audience. Trump is making a mockery of the show, and the Wolf Blitzers and Anderson Coopers of the world seem appalled. How dare he demean the presidency with his antics?

But they've all got it backward. The presidency is serious. The presidential electoral process, however, is a sick joke, in which everyone loses except the people behind the rope line. And every time some pundit or party spokesman tries to deny it, Trump picks up another vote.

•    •    •

The ninth Republican debate, in Greenville, South Carolina, is classic Trump. He turns these things into WWE contests, and since he has actual WWE experience after starring in Wrestlemania in 2007, he knows how to play these moments like a master.

Interestingly, a lot of Trump's political act seems lifted from bully-wrestlers. A clear influence is "Ravishing" Rick Rude, an eighties champ whose shtick was to insult the audience. He would tell ticket holders they were "fat, ugly sweat hogs," before taking off his robe to show them "what a real sexy man looks like."

In Greenville, Donald "The Front-Runner" Trump started off the debate by jumping on his favorite wrestling foil, Prince Dinkley McBirthright, a.k.a. Jeb Bush. Trump seems to genuinely despise Bush. He never missed a chance to rip him for being a "low-energy," "stiff," and "dumb as a rock" weenie who lets his Mexican wife push him around. But if you watch Trump long enough, it starts to seem gratuitous.

Trump's basic argument is the same one every successful authoritarian movement in recent Western history has made: that the regular guy has been screwed by a conspiracy of incestuous elites. The Bushes are half that conspiratorial picture, fronts for a Republican Party establishment and whose sum total of accomplishments, dating back nearly thirty years, are two failed presidencies, the sweeping loss of manufacturing jobs, and a pair of pitiable Middle Eastern military adventures—the second one achieving nothing but dead American kids and Junior's reelection.

Trump picked on Jeb because Jeb is a symbol. The Bushes are a dissolute monarchy, down to offering their last genetic screw-up to the throne.

Jeb took the high road for most of the past calendar year, but Trump used his gentlemanly dignity against him. What Trump understands better than his opponents is that NASCAR America, WWE America, always loves seeing the preening self-proclaimed good guy get whacked with a chair. In Greenville, Trump went after Jeb this time on the issue of his brother's invasion of Iraq.

"The war in Iraq was a big f . . . fat mistake, all right?" he snorted. He nearly said, "A big fucking mistake." He added that the George W. Bush administration lied before the war about Iraq having WMDs and that we spent $2 trillion basically for nothing.

Days earlier, Trump had gleefully tweeted that Bush needed his "mommy" after Jeb appeared with Lady Barbara on a morning show.

Jeb now went straight into character as the Man Whose Good Name Had Been Insulted. He defended his family and took exception to Trump having the "gall" to go after his mother.

"I won the lottery when I was born sixty-three years ago and looked up and I saw my mom," Jeb said proudly and lifted his chin. America loves Moms. How could he not win this exchange? But he was walking into a lawn mower.

"My mom is the strongest woman I know," Jeb continued.

"She should be running," Trump snapped.

The crowd booed, but even that was phony. It later came out that more than 900 of the 1,600 seats were given to local and national GOP officials. (Trump mentioned during the debate that he had only his wife and son there in comparison, but few picked up on what he was saying.) Pundits, meanwhile, lined up to congratulate Jeb for "assailing" Trump—"Bush is finally going for it," the *New York Times* wrote—but the exchange really highlighted many of the keys to Trump's success.

Trump had said things that were true and that no other Republican would dare to say. And yet the press congratulated the candidate stuffed with more than $100 million in donor cash who really did take five whole days last year to figure out his position on his own brother's invasion of Iraq.

At a time when there couldn't be more at stake, with the Middle East in shambles, a major refugee crisis, and as many as three Supreme Court seats up for grabs (the death of satanic quail hunter Antonin Scalia underscored this), the Republican Party picked a strange year to turn the presidential race into a potluck affair. The candidates sent forth to take on Trump have been so incompetent they can't even lose properly.

One GOP strategist put it this way: "Maybe 34 [percent] is Trump's ceiling. But 34 in a five-person race wins."

The numbers simply don't work, unless the field unexpectedly narrows before March. Trump has a chokehold on somewhere between 25 and 40 percent of the Republican vote, scoring in one poll across every category: young and old, educated and less so, hardcore conservatives and registered Democrats, with men and with women, Megyn Kelly's "wherever" notwithstanding. Trump the Builder of Anti-Rapist Walls even earns an estimated 25 percent of the GOP Latino vote.

Moreover, there's evidence that human polling undercounts Trump's votes, as people support him in larger numbers when they don't have to admit their leanings to a live human being. Like autoerotic asphyxiation, supporting Donald Trump is an activity many people prefer to enjoy in a private setting, like in a shower or a voting booth.

The path to unseating Trump is consolidation of opposition, forcing him into a two- or three-person race. Things seemed headed that way after Iowa, when Ted Cruz won and Marco Rubio came in third.

Rubio's Iowa celebration was a classic. The toothy Floridian leaped onstage and delivered a rollickingly pretentious speech appropriate not for a candidate who just eked out wins in five Iowa counties, but for a man just crowned king of Jupiter.

"For months, they told us because we offered too much optimism in a time of anger, we had no chance," he thundered. Commentators later noted Rubio's language was remarkably similar to Barack Obama's florid "they said our sights were set too high" 2008 Iowa victory speech.

The national punditry predictably overreacted to Rubio's showing, having been desperate to rally behind a traditional, party-approved GOP candidate.

Why do the media hate Trump? Progressive reporters will say it's because of things like his being crazy and the next Hitler while the Fox types insist it's because he's "not conservative." But reporters mostly loathe Trump because he regularly craps on other reporters.

He called Fox's Kelly a period-crazed bias monster for asking simple questions about Trump's past comments about women and launched a weirdly lengthy crusade against little-known *New Hampshire Union-Leader* publisher Joseph McQuaid for comparing Trump to *Back to the Future* villain Biff Tannen. He even mocked the neurological condition of *Times* reporter Serge Kovaleski for failing to ratify Trump's hilariously fictional recollection of "thousands" of Muslims celebrating after 9/11, doing an ad hoc writhing disabled-person impersonation at a South Carolina rally that left puppies and cancer kids as the only groups untargeted by his campaign. (He later denied the clearly undeniable characterization.)

But Trump's thin-skinned dealings with reporters didn't fully explain the media's efforts to prop up his opponents. We've long been engaged in our own version of the high school put-down game, battering nerds and outsiders like Ron Paul and Dennis Kucinich while elevating "electable," party-approved candidates like John McCain and John Kerry.

Thus it was no surprise that after Iowa, columnists tried to sell the country on the loathsome "Marcomentum" narrative, a paean to the good old days when reporters got to tell the public who was hot and who wasn't—the days of the "Straight Talk Express," "Joementum," etc.

"Marco Rubio Was the Real Winner in Iowa," blared CNN. "Marco Rubio's Iowa Mojo," chimed in *Politico*. "Forget Ted Cruz, Marco Rubio Is the Real Winner of the Iowa Caucuses," agreed *Vanity Fair*.

Rubio, we were told, had zoomed to the front of the "establishment lane" in timely enough fashion to stop Trump. Of course, in the real world, nobody cares about what happens in the "establishment lane" except other journalists. But even the other candidates seemed to believe the narrative. Ohio governor John Kasich staggered out of Iowa in eighth place and was finishing up his ninetieth lonely appearance in New Hampshire when Boston-based reporters caught up to him.

"If we get smoked up there, I'm going back to Ohio," he lamented. Kasich in person puts on a brave face, but he also frequently rolls his eyes in an expression of ostentatious misanthropy that says, "I can't believe I'm losing to these idiots."

But then Rubio went onstage at St. Anselm College in the eighth GOP debate and blew himself up. Within just a few minutes of a vicious exchange with haranguing now-former candidate Chris Christie, he twice delivered the exact same canned twenty-five-second spiel about how Barack Obama "knows exactly what he's doing."

Rubio's face-plant brilliantly reprised Sir Ian Holm's performance in *Alien*, as a malfunctioning, disembodied robot head stammering, "I admire its purity," while covered in milky android goo. It was everything we hate about scripted mannequin candidates captured in a brief crack in the political façade.

Rubio plummeted in the polls, and Kasich, already mentally checked out, was the surprise second-place finisher in New Hampshire, with 15.8 percent of the vote.

"Something big happened tonight," Kasich said vaguely, not seeming sure what that thing was exactly. Even worse from a

Republican point of view, Dinkley McBush somehow finished fourth, above Rubio and in a virtual tie with Iowa winner Ted Cruz.

Now none of the three "establishment lane" candidates could drop out. And the next major contest, South Carolina, was deemed by horse-race experts to have too tiny an "establishment lane" vote to decide which two out of that group should off themselves in time for the third to mount a viable "Stop Trump" campaign.

All of which virtually guarantees Trump will probably enjoy at least a five-horse race through Super Tuesday. So he might have this thing sewn up before the others even figure out in what order they should quit. It's hard to recall a dumber situation in American presidential politics.

"If you're Trump, you're sending flowers to all of them for staying in," the GOP strategist tells me. "The more the merrier. And they're running out of time to figure it out."

The day after Rubio's implosion, Trump is upstate in New Hampshire, addressing what for him is a modest crowd of about 1,500 to 2,000 in the gym at Plymouth State University. The crowd here is more full-blown New England townie than you'll find at his Manchester events: lots of work boots, Pats merch and f-bombs.

Trump's speeches are never scripted, never exactly the same twice. Instead he just riffs and feels his way through crowds. He's no orator—as anyone who's read his books knows, he's not really into words, especially long ones—but he has an undeniable talent for commanding a room.

Today, knowing the debate news is in the air, he makes sure to plunge a finger into Rubio's wound, mocking candidates who need scripts.

"Honestly, I don't have any teleprompters, I don't have a speech I'm reading to you," Trump says. Then he switches into a nasal, weenie-politician voice, and imitates someone reading tiny text from a crib sheet: "Ladies and gentlemen, it's so nice to be here in New Hampshire, please vote for me or I'll never speak to you again . . ."

The crowd laughs. Trump also makes sure to point a finger at the omnipresent Giant Media Throng.

"See all those cameras back there?" he says. "They've never driven so far to a location."

The crowd turns to gape and sneer at the hated press contingent, which seems glad to be behind a rope. Earlier, Trump had bragged about how these same reporters had begrudgingly admitted that he'd won the St. Anselm debate. "They hate it, but they gave me very high grades."

It's simple transitive-property rhetoric, and it works. The press went gaga for Rubio after Iowa because—why? Because he's an unthreatening, blow-dried, cliché-spouting, dial-surveying phony of the type campaign journalists always approve of.

And when Rubio gets exposed in the debate as a talking haircut, a political Speak n' Spell, suddenly the throng of journalists who spent the past two weeks trying to sell America on "Marcomentum" and the all-important "establishment lane" looks very guilty indeed. Voters were supposed to take *this* seriously?

Trump knows the public sees through all of this, grasps the press's role in it and rightly hates us all. When so many Trump supporters point to his stomping of the carpetbagging snobs in the national media as the main reason they're going to vote for him, it should tell us in the press something profound about how much people think we suck.

Jay Matthews, a Plymouth native with a long beard and a Trump sign, cites Trump's press beat-downs as the first reason he's voting Donald.

"He's gonna be his own man," he says. "He's proving that now with how he's getting all the media. He's paying nothing and getting all the coverage. He's not paying one dime."

Reporters have focused quite a lot on the crazy/race-baiting/nativist themes in Trump's campaign, but these comprise a very small part of his usual presentation. His speeches increasingly are strikingly populist in their content.

His pitch is: He's rich, he won't owe anyone anything upon election, and therefore he won't do what both Democratic and Republican politicians unfailingly do upon taking office, i.e., approve rotten/regressive policies that screw ordinary people.

He talks, for instance, about the anti-trust exemption enjoyed by insurance companies, an atrocity dating back more than half a century, to the McCarran-Ferguson Act of 1945. This law, sponsored by one of the most notorious legislators in our history (Nevada Sen. Pat McCarran was thought to be the inspiration for the corrupt Sen. Pat Geary in *The Godfather II*), allows insurance companies to share information and collude to divvy up markets.

Neither the Republicans nor the Democrats made a serious effort to overturn this indefensible loophole during the debate over the Affordable Care Act.

Trump pounds home this theme in his speeches, explaining things from his perspective as an employer. "The insurance companies," he says, "they'd rather have monopolies in each state than hundreds of companies going all over the place bidding . . . It's so hard for me to make deals . . . because I can't get bids."

He goes on to explain that prices would go down if the state-by-state insurance fiefdoms were eliminated, but that's impossible because of the influence of the industry. "I'm the only one that's self-funding . . . Everyone else is taking money from, I call them the bloodsuckers."

Trump isn't lying about any of this. Nor is he lying when he mentions that the big-pharma companies have such a stranglehold on both parties that they've managed to get the federal government to bar itself from negotiating Medicare prescription-drug prices in bulk.

"I don't know what the reason is—I do know what the reason is, but I don't know how they can sell it," he says. "We're not allowed to negotiate drug prices. We pay $300 billion more than if we negotiated the price."

It's actually closer to $16 billion a year more, but the rest of it is true enough. Trump then goes on to personalize this story. He claims (and with Trump we *always* have to use words like "claims") how it was these very big-pharma donors, "fat cats," sitting in the front row of the debate the night before. He steams ahead even more with this tidbit: Woody Johnson, one of the heirs of drug giant Johnson & Johnson (and the laughably incompetent owner of the New York Jets), is the finance chief for the campaign of whipping boy Jeb Bush.

"Now, let's say Jeb won. Which is an impossibility, but let's say . . ."

The crowd explodes in laughter.

"Let's say Jeb won," Trump goes on. "How is it possible for Jeb to say, 'Woody, we're going to go out and fight competitively'?"

This is, what—not true? Of course it's true.

What's Trump's solution? Himself! He's gonna grab the problem by the throat and fix it by force!

Throughout his campaign, he's been telling a story about a $2.5 billion car factory that a Detroit automaker wants to build in Mexico, and how as president he's going to stop it. Humorously, he tried at one point to say he already had stopped it, via his persistent criticism, citing an article on an obscure website that claimed the operation had moved to Youngstown, Ohio.

That turned out to be untrue, but, hey, what candidate for president hasn't impulse-tweeted the completely unprovable fact or two? (Trump, incidentally, will someday be in the Twitter Hall of Fame. His fortune-cookie mind—restless, confrontational, completely lacking the shame/veracity filter—is perfectly engineered for the medium.)

In any case, Trump says he'll call Detroit carmakers into his office and lay down an ultimatum: Either move the jobs back to

America, or eat a 35 percent tax on every car imported back into the U.S. over the Mexican border.

"I'm a free-trader," he says, "but you can only be a free-trader when something's fair."

It's stuff like this that has conservative pundits from places like the *National Review* bent out of shape. Where, they ask, is the M-F'ing love? What about those conservative principles we've spent decades telling you flyover-country hicks you're supposed to have?

"Trump has also promised to use tariffs to punish companies," wrote David McIntosh in the *Review*'s much-publicized, but not-effective-at-all "Conservatives Against Trump" 22-pundit ji-had. "These are not the ideas of a small-government conservative . . . They are, instead, the ramblings of a liberal wanna-be strongman."

What these tweedy Buckleyites at places like the *Review* don't get is that most people don't give a damn about "conservative principles." Yes, millions of people responded to that rhetoric for years. But that wasn't because of the principle itself, but because it was always coupled with the more effective politics of resentment: Big-government liberals are to blame for your problems.

Elections, like criminal trials, are ultimately always about assigning blame. For a generation, conservative intellectuals have successfully pointed the finger at big-government-loving, whale-hugging liberals as the culprits behind American decline.

But the fact that lots of voters hated the Clintons, Sean Penn, the Dixie Chicks and whomever else, did not, ever, mean that they believed in the principle of Detroit carmakers being able to costlessly move American jobs overseas by the thousands.

"We've got to do something to bring jobs back," says one Trump supporter in Plymouth, when asked why tariffs are suddenly a good idea.

Cheryl Donlon says she heard the tariff message loud and clear and she's fine with it, despite the fact that it clashes with traditional conservatism.

"We need someone who is just going to look at what's best for us," she says.

I mention that Trump's plan is virtually identical to Dick Gephardt's idea from way back in the 1988 Democratic presidential race, to fight the Korean Hyundai import wave with retaliatory tariffs.

Donlon says she didn't like that idea then.

Why not?

"I didn't like him," she says.

Trump, though, she likes. And so do a lot of people. No one should be surprised that he's tearing through the Republican primaries, because everything he's saying about his GOP opponents is true. They really are all stooges on the take, unable to stand up to Trump because they're not even people, but are, like Jeb and Rubio, just robo-babbling representatives of unseen donors.

**B**ack in Manchester, an American Legion hall half-full of bored-looking Republicans nurses beers and knocks billiard balls around, awaiting Iowa winner Ted Cruz. The eely Texan is presumably Trump's most serious threat and would later nudge past Trump in one national poll (dismissed by Trump as conducted by people who "don't like me").

But New Hampshire is a struggle for Cruz. The high point in his entire New England run has been his penchant for reciting scenes from *The Princess Bride*, including the entire Billy Crystal "your friend here is only mostly dead" speech for local station WMUR. The one human thing about Cruz seems to be that his movie impersonations are troublingly solid, a consistent B-plus to A-minus.

But stepping into the human zone for even a few minutes backfired. The actor Mandy Patinkin, who played Inigo Montoya in the film, reacted with horror when he learned Cruz was doing his character's famous line "You killed my father, prepare to die." He accused Cruz of deliberately leaving out the key line in Montoya's speech, after he finally slays the man who killed his father: "I've been in the revenge business for so long, now that it's over, I don't know what to do with the rest of my life."

Patinkin believed Cruz didn't do that line because Cruz is himself in the revenge business, promising to "carpet-bomb [ISIS] into oblivion" and wondering if "sand can glow."

Patinkin's criticism of Cruz cut deeply, especially after the Iowa caucuses, when Cruz was accused by Trump and others of spreading a false rumor that Ben Carson was dropping out, in order to steal evangelical votes and pad his lead.

The unwelcome attention seemed to scare Cruz back into scripted-bot mode, where he's a less-than-enthralling presence. Cruz in person is almost physically repellent. *Psychology Today* even ran an article by a neurology professor named Dr. Richard Cytowic about the peculiarly off-putting qualities of Cruz's face.

He used a German term, *backpfeifengesicht*, literally "a face in need of a good punch," to describe Cruz. This may be overstating things a little. Cruz certainly has an odd face—it looks like someone sewed pieces of a waterlogged Reagan mask together at gunpoint—but it's his tone more than anything that gets you. He speaks slowly and loudly and in the most histrionic language possible, as if he's certain you're too stupid to grasp that *he is for freedom.*

"The . . . Constitution . . . ," he says, "serves . . . as . . . chains . . . to . . . bind . . . the . . . mischief . . . of . . . government . . ."

Four years ago, a candidate like this would have just continued along this path, serving up piles of euphuistic Tea Party rhetoric for audiences that at the time were still hot for the tricorner-hat explanation of how Comrade Obama ruined the American Eden.

But now, that's not enough. In the age of Trump, the Cruzes of the world also have to be rebels against the "establishment." This requirement makes for some almost unbelievable rhetorical contortions.

"Government," Cruz now ventures, "should not be about re-distributing wealth and benefiting the corporations and the special interests."

This absurd Swiss Army cliché perfectly encapsulates the predicament of the modern GOP. In one second, Cruz is against "redistributionism," which in the Obama years was code for "government spending on minorities." In the next second, he's against corporations and special interests, the villains du jour in the age of Bernie Sanders and Trump, respectively.

He's against everything all at once. Welfare! Corporations! Special Interests! Government! The Establishment! He's that escort who'll be into whatever you want, for an hour.

Trump meanwhile wipes out Cruz in his speeches in a single, drop-the-mic line.

"They give Ted $5 million," he says, bringing to mind loans Cruz took from a pair of banks, Goldman Sachs and Citibank.

The total was closer to $1.2 million, but Trump's point, that even the supposed "outsider" GOP candidate is just another mindless payola machine, is impossible to counter.

The unexpectedly thrilling Democratic Party race between Hillary Clinton and Bernie Sanders, too, is breaking just right for Trump. It's exposing deep fissures in the Democratic strategy that Trump is already exploiting.

Every four years, some Democrat who's been a lifelong friend of labor runs for president. And every four years, that Democrat gets thrown over by national labor bosses in favor of some party lifer with his signature on a half-dozen job-exporting free-trade agreements.

It's called "transactional politics," and the operating idea is that workers should back the winner, rather than the most union-friendly candidate.

This year, national leaders of several prominent unions went with Hillary Clinton—who, among other things, supported her husband's efforts to pass NAFTA—over Bernie Sanders. Pissed, the rank and file in many locals revolted. In New Hampshire, for instance, a Service Employees International Union local backed Sanders despite the national union's endorsement of

Clinton, as did an International Brotherhood of Electrical Workers chapter.

Trump is already positioning himself to take advantage of the political opportunity afforded him by "transactional politics." He regularly hammers the NAFTA deal in his speeches, applying to it his favorite word, "disaster." And he just as regularly drags Hillary Clinton into his hypothetical tales of job-saving, talking about how she could never convince Detroit carmakers out of moving a factory to Mexico.

Unions have been abused so much by both parties in the past decades that even mentioning themes union members care about instantly grabs the attention of workers. That's true even when it comes from Donald Trump, a man who kicked off the fourth GOP debate saying "wages [are] too high" and who had the guts to tell the *Detroit News* that Michigan autoworkers make too much money.

You will find union members scattered at almost all of Trump's speeches. And there have been rumors of unions nationally considering endorsing Trump. SEIU president Mary Kay Henry even admitted in January that Trump appeals to members because of the "terrible anxiety" they feel about jobs.

"I know guys, union guys, who talk about Trump," says Rand Wilson, an activist from the Labor for Bernie organization. "I try to tell them about Sanders, and they don't know who he is. Or they've just heard he's a socialist. Trump they've heard of."

This is part of a gigantic subplot to the Trump story, which is that many of his critiques of the process are the same ones being made by Bernie Sanders. The two men, of course, are polar opposites in just about every way—Sanders worries about the poor, while Trump would eat a child in a lifeboat—but both are laser-focused on the corrupting role of money in politics.

Both propose "revolutions" to solve the problem, the difference being that Trump's is an authoritarian revolt, while Sanders proposes a democratic one. If it comes down to a Sanders-Trump general election, the matter will probably be decided by which candidate the national press turns on first: the flatulent narcissist with cattle-car fantasies or the Democrat who gently admires Scandinavia. Would you bet your children on that process playing out sensibly?

In the meantime, Trump is cannily stalking the Sanders vote. While the rest of the GOP clowns just roll their eyes at Sanders, going for cheap groans with bits about socialism, Trump goes a different route. He hammers Hillary and compliments Sanders. "I agree with [Sanders] on two things," he says. "On trade, he said we're being ripped off. He just doesn't know how much."

He goes on. "And he's right with Hillary because, look, she's receiving a fortune from a lot of people."

At a Democratic town hall in Derry, New Hampshire, Hillary's strangely pathetic answer about why she accepted $675,000 from Goldman to give speeches—"That's what they offered"—seemed doomed to become a touchstone for the general-election contest. Trump would go out on Day One of that race and blow $675,000 on a pair of sable underwear, or a solid-gold happy-face necktie. And he'd wear it 24 hours a day, just to remind voters that his opponent sold out for the Trump equivalent of lunch money.

Trump will surely argue that the Clintons are the other half of the dissolute-conspiracy story he's been selling, representing a workers' party that abandoned workers and turned the presidency into a vast cash-for-access enterprise, avoiding scrutiny by making Washington into Hollywood East and turning labor leaders and journalists alike into starstruck courtiers. As with everything else, Trump personalizes this, making his stories of buying Hillary's presence at his wedding a part of his stump speech. A race against Hillary Clinton in the general, if it happens, will be a pitch right in Trump's wheelhouse—and if Bill Clinton is complaining about the "vicious" attacks by the campaign of pathological nice guy Bernie Sanders, it's hard to imagine what will happen once they get hit by the Trumpdozer.

The electoral roadshow, that giant ball of corrupt self-impor-tance, gets bigger and more grandiloquent every four years. This time around, there was so much press at the Manchester Radis-son, you could have wiped out the entire cable-news industry by detonating a single Ryder truck full of fertilizer.

Like the actual circus, this is a roving business. Cash flows to campaigns from people and donors; campaigns buy ads; ads pay for journalists; journalists assess candidates. Somewhat unsur-prisingly, the ever-growing press corps tends in most years to like—or at least deem "most serious"—the candidates who buy the most ads. Nine out of 10 times in America, the candidate who raises the most money wins. And those candidates then owe the most favors.

Meaning that for the pleasure of being able to watch insincere campaign coverage and see manipulative political ads on TV for free, we end up having to pay inflated Medicare drug prices, fund bank bailouts with our taxes, let billionaires pay 17 percent tax rates, and suffer a thousand other indignities. Trump is right: Because Jeb Bush can't afford to make his own commercials, he would go into the White House in the pocket of a drug manu-facturer. It really is that stupid.

The triumvirate of big media, big donors and big political parties has until now successfully excluded every challenge to its authority. But like every aristocracy, it eventually got lazy and profligate, too sure it was loved by the people. It's now shocked that voters in depressed ex-factory towns won't keep pulling the lever for "conservative principles," or that union members bitten a dozen times over by a trade deal won't just keep voting Demo-cratic on cue.

Trump isn't the first rich guy to run for office. But he is the first to realize the weakness in the system, which is that the watchdogs in the political media can't resist a car wreck. The more he insults the press, the more they cover him: He's pulling 33 times as much coverage on the major networks as his next-closest GOP competitor, and twice as much as Hillary.

Trump found the flaw in the American Death Star. It doesn't know how to turn the cameras off, even when it's filming its own demise.

The problem, of course, is that Trump is crazy. He's like every other corporate tyrant in that his solution to most things follows the logic of Stalin: no person, no problem. You're fired! Except as president he'd have other people-removing options, all of which he likes: torture, mass deportations, the banning of 23 percent of the Earth's population from entering the United States, etc.

He seems to be coming around to the idea that having an ego smaller than that of, say, an Egyptian Pharaoh would be a sign of weakness. So of late, his already-insane idea to build a "beautiful" wall across the Mexican border has evolved to the point where he also wants the wall to be named after him. He told Maria Bartiromo he wanted to call it the "Great Wall of Trump."

In his mind, it all makes sense. Drugs come from Mexico; the wall will keep out Mexicans; therefore, no more drugs. "We're gonna stop it," he says. "You're not going to have the drugs coming in destroying your children. Your kids are going to look all over the place and they're not going to be able to find them."

Obviously! Because no one's ever tried wide-scale drug prohibition before.

And as bad as our media is, Trump is trying to replace it with a worse model. He excommunicates every reporter who so much as raises an eyebrow at his insanity, leaving him with a small-but-dependable crowd of groveling supplicants who in a Trump presidency would be the royal media. He even waves at them during his speeches.

"Mika and Joe are here!" he chirped at the MSNBC morning hosts at a New Hampshire event. The day after he won the New Hampshire primary, he called in to their show to thank them for being "supporters." To her credit, Mika Brzezinski tried to object to the characterization, interrupting Joe Scarborough, who by then had launched into a minute-long homily about how happy he was to be a bug on the windshield of the Trump phenomenon.

You think the media sucks now? Just wait until reporters have to kiss a brass Trump-sphinx before they enter the White House press room.

"He has all these crazy ideas, and [reporters] are so scared of him, they don't ask him any details," says Michael Pleyte, an Iraq vet who came all the way from Michigan to watch the New Hampshire primary in person. "Forget about A to Z, they don't even ask him to go A to Trump."

King Trump. Brace yourselves, America. It's really happening.


# "Appetite for Destruction"

July 22, 2016

Hell, yes, it was crazy. You rubbed your eyes at the sight of it, as in, "Did *that* really just happen?"

It wasn't what we expected. We thought Donald Trump's version of the Republican National Convention would be a brilliantly bawdy exercise in Nazistic excess.

We expected thousand-foot light columns, a 400-piece horn section where the delegates usually sit (they would be in cages out back with guns to their heads). Onstage, a chorus line of pageant girls in gold bikinis would be twerking furiously to a techno version of "New York, New York" while an army of Broadway dancers spent all four days building a Big Beautiful Wall that read winning, the ceremonial last brick timed to the start of Donald's acceptance speech . . .

But nah. What happened instead was just sad and weird, very weird. The lineup for the 2016 Republican National Convention to nominate Trump felt like a fallback list of speakers for some ancient UHF telethon, on behalf of a cause like plantar-wart research.

Was one of the headliners really Ultimate Fighting chief Dana White, head all swollen and shouting into the microphone like a man having a road-rage dispute?

Was that really *General Hospital* star and Calvin Klein underwear model Antonio Sabato Jr. warning gravely that "our rights have been trampled and our security threatened" by President Obama's policies? And were there really two soap stars in the lineup, the second being Kimberlin Brown, of *The Young and the Restless*, who drove a spear through the grave of Henny Youngman with an agonizing attempt at warm-up humor?

"Many of you know me from one of your favorite soap operas," she said. "But since we only have one life to live . . . I decided to follow other dreams!" Punchline: She grows avocados now, and loves Donald Trump.

There were four categories of speakers. First, the Trump family members, including poor wife Melania, whose speechwriters pushed her into a media buzz saw on opening night.

Then, there were even a few Republican politicians who seemed to want to be there voluntarily, people like crazed Alabama Sen. Jeff Sessions, who came off like a shaved and slightly angrier version of Yosemite Sam. Ex-candidate Ben Carson emerged from a grain-storage chamber somewhere to connect Hillary Clinton to Lucifer and say things about transgender people so outrageous that even Orrin Hatch rushed to their defense.

The third group consisted of Republican officials who had no choice but to be there. People like Republican Party chief Reince Priebus and House Majority Leader Paul Ryan rarely spoke Trump's name and seemed pained throughout, aware they might spend eternity giving each other back rubs in hell as punishment for participating in this event.

The rest were basically personal friends of Trump's who owed him a favor.

The nominee seemed to mine the very bottom of his Rolodex for the exercise, to the point where we even heard a testimonial from Natalie Gulbis, the world's 492nd-ranked professional woman golfer.

"The first time I played golf with him, in 2005, I shared two things I had told countless CEOs, billionaires and politicians before him," said Gulbis. The two things sort of turned out to be one thing, i.e., that she wanted to open a Boys & Girls Club and she was tired of having such business ideas rejected.

"Those words previously fell on deaf, albeit well-intentioned ears," she went on. "But that day was different. They finally fell on ears that cared enough to take action." Trump funded her Boys & Girls Club!

"Trump's ears cared?" cracked a nearby reporter, stuffing his face with yogurt peanuts while Googling "Natalie Gulbis naked" on his cellphone.

Then there was Scott Baio. Scott Baio, ladies and gentlemen! Not the Fonz or Richie or even Pinky Tuscadero, but the man who played Chachi, a gimmick character in a show about an America that never existed, a time when there were no black people and the last gasps of our apartheid state were called *Happy Days*.

Republicans have been selling a return to that mythical Fifties golden age for the past half-century, but it took Donald Trump for the sales pitch to come out as such extreme comedy. Make America's Days Happy Again!

Trump had Baio in the convention lineup just days after wired-on-Jesus former Congresskook Michelle Bachmann described the nominee as a man with "1950s sensibilities," who grew up in an era when "even . . . Jews would say Merry Christmas." Why can't we go back to those days?

"Let's make America America again!" is how Baio put it in his speech.

The next day, Baio labored through a confused and contentious appearance on MSNBC with host Tamron Hall. The headline that emerged from that uncomfortable segment involved Hall confronting Baio over a tweet in which he appeared to call Hillary Clinton a "cunt." But the real shocker came at the beginning of the interview.

"Did you write your own speech?" Hall asked.

"I did," said Baio. "I was asked to do this Thursday. I wrote my speech in church on Sunday morning."

Donald Trump did not nail down Scott Baio, perhaps Earth's most conspicuously available actor, as a speaker for opening night of the Republican Party Convention until four days before it started!

It didn't get any better when the so-called professional politicians spoke. As if in one voice, they all repeated a mantra more appropriate for a megachurch full of Rapture-ready Christians than a political convention: We are not safe, the end is nigh, run for the hills and vote Trump on your way out.

"There's no next election—this is it," screeched Rudy Giuliani (or "9/11's Rudy Giuliani," as he is jokingly dubbed in the press section).

The former New York mayor's "there are terrorists trimming their beards under your bed as we speak" act has been seen a million times before by this political press corps, but even that jaded group was stunned by the hysterical heights—or depths?—to which he rose/sank in his appearance for Trump.

"To defeat Islamic extremist terrorists, we must put them on defense!" he shouted, with his usual bluster at first.

Then, suddenly, in a frenzy of violent hand gestures, Giuliani found another gear. *"We must commit ourselves to unconditional victory against them!"* he bellowed, with a flourish that could only be described as Hitlerian. It was a daring performance that met with some roars on the floor, but also plenty of murmuring.

The thing is, the convention crowd wasn't exactly the fevered revolutionary rally the press had been predicting for months. It was, in fact, a sadly muted affair, with many delegates quietly despairing at what had happened to the Grand Old Party.

The Republican Party under Trump has become the laughingstock of the world, and it happened in front of an invading force of thousands of mocking reporters who made sure that not one single excruciating moment was left uncovered.

So, yes, it was weird, and pathetic, but it was also disturbing, and not just for the reasons you might think. Trump's implosion left the Republican Party in schism, but it also created an unprecedented chattering-class consensus and a dangerous political situation.

Everyone piled on the Republicans, with pundits from George Will to David Brooks to Dan Savage all on the same side now, and nobody anywhere seeming to worry about the obvious subtext to Trump's dumpster-fire convention: In a two-party state, when one collapses, doesn't that mean only one is left? And isn't that a bad thing?

Day two of the Republican National Convention in Cleveland, a little after 6:30 p.m. Roll has been called, states are announcing their support for the Donald, and the floor is filled with TV crews breathlessly looking for sexy backdrops for the evolving train wreck that is the Republican Party.

Virtually every major publication in America has run with some version of the "Man, has this convention been one giant face-plant, or what?" story, often citing the sanitized, zero-debate conventions of the past as a paradise now lost to the GOP.

"The miscues, mistakes [and] mishandled dissent," wrote Elizabeth Sullivan in Cleveland's *Plain Dealer*, "did not augur well for the sort of smoothly scripted, expertly choreographed nominating conventions our mainstream political parties prefer."

The odd thing is that once upon a time, conventions were a site of fierce debates, not only over the content of the party platform but even the choice of candidates themselves. And this was regarded as the healthy exercise of democracy.

It wasn't until the television era, when conventions became intolerably dull pro-forma infomercials stage-managed for the networks to consume as fake shows of unity, that we started to measure the success of conventions by their lack of activity, debate and new ideas.

A Wyoming delegate named Rick Shanor shakes his head as he leans against a wall, staying out of the way of the crews zooming to and fro. He insists dissent is always part of the process, and maybe it's just that nobody cared before.

"It's beautiful," he says. "You've got to have the discourse. You've got to have arguments about this and that. That's the way we work in the Republican Party. We yak and yak, but we coalesce."

The Republican Convention in Cleveland was supposed to be the site of revolts and unprecedented hijinks on the part of delegates. But on the floor of Chez LeBron, a.k.a. the Quicken Loans Arena, a.k.a. the "Q," it's the journalists who are acting like fanatics, buttonholing every delegate in sight for embarrassed quotes about things like Melania's plagiarism flap.

"The only safe place to stand is, like, in the middle row of your delegation," one delegate says, eyeing the media circling the edges of the floor like a school of sharks. "If you go out to get nachos or take a leak, they come after you."

A two-person crew, a camera and a coiffed on-air hack, blows through a portion of the Washington state delegation, a bunch of princely old gentlemen in zany foam tree-hats. The trees separate briefly, then return to formation.

Meanwhile, the TV crew has set up and immediately begun babbling still more about last night's story, Melania Trump's plagiarism, which *Esquire*'s Charlie Pierce correctly quipped was a four-hour story now stretching toward multiple days.

Nearby, watching the reporters, one delegate from a Midwestern state turns to another.

"This is like a NAMBLA convention," he says with a sigh. "And we're the kiddies."

Outside, it's not much better.

The vast demilitarized zone set up between the Q and anywhere in the city that contains people is an inert, creepy place to visit. Towering metal barricades line streets cleansed of people, with the only movement being the wind blowing the occasional discarded napkin or pamphlet excerpt of *The Conservative Heart* (the president of the American Enterprise Institute's hilarious text about tough-love cures for poverty first littered the floor of the Q, then the grounds outside it).

Thus the area around the convention feels like some other infamous de-peopled landscapes, like Hitler's paintings, or downtown New Orleans after Katrina. You have to walk a long way, sometimes climbing barriers and zigzagging through the multiple absurd metal mazes of the DMZ, to even catch a glimpse of anyone lacking the credentials to get into this most exclusive of clubs: American democracy.

Concepts like "free speech zones" or the idea that the general public may not come within a half-mile or so of the actual event seemed insane when they were first introduced years ago. But the public has since become inured to the notion, which perhaps is a reason the protests here have been far tamer than in years past.

In 2004, the first year that both parties were unembarrassed enough to actually use the Orwellian term "free speech zones," there were large demonstrations for and against issues like the Iraq War, and the zones themselves.

But this time around, it is only the press that turned out in massive numbers, apparently hoping to catch a repeat of 1968, when a violent street ruckus upended the Democratic Convention. But 1968 was exactly the sort of televisable show of dangerous dissent these zones are designed to preclude.

Eleven a.m., Day Three, Cleveland's Soldiers' and Sailors' Monument. Rumors had circulated that something big was going to happen here this morning, like thousands of Latinos building a human wall around the Q.

But at the appointed time, there are just a few dozen protesters wearing hand-painted burlap "Wall Off Trump" costumes . . . and about a million journalists.

The joke in the past few days had been that there were 10 cops for every reporter and 10 reporters for every protester. But under the monument at this moment, you can actually see the math.

"Welcome to the photographers' convention!" seethes videographer James Woods, a.k.a. James FromTheInternet (no relation to the unhinged actor).

An executive producer at the popular indie press outlet act.tv, the burly, bearded Woods is a fixture on the protest circuit, a one-man TV production unit who has been spotted chronicling everything from the Ferguson riots to anti-war marches to the unrest that rocked New York after the Eric Garner grand jury.

Woods came to the RNC on the off chance that some real anarchist craziness might finally happen. But he was quickly dispirited when it became a scene where everyone in America with a blog or an iPhone showed up to take selfies while "covering" the historic event, a kind of journo-tourism.

"It's like everyone who's been sitting around for four years decided to scrape the dust off their cameras and show up here," he says, shaking his head.

After a brief attempt at an interlocking-hand "wall" that stretches for perhaps 15 people, the anti-Trump group begins moving in a single row toward the Q, chanting, "Wall off Trump! Wall off Trump!"

They are followed, no joke, by groups of reporters six or seven rows deep on both sides. And when a pair of pro-Trumpers show up quietly holding American flags along the street's edge, they are suddenly set upon by photographers in search of a confrontation.

One of the pro-Trumpers, a 31-year-old Los Angeleno named Shawn Witte, is walking in silence carrying a flag. "Just fucking walking," as he puts it. But the mass of reporters, detecting him, seem anxious to clear a lane between him and the human wall, perhaps hoping they will bite one another or something.

The day before, Witte says, the same thing had happened. When he went outside with his flag, reporters rushed back and forth between Witte and some Black Lives Matter protesters, pointing them out to each other.

"Everybody in Black Lives Matter, they were cool with it," Witte says. "They were like, 'Right on, man. I don't agree with what you're saying, but you have a personal right.' Media was trying to hype that shit up."

The 1968 narrative never materializes, much to the obvious chagrin of the monstrous press contingent (the "human centipede of bastards," as one sketch artist dubbed them). Handfuls of protesters do their thing peacefully, on the permitted side of the DMZ, and it is weak-beer TV no matter how you look at it.

That the press seemed let down by the lack of turmoil on the streets was odd, given that the Trump convention itself was, after all, a historic revolt.

Thirteen million and three hundred thousand Republican voters had defied the will of their party and soundly rejected hundred-million-dollar insider favorites like Jeb Bush to re-seize control of their own political destiny. That they made perhaps the most ridiculous choice in the history of democracy was really a secondary issue.

It was a tremendous accomplishment that real-life conservative voters did what progressives could not quite do in the Democratic primaries. Republican voters penetrated the many layers of money and political connections and corporate media policing that, like the labyrinth of barricades around the Q, are designed to keep the riffraff from getting their mitts on the political process.

But it wasn't covered that way. What started a year ago as an amusing story about a clown car full of bumbling primary hopefuls was about to be described to the world not as a groundbreaking act of defiance, but as a spectacular failure of democracy.

The once-divided media class now came together to gang-troll flyover America for its preposterous decision, turning the coverage of the convention into a parable on the evil of letting voters make up their own dumb minds. This was the *Fatal Attraction* of political coverage, a warning disguised as a story: Look what happens, you rubes, when you step outside the lines.

One of the great propaganda successes of the past few decades has been the myth of the liberal media. The idea that a monolithic herd of leftist snobs somehow controlled the news spread in part because of a seemingly key but really irrelevant demographic truth, i.e., that most individual reporters lean blue in their personal politics.

Moreover, from *All the President's Men* to *The Insider* to *Good Night, and Good Luck* to *Spotlight*, Hollywood portrayals of the media always involve prudish conservative villains upended by chain-smoking/disheveled/wisecracking lefty heroes, Robert Redford's amusingly hunky representation of then-Republican Bob Woodward notwithstanding.

But whatever their personal leanings, influential reporters mostly work in nihilistic corporations, to whom the news is a non-ideological commodity, to be sold the same way we hawk cheeseburgers or Marlboro Lights. Wars, scandals and racial conflicts sell, while poverty and inequality do not. So reporters chase one and not the other. It's just business.

Previously, at conventions like this, pundits always played up the differences between Republicans and Democrats (abortion, religion, immigration), while ignoring the many areas of consensus (trade, military spending, surveillance, the Drug War, non-enforcement of financial crime, corporate tax holidays, etc.).

Any halfway decent boxing promoter will tell you the public must be made to believe the fighters hate each other in order to sell the fight. The fighters also must be hyped as both having a good shot to win. Otherwise, why watch?

The same principle applies in politics. Or at least it did, until Donald Trump arrived in Cleveland.

Thanks to Trump, we in the media can no longer cast politics as a sports story, because the illusion that both sides have a compelling chance at victory is now a tougher sell.

Instead, we will sell it as a freak show, a tent full of bearded ladies and pinheads at which to gape. Next to sports, freak shows are what the media do best, so it'll be an easy switch. Shows like *Anderson Cooper 360°* will become high-tech versions of *Here Comes Honey Boo Boo* or *The Biggest Loser*, destinations for Americans to tune in for a bit to feel superior to the mutants debasing themselves onscreen.

And it's here that the irony of a reality-TV star like Donald Trump winning the nomination comes full circle. Trump won because he grasped instinctively that the campaign trail was more TV show than democracy.

He rolled through primary season simply by being a better and more magnetic reality character than the likes of Scott Walker, Lindsey Graham and Jeb Bush. (You couldn't build a successful reality show around those pols even if you locked them in a hyena cage with Ryan Seacrest and Tila Tequila.)

Then he went to his convention, and his lineup of speakers, minus the handful of "real" politicians who held their noses through the thing, read suspiciously like an episode of *The Apprentice* or *Flavor of Love*. His celebrity guests were a bunch of D-listers ready to eat snails, walk on coals, swap wives or (in this case) publicly support Donald Trump to keep their fading celebrity alive.

The big exception was *Duck Dynasty*'s Willie Robertson, an actual huge star who scored cheers attacking the media.

"It's been a rough year for the media experts," he said. "They don't hang out with folks like us who like to hunt, and fish, and pray, and actually work for a living. I don't even know if they know how to talk to people from Middle America."

It was hard to listen to Robertson's defiant spiel and not wonder at the fact that both he and his most ardent fans probably still have no idea that he was put on TV to be laughed at. *Duck Dynasty* viewers think they're the experts on hunting, but actually they're the hunted ones, just another dumb demographic to be captured, laughed at and force-fed commercials for Geico and Home Depot by the Smart People in New York and L.A.

Trump's voters will almost certainly share the same fate. They will be mined by cable news shows for their entertainment value before ultimately being held up as dangerous loons whose noisy little revolt will serve as the rationale for a generation of Democratic Party rule at the White House level.

Of course, the Republicans blew the one chance they had to save themselves. They could have turned the internal discord to their advantage and held an open convention of ideas, dispensing with the pretense of unity and presenting themselves instead as a big enough tent to embrace and accept many different viewpoints.

Trump should have invited his fiercest critics, the Mike Lees and George Wills of the world, to come onstage and explain why they so fervently disagreed with his tactics and rhetoric. He even should have stopped short of demanding endorsements from all of them. A smart Donald Trump—such a thing is difficult to imagine, but let's say—would have given his opponents a forum to just whale away at him, even removing time constraints. It would have helped make Trump look more like presidential material.

And this would have accomplished two other things.

First, and most important, it would have rescued the immediate future of the party in the highly likely event that Trump goes on to lose in November.

The Republican leadership from Ryan on down could have walked away from this convention with their pseudo-dignity intact, having spoken out against Trump's more naked and vulgar form of racism, standing instead on the principle of a more covert, more subterranean, more dog-whistle-y form of race politics—you know, like Mitt Romney lecturing the NAACP about black people wanting "free stuff."

Second, it would have made for a fascinating run-up to Trump's final address. Here was a man famous for being so thin-skinned that he stays up at night tweeting insults at judges and editors of New Hampshire newspapers, giving the world's biggest stage to his critics.

Then he could have ascended the podium on the concluding night and delivered his apocalyptic argument, which he'd describe as believing in so strongly he stacked it up against his fiercest critics. And he'd have plenty of fodder to swing back at, with decades of Republican inaction, corruption and failure to save American jobs to use in service of his case for a radical change of leadership.

Alas, exactly the opposite happened, and everybody, to the last speaker, came out looking smaller than before.

Priebus and Ryan hanged themselves at the start, endorsing Trump despite clearly not wanting to do so. If Trump loses, they go down the drain of history as pathetic quislings. In the unlikely event that Trump wins, a triumphant Donald would replace them at the first opportunity with horses or WWE ring doctors or anyone who didn't make such a big show of being reluctant supporters when the chips were down.

Some say Ted Cruz was the only winner, given that he came the closest to openly defying the nominee. Cruz refused to endorse Trump, giving a remarkably poisonous and self-serving speech in which he preened like a bully wrestler and told people to "vote your conscience, vote for candidates up and down the ticket," instantly drawing boos from the crowd. Chris Christie, another quisling whose career will soon be over, felt compelled to shake his head in disbelief, while Cruz went on to repulse the crowd with his 10 gazillionth recitation of his Inspirational Family History, including what trail reporters derisively call "the underpants fable."

"Love of freedom has allowed millions to achieve their dreams," he said. "Like my mom, the first in her family to go to college, and my dad, who's here tonight, who fled prison and torture in Cuba, coming to Texas with just $100 sewn into his underwear . . . "

"Fuck your mom!" grumbled someone in the cheap seats.

"You suck!" shouted another.

Trump should have let this all play out, but instead he tried to screw with Cruz's rhythm by entering the hall mid-speech and giving a thumb's-up. Later, Cruz's wife, Heidi, was heckled by Trump supporters who yelled, "Goldman Sachs! Goldman Sachs!" at her, which was both amusing and kind of revolting. Why not yell it at her husband?

But even Cruz wasn't denouncing Trump's belittling of Mexicans, veterans, the Chinese, the disabled, Jewish people, Megyn Kelly's wherever, Carly Fiorina's face, Super Bowl 50 ("Boring!") or any of the hundreds of other groups, people and things targeted by the nominee in the past year.

Instead, the next day, Cruz said that he was not "in the habit" of supporting candidates who attacked his family. This was a sensible enough position but not one that particularly marked him as having stood on principle, especially given that his politics are basically identical to Trump's, minus the oddball insults. If Cruz turns out to be the one Republican who survives this mess, that will be the cruelest blow of all.

By the time Cruz's speech was done, it felt as though an improbable collection of America's most obnoxious, vapid, mean-spirited creeps had somehow been talked into assembling at the Q for the sheer novelty of it ("like X-Men, but for assholes" is how one reporter put it).

As for the subsequent speech by VP hopeful Mike Pence, there's little to report beyond that it happened and he'll someday regret it. Pence redefines boring. He makes Al Gore seem like the Wu-Tang Clan. His one desperate attempt at a Hillary takedown—calling her "the secretary of the Status Quo"—was so painful that people visibly winced in the stands. And when it was all over, he left Trump hanging for an excruciating unexecuted air kiss that immediately became the most mocked thing on Twitter since anything ever. It was a mathematically inexpressible level of Awkward.

All of these awful happenings left only one possibility for salvation: Trump's speech. Unfortunately, by Thursday the multitudinous letdowns had already dented the TV ratings and all but wiped out the possibility of a saving last-night performance. But if anyone could make a bad situation worse, it was Trump. If only for that reason, it was worth attending.

The buzz in the hall on the final night was that Trump might screw things up—how could he not? On the primary trail we had never seen anything like him: impulsive, lewd, grandiose, disgusting, horrible, narcissistic and dangerous, but also usually unscripted and 10 seconds ahead of the news cycle.

We could never quite tell what he was: possibly the American Hitler, but just as possibly punking the whole world in the most ambitious prank/PR stunt of all time. Or maybe he was on the level, birthing a weird new rightist/populist movement, a cross of Huey Long, Pinochet and David Hasselhoff. He was probably a monster, but whatever he was, he was original.

Then came Thursday night.

With tens of millions of eyes watching, Trump the Beltway conqueror turtled and wrapped his arms around the establishment's ankles. He spent the entirety of his final address huddled inside five decades of Republican Party clichés, apparently determined to hide in there until Election Day.

And not just any clichés, either. Trump ripped off the Republican Party's last-ditch emergency maneuver, a scare-the-whitefolks spiel used by a generation of low-charisma underdogs trailing in the polls.

Many observers called it the most terrifying speech they'd ever seen, but that had a lot to do with its hysterical tenor (the *Times* amusingly called it "almost angry"), the Mussolinian head-bobs, the draped-in-flags Caesarean imagery, and his strongman promises. It was a relentlessly negative speech, pure horror movie, with constant references to murder and destruction. If you bought any of it, you probably turned off the tube ready to blow your head off.

But it wasn't new, not one word. Trump cribbed his ideas from the Republicans he spent a year defaming. Trump had merely reprised Willie Horton, Barry Goldwater's "marauders" speech, Jesse Helms' "White Hands" ad, and most particularly Richard Nixon's 1968 "law and order" acceptance address, the party's archetypal fear-based appeal from which Trump borrowed in an intellectual appropriation far more sweeping and shameless than Melania's much-hyped mistake.

He even used the term "law and order" four times, and rehashed a version of Nixon's somber "let us begin by committing ourselves to the truth" intro, promising to "honor the American people with the truth, and nothing else."

In place of Nixon's "merchants of crime," Trump spoke of 180,000 illegal immigrants roaming the countryside like zombies, hungry for the brains of decent folk.

"The number of new illegal-immigrant families who have crossed the border so far this year already exceeds the entire total from 2015," he cried. "They are being released by the tens of thousands into our communities, with no regard for the impact on public safety or resources." The tragic story of Sarah Root, killed by a released immigrant, was just Willie Horton without the picture.

He mentioned cities in crisis, a rising crime rate, and an opponent who promised "death, destruction, terrorism and weakness" for America. His argument really came down to that: Vote for me or die.

As for his populist critiques of money in politics and the pay-for-play corruption in both parties that made up so much of his stump speeches, the same critiques that Bernie Sanders used to throw a scare into Hillary Clinton, they took a back seat in crunch time.

Trump was always just smart enough to see that the same money backs the Jeb Bushes and Hillary Clintons of the world. But he never had the vision or the empathy to understand, beyond the level of a punchline, the frustrations linking disenfranchised voters on both the left and right.

Presented with a rare opportunity to explain how the two parties stoke divisions on social issues to keep working people from realizing their shared economic dilemmas, Trump backed down. Even if he didn't believe it, he could have turned such truths into effective campaign rhetoric. But such great themes are beyond his pampered, D-minus mind. Instead, he tried to poach Sanders voters simply by chanting Bernie's name like a magic word.

In the end, Trump's populism was as fake as everything else about him, and he emerged as just another in a long line of Republican hacks, only dumber and less plausible to the political center.

Which meant that after all that we went through last year, after that crazy cycle of insults and bluster and wife wars and penis-measuring contests and occasionally bloody street battles, after the insane media tornado that destroyed the modern Republican establishment, Trump concluded right where the party started 50 years ago, meekly riding Nixon's Southern Strategy. It was all just one very noisy ride in a circle. All that destruction and rebellion went for nothing. Officially now, he's just another party schmuck.

Archibald MacLeish once wrote a poem called "The End of the World," about a circus interrupted when the big top blows away. The freaks and lion-tamers and acrobats are frozen mid-performance, and the "thousands of white faces" in the audience gasp as they look up at the vast sky to see, after all the fantastical performances in the ring, the ultimate showstopper: emptiness, an endless black sky, "nothing, nothing, nothing—nothing at all."

Trump's finale was like that. When we finally pulled the lid off this guy, there was nothing there. Just a cheap fraud and TV huckster who got in way over his head, and will now lead his hoodwinked followers off the cliff of history.

# The Fury and Failure of Donald Trump

October 14, 2016

Saturday, early October, at a fairground 40 minutes southwest of Milwaukee. The very name of this place, Elkhorn, conjures images of past massacres on now-silent fields across our blood-soaked history. Nobody will die here; this is not Wounded Knee, but it is the end of an era. The modern Republican Party will perish on this stretch of grass.

Trump had been scheduled to come here today, to kiss defenseless babies and pose next to pumpkins and haystacks at Wisconsin congressman and House Speaker Paul Ryan's annual "GOP Fall Fest."

Instead, the two men declared war on each other. The last straw was the release of a tape capturing Donald Trump uttering five words—"Grab them by the pussy"—during an off-camera discussion with former *Access Hollywood* host Billy Bush about what you can do to women when you're a star.

Keeping up with Trump revelations is exhausting. By late October, he'll be caught whacking it outside a nunnery. There are not many places left for this thing to go that don't involve kids or cannibalism. We wait, miserably, for the dong shot.

Ryan, recoiling from Trump's remarks, issued a denunciation ("Women are to be championed and revered, not objectified"), disinviting Trump from his Elkhorn celebration, which was to be the first joint campaign appearance by the country's two highest-ranking Republicans.

As a result, the hundreds of Republican faithful who came spoiling for Trumpian invective, dressed in T-shirts reading things like DEPLORABLE LIVES MATTER and BOMB THE SHIT OUT OF ISIS, and even FUCK OFF, WE'RE FULL (a message for immigrants), ended up herded out here, as if by ruse, to get a big dose of the very thing they'd rebelled against.

They sat through a succession of freedom-and-God speeches by Wisconsin Republicans like Rep. Jim Sensenbrenner, Sen. Ron Johnson, Gov. Scott Walker and Ryan, who collectively represented the party establishment closing ranks and joining the rest of the country in denouncing the free-falling Trump. Once an unstoppable phenomenon who had the media eating out of his controversial-size hands, Trump, in the space of a few hours, had become the mother of all pop-culture villains, a globally despised cross of Dominique Strauss-Kahn, Charlie Sheen and Satan.

To the self-proclaimed "Deplorables" who came out to see Trump anyway, Ryan's decision was treason, the latest evidence that no matter what their party affiliation, Washington politicians have more in common with one another than with regular people.

"Small-ball Ryan," groused Trump supporter Mike Goril, shaking his head, adding to this election cycle's unsurpassable all-time record for testicular innuendo.

Speaker after speaker ascended the stage to urge Republican voters to vote. But with the exception of Attorney General Brad Schimel, who got a round of applause when he grudgingly asked the audience to back Trump for the sake of the Supreme Court, every last one of them tiptoed past the party nominee's name. One by one, they talked around Trump, like an unmentionable uncle carted off on a kiddie-porn rap just before Thanksgiving dinner.

Metaphorically anyway, Trump supporters like Goril were right. Not one of these career politicians had the gumption to be frank with this crowd about what had happened to their party. Instead, the strategy seemed to be to pretend none of it had happened, and to hide behind piles of the same worn clichés that had driven these voters to rebel in the first place.

The party schism burst open in the middle of a speech by Wisconsin's speaker of the State Assembly, Robin Vos. Vos is the Billy Mays of state budget hawks. He's a mean-spirited little ball of energy who leaped onto the stage reminding the crowd that he wanted to eliminate the office of the treasurer to SAVE YOU MONEY!

Vos went on to brag about having wiped out tenure for University of Wisconsin professors, before dismounting with yet another superawkward Trumpless call for Republicans to turn out to vote.

"I have no doubt that with all of you standing behind us," he shouted, "and with the fantastic record of achievement that we have, we're going to go on to an even bigger and better victory than before!"

There was scattered applause, then someone from the crowd called out:

"You uninvited Donald Trump!"

Boos and catcalls, both for and against Vos and the Republicans. Most in the crowd were Trump supporters, but others were angry with Trump for perhaps saddling them with four years of Hillary Clinton. These camps now battled it out across the field. A competing chant of "U-S-A! U-S-A!" started on the opposite end of the stands, only to be met by chants from the pro-Trumpers.

"We want Trump! We want Trump!" "U-S-A! U-S-A!"

Ryan, the last speaker, tried to cut the tension with a leaden joke about the "elephant in the room." But he still refused to speak Trump's name, or do more than refer the crowd to a written statement. He just smiled like it was all OK, and talked about what a beautiful day it was.

Ryan's cowardly play was reflective of the party as a whole, which has yet to own its role in the Trump story. Republican ineptitude and corruption represented the first crack in the facade of a crumbling political system that made Trump's rise possible. As toxic as Trump was, many outside observers were slow to pick up on the threat because they were so focused on how much Republicans like Ryan deserved him.

Trump's early rampage through the Republican field made literary sense. It was classic farce. He was the lewd, unwelcome guest who horrified priggish, decent society, a theme that has mesmerized audiences for centuries, from *Vanity Fair* to *The Government Inspector* to (closer to home) *Fear and Loathing in Las Vegas*. When you let a hands-y, drunken slob loose at an aristocrats' ball, the satirical power of the story comes from the aristocrats deserving what comes next. And nothing has ever deserved a comeuppance quite like the American presidential electoral process, which had become as exclusive and cut off from the people as a tsarist shooting party.

The first symptom of a degraded aristocracy is a lack of capable candidates for the throne. After years of indulgence, ruling families become frail, inbred and isolated, with no one but mystics, impotents and children to put forward as kings. Think of Nikolai Romanov reading fortunes as his troops starved at the front. Weak princes lead to popular uprisings. Which brings us to this year's Republican field.

There wasn't one capable or inspiring person in the infamous "Clown Car" lineup. All 16 of the non-Trump entrants were dunces, religious zealots, wimps or tyrants, all equally out of touch with voters. Scott Walker was a lipless sadist who in centuries past would have worn a leather jerkin and thrown dogs off the castle walls for recreation. Marco Rubio was the young rake with debts. Jeb Bush was the last offering in a fast-diminishing hereditary line. Ted Cruz was the Zodiac Killer. And so on.

The party spent 50 years preaching rich people bromides like "trickle-down economics" and "picking yourself up by your bootstraps" as solutions to the growing alienation and financial privation of the ordinary voter. In place of jobs, exported overseas by the millions by their financial backers, Republicans glibly offered the flag, Jesus and Willie Horton.

In recent years it all went stale. They started to run out of lines to sell the public. Things got so desperate that during the Tea Party phase, some GOP candidates began dabbling in the truth. They told voters that all Washington politicians, including their own leaders, had abandoned them and become whores for special interests. It was a slapstick routine: Throw us bums out!

Republican voters ate it up and spent the whole of last primary season howling for blood as Trump shredded one party-approved hack after another. By the time the other 16 candidates finished their mass-suicide-squad routine, a tail-chasing, sewer-mouthed septuagenarian New Yorker was accepting the nomination of the Family Values Party.

Now, months later, as Trump was imploding, Ryan was retreating to ancient supply-side clichés about how cutting taxes will bring the jobs back. "We've got to scrap this tax code and start over," he said.

As Ryan droned on, well back behind the stands, two heavy-set middle-aged women in Trump/Pence T-shirts shook their heads in boredom. One elbowed the other.

"Wanna grab my crotch?"

This is Wisconsin, after all. You can tell immigrants to fuck off, but you can't say the p-word the day before church, or a Packers game.

The other woman chuckled, then reached down to her own, as if to say, "Grab this!"

Both women busted out laughing. When the event was done, as the crowd of other seething Deplorables filed past them, they and a few others remained in their chairs, staring fatalistically at the empty stage.

The scene couldn't have been more poignant. Duped for a generation by a party that kowtowed to the wealthy while offering scraps to voters, then egged on to a doomed rebellion by a third-rate con man who wilted under pressure and was finally incinerated in a fireball of his own stupidity, people like this found themselves, in the end, represented by literally no one.

Not many people are shedding tears for the Republican voter these days, perhaps rightly so. But the sudden crash-ending of the Trump campaign only made official what these voters have suspected for years: They've been represented by an empty stage all along. Why not sit there and stare at it for a little longer?

Wilkes-Barre, Pennsylvania, the Mohegan Sun Arena, two days later. As he has done multiple times in the past year, Trump has seemingly rebounded from certain disaster. A second debate with Hillary Clinton did not go quite so disastrously as the first, despite horrible optics (he appeared obese from stress and stalked Clinton onstage, as if wanting to bite her back á la Marv Albert) and even worse behavior (he threatened to jail his opponent, a straight-up dictator move you'd expect from a Mobutu, Pinochet or Putin).

Whether or not he "won" the debate was immaterial. He at least impressed pious Mike Pence, Trump's sad-sack running mate, who reportedly had been considering withdrawing from the ticket over the whole pussy thing. "Big debate win!" Pence tweeted, ending rumors of an internal mutiny. "Proud to stand with you as we #MAGA!"

That's hashtag Make America Great Again, in case you didn't believe Mike Pence is hip. (The new white-power movement, like a lot of fraternities, is short on brains, but long on secret pass-words and handshakes.) The man who once opposed clean nee-dles on moral grounds was now ready to march through history with a serial groper and tit-gazer.

In Wilkes-Barre, home to a recent Klan leafleting, and a key electoral-map battleground, the turnout for Trump's rally was a vast sea of white faces and profane signage. SHE'S A CUNT—VOTE TRUMP read the T-shirt of one attendee. BILL! MONICA GAVE YOU WHAT? read the caption over a photo of a grinning Hillary, plastered on the side of one of a scary triad of 18-wheel-ers decked out in anti-Clinton invective. On line going into the event, some more mild-mannered visitors explained why there was nothing that could dissuade them from voting Trump. "Even if it's small, there's a chance that he's going to do something com-pletely different, and that's why I like him," said Trent Gower, a soft-spoken young man. "And when he talks, I actually under-stand what he's saying. But, like, when fricking Hillary Clinton talks, it just sounds like a bunch of bullshit." Inside the arena, passions were running high. Kids zoomed back and forth in Trump/Pence shirts. Some future visitors to probate court even brought their little boy to the event dressed in Trump garb, with a blazer and a power tie. Trump called the lad up onstage.

"Would you like to go back to your parents, or stay with Trump?" Trump asked. No one since Rickey "Rickey can't find Rickey's limo" Henderson has referred to himself in the third person with the same zeal as Trump.

The boy paused.

"Trump!" he said finally, to monstrous applause.

That was the highlight of the evening, unless you want to count Rudy Giuliani's time onstage, with his eyes spinning and arms flailing like a man who'd come to a hospital lost-and-found in search of his medulla oblongata. In recent weeks, Giuliani has looked as though he's been experimenting with recreational Botox. His new thing is to say something insane and then let his face freeze for a second, as if for the last time. In Wilkes-Barre, he started saying something rude about the Clinton Foundation: "Boy, that is phony as . . . I can't say the word because I have to be . . . nice."

He stared helplessly at the crowd for a moment, then pointed upward, like he remembered something. "I might say it in the locker room!" he said, to cheers.

How Giuliani isn't Trump's running mate, no one will ever understand. Theirs is the most passionate television love story since Beavis and Butthead. Every time Trump says something nuts, Giuliani either co-signs it or outdoes him. They will probably spend the years after the election doing prostate-medicine commercials together.

In the far-right world, every successive villain has always been worse than the last. It's quaint now to think about how Al Gore was once regarded as the second coming of Lenin, or that John Kerry was a secret communist agent. Then the race element took Obama-hatred to new and horrifying places. But Trumpian license has pushed hatred of Hillary Clinton beyond all reason. If you don't connect with it emotionally, you won't get it. For grown men and women to throw around words like "bitch" and "cunt" in front of their kids, it means things have moved way beyond the analytical.

Where is it all coming from? The most generous conceivable explanation is that the anger stems from a sense of abandonment and betrayal by the political class. This doesn't explain the likes of Giuliani and Trump, but if you squint really hard, it maybe explains some of what's going on with his supporters.

Although a lot of Clinton backers believe she's being unfairly weighed down by negative reports about the Clinton Foundation and her e-mails, her most serious obstacles this year were less her faults than her virtues. The best argument for a Clinton presidency is that she's virtually guaranteed to be a capable steward of the status quo, at a time of relative stability and safety. There are criticisms to make of Hillary Clinton, but the grid isn't going to collapse while she's in office, something no one can say with even mild confidence about Donald Trump.

But nearly two-thirds of the population was unhappy with the direction of the country entering the general-election season, and nothing has been more associated with the political inside than the Clinton name.

The suspicions heightened on the same day that Trump's infamous "pussy" tape leaked, when WikiLeaks released papers purporting to be excerpts of Clinton's speeches to corporate and financial titans like Goldman Sachs, Deutsche Bank and GE. Her campaign had stalwartly refused to release these during the primary against Bernie Sanders. After the Wiki release, however, one had to wonder why the Clinton camp had bothered to keep the papers secret.

The "secret" speeches in some ways showed Hillary Clinton in a more sympathetic light than her public persona usually allows. Speaking to bankers and masters of the corporate universe, she came off as relaxed, self-doubting, reflective, honest, philosophical rather than political, and unafraid to admit she lacked all the answers.

The transcripts read like freewheeling discussions with friends about how to navigate an uncertain future. In one speech, she conceded a sense of disconnect between the wealthy and the middle class to which she used to belong. This, she said, was a feeling she never had growing up, when the country seemed to be more united.

"And now, obviously," she told executives from Goldman, "I'm kind of far removed because of the life I've lived and the economic . . . fortunes that my husband and I now enjoy."

This frank, almost regretful admission rendered her more real in a few sentences than those cliché-ridden speeches about her hardscrabble background as the granddaughter of a Scranton lace-factory worker.

In a speech before the Brazilian Banco Itaú, Clinton talked about her vision for the future. "My dream is a hemispheric common market, with open trade and open borders," she reportedly said. She wanted this economy "as green and sustainable as we can get it, powering growth and opportunity for every person in the hemisphere."

In classic Clintonian fashion, her camp refused to confirm the authenticity of the emails, while also not denying them either. But why not just own the e-mails? Why all the cagey non-denial denials?

The themes Clinton discussed with the banks were awesome, sweeping and of paramount importance, especially coming from someone in such a unique position to shape the world's future. They collectively represented exactly the honest discussion about what is ahead for all of us that no one in power has ever really had with the rest of the country.

The "scandal" of the Wiki papers, if you can call it that, is that it captured how at ease Clinton was talking to bankers and industrialists about the options for the organization of a global society. Even in transcript form, it's hard not to realize that the people in these rooms are all stakeholders in this vast historical transformation.

Left out of the discussion over the years have been people like Trump's voters, who coincidentally took the first hit along the way in the form of lowered middle-class wages and benefits. They were also never told that things they cared about, like their national identity as Americans, were to have diluted meaning in the more borderless future.

This is why the "basket of deplorables" comment rankled so badly. It's not like it was anywhere near as demeaning or vicious as any of 10,000 Trump insults. But it spoke to a factual disconnnect.

It isn't just that the likely next president feels alienated from people in places like Wilkes-Barre, so close to her ancestral home. It's that, plus the fact that she feels comfortable admitting this to the likes of Goldman's Lloyd Blankfein, to whom she complained about the "bias against people who have led successful and/or complicated lives."

All of which is interesting, and maybe a problem we Americans can have a sober discussion about once we finish bayoneting each other over "pussy" or Miss Universe's weight or the Central Park Five (only Trump could go back in time and revictimize the survivors of one of the most infamous law-enforcement mistakes of all time), or whatever other lunacies we'll be culture-warring over in the last weeks of this mercifully soon-to-end campaign.

It is true that if you talk to enough Trump supporters, you will eventually find an ex-Democrat or two who'll cop to being disillusioned by the party's turn away from the middle class. "My parents were FDR Democrats," says Tim Kallas of Oak Creek, Wisconsin. "I was born and raised to believe that Democrats were for the workingman." A self-described "child of the MTV generation" who has plenty of liberal friends and rocks a long silver ponytail, Kallas says he became disenchanted with the Democrats sometime during Bill Clinton's second term. He was troubled by the Wiki speeches, and says he never signed up for the globalist program. "If you look at what's going on in Europe with the Brexit vote, it's the same conclusion that voters in England came to," he says. "Why are the problems in Greece, or whatever, my problem?"

This sounds sensible enough, but it stops computing when you get to the part where the solution to the vast and complex dilemmas facing humanity is Donald Trump, a man who stays up at night tweeting about whether or not Robert Pattinson should take back Kristen Stewart. (He shouldn't, says Trump: "She cheated on him like a dog and will do it again—just watch. He can do much better!") This is a man who can't remember what he did ten seconds ago, much less decide the fate of the nation-state.

Whatever the original source of disaffection among these Republican voters, the battle has morphed into something else, as Trump himself proved the morning after Wilkes-Barre. He went on one of his trademark Twitter rampages, this time directed at Ryan.

The House speaker had held a conference call with elected Republicans, telling them they were free to yank support from Trump if they thought it would help them win in November. This sounds like a good decision, until you consider that it's one he should have made the moment Trump sealed the nomination. As always, the Republicans acted far too late in disavowing vicious and disgusting behavior in their ranks. Then again, it's hard to keep the loons out when you're scraping to find people willing to sell rich-friendly policies to a broke population. The reaction among hard-line legislators was predictable: You're telling us *now* we can't be pigs?

Arizona Rep. Trent Franks told Ryan that Clinton reaching the White House would result in fetuses being torn "limb to limb," while Southern California's cretinous boob Dana Rohrabacher called Ryan "cowardly," and said Trump's "pussy" comment was just a "60-[year-old] expressing sexual attitude to a younger man."

Trump, meanwhile, unleashed an inevitable string of self-destructive tweets.

9:05 a.m.: "Our very weak and ineffective leader, Paul Ryan, had a bad conference call where his members went wild at his disloyalty."

10 a.m.: "It is so nice that the shackles have been taken off me and I can now fight for America the way I want to."

Shackled! Only in America can a man martyr himself on a cross of pussy.

There's an old Slavic saying about corruption: One thief sits atop another thief, using a third thief for a whip. The campaign trail is similarly a stack of deceptions, with each implicit lie of the horse race driving the next.

Lie No. 1 is that there are only two political ideas in the world, Republican and Democrat. Lie No. 2 is that the parties are violent ideological opposites, and that during campaign season we can only speak about the areas where they differ (abortion, guns, etc.) and never the areas where there's typically consensus (defense spending, surveillance, torture, trade, and so on). Lie No. 3, a corollary to No. 2, is that all problems are the fault of one party or the other, and never both. Assuming you watch the right channels, everything is always someone else's fault. Lie No. 4, the reason America in campaign seasons looks like a place where everyone has great teeth and $1,000 haircuts, is that elections are about political personalities, not voters.

These are the rules of the Campaign Reality Show as it has evolved over the years. The program is designed to reduce political thought to a simple binary choice and force more than 100 million adults to commit to one or the other. Like every TV contest, it discourages subtlety, reflection and reconciliation, and encourages belligerence, action and conflict.

Trump was the ultimate contestant in this show. It's no accident that his first debate with Hillary Clinton turned into the Ali-Frazier of political events, with a breathtaking 84 million people tuning in, making it the most watched political program in American history.

Anyone who takes a close-enough look at how we run elections in this country will conclude that the process is designed to be regressive. It distracts us with trivialities and drives us apart during two years of furious arguments. It's a divide-and-conquer mechanism that keeps us from communicating with one another, and prevents us from examining the broader, systemic problems we all face together.

In the good old days, when elections were merely stupid and not also violent and terrifying, we argued over which candidate we'd rather have a beer with, instead of wondering why both parties were getting hundreds of millions of dollars from the same people.

Trump, ironically, was originally a rebel against this process, the first-ever party-crasher to bulldoze his way past the oligarchical triad of donors, party leaders and gatekeeping media. But once he got in, he became the ultimate servant of the horse race, simultaneously creating the most-watched and most regressive election ever.

He was unable to stop being a reality star. Trump from the start had been playing a part, but his acting got worse and worse as time went on, until finally he couldn't keep track: Was he supposed to be a genuine traitor to his class and the savior of the common man, or just be himself, i.e., a bellicose pervert with too much time on his hands? Or were the two things the same thing? He was too dumb to figure it out, and that paralysis played itself out on the Super Bowl of political stages. It was great television. It was also the worst thing that ever happened to our electoral system.

Trump's shocking rise and spectacular fall have been a singular disaster for U.S. politics. Built up in the press as the American Hitler, he was unmasked in the end as a pathetic little prankster who ruined himself, his family and half of America's two-party political system for what was probably a half-assed ego trip all along, adventure tourism for the idiot rich.

That such a small man would have such an awesome impact on our nation's history is terrible, but it makes sense if you believe in the essential ridiculousness of the human experience. Trump picked exactly the wrong time to launch his mirror-gazing rampage to nowhere. He ran at a time when Americans on both sides of the aisle were experiencing a deep sense of betrayal by the political class, anger that was finally ready to express itself at the ballot box.

The only thing that could get in the way of real change—if not now, then surely very soon—was a rebellion so maladroit, illconceived and irresponsible that even the severest critics of the system would become zealots for the status quo.

In the absolute best-case scenario, the one in which he loses, this is what Trump's run accomplished. He ran as an outsider antidote to a corrupt two-party system, and instead will leave that system more entrenched than ever. If he goes on to lose, he will be our Bonaparte, the monster who will continue to terrify us even in exile, reinforcing the authority of kings.

If you thought lesser-evilism was bad before, wait until the answer to every question you might have about your political leaders becomes, "Would you rather have Trump in office?"

Trump can't win. Our national experiment can't end because one aging narcissist got bored of sex and food. Not even America deserves that. But that doesn't mean we come out ahead. We're more divided than ever, sicker than ever, dumber than ever. And there's no reason to think it won't be worse the next time.

## New York

FINALIST—ESSAYS AND
CRITICISM

*Andrew Sullivan put the rise of Donald Trump—he was days away from securing the nomination when this piece was published—in alarming perspective. Drawing from sources ranging from Plato to Sinclair Lewis, Sullivan wrote that the expansion of freedom in the United States made Trump all but inevitable. "Sullivan lays out the stakes in the general election with devastating prescience, deeming a Trump victory 'an extinction-level event' for our liberal democracy," wrote the Ellies judges. Sullivan is one of the rare Ellie honorees to win recognition as both a writer and an editor*—The New Republic *won the award for Public Interest in 1995 while he was editor. Sullivan shuttered his blog* The Daily Dish, *in 2015; he now writes a column for* New York.

Andrew Sullivan

# Democracies End When They Are Too Democratic

As this dystopian election campaign has unfolded, my mind keeps being tugged by a passage in Plato's *Republic*. It has unsettled—even surprised—me from the moment I first read it in graduate school. The passage is from the part of the dialogue where Socrates and his friends are talking about the nature of different political systems, how they change over time, and how one can slowly evolve into another. And Socrates seemed pretty clear on one sobering point: that "tyranny is probably established out of no other regime than democracy." What did Plato mean by that? Democracy, for him, I discovered, was a political system of maximal freedom and equality, where every lifestyle is allowed and public offices are filled by a lottery. And the longer a democracy lasted, Plato argued, the more democratic it would become. Its freedoms would multiply; its equality spread. Deference to any sort of authority would wither; tolerance of any kind of inequality would come under intense threat; and multiculturalism and sexual freedom would create a city or a country like "a many-colored cloak decorated in all hues."

This rainbow-flag polity, Plato argues, is, for many people, the fairest of regimes. The freedom in that democracy has to be experienced to be believed—with shame and privilege in particular emerging over time as anathema. But it is inherently unstable. As the authority of elites fades, as establishment values cede to popular ones, views and identities can become so magnificently diverse as to be mutually uncomprehending. And when all the barriers to equality, formal and informal, have been removed; when everyone is equal; when elites are despised and full license is established to do "whatever one wants," you arrive at what might be called late-stage democracy. There is no kowtowing to authority here, let alone to political experience or expertise.

The very rich come under attack as inequality becomes increasingly intolerable. Patriarchy is also dismantled: "We almost forgot to mention the extent of the law of equality and of freedom in the relations of women with men and men with women." Family hierarchies are inverted: "A father habituates himself to be like his child and fear his sons, and a son habituates himself to be like his father and to have no shame before or fear of his parents." In classrooms, "as the teacher . . . is frightened of the pupils and fawns on them, so the students make light of their teachers." Animals are regarded as equal to humans; the rich mingle freely with the poor in the streets and try to blend in. The foreigner is equal to the citizen.

And it is when a democracy has ripened as fully as this, Plato argues, that a would-be tyrant will often seize his moment.

He is usually of the elite but has a nature in tune with the time—given over to random pleasures and whims, feasting on plenty of food and sex, and reveling in the nonjudgment that is democracy's civil religion. He makes his move by "taking over a particularly obedient mob" and attacking his wealthy peers as corrupt. If not stopped quickly, his appetite for attacking the rich on behalf of the people swells further. He is a traitor to his class—and soon, his elite enemies, shorn of popular legitimacy, find a way to appease him or are forced to flee. Eventually, he stands alone, promising to cut through the paralysis of democratic incoherence. It's as if he were offering the addled, distracted, and self-indulgent citizens a kind of relief from democracy's endless choices and insecurities. He rides a backlash to excess—"too much freedom seems to change into nothing but too much slavery"—and offers himself as the personified answer to the internal conflicts of the democratic mess. He pledges, above all, to take on the increasingly despised elites. And as the people thrill to him as a kind of solution, a democracy willingly, even impetuously, repeals itself.

And so, as I chitchatted over cocktails at a Washington office Christmas party in December, and saw, looming above our heads, the pulsating, angry televised face of Donald Trump on Fox News, I couldn't help but feel a little nausea permeate my stomach. And as I watched frenzied Trump rallies on C-SPAN in the spring, and saw him lay waste to far more qualified political peers in the debates by simply calling them names, the nausea turned to dread. And when he seemed to condone physical violence as a response to political disagreement, alarm bells started to ring in my head. Plato had planted a gnawing worry in my mind a few decades ago about the intrinsic danger of late-democratic life. It was increasingly hard not to see in Plato's vision a murky reflection of our own hyperdemocratic times and in Trump a demagogic, tyrannical character plucked directly out of one of the first books about politics ever written.

Could it be that the Donald has emerged from the populist circuses of pro wrestling and New York City tabloids, via reality television and Twitter, to prove not just Plato but also James Madison right, that democracies "have ever been spectacles of turbulence and contention . . . and have in general been as short in their lives as they have been violent in their deaths"? Is he testing democracy's singular weakness—its susceptibility to the demagogue—by blasting through the firewalls we once had in place to prevent such a person from seizing power? Or am I overreacting?

Perhaps. The nausea comes and goes, and there have been days when the news algorithm has actually reassured me that "peak Trump" has arrived. But it hasn't gone away, and neither has Trump. In the wake of his most recent primary triumphs, at a time when he is perilously close to winning enough delegates to grab the Republican nomination outright, I think we must confront this dread and be clear about what this election has already revealed about the fragility of our way of life and the threat late-stage democracy is beginning to pose to itself.

.　　　.　　　.

Plato, of course, was not clairvoyant. His analysis of how democracy can turn into tyranny is a complex one more keyed toward ancient societies than our own (and contains more wrinkles and eddies than I can summarize here). His disdain for democratic life was fueled in no small part by the fact that a democracy had executed his mentor, Socrates. And he would, I think, have been astonished at how American democracy has been able to thrive with unprecedented stability over the last couple of centuries even as it has brought more and more people into its embrace. It remains, in my view, a miracle of constitutional craftsmanship and cultural resilience. There is no place I would rather live. But it is not immortal, nor should we assume it is immune to the forces that have endangered democracy so many times in human history.

Part of American democracy's stability is owed to the fact that the Founding Fathers had read their Plato. To guard our democracy from the tyranny of the majority and the passions of the mob, they constructed large, hefty barriers between the popular will and the exercise of power. Voting rights were tightly circumscribed. The president and vice president were not to be popularly elected but selected by an Electoral College, whose representatives were selected by the various states, often through state legislatures. The Senate's structure (with two members from every state) was designed to temper the power of the more populous states, and its term of office (six years, compared with two for the House) was designed to cool and restrain temporary populist passions. The Supreme Court, picked by the president and confirmed by the Senate, was the final bulwark against any democratic furies that might percolate up from the House and threaten the Constitution. This separation of powers was designed precisely to create sturdy firewalls against democratic wildfires.

Over the centuries, however, many of these undemocratic rules have been weakened or abolished. The franchise has been extended far beyond propertied white men. The presidency is now effectively elected through popular vote, with the Electoral College almost always reflecting the national democratic will. And these formal democratic advances were accompanied by informal ones, as the culture of democracy slowly took deeper root. For a very long time, only the elites of the political parties came to select their candidates at their quadrennial conventions, with the vote largely restricted to party officials from the various states (and often decided in, yes, smoke-filled rooms in large hotel suites). Beginning in the early 1900s, however, the parties began experimenting with primaries, and after the chaos of the 1968 Democratic convention, today's far more democratic system became the norm.

Direct democracy didn't just elect Congress and the president anymore; it expanded the notion of who might be qualified for public office. Once, candidates built a career through experience in elected or cabinet positions or as military commanders; they were effectively selected by peer review. That elitist sorting mechanism has slowly imploded. In 1940, Wendell Willkie, a businessman with no previous political office, won the Republican nomination for president, pledging to keep America out of war and boasting that his personal wealth inoculated him against corruption: "I will be under obligation to nobody except the people." He lost badly to Franklin D. Roosevelt, but nonetheless, since then, nonpolitical candidates have proliferated, from Ross Perot and Jesse Jackson, to Steve Forbes and Herman Cain, to this year's crop of Ben Carson, Carly Fiorina, and, of course, Donald J. Trump. This further widening of our democracy—our increased openness to being led by anyone; indeed, our accelerating preference for outsiders—is now almost complete.

The barriers to the popular will, especially when it comes to choosing our president, are now almost nonexistent. In 2000, George W. Bush lost the popular vote and won the election thanks to Electoral College math and, more egregiously, to a partisan Supreme Court vote. Al Gore's eventual concession spared the nation a constitutional crisis, but the episode generated widespread unease, not just among Democrats. And this year, the delegate system established by our political parties is also under assault. Trump has argued that the candidate with the most votes should get the Republican nomination, regardless of the rules in place. It now looks as if he won't even need to win that argument—that he'll bank enough delegates to secure the nomination uncontested—but he's won it anyway. Fully half of Americans now believe the traditional nominating system is rigged.

Many contend, of course, that American democracy is actually in retreat, close to being destroyed by the vastly more unequal economy of the last quarter century and the ability of the very rich to purchase political influence. This is Bernie Sanders's core critique. But the past few presidential elections have demonstrated that, in fact, money from the ultrarich has been mostly a dud. Barack Obama, whose 2008 campaign was propelled by small donors and empowered by the Internet, blazed the trail of the modern-day insurrectionist, defeating the prohibitive favorite in the Democratic primary and later his Republican opponent (both pillars of their parties' establishments and backed by moneyed elites). In 2012, the fund-raising power behind Mitt Romney—avatar of the one percent—failed to dislodge Obama from office. And in this presidential cycle, the breakout candidates of both parties have soared without financial support from the elites. Sanders, who is sustaining his campaign all the way to California on the backs of small donors and large crowds, is, to put it bluntly, a walking refutation of his own argument. Trump, of course, is a largely self-funding billionaire—but like Willkie, he argues that his wealth uniquely enables him to resist the influence of the rich and their lobbyists. Those despairing over the influence of Big Money in American politics must also explain the swift, humiliating demise of Jeb Bush and the struggling establishment campaign of Hillary Clinton. The evidence suggests that direct democracy, far from being throttled, is actually intensifying its grip on American politics.

None of this is necessarily cause for alarm, even though it would be giving the Founding Fathers palpitations. The emergence of the first black president—unimaginable before our more inclusive democracy—is miraculous, a strengthening, rather than weakening, of the system. The days when party machines just fixed things or rigged elections are mercifully done with. The way in which outsider candidates, from Obama to Trump and Sanders, have brought millions of new people into the electoral process is an unmitigated advance. The inclusion of previously excluded voices helps, rather than impedes, our public deliberation. But it is precisely because of the great accomplishments of our democracy that we should be vigilant about its specific, unique vulnerability: its susceptibility, in stressful times, to the appeal of a shameless demagogue.

•     •     •

What the twenty-first century added to this picture, it's now blindingly obvious, was media democracy—in a truly revolutionary form. If late-stage political democracy has taken two centuries to ripen, the media equivalent took around two decades, swiftly erasing almost any elite moderation or control of our democratic discourse. The process had its origins in partisan talk radio at the end of the past century. The rise of the Internet—an event so swift and pervasive its political effect is only now beginning to be understood—further democratized every source of information, dramatically expanded each outlet's readership, and gave everyone a platform. All the old barriers to entry—the cost of print and paper and distribution—crumbled.

So much of this was welcome. I relished it myself in the early aughts, starting a blog and soon reaching as many readers, if not more, as some small magazines do. Fusty old-media institutions, grown fat and lazy, deserved a drubbing. The early independent blogosphere corrected facts, exposed bias, earned scoops. And as the medium matured, and as Facebook and Twitter took hold, everyone became a kind of blogger. In ways no twentieth-century journalist would have believed, we all now have our own virtual newspapers on our Facebook newsfeeds and Twitter timelines—picking stories from countless sources and creating a peer-to-peer media almost completely free of editing or interference by elites. This was bound to make politics more fluid. Political organizing—calling a meeting, fomenting a rally to advance a cause—used to be extremely laborious. Now you could bring together a virtual mass movement with a single webpage. It would take you a few seconds.

The web was also uniquely capable of absorbing other forms of media, conflating genres and categories in ways never seen before. The distinction between politics and entertainment became fuzzier; election coverage became even more modeled on sportscasting; your Pornhub jostled right next to your mother's Facebook page. The web's algorithms all but removed any editorial judgment, and the effect soon had cable news abandoning even the pretense of asking "Is this relevant?" or "Do we really need to cover this live?" in the rush toward ratings bonanzas. In the end, all these categories were reduced to one thing: traffic, measured far more accurately than any other medium had ever done before.

And what mainly fuels this is precisely what the Founders feared about democratic culture: feeling, emotion, and narcissism, rather than reason, empiricism, and public-spiritedness. Online debates become personal, emotional, and irresolvable almost as soon as they begin. Godwin's Law—it's only a matter of time before a comments section brings up Hitler—is a reflection of the collapse of the reasoned deliberation the Founders saw as indispensable to a functioning republic.

Yes, occasional rational points still fly back and forth, but there are dramatically fewer elite arbiters to establish which of those points is actually true or valid or relevant. We have lost authoritative sources for even a common set of facts. And without such common empirical ground, the emotional component of politics becomes inflamed and reason retreats even further. The more emotive the candidate, the more supporters he or she will get.

Politically, we lucked out at first. Obama would never have been nominated for the presidency, let alone elected, if he hadn't harnessed the power of the Web and the charisma of his media celebrity. But he was also, paradoxically, a very elite figure, a former state and U.S. senator, a product of Harvard Law School, and, as it turned out, blessed with a preternaturally rational and calm disposition. So he has masked, temporarily, the real risks in the system that his pioneering campaign revealed. Hence many Democrats' frustration with him. Those who saw in his campaign the seeds of revolutionary change, who were drawn to him by their own messianic delusions, came to be bitterly disappointed by his governing moderation and pragmatism.

The climate Obama thrived in, however, was also ripe for far less restrained opportunists. In 2008, Sarah Palin emerged as proof that an ardent Republican, branded as an outsider, tailor-made for reality TV, proud of her own ignorance about the world, and reaching an audience directly through online media, could also triumph in this new era. She was, it turned out, a John the Baptist for the true messiah of conservative populism, waiting patiently and strategically for his time to come.

. . .

Trump, we now know, had been considering running for president for decades. Those who didn't see him coming—or kept treating him as a joke—had not yet absorbed the precedents of Obama and Palin or the power of the new wide-open system to change the rules of the political game. Trump was as underrated for all of 2015 as Obama was in 2007—and for the same reasons. He intuitively grasped the vanishing authority of American political and media elites, and he had long fashioned a public persona perfectly attuned to blast past them.

Despite his immense wealth and inherited privilege, Trump had always cultivated a common touch. He did not hide his wealth in the late twentieth century—he flaunted it in a way that connected with the masses. He lived the rich man's life most working men dreamed of—endless glamour and women, for example—without sacrificing a way of talking about the world that would not be out of place on the construction sites he regularly toured. His was a cult of democratic aspiration. His 1987 book, *The Art of the Deal*, promised its readers a path to instant success; his appearances on *The Howard Stern Show* cemented his appeal. His friendship with Vince McMahon offered him an early entrée into the world of professional wrestling, with its fusion of sports and fantasy. He was a macho media superstar.

One of the more amazing episodes in Sarah Palin's early political life, in fact, bears this out. She popped up in the Anchorage *Daily News* as "a commercial fisherman from Wasilla" on April 3, 1996. Palin had told her husband she was going to Costco but had sneaked into J.C. Penney in Anchorage to see . . . one Ivana Trump, who, in the wake of her divorce, was touting her branded perfume. "We want to see Ivana," Palin told the paper, "because we are so desperate in Alaska for any semblance of glamour and culture."

Trump assiduously cultivated this image and took to reality television as a natural. Each week, for fourteen seasons of *The Apprentice*, he would look someone in the eye and tell them, "You're fired!" The conversation most humane bosses fear to have with an employee was something Trump clearly relished, and the cruelty became entertainment. In retrospect, it is clear he was training—both himself and his viewers. If you want to understand why a figure so widely disliked nonetheless powers toward the election as if he were approaching a reality-TV-show finale, look no further. His television tactics, as applied to presidential debates, wiped out rivals used to a different game. And all our reality-TV training has conditioned us to hope he'll win—or at least stay in the game till the final round. In such a shame-free media environment, the assholes often win. In the end, you support them because they're assholes.

·　　·　　·

In Eric Hoffer's classic 1951 tract, *The True Believer*, he sketches the dynamics of a genuine mass movement. He was thinking of the upheavals in Europe in the first half of the century, but the book remains sobering, especially now. Hoffer's core insight was to locate the source of all truly mass movements in a collective sense of acute frustration. Not despair, or revolt, or resignation—but frustration simmering with rage. Mass movements, he notes (as did Tocqueville centuries before him), rarely arise when oppression or misery is at its worst (say, 2009); they tend to appear when the worst is behind us but the future seems not so much better (say, 2016). It is when a recovery finally gathers speed and some improvement is tangible but not yet widespread that the anger begins to rise. After the suffering of recession or unemployment, and despite hard work with stagnant or dwindling pay, the future stretches ahead with relief just out of reach. When those who helped create the last recession face no consequences but renewed fabulous wealth, the anger reaches a crescendo.

The deeper, long-term reasons for today's rage are not hard to find, although many of us elites have shamefully found ourselves able to ignore them. The jobs available to the working class no longer contain the kind of craftsmanship or satisfaction or meaning that can take the sting out of their low and stagnant wages. The once-familiar avenues for socialization—the church, the union hall, the VFW—have become less vibrant and social isolation more common. Global economic forces have pummeled blue-collar workers more relentlessly than almost any other segment of society, forcing them to compete against hundreds of millions of equally skilled workers throughout the planet. No one asked them in the 1990s if this was the future they wanted. And the impact has been more brutal than many economists predicted. No wonder suicide and mortality rates among the white working poor are spiking dramatically.

"It is usually those whose poverty is relatively recent, the 'new poor,' who throb with the ferment of frustration," Hoffer argues. Fundamentalist religion long provided some emotional support for those left behind (for one thing, it invites practitioners to defy the elites as unholy), but its influence has waned as modernity has penetrated almost everything and the great culture wars of the 1990s and 2000s have ended in a rout. The result has been a more diverse mainstream culture—but also, simultaneously, a subculture that is even more alienated and despised, and ever more infuriated and bloody-minded.

This is an age in which a woman might succeed a black man as president but also one in which a member of the white working class has declining options to make a decent living. This is a time when gay people can be married in fifty states, even as working-class families are hanging by a thread. It's a period in which we have become far more aware of the historic injustices that still haunt African Americans and yet we treat the desperate plight of today's white working class as an afterthought. And so late-stage capitalism is creating a righteous, revolutionary anger that late-stage democracy has precious little ability to moderate or constrain—and has actually helped exacerbate.

For the white working class, having had their morals roundly mocked, their religion deemed primitive, and their economic prospects decimated, now find their very gender and race, indeed the very way they talk about reality, described as a kind of problem for the nation to overcome. This is just one aspect of what Trump has masterfully signaled as "political correctness" run amok, or what might be better described as the newly rigid progressive passion for racial and sexual equality of outcome, rather than the liberal aspiration to mere equality of opportunity.

Much of the newly energized left has come to see the white working class not as allies but primarily as bigots, misogynists, racists, and homophobes, thereby condemning those often at the near-bottom rung of the economy to the bottom rung of the culture as well. A struggling white man in the heartland is now told to "check his privilege" by students at Ivy League colleges. Even if you agree that the privilege exists, it's hard not to empathize with the object of this disdain. These working-class communities, already alienated, hear—how can they not?—the glib and easy dismissals of "white straight men" as the ultimate source of all our woes. They smell the condescension and the broad generalizations about them—all of which would be repellent if directed at racial minorities—and see themselves, in Hoffer's words, "disinherited and injured by an unjust order of things."

And so they wait and they steam and they lash out. This was part of the emotional force of the tea party: not just the advancement of racial minorities, gays, and women but the simultaneous demonization of the white working-class world, its culture and way of life. Obama never intended this, but he became a symbol to many of this cultural marginalization. The Black Lives Matter left stoked the fires still further; so did the gay left, for whom the word *magnanimity* seems unknown, even in the wake of stunning successes. And as the Tea Party swept through Washington in 2010, as its representatives repeatedly held the government budget hostage, threatened the very credit of the United States, and refused to hold hearings on a Supreme Court nominee, the American political and media establishment mostly chose to interpret such behavior as something other than unprecedented. But Trump saw what others didn't, just as Hoffer noted: "The frustrated individual and the true believer make better prognosticators than those who have reason to want the preservation of the status quo."

.   .   .

Mass movements, Hoffer argues, are distinguished by a "facility for make-believe . . . credulity, a readiness to attempt the impossible." What, one wonders, could be more impossible than suddenly vetting every single visitor to the United States for traces of Islamic belief? What could be more make-believe than a big, beautiful wall stretching across the entire Mexican border, paid for by the Mexican government? What could be more credulous than arguing that we could pay off our national debt through a global trade war? In a conventional political party, and in a rational political discourse, such ideas would be laughed out of contention, their self-evident impossibility disqualifying them from serious consideration. In the emotional fervor of a democratic mass movement, however, these impossibilities become icons of hope, symbols of a new way of conducting politics. Their very impossibility is their appeal.

But the most powerful engine for such a movement—the thing that gets it off the ground, shapes and solidifies and entrenches it—is always the evocation of hatred. It is, as Hoffer put it, "the most accessible and comprehensive of all unifying elements." And so Trump launched his campaign by calling undocumented Mexican immigrants a population largely of rapists and murderers. He moved on to Muslims, both at home and abroad. He has now added to these enemies—with sly brilliance—the Republican establishment itself. And what makes Trump uniquely dangerous in the history of American politics—with far broader national appeal than, say, Huey Long or George Wallace—is his response to all three enemies. It's the threat of blunt coercion and dominance.

And so after demonizing most undocumented Mexican immigrants, he then vowed to round up and deport all 11 million of them by force. "They have to go" was the typically blunt phrase he used—and somehow people didn't immediately recognize the monstrous historical echoes. The sheer scale of the police and military operation that this policy would entail boggles the mind. Worse, he emphasized, after the mass murder in San Bernardino, that even the Muslim Americans you know intimately may turn around and massacre you at any juncture. "There's something going on," he declaimed ominously, giving legitimacy to the most hysterical and ugly of human impulses.

To call this fascism doesn't do justice to fascism. Fascism had, in some measure, an ideology and occasional coherence that Trump utterly lacks. But his movement is clearly fascistic in its demonization of foreigners, its hyping of a threat by a domestic minority (Muslims and Mexicans are the new Jews), its focus on a single supreme leader of what can only be called a cult, and its deep belief in violence and coercion in a democracy that has heretofore relied on debate and persuasion. This is the Weimar aspect of our current moment. Just as the English Civil War ended with a dictatorship under Oliver Cromwell, and the French Revolution gave us Napoleon Bonaparte, and the unstable chaos of Russian democracy yielded to Vladimir Putin, and the most recent burst of Egyptian democracy set the conditions for General el-Sisi's coup, so our paralyzed, emotional hyperdemocracy leads the stumbling, frustrated, angry voter toward the chimerical panacea of Trump.

His response to his third vaunted enemy, the RNC, is also laced with the threat of violence. There will be riots in Cleveland if he doesn't get his way. The RNC will have "a rough time" if it doesn't cooperate. "Paul Ryan, I don't know him well, but I'm sure I'm going to get along great with him," Trump has said. "And if I don't? He's gonna have to pay a big price, okay?" The past month has seen delegates to the Cleveland convention receiving death threats; one of Trump's hatchet men, Roger Stone, has already threatened to publish the hotel rooms of delegates who refuse to vote for Trump.

And what's notable about Trump's supporters is precisely what one would expect from members of a mass movement: their intense loyalty. Trump is their man, however inarticulate they are when explaining why. He's tough, he's real, and they've got his back, especially when he is attacked by all the people they have come to despise: liberal Democrats and traditional Republicans. At rallies, whenever a protester is hauled out, you can almost sense the rising rage of the collective identity venting itself against a lone dissenter and finding a catharsis of sorts in the brute force a mob can inflict on an individual. Trump tells the crowd he'd like to punch a protester in the face or have him carried out on a stretcher. No modern politician who has come this close to the presidency has championed violence in this way. It would be disqualifying if our hyperdemocracy hadn't already abolished disqualifications.

And while a critical element of twentieth-century fascism— its organized street violence—is missing, you can begin to see it in embryonic form. The phalanx of bodyguards around Trump grows daily; plainclothes bouncers in the crowds have emerged as pseudocops to contain the incipient unrest his candidacy will only continue to provoke; supporters have attacked hecklers with sometimes stunning ferocity. Every time Trump legitimizes potential violence by his supporters by saying it comes from a love of country, he sows the seeds for serious civil unrest.

Trump celebrates torture—the one true love of tyrants everywhere—not because it allegedly produces intelligence but because it has a demonstration effect. At his rallies he has recounted the mythical acts of one General John J. Pershing when confronted with an alleged outbreak of Islamist terrorism in the Philippines. Pershing, in Trump's telling, lines up fifty Muslim prisoners, swishes a series of bullets in the corpses of freshly slaughtered pigs, and orders his men to put those bullets in their rifles and kill forty-nine of the captured Muslim men. He spares one captive solely so he can go back and tell his friends. End of the terrorism problem.

In some ways, this story contains all the elements of Trump's core appeal. The vexing problem of tackling jihadist terror? Torture and murder enough terrorists and they will simply go away. The complicated issue of undocumented workers, drawn by jobs many Americans won't take? Deport every single one of them and build a wall to stop the rest. Fuck political correctness. As one of his supporters told an obtuse reporter at a rally when asked if he supported Trump: "Hell yeah! He's no bullshit. All balls. Fuck you all balls. That's what I'm about." And therein lies the appeal of tyrants from the beginning of time. Fuck you all balls. Irrationality with muscle.

The racial aspect of this is also unmissable. When the enemy within is Mexican or Muslim, and your ranks are extremely white, you set up a rubric for a racial conflict. And what's truly terrifying about Trump is that he does not seem to shrink from such a prospect; he relishes it.

For, like all tyrants, he is utterly lacking in self-control. Sleeping a handful of hours a night, impulsively tweeting in the early hours, improvising madly on subjects he knows nothing about, Trump rants and raves as he surfs an entirely reactive media landscape. Once again, Plato had his temperament down: A tyrant is a man "not having control of himself [who] attempts to rule others"; a man flooded with fear and love and passion, while having little or no ability to restrain or moderate them; a "real slave to the greatest fawning," a man who "throughout his entire life . . . is full of fear, overflowing with convulsions and pains." Sound familiar? Trump is as mercurial and as unpredictable and as emotional as the daily Twitter stream. And we are contemplating giving him access to the nuclear codes.

•     •     •

Those who believe that Trump's ugly, thuggish populism has no chance of ever making it to the White House seem to me to be missing this dynamic. Neofascist movements do not advance gradually by persuasion; they first transform the terms of the debate, create a new movement based on untrammeled emotion, take over existing institutions, and then ruthlessly exploit events. And so current poll numbers are only reassuring if you ignore the potential impact of sudden, external events—an economic downturn or a terror attack in a major city in the months before November. I have no doubt, for example, that Trump is sincere in his desire to "cut the head off" ISIS, whatever that can possibly mean. But it remains a fact that the interests of ISIS and the Trump campaign are now perfectly aligned. Fear is always the would-be tyrant's greatest ally.

And though Trump's unfavorables are extraordinarily high (around 65 percent), he is already showing signs of changing his tune, pivoting (fitfully) to the more presidential mode he envisages deploying in the general election. I suspect this will, to some fools on the fence, come as a kind of relief, and may open their minds to him once more. Tyrants, like mob bosses, know the value of a smile: Precisely because of the fear he's already generated, you desperately want to believe in his new warmth. It's part of the good-cop-bad-cop routine that will be familiar to anyone who has studied the presidency of Vladimir Putin.

With his appeal to his own base locked up, Trump may well also shift to more moderate stances on social issues like abortion (he already wants to amend the GOP platform to a less draconian position) or gay and even transgender rights. He is consistent in his inconsistency, because, for him, winning is what counts. He has had a real case against Ted Cruz—that the senator has no base outside ideological-conservative quarters and is even less likely to win a general election. More potently, Trump has a worryingly strong argument against Clinton herself—or "crooked Hillary," as he now dubs her.

His proposition is a simple one. Remember James Carville's core question in the 1992 election: Change versus more of the same? That sentiment once elected Clinton's husband; it could also elect her opponent this fall. If you like America as it is, vote Clinton. After all, she has been a member of the American political elite for a quarter-century. Clinton, moreover, has shown no ability to inspire or rally anyone but her longtime loyalists. She is lost in the new media and has struggled to put away a seventy-four-year-old socialist who is barely a member of her party. Her own unfavorables are only eleven points lower than Trump's (far higher than Obama's, John Kerry's, or Al Gore's were at this point in the race), and the more she campaigns, the higher her unfavorables go (including in her own party). She has a Gore problem. The idea of welcoming her into your living room for the next four years can seem, at times, positively masochistic.

It may be that demographics will save us. America is no longer an overwhelmingly white country, and Trump's signature issue—illegal immigration—is the source of his strength but also of his weakness. Nonetheless, it's worth noting how polling models have consistently misread the breadth of his support, especially in these past few weeks; he will likely bend over backward to include minorities in his fall campaign; and those convinced he cannot bring a whole new swath of white voters back into the political process should remember 2004, when Karl Rove helped engineer anti-gay-marriage state constitutional amendments that increased conservative voter turnout. All Trump needs is a sliver of minority votes inspired by the new energy of his campaign and the alleged dominance of the Obama coalition could crack (especially without Obama). Throughout the West these past few years, from France to Britain and Germany, the polls have kept missing the power of right-wing insurgency.

Were Trump to win the White House, the defenses against him would be weak. He would likely bring a GOP majority in the House, and Republicans in the Senate would be subjected to almighty popular fury if they stood in his way. The 4–4 stalemate in the Supreme Court would break in Trump's favor. (In large part, of course, this would be due to the GOP's unprecedented decision to hold a vacancy open "for the people to decide," another massive hyperdemocratic breach in our constitutional defenses.) And if Trump's policies are checked by other branches of government, how might he react? Just look at his response to the rules of the GOP nomination process. He's not interested in rules. And he barely understands the Constitution. In one revealing moment earlier this year, when asked what he would do if the military refused to obey an illegal order to torture a prisoner, Trump simply insisted that the man would obey: "They won't refuse. They're not going to refuse, believe me." He later amended his remark, but it speaks volumes about his approach to power. Dick Cheney gave illegal orders to torture prisoners and coerced White House lawyers to cook up absurd "legal" defenses. Trump would make Cheney's embrace of the dark side and untrammeled executive power look unambitious.

.     .     .

In his 1935 novel, *It Can't Happen Here,* Sinclair Lewis wrote a counterfactual about what would happen if fascism as it was then spreading across Europe were to triumph in America. It's not a good novel, but it remains a resonant one. The imagined American fascist leader—a senator called Buzz Windrip—is a "Professional Common Man. . . . But he was the Common Man twenty-times-magnified by his oratory, so that while the other Commoners could understand his every purpose, which was exactly the same as their own, they saw him towering among them, and they raised hands to him in worship."

He "was vulgar, almost illiterate, a public liar easily detected, and in his 'ideas' almost idiotic." " 'I know the Press only too well,'" Windrip opines at one point. " 'Almost all editors hide away in spider-dens, men without thought of Family or Public Interest . . . plotting how they can put over their lies, and advance their own positions and fill their greedy pocketbooks.' "

He is obsessed with the balance of trade and promises instant economic success: " 'I shall not be content till this country can produce every single thing we need. . . . We shall have such a balance of trade as will go far to carry out my often-criticized yet completely sound idea of from $3000 to $5000 per year for every single family.'" However fantastical and empty his promises, he nonetheless mesmerizes the party faithful at the nominating convention (held in Cleveland!): "Something in the intensity with which Windrip looked at his audience, looked at all of them, his glance slowly taking them in from the highest-perched seat to the nearest, convinced them that he was talking to each individual, directly and solely; that he wanted to take each of them into his heart; that he was telling them the truths, the imperious and dangerous facts, that had been hidden from them."

And all the elites who stood in his way? Crippled by their own failures, demoralized by their crumbling stature, they first mock and then cave. As one lone journalist laments before the election (he finds himself in a concentration camp afterward): "I've got to keep remembering . . . that Windrip is only the lightest cork on the whirlpool. He didn't plot all this thing. With all the justified discontent there is against the smart politicians and the Plush Horses of Plutocracy—oh, if it hadn't been one Windrip, it'd been another. . . . We had it coming, we Respectables."

And, eighty-one years later, many of us did. An American elite that has presided over massive and increasing public debt, that failed to prevent 9/11, that chose a disastrous war in the Middle East, that allowed financial markets to nearly destroy the global economy, and that is now so bitterly divided the Congress is effectively moot in a constitutional democracy: "We Respectables" deserve a comeuppance. The vital and valid lesson of the Trump phenomenon is that if the elites cannot govern by compromise, someone outside will eventually try to govern by popular passion and brute force.

But elites still matter in a democracy. They matter not because they are democracy's enemy but because they provide the critical ingredient to save democracy from itself. The political establishment may be battered and demoralized, deferential to the algorithms of the Web and to the monosyllables of a gifted demagogue, but this is not the time to give up on America's near-unique and stabilizing blend of democracy and elite responsibility. The country has endured far harsher times than the present without succumbing to rank demagoguery; it avoided the fascism that destroyed Europe; it has channeled extraordinary outpourings of democratic energy into constitutional order. It seems shocking to argue that we need elites in this democratic age—especially with vast inequalities of wealth and elite failures all around us.

But we need them precisely to protect this precious democracy from its own destabilizing excesses.

And so those Democrats who are gleefully predicting a Clinton landslide in November need to both check their complacency and understand that the Trump question really isn't a cause for partisan schadenfreude anymore. It's much more dangerous than that. Those still backing the demagogue of the left, Bernie Sanders, might want to reflect that their critique of Clinton's experience and expertise—and their facile conflation of that with corruption—is only playing into Trump's hands. That it will fall to Clinton to temper her party's ambitions will be uncomfortable to watch, since her willingness to compromise and equivocate is precisely what many Americans find so distrustful. And yet she may soon be all we have left to counter the threat. She needs to grasp the lethality of her foe, moderate the kind of identity politics that unwittingly empowers him, make an unapologetic case that experience and moderation are not vices, address much more directly the anxieties of the white working class—and Democrats must listen.

More to the point, those Republicans desperately trying to use the long-standing rules of their own nominating process to thwart this monster deserve our passionate support, not our disdain. This is not the moment to remind them that they partly brought this on themselves. This is a moment to offer solidarity, especially as the odds are increasingly stacked against them. Ted Cruz and John Kasich face their decisive battle in Indiana on May 3. But they need to fight on, with any tactic at hand, all the way to the bitter end. The Republican delegates who are trying to protect their party from the whims of an outsider demagogue are, at this moment, doing what they ought to be doing to prevent civil and racial unrest, an international conflict, and a constitutional crisis. These GOP elites have every right to deploy whatever rules or procedural roadblocks they can muster, and they should refuse to be intimidated.

And if they fail in Indiana or Cleveland, as they likely will, they need, quite simply, to disown their party's candidate. They should resist any temptation to loyally back the nominee or to sit this election out. They must take the fight to Trump at every opportunity, unite with Democrats and Independents against him, and be prepared to sacrifice one election in order to save their party and their country.

For Trump is not just a wacky politician of the far right or a riveting television spectacle or a Twitter phenom and bizarre working-class hero. He is not just another candidate to be parsed and analyzed by TV pundits in the same breath as all the others. In terms of our liberal democracy and constitutional order, Trump is an extinction-level event. It's long past time we started treating him as such.

## The Atlantic

FINALIST—REPORTING

*Jeffrey Goldberg's reporting on the decision making of the forty-fourth president of the United States was built on relationships Goldberg had worked years to cultivate. The result in "The Obama Doctrine" was, the Ellie judges said, "a profound understanding of the subject matter, coupled with skillful questioning that pierced the psyche of a president many found inscrutable." Goldberg's two-part series on Hezbollah, "In the Party of God," won the Ellie for Reporting for* The New Yorker *in 2003. His essay for* The Atlantic *"Is It Time for the Jews to Leave Europe" was nominated for the same award last year. After nine years as a writer and reporter for* The Atlantic, *Goldberg was named editor in chief of the magazine in October 2016.*

Jeffrey Goldberg

# The Obama Doctrine

Friday, August 30, 2013, the day the feckless Barack Obama brought to a premature end America's reign as the world's sole indispensable superpower—or, alternatively, the day the sagacious Barack Obama peered into the Middle Eastern abyss and stepped back from the consuming void—began with a thundering speech given on Obama's behalf by his secretary of state, John Kerry, in Washington, D.C. The subject of Kerry's uncharacteristically Churchillian remarks, delivered in the Treaty Room at the State Department, was the gassing of civilians by the president of Syria, Bashar al-Assad.

Obama, in whose cabinet Kerry serves faithfully, but with some exasperation, is himself given to vaulting oratory, but not usually of the martial sort associated with Churchill. Obama believes that the Manichaeanism, and eloquently rendered bellicosity, commonly associated with Churchill were justified by Hitler's rise, and were at times defensible in the struggle against the Soviet Union. But he also thinks rhetoric should be weaponized sparingly, if at all, in today's more ambiguous and complicated international arena. The president believes that Churchillian rhetoric and, more to the point, Churchillian habits of thought, helped bring his predecessor, George W. Bush, to ruinous war in Iraq. Obama entered the White House bent on getting out of Iraq and Afghanistan; he was not seeking new dragons to slay. And he was particularly mindful of promising victory in conflicts he believed to be unwinnable. "If you were to say, for instance, that we're going to rid Afghanistan of the Taliban and build a prosperous democracy instead, the president is aware that someone, seven years later, is going to hold you to that promise," Ben Rhodes, Obama's deputy national-security adviser, and his foreign-policy amanuensis, told me not long ago.

But Kerry's rousing remarks on that August day, which had been drafted in part by Rhodes, were threaded with righteous anger and bold promises, including the barely concealed threat of imminent attack. Kerry, like Obama himself, was horrified by the sins committed by the Syrian regime in its attempt to put down a two-year-old rebellion. In the Damascus suburb of Ghouta nine days earlier, Assad's army had murdered more than 1,400 civilians with sarin gas. The strong sentiment inside the Obama administration was that Assad had earned dire punishment. In Situation Room meetings that followed the attack on Ghouta, only the White House chief of staff, Denis McDonough, cautioned explicitly about the perils of intervention. John Kerry argued vociferously for action.

"As previous storms in history have gathered, when unspeakable crimes were within our power to stop them, we have been warned against the temptations of looking the other way," Kerry said in his speech. "History is full of leaders who have warned against inaction, indifference, and especially against silence when it mattered most."

Kerry counted President Obama among those leaders. A year earlier, when the administration suspected that the Assad regime was contemplating the use of chemical weapons, Obama had declared: "We have been very clear to the Assad regime . . . that a red line for us is we start seeing a whole bunch of chemical weapons moving around or being utilized. That would change my calculus. That would change my equation."

Despite this threat, Obama seemed to many critics to be coldly detached from the suffering of innocent Syrians. Late in the summer of 2011, he had called for Assad's departure. "For the sake of the Syrian people," Obama said, "the time has come for President Assad to step aside." But Obama initially did little to bring about Assad's end.

He resisted demands to act in part because he assumed, based on the analysis of U.S. intelligence, that Assad would fall without his help. "He thought Assad would go the way Mubarak went," Dennis Ross, a former Middle East adviser to Obama, told me, referring to the quick departure of Egyptian president Hosni Mubarak in early 2011, a moment that represented the acme of the Arab Spring. But as Assad clung to power, Obama's resistance to direct intervention only grew. After several months of deliberation, he authorized the CIA to train and fund Syrian rebels, but he also shared the outlook of his former defense secretary, Robert Gates, who had routinely asked in meetings, "Shouldn't we finish up the two wars we have before we look for another?"

The current U.S. ambassador to the United Nations, Samantha Power, who is the most dispositionally interventionist among Obama's senior advisers, had argued early for arming Syria's rebels. Power, who during this period served on the National Security Council staff, is the author of a celebrated book excoriating a succession of U.S. presidents for their failures to prevent genocide. The book, *A Problem from Hell*, published in 2002, drew Obama to Power while he was in the U.S. Senate, though the two were not an obvious ideological match. Power is a partisan of the doctrine known as "responsibility to protect," which holds that sovereignty should not be considered inviolate when a country is slaughtering its own citizens. She lobbied him to endorse this doctrine in the speech he delivered when he accepted the Nobel Peace Prize in 2009, but he declined. Obama generally does not believe a president should place American soldiers at great risk in order to prevent humanitarian disasters, unless those disasters pose a direct security threat to the United States.

Power sometimes argued with Obama in front of other National Security Council officials, to the point where he could no longer conceal his frustration. "Samantha, enough, I've already read your book," he once snapped.

Obama, unlike liberal interventionists, is an admirer of the foreign-policy realism of President George H. W. Bush and, in particular, of Bush's national-security adviser, Brent Scowcroft ("I love that guy," Obama once told me). Bush and Scowcroft removed Saddam Hussein's army from Kuwait in 1991, and they deftly managed the disintegration of the Soviet Union; Scowcroft also, on Bush's behalf, toasted the leaders of China shortly after the slaughter in Tiananmen Square. As Obama was writing his campaign manifesto, *The Audacity of Hope*, in 2006, Susan Rice, then an informal adviser, felt it necessary to remind him to include at least one line of praise for the foreign policy of President Bill Clinton, to partially balance the praise he showered on Bush and Scowcroft.

At the outset of the Syrian uprising, in early 2011, Power argued that the rebels, drawn from the ranks of ordinary citizens, deserved America's enthusiastic support. Others noted that the rebels were farmers and doctors and carpenters, comparing these revolutionaries to the men who won America's war for independence.

Obama flipped this plea on its head. "When you have a professional army," he once told me, "that is well armed and sponsored by two large states"—Iran and Russia—"who have huge stakes in this, and they are fighting against a farmer, a carpenter, an engineer who started out as protesters and suddenly now see themselves in the midst of a civil conflict . . ." He paused. "The notion that we could have—in a clean way that didn't commit U.S. military forces—changed the equation on the ground there was never true." The message Obama telegraphed in speeches and interviews was clear: He would not end up like the second President Bush—a president who became tragically overextended in the Middle East, whose decisions filled the wards of Walter Reed with grievously wounded soldiers, who was helpless to stop the obliteration of his reputation, even when he recalibrated his policies in his second term. Obama would say privately that the first task of an American president in the post-Bush international arena was "Don't do stupid shit."

Obama's reticence frustrated Power and others on his national-security team who had a preference for action. Hillary Clinton, when she was Obama's secretary of state, argued for an early and assertive response to Assad's violence. In 2014, after she left office, Clinton told me that "the failure to help build up a credible fighting force of the people who were the originators of the protests against Assad . . . left a big vacuum, which the jihadists have now filled." When *The Atlantic* published this statement, and also published Clinton's assessment that "great nations need organizing principles, and 'Don't do stupid stuff' is not an organizing principle," Obama became "rip-shit angry," according to one of his senior advisers. The president did not understand how "Don't do stupid shit" could be considered a controversial slogan. Ben Rhodes recalls that "the questions we were asking in the White House were 'Who exactly is in the stupid-shit caucus? Who is pro–stupid shit?'" The Iraq invasion, Obama believed, should have taught Democratic interventionists like Clinton, who had voted for its authorization, the dangers of doing stupid shit. (Clinton quickly apologized to Obama for her comments, and a Clinton spokesman announced that the two would "hug it out" on Martha's Vineyard when they crossed paths there later.)

Syria, for Obama, represented a slope potentially as slippery as Iraq. In his first term, he came to believe that only a handful of threats in the Middle East conceivably warranted direct U.S. military intervention. These included the threat posed by al-Qaeda; threats to the continued existence of Israel ("It would be a moral failing for me as president of the United States" not to defend Israel, he once told me); and, not unrelated to Israel's security, the threat posed by a nuclear-armed Iran. The danger to the United States posed by the Assad regime did not rise to the level of these challenges.

Given Obama's reticence about intervention, the bright-red line he drew for Assad in the summer of 2012 was striking. Even his own advisers were surprised. "I didn't know it was coming," his secretary of defense at the time, Leon Panetta, told me. I was told that Vice President Joe Biden repeatedly warned Obama against drawing a red line on chemical weapons, fearing that it would one day have to be enforced.

Kerry, in his remarks on August 30, 2013, suggested that Assad should be punished in part because the "credibility and the future interests of the United States of America and our allies" were at stake. "It is directly related to our credibility and whether countries still believe the United States when it says something. They are watching to see if Syria can get away with it, because then maybe they too can put the world at greater risk."

Ninety minutes later, at the White House, Obama reinforced Kerry's message in a public statement: "It's important for us to recognize that when over 1,000 people are killed, including hundreds of innocent children, through the use of a weapon that 98 or 99 percent of humanity says should not be used even in war, and there is no action, then we're sending a signal that that international norm doesn't mean much. And that is a danger to our national security."

It appeared as though Obama had drawn the conclusion that damage to American credibility in one region of the world would bleed into others, and that U.S. deterrent credibility was indeed at stake in Syria. Assad, it seemed, had succeeded in pushing the president to a place he never thought he would have to go. Obama generally believes that the Washington foreign-policy establishment, which he secretly disdains, makes a fetish of "credibility"—

particularly the sort of credibility purchased with force. The preservation of credibility, he says, led to Vietnam. Within the White House, Obama would argue that "dropping bombs on someone to prove that you're willing to drop bombs on someone is just about the worst reason to use force."

American national-security credibility, as it is conventionally understood in the Pentagon, the State Department, and the cluster of think tanks headquartered within walking distance of the White House, is an intangible yet potent force—one that, when properly nurtured, keeps America's friends feeling secure and keeps the international order stable.

In White House meetings that crucial week in August, Biden, who ordinarily shared Obama's worries about American overreach, argued passionately that "big nations don't bluff." America's closest allies in Europe and across the Middle East believed Obama was threatening military action, and his own advisers did as well. At a joint press conference with Obama at the White House the previous May, David Cameron, the British prime minister, had said, "Syria's history is being written in the blood of her people, and it is happening on our watch." Cameron's statement, one of his advisers told me, was meant to encourage Obama toward more-decisive action. "The prime minister was certainly under the impression that the president would enforce the red line," the adviser told me. The Saudi ambassador in Washington at the time, Adel al-Jubeir, told friends, and his superiors in Riyadh, that the president was finally ready to strike. Obama "figured out how important this is," Jubeir, who is now the Saudi foreign minister, told one interlocutor. "He will definitely strike."

Obama had already ordered the Pentagon to develop target lists. Five Arleigh Burke–class destroyers were in the Mediterranean, ready to fire cruise missiles at regime targets. French president François Hollande, the most enthusiastically pro-intervention among Europe's leaders, was preparing to strike as well. All week,

White House officials had publicly built the case that Assad had committed a crime against humanity. Kerry's speech would mark the culmination of this campaign.

But the president had grown queasy. In the days after the gassing of Ghouta, Obama would later tell me, he found himself recoiling from the idea of an attack unsanctioned by international law or by Congress. The American people seemed unenthusiastic about a Syria intervention; so too did one of the few foreign leaders Obama respects, Angela Merkel, the German chancellor. She told him that her country would not participate in a Syria campaign. And in a stunning development, on Thursday, August 29, the British Parliament denied David Cameron its blessing for an attack. John Kerry later told me that when he heard that, "internally, I went, *Oops.*"

Obama was also unsettled by a surprise visit early in the week from James Clapper, his director of national intelligence, who interrupted the President's Daily Brief, the threat report Obama receives each morning from Clapper's analysts, to make clear that the intelligence on Syria's use of sarin gas, while robust, was not a "slam dunk." He chose the term carefully. Clapper, the chief of an intelligence community traumatized by its failures in the run-up to the Iraq War, was not going to overpromise, in the manner of the onetime CIA director George Tenet, who famously guaranteed George W. Bush a "slam dunk" in Iraq.

While the Pentagon and the White House's national-security apparatuses were still moving toward war (John Kerry told me he was expecting a strike the day after his speech), the president had come to believe that he was walking into a trap—one laid both by allies and by adversaries, and by conventional expectations of what an American president is supposed to do.

Many of his advisers did not grasp the depth of the president's misgivings; his cabinet and his allies were certainly unaware of them. But his doubts were growing. Late on Friday afternoon, Obama determined that he was simply not prepared to authorize a strike. He asked McDonough, his chief of staff, to take a walk with him on the South Lawn of the White House. Obama did not choose McDonough randomly: He is the Obama aide most averse to U.S. military intervention and someone who, in the words of one of his colleagues, "thinks in terms of traps." Obama, ordinarily a preternaturally confident man, was looking for validation and trying to devise ways to explain his change of heart, both to his own aides and to the public. He and McDonough stayed outside for an hour. Obama told him he was worried that Assad would place civilians as "human shields" around obvious targets. He also pointed out an underlying flaw in the proposed strike: U.S. missiles would not be fired at chemical-weapons depots, for fear of sending plumes of poison into the air. A strike would target military units that had delivered these weapons but not the weapons themselves.

Obama also shared with McDonough a long-standing resentment: He was tired of watching Washington unthinkingly drift toward war in Muslim countries. Four years earlier, the president believed, the Pentagon had "jammed" him on a troop surge for Afghanistan. Now, on Syria, he was beginning to feel jammed again.

When the two men came back to the Oval Office, the president told his national-security aides that he planned to stand down. There would be no attack the next day; he wanted to refer the matter to Congress for a vote. Aides in the room were shocked. Susan Rice, now Obama's national-security adviser, argued that the damage to America's credibility would be serious and lasting. Others had difficulty fathoming how the president could reverse himself the day before a planned strike. Obama, however, was completely calm. "If you've been around him, you know when he's ambivalent about something, when it's a 51–49 decision," Ben Rhodes told me. "But he was completely at ease."

Not long ago, I asked Obama to describe his thinking on that day. He listed the practical worries that had preoccupied him.

"We had UN inspectors on the ground who were completing their work, and we could not risk taking a shot while they were there. A second major factor was the failure of Cameron to obtain the consent of his parliament."

The third, and most important, factor, he told me, was "our assessment that while we could inflict some damage on Assad, we could not, through a missile strike, eliminate the chemical weapons themselves, and what I would then face was the prospect of Assad having survived the strike and claiming he had successfully defied the United States, that the United States had acted unlawfully in the absence of a UN mandate, and that that would have potentially strengthened his hand rather than weakened it."

The fourth factor, he said, was of deeper philosophical importance. "This falls in the category of something that I had been brooding on for some time," he said. "I had come into office with the strong belief that the scope of executive power in national-security issues is very broad, but not limitless."

Obama knew his decision not to bomb Syria would likely upset America's allies. It did. The prime minister of France, Manuel Valls, told me that his government was already worried about the consequences of earlier inaction in Syria when word came of the stand-down. "By not intervening early, we have created a monster," Valls told me. "We were absolutely certain that the U.S. administration would say yes. Working with the Americans, we had already seen the targets. It was a great surprise. If we had bombed as was planned, I think things would be different today." The crown prince of Abu Dhabi, Mohammed bin Zayed al-Nahyan, who was already upset with Obama for "abandoning" Hosni Mubarak, the former president of Egypt, fumed to American visitors that the U.S. was led by an "untrustworthy" president. The king of Jordan, Abdullah II—already dismayed by what he saw as Obama's illogical desire to distance the United States from its traditional Sunni Arab allies and create a new alliance with Iran, Assad's Shia sponsor—complained privately, "I think

I believe in American power more than Obama does." The Saudis, too, were infuriated. They had never trusted Obama—he had, long before he became president, referred to them as a "so-called ally" of the United States. "Iran is the new great power of the Middle East, and the U.S. is the old," Jubeir, the Saudi ambassador in Washington, told his superiors in Riyadh.

Obama's decision caused tremors across Washington as well. John McCain and Lindsey Graham, the two leading Republican hawks in the Senate, had met with Obama in the White House earlier in the week and had been promised an attack. They were angered by the about-face. Damage was done even inside the administration. Neither Chuck Hagel, then the secretary of defense, nor John Kerry was in the Oval Office when the president informed his team of his thinking. Kerry would not learn about the change until later that evening. "I just got fucked over," he told a friend shortly after talking to the president that night. (When I asked Kerry recently about that tumultuous night, he said, "I didn't stop to analyze it. I figured the president had a reason to make a decision and, honestly, I understood his notion.")

The next few days were chaotic. The president asked Congress to authorize the use of force—the irrepressible Kerry served as chief lobbyist—and it quickly became apparent in the White House that Congress had little interest in a strike. When I spoke with Biden recently about the red-line decision, he made special note of this fact. "It matters to have Congress with you, in terms of your ability to sustain what you set out to do," he said. Obama "didn't go to Congress to get himself off the hook. He had his doubts at that point, but he knew that if he was going to do anything, he better damn well have the public with him, or it would be a very short ride." Congress's clear ambivalence convinced Biden that Obama was correct to fear the slippery slope. "What happens when we get a plane shot down? Do we not go in and rescue?" Biden asked. "You need the support of the American people."

Amid the confusion, a deus ex machina appeared in the form of the Russian president, Vladimir Putin. At the G20 summit in St. Petersburg, which was held the week after the Syria reversal, Obama pulled Putin aside, he recalled to me, and told the Russian president "that if he forced Assad to get rid of the chemical weapons, that that would eliminate the need for us taking a military strike." Within weeks, Kerry, working with his Russian counterpart, Sergey Lavrov, would engineer the removal of most of Syria's chemical-weapons arsenal—a program whose existence Assad until then had refused to even acknowledge.

The arrangement won the president praise from, of all people, Benjamin Netanyahu, the Israeli prime minister, with whom he has had a consistently contentious relationship. The removal of Syria's chemical-weapons stockpiles represented "the one ray of light in a very dark region," Netanyahu told me not long after the deal was announced.

John Kerry today expresses no patience for those who argue, as he himself once did, that Obama should have bombed Assad-regime sites in order to buttress America's deterrent capability. "You'd still have the weapons there, and you'd probably be fighting ISIL" for control of the weapons, he said, referring to the Islamic State, the terror group also known as ISIS. "It just doesn't make sense. But I can't deny to you that this notion about the red line being crossed and [Obama's] not doing anything gained a life of its own."

Obama understands that the decision he made to step back from air strikes, and to allow the violation of a red line he himself had drawn to go unpunished, will be interrogated mercilessly by historians. But today that decision is a source of deep satisfaction for him.

"I'm very proud of this moment," he told me. "The overwhelming weight of conventional wisdom and the machinery of our national-security apparatus had gone fairly far. The perception was that my credibility was at stake, that America's credibility was at stake. And so for me to press the pause button at that moment, I knew, would cost me politically. And the fact that I was able to pull back from the immediate pressures and think through in my own mind what was in America's interest, not only with respect to Syria but also with respect to our democracy, was as tough a decision as I've made—and I believe ultimately it was the right decision to make."

This was the moment the president believes he finally broke with what he calls, derisively, the "Washington playbook."

"Where am I controversial? When it comes to the use of military power," he said. "That is the source of the controversy. There's a playbook in Washington that presidents are supposed to follow. It's a playbook that comes out of the foreign-policy establishment. And the playbook prescribes responses to different events, and these responses tend to be militarized responses. Where America is directly threatened, the playbook works. But the playbook can also be a trap that can lead to bad decisions. In the midst of an international challenge like Syria, you get judged harshly if you don't follow the playbook, even if there are good reasons why it does not apply."

I have come to believe that, in Obama's mind, August 30, 2013, was his liberation day, the day he defied not only the foreign-policy establishment and its cruise-missile playbook, but also the demands of America's frustrating, high-maintenance allies in the Middle East—countries, he complains privately to friends and advisers, that seek to exploit American "muscle" for their own narrow and sectarian ends. By 2013, Obama's resentments were well developed. He resented military leaders who believed they could fix any problem if the commander in chief would simply give them what they wanted, and he resented the foreign-policy think-tank complex. A widely held sentiment inside the White House is that many of the most prominent foreign-policy think tanks in Washington are doing the bidding of their Arab and pro-Israel funders. I've heard one administration official refer to Massachusetts Avenue, the home of many of these think tanks, as "Arab-occupied territory."

For some foreign-policy experts, even within his own administration, Obama's about-face on enforcing the red line was a dispiriting moment in which he displayed irresolution and naïveté and did lasting damage to America's standing in the world. "Once the commander in chief draws that red line," Leon Panetta, who served as CIA director and then as secretary of defense in Obama's first term, told me recently, "then I think the credibility of the commander in chief and this nation is at stake if he doesn't enforce it." Right after Obama's reversal, Hillary Clinton said privately, "If you say you're going to strike, you have to strike. There's no choice."

"Assad is effectively being rewarded for the use of chemical weapons, rather than 'punished' as originally planned." Shadi Hamid, a scholar at the Brookings Institution, wrote for *The Atlantic* at the time. "He has managed to remove the threat of U.S. military action while giving very little up in return."

Even commentators who have been broadly sympathetic to Obama's policies saw this episode as calamitous. Gideon Rose, the editor of *Foreign Affairs*, wrote recently that Obama's handling of this crisis—"first casually announcing a major commitment, then dithering about living up to it, then frantically tossing the ball to Congress for a decision—was a case study in embarrassingly amateurish improvisation."

Obama's defenders, however, argue that he did no damage to U.S. credibility, citing Assad's subsequent agreement to have his chemical weapons removed. "The threat of force was credible enough for them to give up their chemical weapons," Tim Kaine, a Democratic senator from Virginia, told me. "We threatened military action and they responded. That's deterrent credibility."

History may record August 30, 2013, as the day Obama prevented the U.S. from entering yet another disastrous Muslim civil war and the day he removed the threat of a chemical attack on Israel, Turkey, or Jordan. Or it could be remembered as the day he let the Middle East slip from America's grasp, into the hands of Russia, Iran, and ISIS.

.        .        .

I first spoke with Obama about foreign policy when he was a U.S. senator, in 2006. At the time, I was familiar mainly with the text of a speech he had delivered four years earlier, at a Chicago anti-war rally. It was an unusual speech for an antiwar rally in that it was not antiwar; Obama, who was then an Illinois state senator, argued only against one specific and, at the time, still theoretical, war. "I suffer no illusions about Saddam Hussein," he said. "He is a brutal man. A ruthless man. . . . But I also know that Saddam poses no imminent and direct threat to the United States or to his neighbors." He added, "I know that an invasion of Iraq without a clear rationale and without strong international support will only fan the flames of the Middle East, and encourage the worst, rather than best, impulses of the Arab world, and strengthen the recruitment arm of al-Qaeda."

This speech had made me curious about its author. I wanted to learn how an Illinois state senator, a part-time law professor who spent his days traveling between Chicago and Springfield, had come to a more prescient understanding of the coming quagmire than the most experienced foreign-policy thinkers of his party, including such figures as Hillary Clinton, Joe Biden, and John Kerry, not to mention, of course, most Republicans and many foreign-policy analysts and writers, including me.

Since that first meeting in 2006, I've interviewed Obama periodically, mainly on matters related to the Middle East. But over the past few months, I've spent several hours talking with him about the broadest themes of his "long game" foreign policy, including the themes he is most eager to discuss—namely, the ones that have nothing to do with the Middle East.

"ISIS is not an existential threat to the United States," he told me in one of these conversations. "Climate change is a potential existential threat to the entire world if we don't do something about it." Obama explained that climate change worries him in particular because "it is a political problem perfectly designed to repel government intervention. It involves every single country, and it is a comparatively slow-moving emergency, so there is always something seemingly more urgent on the agenda."

At the moment, of course, the most urgent of the "seemingly more urgent" issues is Syria. But at any given moment, Obama's entire presidency could be upended by North Korean aggression or an assault by Russia on a member of NATO or an ISIS-planned attack on U.S. soil. Few presidents have faced such diverse tests on the international stage as Obama has, and the challenge for him, as for all presidents, has been to distinguish the merely urgent from the truly important and to focus on the important.

My goal in our recent conversations was to see the world through Obama's eyes and to understand what he believes America's role in the world should be. This article is informed by our recent series of conversations, which took place in the Oval Office; over lunch in his dining room; aboard *Air Force One*; and in Kuala Lumpur during his most recent visit to Asia, in November. It is also informed by my previous interviews with him and by his speeches and prolific public ruminations, as well as by conversations with his top foreign-policy and national-security advisers, foreign leaders and their ambassadors in Washington, friends of the president and others who have spoken with him about his policies and decisions, and his adversaries and critics.

Over the course of our conversations, I came to see Obama as a president who has grown steadily more fatalistic about the constraints on America's ability to direct global events, even as he has, late in his presidency, accumulated a set of potentially historic foreign-policy achievements—controversial, provisional achievements, to be sure, but achievements nonetheless: the opening to Cuba, the Paris climate-change accord, the Trans-Pacific Partnership trade agreement, and, of course, the Iran nuclear deal. These he accomplished despite his growing sense that larger forces—the riptide of tribal feeling in a world that should have already shed its atavism; the resilience of small men who rule large countries in ways contrary to their own best interests; the persistence of fear as a governing human emotion—frequently conspire against the best of America's intentions. But he also has come to learn, he told me, that very little is accomplished in international affairs without U.S. leadership.

Obama talked me through this apparent contradiction. "I want a president who has the sense that you can't fix everything," he said. But on the other hand, "if we don't set the agenda, it doesn't happen." He explained what he meant. "The fact is, there is not a summit I've attended since I've been president where we are not setting the agenda, where we are not responsible for the key results," he said. "That's true whether you're talking about nuclear security, whether you're talking about saving the world financial system, whether you're talking about climate."

One day, over lunch in the Oval Office dining room, I asked the president how he thought his foreign policy might be understood by historians. He started by describing for me a four-box grid representing the main schools of American foreign-policy thought. One box he called isolationism, which he dismissed out of hand. "The world is ever-shrinking," he said. "Withdrawal is untenable." The other boxes he labeled realism, liberal interventionism, and internationalism. "I suppose you could call me a realist in believing we can't, at any given moment, relieve all the world's misery," he said. "We have to choose where we can make a real impact." He also noted that he was quite obviously an internationalist, devoted as he is to strengthening multilateral organizations and international norms.

I told him my impression was that the various traumas of the past seven years have, if anything, intensified his commitment to realist-driven restraint. Had nearly two full terms in the White House soured him on interventionism?

"For all of our warts, the United States has clearly been a force for good in the world," he said. "If you compare us to previous superpowers, we act less on the basis of naked self-interest, and have been interested in establishing norms that benefit everyone. If it is possible to do good at a bearable cost, to save lives, we will do it."

If a crisis, or a humanitarian catastrophe, does not meet his stringent standard for what constitutes a direct national-security threat, Obama said, he doesn't believe that he should be forced into silence. He is not so much the realist, he suggested, that he won't pass judgment on other leaders. Though he has so far ruled out the use of direct American power to depose Assad, he was not wrong, he argued, to call on Assad to go. "Oftentimes when you get critics of our Syria policy, one of the things that they'll point out is 'You called for Assad to go, but you didn't force him to go. You did not invade.' And the notion is that if you weren't going to overthrow the regime, you shouldn't have said anything. That's a weird argument to me, the notion that if we use our moral authority to say 'This is a brutal regime, and this is not how a leader should treat his people,' once you do that, you are obliged to invade the country and install a government you prefer."

"I am very much the internationalist," Obama said in a later conversation. "And I am also an idealist insofar as I believe that we should be promoting values, like democracy and human rights and norms and values, because not only do they serve our interests the more people adopt values that we share—in the same way that, economically, if people adopt rule of law and property rights and so forth, that is to our advantage—but because it makes the world a better place. And I'm willing to say that in a very corny way, and in a way that probably Brent Scowcroft would not say.

"Having said that," he continued, "I also believe that the world is a tough, complicated, messy, mean place, and full of hardship and tragedy. And in order to advance both our security interests and those ideals and values that we care about, we've got to be hardheaded at the same time as we're bighearted, and pick and choose our spots, and recognize that there are going to be times where the best that we can do is to shine a spotlight on something that's terrible, but not believe that we can automatically solve it. There are going to be times where our security interests conflict with our concerns about human rights. There are going to be times where we can do something about innocent people being killed, but there are going to be times where we can't."

If Obama ever questioned whether America really is the world's one indispensable nation, he no longer does so. But he is the rare president who seems at times to resent indispensability rather than embrace it. "Free riders aggravate me," he told me. Recently, Obama warned that Great Britain would no longer be able to claim a "special relationship" with the United States if it did not commit to spending at least 2 percent of its GDP on defense. "You have to pay your fair share," Obama told David Cameron, who subsequently met the 2 percent threshold.

Part of his mission as president, Obama explained, is to spur other countries to take action for themselves, rather than wait for the United States to lead. The defense of the liberal international order against jihadist terror, Russian adventurism, and Chinese bullying depends in part, he believes, on the willingness of other nations to share the burden with the United States. This is why the controversy surrounding the assertion—made by an anonymous administration official to *The New Yorker* during the Libya crisis of 2011—that his policy consisted of "leading from behind" perturbed him. "We don't have to always be the ones who are up front," he told me. "Sometimes we're going to get what we want precisely because we are sharing in the agenda. The irony is that it was precisely in order to prevent the Europeans and the Arab states from holding our coats while we did all the fighting that we, by design, insisted" that they lead during the mission to remove Muammar Qaddafi from power in Libya. "It was part of the anti-free-rider campaign."

The president also seems to believe that sharing leadership with other countries is a way to check America's more unruly impulses. "One of the reasons I am so focused on taking action multilaterally where our direct interests are not at stake is that multilateralism regulates hubris," he explained. He consistently invokes what he understands to be America's past failures overseas as a means of checking American self-righteousness. "We have history," he said. "We have history in Iran, we have history in Indonesia and Central America. So we have to be mindful of our history when we start talking about intervening, and understand the source of other people's suspicions."

In his efforts to off-load some of America's foreign-policy responsibilities to its allies, Obama appears to be a classic retrenchment president in the manner of Dwight D. Eisenhower and Richard Nixon. Retrenchment, in this context, is defined as "pulling back, spending less, cutting risk, and shifting burdens to allies," Stephen Sestanovich, an expert on presidential foreign policy at the Council on Foreign Relations, explained to me. "If John McCain had been elected in 2008, you would still have seen some degree of retrenchment," Sestanovich said. "It's what the country wanted. If you come into office in the middle of a war that is not going well, you're convinced that the American people have hired you to do less." One difference between Eisenhower and Nixon, on the one hand, and Obama, on the other, Sestanovich said, is that Obama "appears to have had a personal, ideological commitment to the idea that foreign policy had consumed too much of the nation's attention and resources."

I asked Obama about retrenchment. "Almost every great world power has succumbed" to overextension, he said. "What I think is not smart is the idea that every time there is a problem, we send in our military to impose order. We just can't do that."

But once he decides that a particular challenge represents a direct national-security threat, he has shown a willingness to act unilaterally. This is one of the larger ironies of the Obama presidency: He has relentlessly questioned the efficacy of force, but he has also become the most successful terrorist-hunter in the history of the presidency, one who will hand to his successor a set of tools an accomplished assassin would envy. "He applies different standards to direct threats to the U.S.," Ben Rhodes says. "For instance, despite his misgivings about Syria, he has not had a second thought about drones." Some critics argue he should have had a few second thoughts about what they see as the overuse of drones. But John Brennan, Obama's CIA director, told me recently that he and the president "have similar views. One of them is that sometimes you have to take a life to save even more lives. We have a similar view of just-war theory. The president requires near-certainty of no collateral damage. But if he believes it is necessary to act, he doesn't hesitate."

Those who speak with Obama about jihadist thought say that he possesses a no-illusions understanding of the forces that drive apocalyptic violence among radical Muslims, but he has been careful about articulating that publicly, out of concern that he will exacerbate anti-Muslim xenophobia. He has a tragic realist's understanding of sin, cowardice, and corruption, and a Hobbesian appreciation of how fear shapes human behavior. And yet he consistently, and with apparent sincerity, professes optimism that the world is bending toward justice. He is, in a way, a Hobbesian optimist.

The contradictions do not end there. Though he has a reputation for prudence, he has also been eager to question some of the long-standing assumptions undergirding traditional U.S. foreign-policy thinking. To a remarkable degree, he is willing to question why America's enemies are its enemies or why some of its friends are its friends. He overthrew half a century of bipartisan consensus in order to reestablish ties with Cuba. He questioned why the United States should avoid sending its forces into Pakistan to kill al-Qaeda leaders, and he privately questions why Pakistan, which he believes is a disastrously dysfunctional country, should be considered an ally of the United States at all. According to Leon Panetta, he has questioned why the United States should maintain Israel's so-called qualitative military edge, which grants it access to more sophisticated weapons systems than America's Arab allies receive, but he has also questioned, often harshly, the role that America's Sunni Arab allies play in fomenting anti-American terrorism. He is clearly irritated that foreign-policy orthodoxy compels him to treat Saudi Arabia as an ally. And of course he decided early on, in the face of great criticism, that he wanted to reach out to America's most ardent Middle Eastern foe, Iran. The nuclear deal he struck with Iran proves, if nothing else, that Obama is not risk-averse. He has bet global security and his own legacy that one of the world's leading state sponsors of terrorism will adhere to an agreement to curtail its nuclear program.

It is assumed, at least among his critics, that Obama sought the Iran deal because he has a vision of a historic American-Persian rapprochement. But his desire for the nuclear agreement was born of pessimism as much as it was of optimism. "The Iran deal was never primarily about trying to open a new era of relations between the U.S. and Iran," Susan Rice told me. "It was far more pragmatic and minimalist. The aim was very simply to make a dangerous country substantially less dangerous. No one had any expectation that Iran would be a more benign actor."

.   .   .

I once mentioned to Obama a scene from *The Godfather: Part III*, in which Michael Corleone complains angrily about his failure to escape the grasp of organized crime. I told Obama that the Middle East is to his presidency what the Mob is to Corleone, and I started to quote the Al Pacino line: "Just when I thought I was out—"

"It pulls you back in," Obama said, completing the thought.

The story of Obama's encounter with the Middle East follows an arc of disenchantment. In his first extended spree of fame, as a presidential candidate in 2008, Obama often spoke with hope about the region. In Berlin that summer, in a speech to 200,000 adoring Germans, he said, "This is the moment we must help answer the call for a new dawn in the Middle East."

The next year, as president, he gave a speech in Cairo meant to reset U.S. relations with the world's Muslims. He spoke about Muslims in his own family and his childhood years in Indonesia and confessed America's sins even as he criticized those in the Muslim world who demonized the United States. What drew the most attention, though, was his promise to address the Israeli-Palestinian conflict, which was then thought to be the central animating concern of Arab Muslims. His sympathy for the Palestinians moved the audience but complicated his relations with Benjamin Netanyahu, the Israeli prime minister—especially because Obama had also decided to bypass Jerusalem on his first presidential visit to the Middle East.

When I asked Obama recently what he had hoped to accomplish with his Cairo reset speech, he said that he had been trying—unsuccessfully, he acknowledged—to persuade Muslims to more closely examine the roots of their unhappiness.

"My argument was this: Let's all stop pretending that the cause of the Middle East's problems is Israel," he told me. "We want to work to help achieve statehood and dignity for the Palestinians, but I was hoping that my speech could trigger a discussion, could create space for Muslims to address the real problems they are confronting—problems of governance, and the fact that some currents of Islam have not gone through a reformation that would help people adapt their religious doctrines to modernity. My thought was, I would communicate that the U.S. is not standing in the way of this progress, that we would help, in whatever way possible, to advance the goals of a practical, successful Arab agenda that provided a better life for ordinary people."

Through the first flush of the Arab Spring, in 2011, Obama continued to speak optimistically about the Middle East's future, coming as close as he ever would to embracing the so-called freedom agenda of George W. Bush, which was characterized in part by the belief that democratic values could be implanted in the Middle East. He equated protesters in Tunisia and Tahrir Square with Rosa Parks and the "patriots of Boston."

"After decades of accepting the world as it is in the region, we have a chance to pursue the world as it should be," he said in a speech at the time. "The United States supports a set of universal rights. And these rights include free speech, the freedom of peaceful assembly, the freedom of religion, equality for men and women under the rule of law, and the right to choose your own leaders. . . . Our support for these principles is not a secondary interest."

But over the next three years, as the Arab Spring gave up its early promise, and brutality and dysfunction overwhelmed the Middle East, the president grew dISILlusioned. Some of his deepest disappointments concern Middle Eastern leaders themselves. Benjamin Netanyahu is in his own category: Obama has long believed that Netanyahu could bring about a two-state solution that would protect Israel's status as a Jewish-majority democracy but is too fearful and politically paralyzed to do so. Obama has also not had much patience for Netanyahu and other Middle Eastern leaders who question his understanding of the region. In one of Netanyahu's meetings with the president, the Israeli prime minister launched into something of a lecture about the dangers of the brutal region in which he lives, and Obama felt that Netanyahu was behaving in a condescending fashion and was also avoiding the subject at hand: peace negotiations. Finally, the president inter-rupted the prime minister: "Bibi, you have to understand some-thing," he said. "I'm the African American son of a single mother, and I live here, in this house. I live in the White House. I managed to get elected president of the United States. You think I don't un-derstand what you're talking about, but I do." Other leaders also frustrate him immensely. Early on, Obama saw Recep Tayyip Erdoğan, the president of Turkey, as the sort of moderate Muslim leader who would bridge the divide between East and West—but Obama now considers him a failure and an authoritarian, one who refuses to use his enormous army to bring stability to Syria. And on the sidelines of a NATO summit in Wales in 2014, Obama pulled aside King Abdullah II of Jordan. Obama said he had heard that Abdullah had complained to friends in the U.S. Congress about his leadership and told the king that if he had complaints, he should raise them directly. The king denied that he had spoken ill of him.

In recent days, the president has taken to joking privately, "All I need in the Middle East is a few smart autocrats." Obama has always had a fondness for pragmatic, emotionally contained technocrats, telling aides, "If only everyone could be like the Scandinavians, this would all be easy."

The unraveling of the Arab Spring darkened the president's view of what the United States could achieve in the Middle East, and made him realize how much the chaos there was distracting from other priorities. "The president recognized during the course of the Arab Spring that the Middle East was consuming us," John Brennan, who served in Obama's first term as his chief counterterrorism adviser, told me recently.

But what sealed Obama's fatalistic view was the failure of his administration's intervention in Libya, in 2011. That intervention was meant to prevent the country's then-dictator, Muammar Qa-ddafi, from slaughtering the people of Benghazi, as he was threat-ening to do. Obama did not want to join the fight; he was counseled by Joe Biden and his first-term secretary of defense Robert Gates, among others, to steer clear. But a strong faction within the national-security team—Secretary of State Hillary Clinton and Susan Rice, who was then the ambassador to the United Nations, along with Samantha Power, Ben Rhodes, and Antony Blinken, who was then Biden's national-security adviser—lobbied hard to protect Benghazi, and prevailed. (Biden, who is acerbic about Clinton's foreign-policy judgment, has said privately, "Hillary just wants to be Golda Meir.") American bombs fell, the people of Benghazi were spared from what may or may not have been a massacre, and Qaddafi was captured and executed.

But Obama says today of the intervention, "It didn't work." The United States, he believes, planned the Libya operation carefully—and yet the country is still a disaster.

Why, given what seems to be the president's natural reticence toward getting militarily ensnared where American national security is not directly at stake, did he accept the recommendation of his more activist advisers to intervene?

"The social order in Libya has broken down," Obama said, explaining his thinking at the time. "You have massive protests against Qaddafi. You've got tribal divisions inside of Libya. Benghazi is a focal point for the opposition regime. And Qaddafi is marching his army toward Benghazi, and he has said, 'We will kill them like rats.'

"Now, option one would be to do nothing, and there were some in my administration who said, as tragic as the Libyan situation may be, it's not our problem. The way I looked at it was that it would be our problem if, in fact, complete chaos and civil war broke out in Libya. But this is not so at the core of U.S. interests that it makes sense for us to unilaterally strike against the Qaddafi regime. At that point, you've got Europe and a number of Gulf countries who despise Qaddafi, or are concerned on a humanitarian basis, who are calling for action. But what has been a habit over the last several decades in these circumstances is people pushing us to act but then showing an unwillingness to put any skin in the game."

"Free riders?," I interjected.

"Free riders," he said, and continued. "So what I said at that point was, we should act as part of an international coalition. But because this is not at the core of our interests, we need to get a UN mandate; we need Europeans and Gulf countries to be actively involved in the coalition; we will apply the military capabilities that are unique to us, but we expect others to carry their weight. And we worked with our defense teams to ensure that we could execute a strategy without putting boots on the ground and without a long-term military commitment in Libya.

"So we actually executed this plan as well as I could have expected: We got a UN mandate, we built a coalition, it cost us $1 billion—which, when it comes to military operations, is very cheap. We averted large-scale civilian casualties, we prevented what almost surely would have been a prolonged and bloody civil conflict. And despite all that, Libya is a mess."

*Mess* is the president's diplomatic term; privately, he calls Libya a "shit show," in part because it's subsequently become an ISIS haven—one that he has already targeted with air strikes. It became a shit show, Obama believes, for reasons that had less to do with American incompetence than with the passivity of America's allies and with the obdurate power of tribalism.

"When I go back and I ask myself what went wrong," Obama said, "there's room for criticism, because I had more faith in the Europeans, given Libya's proximity, being invested in the follow-up," he said. He noted that Nicolas Sarkozy, the French president, lost his job the following year. And he said that British prime minister David Cameron soon stopped paying attention, becoming "distracted by a range of other things." Of France, he said, "Sarkozy wanted to trumpet the flights he was taking in the air campaign, despite the fact that we had wiped out all the air defenses and essentially set up the entire infrastructure" for the intervention. This sort of bragging was fine, Obama said, because it allowed the United States to "purchase France's involvement in a way that made it less expensive for us and less risky for us." In other words, giving France extra credit in exchange for less risk and cost to the United States was a useful trade-off—except that "from the perspective of a lot of the folks in the foreign-policy establishment, well, that was terrible. If we're going to do something, obviously we've got to be up front, and nobody else is sharing in the spotlight."

Obama also blamed internal Libyan dynamics. "The degree of tribal division in Libya was greater than our analysts had expected. And our ability to have any kind of structure there that we could interact with and start training and start providing resources broke down very quickly."

Libya proved to him that the Middle East was best avoided. "There is no way we should commit to governing the Middle East and North Africa," he recently told a former colleague from the Senate. "That would be a basic, fundamental mistake."

.    .    .

President Obama did not come into office preoccupied by the Middle East. He is the first child of the Pacific to become president—born in Hawaii, raised there and, for four years, in Indonesia—and he is fixated on turning America's attention to Asia. For Obama, Asia represents the future. Africa and Latin America, in his view, deserve far more U.S. attention than they receive. Europe, about which he is unromantic, is a source of global stability that requires, to his occasional annoyance, American hand-holding. And the Middle East is a region to be avoided—one that, thanks to America's energy revolution, will soon be of negligible relevance to the U.S. economy.

It is not oil but another of the Middle East's exports, terrorism, that shapes Obama's understanding of his responsibilities there. Early in 2014, Obama's intelligence advisers told him that

ISIS was of marginal importance. According to administration officials, General Lloyd Austin, then the commander of Central Command, which oversees U.S. military operations in the Middle East, told the White House that the Islamic State was "a flash in the pan." This analysis led Obama, in an interview with *The New Yorker*, to describe the constellation of jihadist groups in Iraq and Syria as terrorism's "jayvee team." (A spokesman for Austin told me, "At no time has General Austin ever considered ISIL a 'flash in the pan' phenomenon.")

But by late spring of 2014, after ISIS took the northern-Iraq city of Mosul, he came to believe that U.S. intelligence had failed to appreciate the severity of the threat and the inadequacies of the Iraqi army, and his view shifted. After ISIS beheaded three American civilians in Syria, it became obvious to Obama that defeating the group was of more immediate urgency to the United States. than overthrowing Bashar al-Assad.

Advisers recall that Obama would cite a pivotal moment in *The Dark Knight*, the 2008 Batman movie, to help explain not only how he understood the role of ISIS but how he understood the larger ecosystem in which it grew. "There's a scene in the beginning in which the gang leaders of Gotham are meeting," the president would say. "These are men who had the city divided up. They were thugs, but there was a kind of order. Everyone had his turf. And then the Joker comes in and lights the whole city on fire. ISIL is the Joker. It has the capacity to set the whole region on fire. That's why we have to fight it."

The rise of the Islamic State deepened Obama's conviction that the Middle East could not be fixed—not on his watch, and not for a generation to come.

•　　　•　　　•

On a rainy Wednesday in mid-November, President Obama appeared on a stage at the Asia-Pacific Economic Cooperation

(APEC) summit in Manila with Jack Ma, the founder of the Chinese e-commerce company Alibaba, and a thirty-one-year-old Filipina inventor named Aisa Mijeno. The ballroom was crowded with Asian CEOs, American business leaders, and government officials from across the region. Obama, who was greeted warmly, first delivered informal remarks from behind a podium, mainly about the threat of climate change.

Obama made no mention of the subject preoccupying much of the rest of the world—the ISIS attacks in Paris five days earlier, which had killed 130 people. Obama had arrived in Manila the day before from a G20 summit held in Antalya, Turkey. The Paris attacks had been a main topic of conversation in Antalya, where Obama held a particularly contentious press conference on the subject.

The traveling White House press corps was unrelenting: "Isn't it time for your strategy to change?" one reporter asked. This was followed by "Could I ask you to address your critics who say that your reluctance to enter another Middle East war, and your preference of diplomacy over using the military, makes the United States weaker and emboldens our enemies?" And then came this imperishable question, from a CNN reporter: "If you'll forgive the language—why can't we take out these bastards?" Which was followed by "Do you think you really understand this enemy well enough to defeat them and to protect the homeland?"

As the questions unspooled, Obama became progressively more irritated. He described his ISIS strategy at length, but the only time he exhibited an emotion other than disdain was when he addressed an emerging controversy about America's refugee policy. Republican governors and presidential candidates had suddenly taken to demanding that the United States block Syrian refugees from coming to America. Ted Cruz had proposed accepting only Christian Syrians. Chris Christie had said that all refugees, including "orphans under five," should be banned from entry until proper vetting procedures had been put in place.

This rhetoric appeared to frustrate Obama immensely. "When I hear folks say that, well, maybe we should just admit the Christians but not the Muslims; when I hear political leaders suggesting that there would be a religious test for which person who's fleeing from a war-torn country is admitted," Obama told the assembled reporters, "that's not American. That's not who we are. We don't have religious tests to our compassion."

*Air Force One* departed Antalya and arrived ten hours later in Manila. That's when the president's advisers came to understand, in the words of one official, that "everyone back home had lost their minds." Susan Rice, trying to comprehend the rising anxiety, searched her hotel television in vain for CNN, finding only the BBC and Fox News. She toggled between the two, looking for the mean, she told people on the trip.

Later, the president would say that he had failed to fully appreciate the fear many Americans were experiencing about the possibility of a Paris-style attack in the United States. Great distance, a frantic schedule, and the jet-lag haze that envelops a globe-spanning presidential trip were working against him. But he has never believed that terrorism poses a threat to America commensurate with the fear it generates. Even during the period in 2014 when ISIS was executing its American captives in Syria, his emotions were in check. Valerie Jarrett, Obama's closest adviser, told him people were worried that the group would soon take its beheading campaign to the United States. "They're not coming here to chop our heads off," he reassured her. Obama frequently reminds his staff that terrorism takes far fewer lives in America than handguns, car accidents, and falls in bathtubs do. Several years ago, he expressed to me his admiration for Israelis' "resilience" in the face of constant terrorism, and it is clear that he would like to see resilience replace panic in American society. Nevertheless, his advisers are fighting a constant rearguard action to keep Obama from placing terrorism in what he considers its "proper" perspective, out of concern that he will seem insensitive to the fears of the American people.

The frustration among Obama's advisers spills over into the Pentagon and the State Department. John Kerry, for one, seems more alarmed about ISIS than the president does. Recently, when I asked the secretary of state a general question—is the Middle East still important to the United States?—he answered by talking exclusively about ISIS. "This is a threat to everybody in the world," he said, a group "overtly committed to destroying people in the West and in the Middle East. Imagine what would happen if we don't stand and fight them, if we don't lead a coalition—as we are doing, by the way. If we didn't do that, you could have allies and friends of ours fall. You could have a massive migration into Europe that destroys Europe, leads to the pure destruction of Europe, ends the European project, and everyone runs for cover and you've got the 1930s all over again, with nationalism and fascism and other things breaking out. Of course we have an interest in this, a huge interest in this."

When I noted to Kerry that the president's rhetoric doesn't match his, he said, "President Obama sees all of this, but he doesn't gin it up into this kind of—he thinks we are on track. He has escalated his efforts. But he's not trying to create hysteria . . . I think the president is always inclined to try to keep things on an appropriate equilibrium. I respect that."

Obama modulates his discussion of terrorism for several reasons: He is, by nature, Spockian. And he believes that a misplaced word or a frightened look or an ill-considered hyperbolic claim, could tip the country into panic. The sort of panic he worries about most is the type that would manifest itself in anti-Muslim xenophobia or in a challenge to American openness and to the constitutional order.

The president also gets frustrated that terrorism keeps swamping his larger agenda, particularly as it relates to rebalancing America's global priorities. For years, the "pivot to Asia" has been a paramount priority of his. America's economic future lies in Asia, he believes, and the challenge posed by China's rise requires constant attention. From his earliest days in office, Obama has been focused on rebuilding the sometimes-threadbare ties between the United States and its Asian treaty partners, and he is perpetually on the hunt for opportunities to draw other Asian nations into the U.S. orbit. His dramatic opening to Burma was one such opportunity; Vietnam and the entire constellation of Southeast Asian countries fearful of Chinese domination presented others.

In Manila, at APEC, Obama was determined to keep the conversation focused on this agenda and not on what he viewed as the containable challenge presented by ISIS. Obama's secretary of defense, Ashton Carter, told me not long ago that Obama has maintained his focus on Asia even as Syria and other Middle Eastern conflicts continue to flare. Obama believes, Carter said, that Asia "is the part of the world of greatest consequence to the American future, and that no president can take his eye off of this." He added, "He consistently asks, even in the midst of everything else that's going on, 'Where are we in the Asia-Pacific rebalance? Where are we in terms of resources?' He's been extremely consistent about that, even in times of Middle East tension."

After Obama finished his presentation on climate change, he joined Ma and Mijeno, who had seated themselves on nearby armchairs, where Obama was preparing to interview them in the manner of a daytime talk-show host—an approach that seemed to induce a momentary bout of status-inversion vertigo in an audience not accustomed to such behavior in their own leaders. Obama began by asking Ma a question about climate change. Ma, unsurprisingly, agreed with Obama that it was a very important issue. Then Obama turned to Mijeno. A laboratory operating in the hidden recesses of the West Wing could not have fashioned a person more expertly designed to appeal to Obama's wonkish enthusiasms than Mijeno, a young engineer who, with her brother, had invented a lamp that is somehow powered by salt water.

"Just to be clear, Aisa, so with some salt water, the device that you've set up can provide—am I right?—about eight hours of lighting?," Obama asked.

"Eight hours of lighting," she responded.

Obama: "And the lamp is twenty dollars—"

Mijeno: "Around twenty dollars."

"I think Aisa is a perfect example of what we're seeing in a lot of countries—young entrepreneurs coming up with leapfrog technologies, in the same ways that in large portions of Asia and Africa, the old landline phones never got set up," Obama said, because those areas jumped straight to mobile phones. Obama encouraged Jack Ma to fund her work. "She's won, by the way, a lot of prizes and gotten a lot of attention, so this is not like one of those infomercials where you order it, and you can't make the thing work," he said, to laughter.

The next day, aboard *Air Force One* en route to Kuala Lumpur, I mentioned to Obama that he seemed genuinely happy to be on-stage with Ma and Mijeno, and then I pivoted away from Asia, asking him if anything about the Middle East makes him happy.

"Right now, I don't think that anybody can be feeling good about the situation in the Middle East," he said. "You have countries that are failing to provide prosperity and opportunity for their people. You've got a violent, extremist ideology, or ideologies, that are turbocharged through social media. You've got countries that have very few civic traditions, so that as autocratic regimes start fraying, the only organizing principles are sectarian."

He went on, "Contrast that with Southeast Asia, which still has huge problems—enormous poverty, corruption—but is filled with striving, ambitious, energetic people who are every single day scratching and clawing to build businesses and get education and find jobs and build infrastructure. The contrast is pretty stark."

In Asia, as well as in Latin America and Africa, Obama says, he sees young people yearning for self-improvement, modernity, education, and material wealth.

"They are not thinking about how to kill Americans," he says. "What they're thinking about is *How do I get a better education? How do I create something of value?*"

He then made an observation that I came to realize was representative of his bleakest, most visceral understanding of the Middle East today—not the sort of understanding that a White House still oriented around themes of hope and change might choose to advertise. "If we're not talking to them," he said, referring to young Asians and Africans and Latin Americans, "because the only thing we're doing is figuring out how to destroy or cordon off or control the malicious, nihilistic, violent parts of humanity, then we're missing the boat."

Obama's critics argue that he is ineffective in cordoning off the violent nihilists of radical Islam because he doesn't understand the threat. He does resist refracting radical Islam through the "clash of civilizations" prism popularized by the late political scientist Samuel Huntington. But this is because, he and his advisers argue, he does not want to enlarge the ranks of the enemy. "The goal is not to force a Huntington template onto this conflict," said John Brennan, the CIA director.

Both François Hollande and David Cameron have spoken about the threat of radical Islam in more Huntingtonesque terms, and I've heard that both men wish Obama would use more-direct language in discussing the threat. When I mentioned this to Obama he said, "Hollande and Cameron have used phrases, like *radical Islam*, that we have not used on a regular basis as our way of targeting terrorism. But I've never had a conversation when they said, 'Man, how come you're not using this phrase the way you hear Republicans say it?'" Obama says he has demanded that Muslim leaders do more to eliminate the threat of violent fundamentalism. "It is very clear what I mean," he told me, "which is that there is a violent, radical, fanatical, nihilistic interpretation of Islam by a faction—a tiny faction—within the Muslim community that is our enemy, and that has to be defeated."

He then offered a critique that sounded more in line with the rhetoric of Cameron and Hollande. "There is also the need for Islam as a whole to challenge that interpretation of Islam, to isolate it, and to undergo a vigorous discussion within their community about how Islam works as part of a peaceful, modern society," he said. But he added, "I do not persuade peaceful, tolerant Muslims to engage in that debate if I'm not sensitive to their concern that they are being tagged with a broad brush."

In private encounters with other world leaders, Obama has argued that there will be no comprehensive solution to Islamist terrorism until Islam reconciles itself to modernity and undergoes some of the reforms that have changed Christianity.

Though he has argued, controversially, that the Middle East's conflicts "date back millennia," he also believes that the intensified Muslim fury of recent years was encouraged by countries considered friends of the United States. In a meeting during APEC with Malcolm Turnbull, the new prime minister of Australia, Obama described how he has watched Indonesia gradually move from a relaxed, syncretistic Islam to a more fundamentalist, unforgiving interpretation; large numbers of Indonesian women, he observed, have now adopted the hijab, the Muslim head covering.

Why, Turnbull asked, was this happening?

Because, Obama answered, the Saudis and other Gulf Arabs have funneled money, and large numbers of imams and teachers, into the country. In the 1990s, the Saudis heavily funded Wahhabist madrassas, seminaries that teach the fundamentalist version of Islam favored by the Saudi ruling family, Obama told Turnbull. Today, Islam in Indonesia is much more Arab in orientation than it was when he lived there, he said.

"Aren't the Saudis your friends?" Turnbull asked.

Obama smiled. "It's complicated," he said.

Obama's patience with Saudi Arabia has always been limited. In his first foreign-policy commentary of note, that 2002 speech at the antiwar rally in Chicago, he said, "You want a fight, President

Bush? Let's fight to make sure our so-called allies in the Middle East—the Saudis and the Egyptians—stop oppressing their own people, and suppressing dissent, and tolerating corruption and inequality." In the White House these days, one occasionally hears Obama's National Security Council officials pointedly reminding visitors that the large majority of 9/11 hijackers were not Iranian, but Saudi—and Obama himself rails against Saudi Arabia's state-sanctioned misogyny, arguing in private that "a country cannot function in the modern world when it is repressing half of its population." In meetings with foreign leaders, Obama has said, "You can gauge the success of a society by how it treats its women."

His frustration with the Saudis informs his analysis of Middle Eastern power politics. At one point I observed to him that he is less likely than previous presidents to axiomatically side with Saudi Arabia in its dispute with its archrival, Iran. He didn't disagree.

"Iran, since 1979, has been an enemy of the United States, and has engaged in state-sponsored terrorism, is a genuine threat to Israel and many of our allies, and engages in all kinds of destructive behavior," the president said. "And my view has never been that we should throw our traditional allies"—the Saudis—"overboard in favor of Iran."

But he went on to say that the Saudis need to "share" the Middle East with their Iranian foes. "The competition between the Saudis and the Iranians—which has helped to feed proxy wars and chaos in Syria and Iraq and Yemen—requires us to say to our friends as well as to the Iranians that they need to find an effective way to share the neighborhood and institute some sort of cold peace," he said. "An approach that said to our friends 'You are right, Iran is the source of all problems, and we will support you in dealing with Iran' would essentially mean that as these sectarian conflicts continue to rage and our Gulf partners, our traditional friends, do not have the ability to put out the flames on their own or decisively win on their own, and would mean that we have to start coming in and using our military power to settle scores. And that would be in the interest neither of the United States nor of the Middle East."

One of the most destructive forces in the Middle East, Obama believes, is tribalism—a force no president can neutralize. Tribalism, made manifest in the reversion to sect, creed, clan, and village by the desperate citizens of failing states, is the source of much of the Muslim Middle East's problems, and it is another source of his fatalism. Obama has deep respect for the destructive resilience of tribalism—part of his memoir, *Dreams from My Father*, concerns the way in which tribalism in postcolonial Kenya helped ruin his father's life—which goes some distance in explaining why he is so fastidious about avoiding entanglements in tribal conflicts.

"It is literally in my DNA to be suspicious of tribalism," he told me. "I understand the tribal impulse, and acknowledge the power of tribal division. I've been navigating tribal divisions my whole life. In the end, it's the source of a lot of destructive acts."

. . .

While flying to Kuala Lumpur with the president, I recalled a passing reference he had once made to me about the Hobbesian argument for strong government as an antidote to the unforgiving state of nature. When Obama looks at swathes of the Middle East, Hobbes's "war of all against all" is what he sees. "I have a recognition that us serving as the Leviathan clamps down and tames some of these impulses," Obama had said. So I tried to reopen this conversation with an unfortunately prolix question about, among other things, "the Hobbesian notion that people organize themselves into collectives to stave off their supreme fear, which is death."

Ben Rhodes and Joshua Earnest, the White House spokesman, who were seated on a couch to the side of Obama's desk on *Air*

*Force One*, could barely suppress their amusement at my discursiveness. I paused and said, "I bet if I asked that in a press conference my colleagues would just throw me out of the room."

"I would be really into it," Obama said, "but everybody else would be rolling their eyes."

Rhodes interjected: "Why can't we get the bastards?" That question, the one put to the president by the CNN reporter at the press conference in Turkey, had become a topic of sardonic conversation during the trip.

I turned to the president: "Well, yeah, and also, why can't we get the bastards?"

He took the first question.

"Look, I am not of the view that human beings are inherently evil," he said. "I believe that there's more good than bad in humanity. And if you look at the trajectory of history, I am optimistic.

"I believe that overall, humanity has become less violent, more tolerant, healthier, better fed, more empathetic, more able to manage difference. But it's hugely uneven. And what has been clear throughout the twentieth and twenty-first centuries is that the progress we make in social order and taming our baser impulses and steadying our fears can be reversed very quickly. Social order starts breaking down if people are under profound stress. Then the default position is tribe—us/them, a hostility toward the unfamiliar or the unknown."

He continued, "Right now, across the globe, you're seeing places that are undergoing severe stress because of globalization, because of the collision of cultures brought about by the Internet and social media, because of scarcities—some of which will be attributable to climate change over the next several decades—because of population growth. And in those places, the Middle East being Exhibit A, the default position for a lot of folks is to organize tightly in the tribe and to push back or strike out against those who are different.

"A group like ISIL is the distillation of every worst impulse along these lines. The notion that we are a small group that defines ourselves primarily by the degree to which we can kill others who are not like us, and attempting to impose a rigid orthodoxy that produces nothing, that celebrates nothing, that really is contrary to every bit of human progress—it indicates the degree to which that kind of mentality can still take root and gain adherents in the twenty-first century."

So your appreciation for tribalism's power makes you want to stay away?, I asked. "In other words, when people say 'Why don't you just go get the bastards?,' you step back?"

"We have to determine the best tools to roll back those kinds of attitudes," he said. "There are going to be times where either because it's not a direct threat to us or because we just don't have the tools in our toolkit to have a huge impact that, tragically, we have to refrain from jumping in with both feet."

I asked Obama whether he would have sent the marines to Rwanda in 1994 to stop the genocide as it was happening, had he been president at the time. "Given the speed with which the killing took place, and how long it takes to crank up the machinery of the U.S. government, I understand why we did not act fast enough," he said. "Now, we should learn from that. I actually think that Rwanda is an interesting test case because it's possible—not guaranteed, but it's possible—that this was a situation where the quick application of force might have been enough."

He related this to Syria: "Ironically, it's probably easier to make an argument that a relatively small force inserted quickly with international support would have resulted in averting genocide [more successfully in Rwanda] than in Syria right now, where the degree to which the various groups are armed and hardened fighters and are supported by a whole host of external actors with a lot of resources requires a much larger commitment of forces."

.   .   .

Obama-administration officials argue that he has a comprehensible approach to fighting terrorism: a drone air force, Special Forces raids, a clandestine CIA-aided army of 10,000 rebels battling in Syria. So why does Obama stumble when explaining to the American people that he, too, cares about terrorism? The Turkey press conference, I told him, "was a moment for you as a politician to say, 'Yeah, I hate the bastards too, and by the way, I *am* taking out the bastards.'" The easy thing to do would have been to reassure Americans in visceral terms that he will kill the people who want to kill them. Does he fear a knee-jerk reaction in the direction of another Middle East invasion? Or is he just inalterably Spockian?

"Every president has strengths and weaknesses," he answered. "And there is no doubt that there are times where I have not been attentive enough to feelings and emotions and politics in communicating what we're doing and how we're doing it."

But for America to be successful in leading the world, he continued, "I believe that we have to avoid being simplistic. I think we have to build resilience and make sure that our political debates are grounded in reality. It's not that I don't appreciate the value of theater in political communications; it's that the habits we—the media, politicians—have gotten into, and how we talk about these issues, are so detached so often from what we need to be doing that for me to satisfy the cable news hype-fest would lead to us making worse and worse decisions over time."

As *Air Force One* began its descent toward Kuala Lumpur, the president mentioned the successful U.S.-led effort to stop the Ebola epidemic in West Africa as a positive example of steady, nonhysterical management of a terrifying crisis.

"During the couple of months in which everybody was sure Ebola was going to destroy the Earth and there was 24/7 coverage of Ebola, if I had fed the panic or in any way strayed from 'Here are the facts, here's what needs to be done, here's how we're handling it, the likelihood of you getting Ebola is very slim, and here's what we need to do both domestically and overseas to stamp out this epidemic,'" then "maybe people would have said 'Obama is taking this as seriously as he needs to be.'" But feeding the panic by overreacting could have shut down travel to and from three African countries that were already cripplingly poor, in ways that might have destroyed their economies—which would likely have meant, among other things, a recurrence of Ebola. He added, "It would have also meant that we might have wasted a huge amount of resources in our public-health systems that need to be devoted to flu vaccinations and other things that actually kill people" in large numbers in America.

The plane landed. The president, leaning back in his office chair with his jacket off and his tie askew, did not seem to notice. Outside, on the tarmac, I could see that what appeared to be a large portion of the Malaysian Armed Forces had assembled to welcome him. As he continued talking, I began to worry that the waiting soldiers and dignitaries would get hot. "I think we're in Malaysia," I said. "It seems to be outside this plane."

He conceded that this was true, but seemed to be in no rush, so I pressed him about his public reaction to terrorism: If he showed more emotion, wouldn't that calm people down rather than rile them up?

"I have friends who have kids in Paris right now," he said. "And you and I and a whole bunch of people who are writing about what happened in Paris have strolled along the same streets where people were gunned down. And it's right to feel fearful. And it's important for us not to ever get complacent. There's a difference between resilience and complacency." He went on to describe another difference—between making considered decisions and making rash, emotional ones. "What it means, actually, is that you care so much that you want to get it right and you're not going to indulge in either impetuous or, in some cases, manufactured responses that make good sound bites but don't produce results. The stakes are too high to play those games."

With that, Obama stood up and said, "Okay, gotta go." He headed out of his office and down the stairs, to the red carpet and the honor guard and the cluster of Malaysian officials waiting to greet him, and then to his armored limousine, flown to Kuala Lumpur ahead of him. (Early in his first term, still unaccustomed to the massive military operation it takes to move a president from one place to another, he noted ruefully to aides, "I have the world's largest carbon footprint.")

The president's first stop was another event designed to highlight his turn to Asia, this one a town-hall meeting with students and entrepreneurs participating in the administration's Young Southeast Asian Leaders Initiative. Obama entered the lecture hall at Taylor's University to huge applause. He made some opening remarks, then charmed his audience in an extended Q&A session.

But those of us watching from the press section became distracted by news coming across our phones about a new jihadist attack, this one in Mali. Obama, busily mesmerizing adoring Asian entrepreneurs, had no idea. Only when he got into his limousine with Susan Rice did he get the news.

Later that evening, I visited the president in his suite at the Ritz-Carlton hotel in downtown Kuala Lumpur. The streets around the hotel had been sealed. Armored vehicles ringed the building; the lobby was filled with SWAT teams. I took the elevator to a floor crowded with Secret Service agents, who pointed me to a staircase; the elevator to Obama's floor was disabled for security reasons. Up two flights, to a hallway with more agents. A moment's wait, and then Obama opened the door. His two-story suite was outlandish: Tara-like drapes, overstuffed couches. It was enormous and lonely and claustrophobic all at once.

"It's like the Hearst Castle," I observed.

"Well, it's a long way from the Hampton Inn in Des Moines," Obama said.

ESPN was playing in the background.

When we sat down, I pointed out to the president a central challenge of his pivot to Asia. Earlier in the day, at the moment he was trying to inspire a group of gifted and eager hijab-wearing Indonesian entrepreneurs and Burmese innovators, attention was diverted by the latest Islamist terror attack.

A writer at heart, he had a suggestion: "It's probably a pretty easy way to start the story," he said, referring to this article.

Possibly, I said, but it's kind of a cheap trick.

"It's cheap, but it works," Obama said. "We're talking to these kids, and then there's this attack going on."

The split-screen quality of the day prompted a conversation about two recent meetings he'd held, one that generated major international controversy and headlines, and one that did not. The one that drew so much attention, I suggested, would ultimately be judged less consequential. This was the Gulf summit in May of 2015 at Camp David, meant to mollify a crowd of visiting sheikhs and princes who feared the impending Iran deal. The other meeting took place two months later, in the Oval Office, between Obama and the general secretary of the Vietnamese Communist Party, Nguyen Phu Trong. This meeting took place only because John Kerry had pushed the White House to violate protocol, since the general secretary was not a head of state. But the goals trumped decorum: Obama wanted to lobby the Vietnamese on the Trans-Pacific Partnership—his negotiators soon extracted a promise from the Vietnamese that they would legalize independent labor unions—and he wanted to deepen cooperation on strategic issues. Administration officials have repeatedly hinted to me that Vietnam may one day soon host a permanent U.S. military presence, to check the ambitions of the country it now fears most, China. The U.S. Navy's return to Cam Ranh Bay would count as one of the more improbable developments in recent American history. "We just moved the Vietnamese Communist Party to recognize labor rights in a way that we could never do by bullying them or scaring them," Obama told me, calling this a key victory in his campaign to replace stick-waving with diplomatic persuasion.

I noted that the 200 or so young Southeast Asians in the room earlier that day—including citizens of communist-ruled countries—seemed to love America. "They do," Obama said. "In Vietnam right now, America polls at 80 percent."

The resurgent popularity of America throughout Southeast Asia means that "we can do really big, important stuff—which, by the way, then has ramifications across the board," he said, "because when Malaysia joins the anti-ISIL campaign, that helps us leverage resources and credibility in our fight against terrorism. When we have strong relations with Indonesia, that helps us when we are going to Paris and trying to negotiate a climate treaty, where the temptation of a Russia or some of these other countries may be to skew the deal in a way that is unhelpful."

Obama then cited America's increased influence in Latin America—increased, he said, in part by his removal of a region-wide stumbling block when he reestablished ties with Cuba—as proof that his deliberate, nonthreatening, diplomacy-centered approach to foreign relations is working. The ALBA movement, a group of Latin American governments oriented around anti-Americanism, has significantly weakened during his time as president. "When I came into office, at the first Summit of the Americas that I attended, Hugo Chávez"—the late anti-American Venezuelan dictator—"was still the dominant figure in the conversation," he said. "We made a very strategic decision early on, which was, rather than blow him up as this ten-foot giant adversary, to right-size the problem and say, 'We don't like what's going on in Venezuela, but it's not a threat to the United States.'"

Obama said that to achieve this rebalancing, the United States had to absorb the diatribes and insults of superannuated Castro manqués. "When I saw Chávez, I shook his hand and he handed me a Marxist critique of the U.S.–Latin America relationship," Obama recalled. "And I had to sit there and listen to Ortega"—

Daniel Ortega, the radical leftist president of Nicaragua—"make an hour-long rant against the United States. But us being there, not taking all that stuff seriously—because it really wasn't a threat to us"—helped neutralize the region's anti-Americanism.

The president's unwillingness to counter the baiting by American adversaries can feel emotionally unsatisfying, I said, and I told him that every so often, I'd like to see him give Vladimir Putin the finger. It's atavistic, I said, understanding my audience.

"It is," the president responded coolly. "This is what they're looking for."

He described a relationship with Putin that doesn't quite conform to common perceptions. I had been under the impression that Obama viewed Putin as nasty, brutish, and short. But, Obama told me, Putin is not particularly nasty.

"The truth is, actually, Putin, in all of our meetings, is scrupulously polite, very frank. Our meetings are very businesslike. He never keeps me waiting two hours like he does a bunch of these other folks." Obama said that Putin believes his relationship with the United States is more important than Americans tend to think. "He's constantly interested in being seen as our peer and as working with us, because he's not completely stupid. He understands that Russia's overall position in the world is significantly diminished. And the fact that he invades Crimea or is trying to prop up Assad doesn't suddenly make him a player. You don't see him in any of these meetings out here helping to shape the agenda. For that matter, there's not a G20 meeting where the Russians set the agenda around any of the issues that are important."

. . .

Russia's invasion of Crimea in early 2014, and its decision to use force to buttress the rule of its client Bashar al-Assad, have been cited by Obama's critics as proof that the post-red-line world no longer fears America.

So when I talked with the president in the Oval Office in late January, I again raised this question of deterrent credibility. "The argument is made," I said, "that Vladimir Putin watched you in Syria and thought, *He's too logical, he's too rational, he's too into retrenchment. I'm going to push him a little bit further in Ukraine.*"

Obama didn't much like my line of inquiry. "Look, this theory is so easily disposed of that I'm always puzzled by how people make the argument. I don't think anybody thought that George W. Bush was overly rational or cautious in his use of military force. And as I recall, because apparently nobody in this town does, Putin went into Georgia on Bush's watch, right smack dab in the middle of us having over 100,000 troops deployed in Iraq." Obama was referring to Putin's 2008 invasion of Georgia, a former Soviet republic, which was undertaken for many of the same reasons Putin later invaded Ukraine—to keep an ex–Soviet republic in Russia's sphere of influence.

"Putin acted in Ukraine in response to a client state that was about to slip out of his grasp. And he improvised in a way to hang on to his control there," he said. "He's done the exact same thing in Syria, at enormous cost to the well-being of his own country. And the notion that somehow Russia is in a stronger position now, in Syria or in Ukraine, than they were before they invaded Ukraine or before he had to deploy military forces to Syria is to fundamentally misunderstand the nature of power in foreign affairs or in the world generally. Real power means you can get what you want without having to exert violence. Russia was much more powerful when Ukraine looked like an independent country but was a kleptocracy that he could pull the strings on."

Obama's theory here is simple: Ukraine is a core Russian interest but not an American one, so Russia will always be able to maintain escalatory dominance there.

"The fact is that Ukraine, which is a non-NATO country, is going to be vulnerable to military domination by Russia no matter what we do," he said.

I asked Obama whether his position on Ukraine was realistic or fatalistic.

"It's realistic," he said. "But this is an example of where we have to be very clear about what our core interests are and what we are willing to go to war for. And at the end of the day, there's always going to be some ambiguity." He then offered up a critique he had heard directed against him, in order to knock it down. "I think that the best argument you can make on the side of those who are critics of my foreign policy is that the president doesn't exploit ambiguity enough. He doesn't maybe react in ways that might cause people to think, *Wow, this guy might be a little crazy.*"

"The 'crazy Nixon' approach," I said: Confuse and frighten your enemies by making them think you're capable of committing irrational acts.

"But let's examine the Nixon theory," he said. "So we dropped more ordnance on Cambodia and Laos than on Europe in World War II, and yet, ultimately, Nixon withdrew, Kissinger went to Paris, and all we left behind was chaos, slaughter, and authoritarian governments that finally, over time, have emerged from that hell. When I go to visit those countries, I'm going to be trying to figure out how we can, today, help them remove bombs that are still blowing off the legs of little kids. In what way did that strategy promote our interests?"

But what if Putin were threatening to move against, say, Moldova—another vulnerable post-Soviet state? Wouldn't it be helpful for Putin to believe that Obama might get angry and irrational about that?

"There is no evidence in modern American foreign policy that that's how people respond. People respond based on what their imperatives are, and if it's really important to somebody, and it's not that important to us, they know that, and we know that," he said. "There are ways to deter, but it requires you to be very clear ahead of time about what is worth going to war for and what is not. Now, if there is somebody in this town that would claim that we would consider going to war with Russia over Crimea and eastern Ukraine, they should speak up and be very clear about it. The idea that talking tough or engaging in some military action that is tangential to that particular area is somehow going to influence the decision making of Russia or China is contrary to all the evidence we have seen over the last fifty years."

Obama went on to say that the belief in the possibilities of projected toughness is rooted in "mythologies" about Ronald Reagan's foreign policy.

"If you think about, let's say, the Iran hostage crisis, there is a narrative that has been promoted today by some of the Republican candidates that the day Reagan was elected, because he looked tough, the Iranians decided, 'We better turn over these hostages,'" he said. "In fact what had happened was that there was a long negotiation with the Iranians and because they so disliked Carter—even though the negotiations had been completed—they held those hostages until the day Reagan got elected. Reagan's posture, his rhetoric, etc., had nothing to do with their release. When you think of the military actions that Reagan took, you have Grenada—which is hard to argue helped our ability to shape world events, although it was good politics for him back home. You have the Iran-Contra affair, in which we supported right-wing paramilitaries and did nothing to enhance our image in Central America, and it wasn't successful at all." He reminded me that Reagan's great foe, Daniel Ortega, is today the unrepentant president of Nicaragua.

Obama also cited Reagan's decision to almost immediately pull U.S. forces from Lebanon after 241 servicemen were killed in a Hezbollah attack in 1983. "Apparently all these things really helped us gain credibility with the Russians and the Chinese," because "that's the narrative that is told," he said sarcastically. "Now, I actually think that Ronald Reagan had a great success in foreign policy, which was to recognize the opportunity that Gorbachev presented and to engage in extensive diplomacy—

which was roundly criticized by some of the same people who now use Ronald Reagan to promote the notion that we should go around bombing people."

· · ·

In a conversation at the end of January, I asked the president to describe for me the threats he worries about most as he prepares, in the coming months, to hand off power to his successor.

"As I survey the next twenty years, climate change worries me profoundly because of the effects that it has on all the other problems that we face," he said. "If you start seeing more severe drought; more significant famine; more displacement from the Indian subcontinent and coastal regions in Africa and Asia; the continuing problems of scarcity, refugees, poverty, disease—this makes every other problem we've got worse. That's above and beyond just the existential issues of a planet that starts getting into a bad feedback loop."

Terrorism, he said, is also a long-term problem "when combined with the problem of failed states."

What country does he consider the greatest challenge to America in the coming decades? "In terms of traditional great-state relations, I do believe that the relationship between the United States and China is going to be the most critical," he said. "If we get that right and China continues on a peaceful rise, then we have a partner that is growing in capability and sharing with us the burdens and responsibilities of maintaining an international order. If China fails; if it is not able to maintain a trajectory that satisfies its population and has to resort to nationalism as an organizing principle; if it feels so overwhelmed that it never takes on the responsibilities of a country its size in maintaining the international order; if it views the world only in terms of regional spheres of influence—then not only do we see the potential for conflict with China, but we will find ourselves having more difficulty dealing with these other challenges that are going to come."

Many people, I noted, want the president to be more forceful in confronting China, especially in the South China Sea. Hillary Clinton, for one, has been heard to say in private settings, "I don't want my grandchildren to live in a world dominated by the Chinese."

"I've been very explicit in saying that we have more to fear from a weakened, threatened China than a successful, rising China," Obama said. "I think we have to be firm where China's actions are undermining international interests, and if you look at how we've operated in the South China Sea, we have been able to mobilize most of Asia to isolate China in ways that have surprised China, frankly, and have very much served our interest in strengthening our alliances."

A weak, flailing Russia constitutes a threat as well, though not quite a top-tier threat. "Unlike China, they have demographic problems, economic structural problems, that would require not only vision but a generation to overcome," Obama said. "The path that Putin is taking is not going to help them overcome those challenges. But in that environment, the temptation to project military force to show greatness is strong, and that's what Putin's inclination is. So I don't underestimate the dangers there." Obama returned to a point he had made repeatedly to me, one that he hopes the country, and the next president, absorbs: "You know, the notion that diplomacy and technocrats and bureaucrats somehow are helping to keep America safe and secure, most people think, *Eh, that's nonsense.* But it's true. And by the way, it's the element of American power that the rest of the world appreciates unambiguously. When we deploy troops, there's always a sense on the part of other countries that, even where necessary, sovereignty is being violated."

•       •       •

Over the past year, John Kerry has visited the White House regularly to ask Obama to violate Syria's sovereignty. On several occasions, Kerry has asked Obama to launch missiles at specific regime targets, under cover of night, to "send a message" to the regime. The goal, Kerry has said, is not to overthrow Assad but to encourage him, and Iran and Russia, to negotiate peace. When the Assad alliance has had the upper hand on the battlefield, as it has these past several months, it has shown no inclination to take seriously Kerry's entreaties to negotiate in good faith. A few cruise missiles, Kerry has argued, might concentrate the attention of Assad and his backers. "Kerry's looking like a chump with the Russians, because he has no leverage," a senior administration official told me.

The United States wouldn't have to claim credit for the attacks, Kerry has told Obama—but Assad would surely know the missiles' return address.

Obama has steadfastly resisted Kerry's requests and seems to have grown impatient with his lobbying. Recently, when Kerry handed Obama a written outline of new steps to bring more pressure to bear on Assad, Obama said, "Oh, another proposal?" Administration officials have told me that Vice President Biden, too, has become frustrated with Kerry's demands for action. He has said privately to the secretary of state, "John, remember Vietnam? Remember how that started?" At a National Security Council meeting held at the Pentagon in December, Obama announced that no one except the secretary of defense should bring him proposals for military action. Pentagon officials understood Obama's announcement to be a brushback pitch directed at Kerry.

One day in January, in Kerry's office at the State Department, I expressed the obvious: He has more of a bias toward action than the president does.

"I do, probably," Kerry acknowledged. "Look, the final say on these things is in his hands . . . I'd say that I think we've had a very symbiotic, synergistic, whatever you call it, relationship, which works very effectively. Because I'll come in with the bias toward 'Let's try to do this, let's try to do that, let's get this done.'"

Obama's caution on Syria has vexed those in the administration who have seen opportunities, at different moments over the past four years, to tilt the battlefield against Assad. Some thought that Putin's decision to fight on behalf of Assad would prompt Obama to intensify American efforts to help antiregime rebels. But Obama, at least as of this writing, would not be moved, in part because he believed that it was not his business to stop Russia from making what he thought was a terrible mistake. "They are overextended. They're bleeding," he told me. "And their economy has contracted for three years in a row, drastically."

In recent National Security Council meetings, Obama's strategy was occasionally referred to as the "Tom Sawyer approach." Obama's view was that if Putin wanted to expend his regime's resources by painting the fence in Syria, the United States should let him. By late winter, though, when it appeared that Russia was making advances in its campaign to solidify Assad's rule, the White House began discussing ways to deepen support for the rebels, though the president's ambivalence about more-extensive engagement remained. In conversations I had with National Security Council officials over the past couple of months, I sensed a foreboding that an event—another San Bernardino–style attack, for instance—would compel the United States to take new and direct action in Syria. For Obama, this would be a nightmare.

If there had been no Iraq, no Afghanistan, and no Libya, Obama told me, he might be more apt to take risks in Syria. "A president does not make decisions in a vacuum. He does not have a blank slate. Any president who was thoughtful, I believe, would recognize that after over a decade of war, with obligations that are still to this day requiring great amounts of resources and attention in Afghanistan, with the experience of Iraq, with the strains that it's placed on our military—any thoughtful president would hesitate about making a renewed commitment in the exact same region of the world with some of the exact same dynamics and the same probability of an unsatisfactory outcome."

Are you too cautious? I asked.

"No," he said. "Do I think that had we not invaded Iraq and were we not still involved in sending billions of dollars and a number of military trainers and advisers into Afghanistan, would I potentially have thought about taking on some additional risk to help try to shape the Syria situation? I don't know."

What has struck me is that, even as his secretary of state warns about a dire, Syria-fueled European apocalypse, Obama has not recategorized the country's civil war as a top-tier security threat.

Obama's hesitation to join the battle for Syria is held out as proof by his critics that he is too naive; his decision in 2013 not to fire missiles is proof, they argue, that he is a bluffer.

This critique frustrates the president. "Nobody remembers bin Laden anymore," he says. "Nobody talks about me ordering 30,000 more troops into Afghanistan." The red-line crisis, he said, "is the point of the inverted pyramid upon which all other theories rest."

One afternoon in late January, as I was leaving the Oval Office, I mentioned to Obama a moment from an interview in 2012 when he told me that he would not allow Iran to gain possession of a nuclear weapon. "You said, 'I'm the president of the United States, I don't bluff.'"

He said, "I don't."

Shortly after that interview four years ago, Ehud Barak, who was then the defense minister of Israel, asked me whether I thought Obama's no-bluff promise was itself a bluff. I answered that I found it difficult to imagine that the leader of the United

States would bluff about something so consequential. But Barak's question had stayed with me. So as I stood in the doorway with the president, I asked: "Was it a bluff?" I told him that few people now believe he actually would have attacked Iran to keep it from getting a nuclear weapon.

"That's interesting," he said, noncommittally.

I started to talk: "Do you—"

He interrupted. "I actually would have," he said, meaning that he would have struck Iran's nuclear facilities. "If I saw them break out."

He added, "Now, the argument that can't be resolved, because it's entirely situational, was what constitutes them getting" the bomb. "This was the argument I was having with Bibi Netanyahu." Netanyahu wanted Obama to prevent Iran from being capable of building a bomb, not merely from possessing a bomb.

"You were right to believe it," the president said. And then he made his key point. "This was in the category of an American interest."

I was reminded then of something Derek Chollet, a former National Security Council official, told me: "Obama is a gambler, not a bluffer."

The president has placed some huge bets. Last May, as he was trying to move the Iran nuclear deal through Congress, I told him that the agreement was making me nervous. His response was telling. "Look, twenty years from now, I'm still going to be around, God willing. If Iran has a nuclear weapon, it's my name on this," he said. "I think it's fair to say that in addition to our profound national-security interests, I have a personal interest in locking this down."

In the matter of the Syrian regime and its Iranian and Russian sponsors, Obama has bet, and seems prepared to continue betting, that the price of direct U.S. action would be higher than the price of inaction. And he is sanguine enough to live with the perilous ambiguities of his decisions. Though in his Nobel Peace Prize speech in 2009, Obama said, "Inaction tears at our conscience and can lead to more costly intervention later," today the opinions of humanitarian interventionists do not seem to move him, at least not publicly. He undoubtedly knows that a next-generation Samantha Power will write critically of his unwillingness to do more to prevent the continuing slaughter in Syria. (For that matter, Samantha Power will also be the subject of criticism from the next Samantha Power.) As he comes to the end of his presidency, Obama believes he has done his country a large favor by keeping it out of the maelstrom—and he believes, I suspect, that historians will one day judge him wise for having done so.

Inside the West Wing, officials say that Obama, as a president who inherited a financial crisis and two active wars from his predecessor, is keen to leave "a clean barn" to whoever succeeds him. This is why the fight against ISIS, a group he considers to be a direct, though not existential, threat to the United States, is his most urgent priority for the remainder of his presidency; killing the so-called caliph of the Islamic State, Abu Bakr al-Baghdadi, is one of the top goals of the American national-security apparatus in Obama's last year.

Of course, ISIS was midwifed into existence, in part, by the Assad regime. Yet by Obama's stringent standards, Assad's continued rule for the moment still doesn't rise to the level of direct challenge to America's national security.

This is what is so controversial about the president's approach, and what will be controversial for years to come—the standard he has used to define what, exactly, constitutes a direct threat.

Obama has come to a number of dovetailing conclusions about the world and about America's role in it. The first is that the Middle East is no longer terribly important to American interests. The second is that even if the Middle East were surpassingly important, there would still be little an American president could do to make it a better place. The third is that the innate American desire to fix the sorts of problems that manifest themselves most drastically in the Middle East inevitably leads to warfare, to the deaths of U.S. soldiers, and to the eventual hemorrhaging of U.S. credibility and power. The fourth is that the world cannot afford to see the diminishment of U.S. power. Just as the leaders of several American allies have found Obama's leadership inadequate to the tasks before him, he himself has found world leadership wanting: global partners who often lack the vision and the will to spend political capital in pursuit of broad, progressive goals and adversaries who are not, in his mind, as rational as he is. Obama believes that history has sides and that America's adversaries—and some of its putative allies—have situated themselves on the wrong one, a place where tribalism, fundamentalism, sectarianism, and militarism still flourish. What they don't understand is that history is bending in his direction.

"The central argument is that by keeping America from immersing itself in the crises of the Middle East, the foreign-policy establishment believes that the president is precipitating our decline," Ben Rhodes told me. "But the president himself takes the opposite view, which is that overextension in the Middle East will ultimately harm our economy, harm our ability to look for other opportunities and to deal with other challenges, and, most important, endanger the lives of American service members for reasons that are not in the direct American national-security interest."

If you are a supporter of the president, his strategy makes eminent sense: Double down in those parts of the world where success is plausible, and limit America's exposure to the rest. His critics believe, however, that problems like those presented by the Middle East don't solve themselves—that, without American intervention, they metastasize.

At the moment, Syria, where history appears to be bending toward greater chaos, poses the most direct challenge to the president's worldview.

George W. Bush was also a gambler, not a bluffer. He will be remembered harshly for the things he did in the Middle East. Barack Obama is gambling that he will be judged well for the things he didn't do.

## *National Geographic*

FINALIST—SINGLE-TOPIC
ISSUE

*The National Magazine Award for Single-Topic Issue is the closest ASME comes to picking a best issue of the year. And in fact, the Ellie judges described the May 2016 edition of* National Geographic, *"Yellowstone: The Battle for the American West," as "magazine making at its best," praising the issue for its "stunning photography; deep, considered reporting; elegant writing; and sharp, engaging infographics." In this abridged version of David Quammen's three-part story from "Yellowstone: The Battle for the American West," readers can sample what the judges so much admired. Quammen is the author of fifteen books, including five works of fiction; his writing also won Ellies for* Outside *in 1987 and 1994 and* National Geographic *in 2005.*

David Quammen

# Yellowstone

## Wild Heart of a Continent

O n August 7, 2015, a ranger found the chewed-upon body of a man near a hiking trail in Yellowstone National Park, not far from one of the park's largest hotels. The deceased was soon identified as Lance Crosby, sixty-three, from Billings, Montana. He had worked seasonally as a nurse at a medical clinic in the park and been reported missing by coworkers that morning.

Investigation revealed that Crosby was hiking alone on the previous day, without bear spray, and ran afoul of a female grizzly with two cubs. The sow, after killing and partially eating him (not necessarily in that order), and allowing the cubs to eat too, cached his remains beneath dirt and pine duff, as grizzlies do when they intend to reclaim a piece of meat. Once trapped and persuasively linked to Crosby by DNA evidence, she was given a sedative and an anesthetic and then executed, on grounds that an adult grizzly bear that has eaten human flesh and cached a body is too dangerous to be spared, even if the fatal encounter wasn't her fault. "We are deeply saddened by this tragedy and our hearts go out to the family and friends of the victim," said Park Super-intendent Dan Wenk, a reasonable man charged with a difficult task: keeping Yellowstone safe for both people and wildlife.

Grizzly bears, clearly, can be dangerous animals. But the danger they represent should be seen in perspective. Lance Crosby's death was just the seventh bear-caused fatality in the park during the past hundred years. In the 144 years since Yellowstone was established, more people have died there of drowning and of scalding in thermal pools, and of suicide, than have been killed by bears. Almost as many people have died from lightning strikes. Two people have been killed by bison.

The real lesson inherent in the death of Lance Crosby, and in the equally regrettable death of the bear that killed him, is a reminder of something too easily forgotten: Yellowstone is a wild place, constrained imperfectly within human-imposed limits. It's filled with wonders of nature—fierce animals, deep canyons, scalding waters—that are magnificent to behold but fretful to engage.

Most of us, when we visit Yellowstone, gaze from our cars at a roadside bear, stand at an overlook above a great river, stroll boardwalks amid the geyser basins. We experience the park as a diorama. But walk just 200 yards off the road into a forested gully or a sagebrush flat, and you had better be carrying, as Lance Crosby wasn't, a canister of bear spray. This is the paradox of Yellowstone, and of most other national parks we have added since: wilderness contained, nature under management, wild animals obliged to abide by human rules. It's the paradox of the cultivated wild.

Question: Can we hope to preserve, in the midst of modern America, any such remnant of our continent's primordial landscape, any such sample of true wildness—a gloriously inhospitable place, full of predators and prey, in which nature is still allowed to be red in tooth and claw? Can that sort of place be reconciled with human demands and human convenience? Time alone, and our choices, will tell. But if the answer is yes, the answer is Yellowstone.

On March 1, 1872, President Ulysses S. Grant, compliant but no great advocate of scenic protection himself, signed a bill creating the world's first national park. That law specified "a public park or pleasuring-ground for the benefit and enjoyment of the people." Within this park "wanton destruction of the fish and game," whatever "wanton" might mean, as well as commercial exploitation of such game, was prohibited. The boundaries were rectilinear, although ecology isn't. The paradox had been framed.

At the outset, the park was an orphan idea with no clarity of purpose, no staff, no budget. Congress seemed to lose interest as soon as the ink of Grant's signature dried. The idea that the park should protect wildlife as well as geysers and canyons was an afterthought. Yellowstone became a disaster zone. Market hunters operated brazenly in the park, killing elk, bison, bighorn sheep, and other ungulates in industrial quantities, until the U.S. Army was brought in to handle enforcement. An elk hide was worth six to eight dollars, serious money, and a man might kill twenty-five to fifty elk in a day. Antlers littered the hillsides. Wagon tourists came and went unsupervised, at low numbers but with relatively high impact, some of them vandalizing geyser cones, carving their names on the scenery, killing a trumpeter swan or other wildlife for the hell of it.

Even after the National Park Service replaced the army in 1916, persecution of the "bad" animals in the park—meaning mostly the predators, as distinct from the gentle herbivores— continued unfettered. One superintendent even encouraged commercial trappers to kill beavers by the hundreds so that they wouldn't build dams and flood his park. Otters were classified as predatory, that damning label, and for a while there was a fatwa against skunks. Wolf killing ended only when the wolves were all gone, not just from Yellowstone (by around 1930) but throughout the American West. Poisoning and shooting of coyotes continued until about 1935.

Bears, especially grizzly bears (though black bears are also present), have always been a different and more complicated matter. Grizzlies are omnivores, smart and opportunistic. From the early years of the park, they learned to accept handouts from passing travelers and to forage on humans' garbage. Later, by the hotels at Old Faithful, on the lake, and near the Grand Canyon, large garbage dumps became theaters where tourists sat on bleacher seats to watch the "bear show" on summer evenings. For eighty years, Yellowstone's grizzlies and black bears consumed food refuse in vast quantities, coming to depend on it unwholesomely, with the blessings of the park managers and to the amusement of the visiting public. The closure of those dumps during the early 1970s, when management ideas shifted toward more "natural" regulation, precipitated a crisis of hungry desperation among grizzlies that brought the population way down and resulted, in 1975, in the bear's listing as "threatened" under the Endangered Species Act.

Today Yellowstone is the eponym of a great ecosystem, the biggest and richest complex of mostly untamed landscape and wildlife within the lower forty-eight states. The Greater Yellowstone Ecosystem is an amoeboid expanse of landscape encompassing two national parks (Grand Teton is the second) as well as national forests, wildlife refuges, and other public and private holdings, the whole shebang amounting to 22.6 million acres, an order of magnitude bigger than Yellowstone Park itself. Surrounding this great amoeba is a modest transition zone, where you will more likely find cattle than elk, more likely see a grain elevator than a grizzly bear, and more likely hear the bark of a black Labrador than the howl of a wolf. Bounding that buffer is twenty-first-century America: highways, towns, parking lots, malls, endlessly sprawling suburbs, golf courses, Starbucks.

Within the ecosystem, everything is connected. That's the first lesson not just of ecology but also of resource politics. The wolf is connected to the grizzly bear by way of their competition for ungulate prey, especially elk calves and adult elk that have been weakened by winter or the rigors of the autumn rut. Because whitebark pine seeds constitute another important food for grizzlies, the bears are connected to the mountain pine beetle, which kills the pines in increasingly severe outbreaks related to climate change. Bison are connected to Montana livestock policy by way of a disease called brucellosis, probably brought to America in cattle.

Such interconnections underscore the truth of a truism: that the ecosystem is an intricate, interactive compoundment of living creatures, relationships, physical factors, geological circumstances, historical accidents, and biological processes. The changes that ricochet through these networks of connection, from animal to plant, predator to prey, one level of the food web to another, are a focus of interest, and disagreement, among scientists who study the wildlife and vegetation of Yellowstone. The details become almost Talmudic in complexity, but what's important to keep in mind is that disturbances have secondary effects, usually unforeseen, and that sometimes those effects are irreversible. Restoring wolves to Yellowstone, for example, does not necessarily fix all the problems that removing wolves from Yellowstone caused. Taking grizzlies off the list of threatened species will have consequences down the road too.

Preservation of the grizzly bear population is arguably the highest and best purpose of Yellowstone Park and the Greater Yellowstone Ecosystem. But that doesn't oblige one to extreme pessimism over the bear's prospects of survival, nor to distrust of agency biologists, many of whom believe that the bear's intelligence and flexibility of behavior will keep it robust and numerous despite changes in the landscape that require greater reliance on some different foods. After all, they say, the grizzly is an omnivore, and although some of its traditionally most used food sources are in decline—spawning cutthroat trout, whitebark pine seeds—because of human-caused impacts on the ecosystem, there are 264 other choices on the known list of grizzly dietary items in Yellowstone. Change may come, these scientists say, but the bear will adapt to the challenge.

For the people who live within it, the Greater Yellowstone Ecosystem is a focus of many hopes, ideals, and fond memories—

but also of many angers, in part because it contains so many different expectations governed by different interests. Some hunters are angry that there aren't enough elk. Some ranchers are angry that there are too many elk. Some wolf lovers are angry that wolves, including those that spend much of their year within the park, now may be hunted or trapped when they roam beyond the park boundaries. Some landowners in Gardiner, Montana, are angry that bison migrate out of the park in winter and into their yards. Some stockmen are angry that migrating bison carry brucellosis, which might be passed to their cows. Some wildlife activists are angry that bison from the park, once they migrate out, may be corralled and shipped to slaughter. Some range scientists are angry about overgrazed grasslands in the two parks, resulting from too many bison and elk. Some fishermen are angry about the slaughter of lake trout, an exotic species that's being suppressed in Yellowstone Lake for the sake of the native cutthroat trout. Somebody somewhere is probably angry about coyotes. Scarcely a season passes, in the gateway towns of Cody and Jackson and Bozeman, without several public meetings, called by the various agencies, at which people express these angers.

Amid that push and pull, however, one important truth must be remembered: that the people who live and work and hunt and fish and hike within the Greater Yellowstone Ecosystem are not the sole possessors of legitimate interest.

This is America's place, and the world's.

Have we vastly improved this great area since the bad old days of commercial poaching and vandalism, governmental neglect, Wild West brigandage, and uncontrolled tourism development—or have we already gone a long way toward making it a big, boring suburb with antler-motif doorknobs?

Passionately dedicated people need to find collaborative solutions and to recognize that righteous intransigence is not a strategy; it's just a satisfying attitude. The various agency members of the Greater Yellowstone Coordinating Committee (the body that tries to oversee the Greater Yellowstone Ecosystem as a comprehensive entity) need to add private groups as partners and to make bold decisions that transcend turf politics. Climate change seems to be hurting Yellowstone—by way of temperature ranges, insect cycles, drought, who knows what else—and we all need to do better on fixing that.

Ha, easier said than done. But if the Yellowstone grizzly bear is expected to adapt, modify its behavior, and cope with new realities, shouldn't we be expected to do that too?

## Mother Jones

WINNER—REPORTING

*When Shane Bauer went to work as a prison guard at the oldest privately operated medium-security facility in the United States, no one seemed interested in his background—as a senior reporter at* Mother Jones *or as the coauthor of* A Sliver of Light, *the story of the two years he spent in an Iranian prison. Only later did they try to stop him from writing this story. Bauer's 26,000-word account of his four months at Winn Correctional Center, supported by another fourteen months of reporting, earned* Mother Jones *the first of the two Ellies it won in 2017. The second was for Magazine of the Year. Judges praised the article not only for its quality but also for emulating the heroic work of investigative journalists from Nellie Bly to Ben Bagdikian.*

Shane Bauer

# My Four Months as a Private Prison Guard

## Chapter 1: "Inmates Run This Bitch"

"Have you ever had a riot?" I ask a recruiter from a prison run by the Corrections Corporation of America (CCA).

"The last riot we had was two years ago," he says over the phone.

"Yeah, but that was with the Puerto Ricans!" says a woman's voice, cutting in. "We got rid of them."

"When can you start?" the man asks.

I tell him I need to think it over.

I take a breath. Am I really going to become a prison guard? Now that it might actually happen, it feels scary and a bit extreme.

I started applying for jobs in private prisons because I wanted to see the inner workings of an industry that holds 131,000 of the nation's 1.6 million prisoners. As a journalist, it's nearly impossible to get an unconstrained look inside our penal system. When prisons do let reporters in, it's usually for carefully managed tours and monitored interviews with inmates. Private prisons are especially secretive. Their records often aren't subject to public-access laws; CCA has fought to defeat legislation that would make private prisons subject to the same disclosure rules as their public counterparts. And even if I could get uncensored information from private prison inmates, how would I verify their claims? I keep coming back to this question: Is there any other way to see what really happens inside a private prison?

CCA certainly seemed eager to give me a chance to join its team. Within two weeks of filling out its online application, using my real name and personal information, several CCA prisons contacted me, some multiple times.

They weren't interested in the details of my résumé. They didn't ask about my job history, my current employment with the Foundation for National Progress, the publisher of *Mother Jones*, or why someone who writes about criminal justice in California would want to move across the country to work in a prison. They didn't even ask about the time I was arrested for shoplifting when I was nineteen.

When I call Winn Correctional Center in Winnfield, Louisiana, the HR lady who answers is chipper and has a smoky Southern voice. "I should tell you upfront that the job only pays nine dollars an hour, but the prison is in the middle of a national forest. Do you like to hunt and fish?"

"I like fishing."

"Well, there is plenty of fishing, and people around here like to hunt squirrels. You ever squirrel hunt?"

"No."

"Well, I think you'll like Louisiana. I know it's not a lot of money, but they say you can go from a CO to a warden in just seven years! The CEO of the company started out as a CO"—a corrections officer.

Ultimately, I choose Winn. Not only does Louisiana have the highest incarceration rate in the world—more than 800 prisoners per 100,000 residents—but Winn is the oldest privately operated medium-security prison in the country.

I phone HR and tell her I'll take the job.

"Well, poop can stick!" she says.

I pass the background check within twenty-four hours.

.     .     .

Two weeks later, in November 2014, having grown a goatee, pulled the plugs from my earlobes, and bought a beat-up Dodge Ram pickup, I pull into Winnfield, a hardscrabble town of 4,600 people three hours north of Baton Rouge. I drive past the former Mexican restaurant that now serves drive-thru daiquiris to people heading home from work, and down a street of collapsed wooden houses, empty except for a tethered dog. About 38 percent of households here live below the poverty line; the median household income is $25,000. Residents are proud of the fact that three governors came from Winnfield. They are less proud that the last sheriff was locked up for dealing meth.

Thirteen miles away, Winn Correctional Center lies in the middle of the Kisatchie National Forest, 600,000 acres of Southern yellow pines crosshatched with dirt roads. As I drive through the thick forest, the prison emerges from the fog. You might mistake the dull expanse of cement buildings and corrugated metal sheds for an oddly placed factory were it not for the office-park-style sign displaying CCA's corporate logo, with the head of a bald eagle inside the "A."

At the entrance, a guard who looks about sixty, a gun on her hip, asks me to turn off my truck, open the doors, and step out. A tall, stern-faced man leads a German shepherd into the cab of my truck. My heart hammers. I tell the woman I'm a new cadet, here to start my four weeks of training. She directs me to a building just outside the prison fence.

"Have a good one, baby," she says as I pull through the gate. I exhale.

I park, find the classroom, and sit down with five other students.

"You nervous?" a nineteen-year-old black guy asks me. I'll call him Reynolds. (I've changed the names and nicknames of the people I met in prison unless noted otherwise.)

"A little," I say. "You?"

"Nah, I been around," he says. "I seen killin'. My uncle killed three people. My brother been in jail, and my cousin." He has scars on his arms. One, he says, is from a shootout in Baton Rouge. The other is from a street fight in Winnfield. He elbowed someone in the face, and the next thing he knew he got knifed from behind. "It was some gang shit." He says he just needs a job until he starts college in a few months. He has a baby to feed. He also wants to put speakers in his truck. They told him he could work on his days off, so he'll probably come in every day. "That will be a fat paycheck." He puts his head down on the table and falls asleep.

The human resources director comes in and scolds Reynolds for napping. He perks up when she tells us that if we recruit a friend to work here, we'll get 500 bucks. She gives us an assortment of other tips: Don't eat the food given to inmates; don't have sex with them or you could be fined $10,000 or get ten years at hard labor; try not to get sick because we don't get paid sick time. If we have friends or relatives incarcerated here, we need to report it. She hands out fridge magnets with the number of a hotline to use if we feel suicidal or start fighting with our families. We get three counseling sessions for free.

I studiously jot down notes as the HR director fires up a video of the company's CEO, Damon Hininger, who tells us what a great opportunity it is to be a corrections officer at CCA. Once a guard himself, he made $3.4 million in 2015, nearly nineteen times the salary of the director of the Federal Bureau of Prisons. "You may be brand new to CCA," Hininger says, "but we need you. We need your enthusiasm. We need your bright ideas. During the academy, I felt camaraderie. I felt a little anxiety too. That is completely normal. The other thing I felt was tremendous excitement."

I look around the room. Not one person—not the recent high school graduate, not the former Walmart manager, not the nurse, not the mother of twins who's come back to Winn after ten years of McDonald's and a stint in the military—looks excited.

"I don't think this is for me," a postal worker says.

## *"Do not run!"*

The next day, I wake up at six a.m. in my apartment in the nearby town where I decided to live to minimize my chances of running into off-duty guards. I feel a shaky, electric nervousness as I put a pen that doubles as an audio recorder into my shirt pocket.

In class that day, we learn about the use of force. A middle-aged black instructor I'll call Mr. Tucker comes into the classroom, his black fatigues tucked into shiny black boots. He's the head of Winn's Special Operations Response Team, or SORT, the prison's SWAT-like tactical unit. "If an inmate was to spit in your face, what would you do?" he asks. Some cadets say they would write him up. One woman, who has worked here for thirteen years and is doing her annual retraining, says, "I would want to hit him. Depending on where the camera is, he might would get hit."

Mr. Tucker pauses to see if anyone else has a response. "If your personality if somebody spit on you is to knock the fuck out of him, you gonna knock the fuck out of him," he says, pacing slowly. "If a inmate hit me, I'm go' hit his ass right back. I don't care if the camera's rolling. If a inmate spit on me, he's gonna have a very bad day." Mr. Tucker says we should call for backup in any confrontation. "If a midget spit on you, guess what? You still supposed to call for backup. You don't supposed to ever get into a one-on-one encounter with anybody. Period. Whether you can take him or not. Hell, if you got a problem with a midget, call me. I'll help you. Me and you can whup the hell out of him."

He asks us what we should do if we see two inmates stabbing each other.

"I'd probably call somebody," a cadet offers.

"I'd sit there and holler 'stop,'" says a veteran guard.

Mr. Tucker points at her. "Damn right. That's it. If they don't pay attention to you, hey, there ain't nothing else you can do."

He cups his hands around his mouth. "Stop fighting," he says to some invisible prisoners. "I said, 'Stop fighting.'" His voice is nonchalant. "Y'all ain't go' to stop, huh?" He makes like he's backing out of a door and slams it shut. "Leave your ass in there!"

"Somebody's go' win. Somebody's go' lose. They both might lose, but hey, did you do your job? Hell yeah!" The classroom erupts in laughter.

We *could* try to break up a fight if we wanted, he says, but since we won't have pepper spray or a nightstick, he wouldn't recommend it. "We are not going to pay you that much," he says emphatically. "The next raise you get is not going to be much more than the one you got last time. The only thing that's important to us is that we go home at the end of the day. Period. So if them fools want to cut each other, well, happy cutting."

When we return from break, Mr. Tucker sets a tear gas launcher and canisters on the table. "On any given day, they can take this facility," he says. "At chow time, there are 800 inmates and just two COs. But with just this class, we could take it back." He passes out sheets for us to sign, stating that we volunteer to be tear-gassed. If we do not sign, he says, our training is over, which means our jobs end right here. (When I later ask CCA if its staff members are required to be exposed to tear gas, spokesman Steven Owen says no.) "Anybody have asthma?" Mr. Tucker says. "Two people had asthma in the last class and I said, 'Okay, well, I'ma spray 'em anyway.' Can we spray an inmate? The answer is yes."

Five of us walk outside and stand in a row, arms linked. Mr. Tucker tests the wind with a finger and drops a tear gas cartridge. A white cloud of gas washes over us. The object is to avoid panicking, staying in the same place until the gas dissipates. My throat is suddenly on fire and my eyes seal shut. I try desperately to breathe, but I can only choke. "Do not run!" Mr. Tucker shouts at a cadet who is stumbling off blindly. I double over. I want to throw up. I hear a woman crying. My upper lip is thick with snot. When our breath starts coming back, the two women linked to me hug each other. I want to hug them too. The three of us laugh a little as tears keep pouring down our cheeks.

### *"Don't ever say thank you"*

Our instructors advise us to carry a notebook to keep track of everything prisoners will ask us for. I keep one in my breast pocket and jet into the bathroom periodically to jot things down. They also encourage us to invest in a watch because when we document rule infractions it is important that we record the time precisely. A few days into training, a wristwatch arrives in the mail. One of the little knobs on its side activates a recorder. On its face there is a tiny camera lens.

On the eighth day, we are pulled from CPR class and sent inside the compound to Elm—one of five single-story brick buildings where the prison's roughly 1,500 inmates live. When we go through security, we are told to empty our pockets and remove our shoes and belts. This is intensely nerve-wracking: I send my watch, pen, employee ID, and pocket change through the X-ray machine. I walk through the metal detector and a CO runs a wand up and down my body and pats down my chest, back, arms, and legs.

The other cadets and I gather at a barred gate and an officer, looking at us through thick glass, turns a switch that opens it slowly. We pass through, and after the gate closes behind us, another opens ahead. On the other side, the CCA logo is emblazoned on the wall along with the words "Respect" and "Integrity" and a mural of two anchors inexplicably floating at sea. Another gate clangs open and our small group steps onto the main outdoor artery of the prison: "the walk."

From above, the walk is shaped like a "T." It is fenced in with chain-link and covered with corrugated steel. Yellow lines divide the pavement into three lanes. Clustered and nervous, we cadets travel up the middle lane from the administration building as prisoners move down their designated side lanes. I greet inmates as they pass, trying hard to appear loose and unafraid. Some say good morning. Others stop in their tracks and make a point of looking the female cadets up and down.

We walk past the squat, dull buildings that house visitation, programming, the infirmary, and a church with a wrought-iron gate shaped into the words "Freedom Chapel." Beyond it there is a mural of a fighter jet dropping a bomb into a mountain lake, water blasting skyward, and a giant bald eagle soaring overhead, backgrounded by an American flag. At the top of the T we take a left, past the chow hall and the canteen, where inmates can buy snacks, toiletries, tobacco, music players, and batteries.

The units sit along the top of the walk. Each is shaped like an "X" and connected to the main walk by its own short, covered walk. Every unit is named after a type of tree. Most are general population units, where inmates mingle in dorm-style halls and can leave for programs and chow. Cypress is the high-security segregation unit, the only one where inmates are confined to cells.

In Dogwood, reserved for the best-behaved inmates, prisoners get special privileges like extra television time, and many work outside the unit in places like the metal shop, the garment factory, or the chow hall. Some "trusties" even get to work in the front office or beyond the fence washing employees' personal cars. Birch holds most of the elderly, infirm, and mentally ill inmates, though it doesn't offer any special services. Then there are Ash and Elm, which inmates call "the projects." The more troublesome prisoners live here.

We enter Elm and walk onto an open, shiny cement floor. The air is slightly sweet and musty, like the clothes of a heavy smoker. Elm can house up to 352 inmates. At the center is an enclosed octagonal control room called "the key." Inside, a "key officer," invariably a woman, watches the feeds of the unit's twenty-seven-odd surveillance cameras, keeps a log of significant occurrences, and writes passes that give inmates permission to go to locations outside the unit, like school or the gym. Also in the key is the office of the unit manager, the "mini-warden" of the unit.

The key stands in the middle of "the floor." Branching out from the floor are the four legs of the X; two tiers run down the length of each leg. Separated from the floor by a locked gate, every tier is an open dormitory that houses up to forty-four men, each with his own narrow bed, thin mattress, and metal locker.

Toward the front of each tier, there are two toilets, a trough-style urinal, and two sinks. There are two showers, open except for a three-foot wall separating them from the common area. Nearby are a microwave, a telephone, and a Jpay machine, where inmates pay to download songs onto their portable players and send short, monitored emails for about thirty cents each. Each tier also has a TV room, which fills up every weekday at twelve-thirty p.m. for the prison's most popular show, *The Young and the Restless*.

At Winn, staff and inmates alike refer to guards as "free people." Like the prisoners, the majority of the COs at Winn are African American. More than half are women, many of them single moms. But in Ash and Elm, the floor officers—who more than anyone else deal with the inmates face-to-face—are exclusively men. Floor officers are both enforcers and a prisoner's first point of contact if he needs something. It is their job to conduct security checks every thirty minutes, walking up and down each tier to make sure nothing is awry. Three times per twelve-hour shift, all movement in the prison stops, and the floor officers count the inmates. There are almost never more than two floor officers per general population unit. That's one per 176 inmates. (CCA later tells me that the Louisiana Department of Corrections, or DOC, considered the "staffing pattern" at Winn "appropriate.")

In Elm, a tall white CO named Christian is waiting for us with a leashed German shepherd. He tells the female cadets to go to the key and the male cadets to line up along the showers and toilets at the front of the tier. We put on latex gloves. The inmates are sitting on their beds. Two ceiling fans turn slowly. The room is filled with fluorescent light. Almost every prisoner is black.

A small group of inmates get up from their beds and file into the shower area. One, his body covered with tattoos, gets in the shower in front of me, pulls off his shirt and shorts, and hands them to me to inspect. "Do a one-finger lift, turn around, bend, squat, cough," Christian orders. In one fluid motion, the man lifts his penis, opens his mouth, lifts his tongue, spins around with his ass facing me, squats, and coughs. He hands me his sandals and shows me the soles of his feet. I hand him his clothes and he puts his shorts on, walks past me, and nods respectfully.

Like a human assembly line, the inmates file in. "Beyond, squawt, cough," Christian drawls. He tells one inmate to open his hand. The inmate uncurls his finger and reveals a SIM card. Christian takes it but does nothing.

Eventually, the TV room is full of prisoners. A guard looks at them and smiles. "Tear 'em up!" he says, gesturing down the tier. Each of us, women included, stops at a bed. Christian tells one cadet to "shake down bed eight real good—just because he pissed me off." He tells us to search everything. I follow the other guards' lead, opening bottles of toothpaste and lotion. Inside a container of Vaseline, I find a one-hitter pipe made out of a pen and ask Christian what to do with it. He takes it from me, mutters "eh," and tosses it on the floor. I go through the mattress, pillow, dirty socks, and underwear. I flip through photos of kids, and of women posing seductively. I move on to new lockers: ramen, chips, dentures, hygiene products, peanut butter, cocoa powder, cookies, candy, salt, moldy bread, a dirty coffee cup. I find the draft of a novel, dedicated to "all the hustlers, bastards, strugglers, and hoodlum childs who are chasing their dreams."

One instructor notices that I am carefully putting each object back where I found it and tells me to pull everything out of the lockers and leave it on the beds. I look down the tier and see mattresses lying on the floor, papers and food dumped across beds. The middle of the floor is strewn with contraband: USB cables refashioned as phone chargers, tubs of butter, slices of cheese, and pills. I find some hamburger patties taken from the cafeteria. A guard tells me to throw them into the pile.

Inmates are glued up against the TV room window, watching a young white cadet named Miss Stirling pick through their stuff. She's pretty and petite, with long, jet-black hair. The attention makes her uncomfortable; she thinks the inmates are gross. Earlier this week, she said she would refuse to give an inmate CPR and won't try the cafeteria food because she doesn't want to "eat AIDS." The more she is around prisoners, though, the more I notice her grapple with an inner conflict. "I don't want to treat everyone like a criminal because I've done things myself," she says.

Miss Stirling says she sometimes wonders if her baby's dad will end up here. She doesn't like doing chokehold escapes in class because they bring back memories of him. He cooked meth in their toolshed and once beat her so badly he dislocated her shoulder and knee. "You know that bone at the bottom of your neck? He pushed it up into my head," she says.

If he ends up in this prison, another cadet assures her, "we could make his life hell."

As we shake down the tier, a prisoner comes out of the TV room to get a better look at Miss Stirling, and she yells at him to go back in. He does.

"Thank you," she says.

"Did she just say thank you?" Christian asks. A bunch of COs scoff.

"Don't ever say thank you," a woman CO tells her. "That takes the power away from it."

*"Ain't no order here"*

Most of our training is uneventful. Some days there are no more than two hours of classes, and then we have to sit and run the clock to four-fifteen p.m. We pass the time discussing each other's lives. I try mostly to stay quiet, but when I slip into describing a backpacking trip I recently took in California, a cadet throws her arms in the air and shouts, "Why are you here?!" I am careful to never lie, instead backing out with generalities like, "I came here for work," or "You never know where life will take you," and no one pries further.

Few of my fellow cadets have traveled farther than nearby Oklahoma. They compare towns by debating the size and quality of their Walmarts. Most are young. They eat candy during break time, write their names on the whiteboard in cutesy lettering, and talk about different ways to get high.

Miss Doucet, a stocky redheaded cadet in her late fifties, thinks that if kids were made to read the Bible in school, fewer would be in prison, but she also sticks pins in a voodoo doll to mete out vengeance. "I swing both ways," she says. She lives in a camper with her daughter and grandkids. With this job, she's hoping to save up for a double-wide trailer.

She worked at the lumber mill in Winnfield for years, but worsening asthma put an end to that. She's been hospitalized several times this year and says she almost died once. "They don't even want me to bring this in," she whispers, leaning in, pulling her inhaler out of her pocket. "I'm not supposed to, but I do. They ain't takin' it away from me." She takes a long drag from her cigarette.

Miss Doucet and others from the class ahead of mine go to the front office to get their paychecks for their first two weeks of work. When they return, the shoulders of a young cadet are slumping. He says his check was for $577, after they took $121 in taxes.

"Dang. That hurts," he says.

Miss Doucet says they withheld $114 from her check.

"They held less for you?!" the young cadet says.

"I'm may-ried!" she says in a singsong voice. "I got a chi-ild!"

Outwardly, Miss Doucet is jovial and cocky, but she is already making mental adjustments to her dreams. The double-wide trailer she imagines her grandkids spreading out in becomes a single-wide. She figures she can get $5,000 for the RV.

At the end of one morning of doing nothing, the training co-ordinator tells us we can go to the gym to watch inmates graduate from trade classes. Prisoners and their families are milling around with plates of cake and cups of fruit punch. An inmate offers a piece of red velvet to Miss Stirling.

I stand around with Collinsworth, an eighteen-year-old cadet with a chubby white baby face hidden behind a brown beard and a wisp of bangs. Before CCA, Collinsworth worked at a Starbucks. When he came to Winnfield to help out with family, this was the first job he could get. Once, Collinsworth was nearly kicked out of class after he jokingly threatened to stab Mr. Tucker with a plastic training knife. He's boasted to me about inmate-management tactics he's learned from seasoned officers. "You just pit 'em against each other and that's the easiest way to get your job done," he tells me. He says one guard told him that inmates should tell troublemakers, "'I'm gonna rape you if you try that shit again.' Or something; whatever it takes."

As Collinsworth and I stand around, inmates gather to look at our watches. One, wearing a cocked gray beanie, asks to buy them. I refuse outright. Collinsworth dithers. "How old you is?" the inmate asks him.

"You never know," Collinsworth says.

"Man, all these fake-ass signals," the inmate says. "The best thing you could do is get to know people in the place."

"I understand it's your home," Collinsworth says. "But I'm at work right now."

"It's your home for twelve hours a day! You trippin'. You 'bout to do half my time with me. You straight with that?"

"It's probably true."

"It ain't no 'probably true.' If you go' be at this bitch, you go' do twelve hours a day." He tells Collinsworth not to bother writing up inmates for infractions: "They ain't payin' you enough for that." Seeming torn between whether to impress me or the inmate, Collinsworth says he will only write up serious offenses, like hiding drugs.

"Drugs?! Don't worry 'bout the drugs." The inmate says he was caught recently with two ounces of "mojo," or synthetic marijuana, which is the drug of choice at Winn. The inmate says guards turn a blind eye to it. They "ain't trippin' on that shit," he says. "I'm telling you, it ain't that type of camp. You can't come change things by yourself. You might as well go with the flow. Get this free-ass, easy-ass money, and go home."

"I'm just here to do my job and take care of my family," Collinsworth says. "I'm not gonna bring stuff in 'cuz even if I don't get caught, there's always the chance that I will."

"Nah. Ain't no chance," the inmate says. "I ain't never heard of nobody movin' good and low-key gettin' caught. Nah. I know a dude still rolling. He been doin' it six years." He looks at Collinsworth. "Easy."

The inmates' families file out the side entrance. A couple of minutes after the last visitors leave, the coach shouts, "All inmates on the bleachers!" A prisoner tosses his graduation certificate dramatically into the trash. Another lifts the podium over his head and runs with it across the gym. The coach shouts, exasperated, as prisoners scramble around.

"You see this chaos?" the inmate in the beanie says to Collinsworth. "If you'd been to other camps, you'd see the order they got. Ain't no order here. Inmates run this bitch, son."

A week later, Mr. Tucker tells us to come in early to do shakedowns. The sky is barely lit as I stand on the walk at six-thirty with the other cadets. Collinsworth tells us another prisoner offered to buy his watch. He said he'd sell it for $600. The inmate declined.

"Don't sell it to him anyway," Miss Stirling admonishes him. "You might get $600, but if they find out, you ain't go' get no more paychecks."

"Nah, I wouldn't actually do it. I just said $600 because I know they don't got $600 to give me."

"Shit," a heavyset black cadet named Willis says. He's our main authority on prison life. He says he served seven and a half years in the Texas State Penitentiary; he won't say what for. (CCA hires former felons whom it deems not to be a security risk; it says all Winn guards' background checks were also reviewed by the DOC.) "Dudes was showing me pictures," says Willis. "They got money in here. One dude in here, don't say nothin', but he got like six to eight thousand dollars. They got it on cards. Little money cards and shit."

Collinsworth jumps up and down. "Dude, I'ma find me one of them damn cards! Hell yeah. And I will not report it."

Officially, inmates are only allowed to keep money in special prison-operated accounts that can be used at the canteen. In these accounts, prisoners with jobs receive their wages, which may be as little as two cents an hour for a dishwasher and as much as twenty cents for a sewing-machine operator at Winn's garment factory. Their families can also deposit money in the accounts.

The prepaid cash cards Willis is referring to are called Green Dots, and they are the currency of the illicit prison economy. Connections on the outside buy them online, then pass on the account numbers in encoded messages through the mail or during visits. Inmates with contraband cell phones can do all these transactions themselves, buying the cards and handing out strips of paper as payments for drugs or phones or whatever else.

Miss Stirling divulges that an inmate gave her the digits of a money card as a Christmas gift. "I'm like, damn! I need a new MK watch. I need a new purse. I need some new jeans."

"There was this one dude in Dogwood," she continues. "He came up to the bars and showed me a stack of hundred-dollar bills folded up, and it was like this—" She makes like she's holding a wad of cash four inches thick. "And I was like, 'I'm not go' say anything.'"

"Dude! I'ma shake him the fuck down!" Collinsworth says. "I don't care if he's cool."

"He had a phone," Miss Stirling says, "and he's like, 'I don't have the time of day to hide it. I just keep it in the open. I really don't give a fuck.'"

Mr. Tucker tells us to follow him. We shake down tiers all morning. By the time we finish at eleven, everyone is exhausted. "I'm not mad we had to do shakedowns. I'm just mad we didn't find anything," Collinsworth says. Christian pulls a piece of paper out of his pocket and reads off a string of numbers in a show-offy way. "A Green Dot," he says. Christian hands the slip of paper to one of the cadets, a middle-aged white woman. "You can have this one," he says. "I have plenty already." She smiles coyly.

## *"We are going to win this unit back"*

"Welcome to the hellhole," a female CO greeted me the first time I visited the segregation unit. A few days later I'm back at Cypress with Collinsworth and Reynolds to shadow some guards. The metal door clicks open and we enter to a cacophony of shouting and pounding on metal. An alarm is sounding and the air smells strongly of smoke.

On one wall is a mural of a prison nestled among dark mountains and shrouded in storm clouds, lightning striking the guard towers and an enormous, screeching bald eagle descending with a giant pair of handcuffs in its talons. Toward the end of a long hall of cells, an officer in a black SWAT-style uniform stands ready with a pepper-ball gun. Another man in black is pulling burnt parts of a mattress out of a cell. Cypress can hold up to 200 inmates; most of the eight-by-eight-foot cells have two prisoners in them. The cells look like tombs; men lie in their bunks, wrapped in blankets, staring at the walls. Many are lit only by the light from the hallway. In one, an inmate is washing his clothes in his toilet.

"How are you doing?" says a smiling white man dressed business casual. He grips my hand. "Thank you for being here." Assistant Warden Parker is new to CCA, but he was once the associate warden of a federal prison. "I know it seems crazy back here now, but you'll learn the ropes," he assures me. "We are going to win this unit back. It's not going to happen in an hour. It's gonna take time, but it will happen." Apparently the segregation unit has been in a state of upheaval for a while, so corporate headquarters has sent in SORT officers from out of state to bring it back under control. SORT teams are trained to suppress riots, rescue hostages, extract inmates from their cells, and neutralize violent prisoners. They deploy an array of "less lethal" weapons like plastic buckshot, electrified shields, and chili-pepper-filled projectiles that burst on contact.

I get a whiff of feces that quickly becomes overpowering. On one of the tiers, a brown liquid oozes out of a bottle on the floor. Food, wads of paper, and garbage are all over the ground. I spot a Coke can, charred black, with a piece of cloth sticking out of it like a fuse. "I use my political voice!" an inmate shouts. "I stand up for my rights. Hahaha! Ain't nowhere like this camp. Shit, y'all's disorganized as fuck up in here."

"That's why we are here," a SORT member says. "We are going to change all that."

"Y'all can't change shit," the prisoner yells back. "They ain't got shit for us here. We ain't got no jobs. No rec time. We just sit in our cells all day. What you think gonna happen when a man got nuttin' to do? That's why we throw shit out on the tier. What else are we going to do? You know how we get these officers to respect us? We throw piss on 'em. That's the only way. Either that or throw them to the floor. Then they respect us."

I ask one of the regular white-shirted COs what an average day in seg looks like. "To be honest with you, normally we just sit here at this table all day long," he tells me. They are supposed to walk up and down the eight tiers every thirty minutes to check on the inmates, but he says they never do that. (CCA says it had no knowledge of guards at Winn skipping security checks before I inquired about it.)

Collinsworth is walking around with a big smile on his face. He's learning how to take inmates out of their cells for disciplinary court, which is inside Cypress. He's supposed to cuff them through the slot in the bars, then tell the CO at the end of the tier to open the gate remotely. "Fuck nah, I ain't coming out of this cell!" an inmate shouts at him. "You go' have to get SORT to bring me up out of here. That's how we do early in the morning. I'll fuck y'all up." The prisoner climbs up on the bars and pounds on the metal above the cell door. The sound explodes down the cement hallway.

Collinsworth and the CO he is shadowing move another inmate from his cell. The inmate tries to walk ahead as the CO holds him. "If that motherfucker starts pulling away from me like that again, I'm gonna make him eat concrete," the CO says to Collinsworth.

"I kind of hope he does mess around again," Collinsworth says, beaming. "That would be fun!"

I take a few inmates out of their cells, too, walking each one a hundred feet or so to disciplinary court with my hand around one of his elbows. One pulls against my grip. "Why you pulling on me, man?" he shouts, spinning around to stand face-to-face with me. A SORT officer rushes over and grabs him. My heart races.

One of the white-shirted officers takes me aside. "Hey, don't let these guys push you around," he says. "If he is pulling away from you, you tell him, 'Stop resisting.' If he doesn't, you stop. If he keeps going, we are authorized to knee him in the back of the leg and drop him to the concrete."

Inmates shout at me as I walk back down the tier. "He has a little twist in his walk. I like them holes in your ears, CO. Come in here with me. Give me that booty!"

At lunchtime, Collinsworth, Reynolds, and I go back to the training room. "I love it here," Collinsworth says dreamily. "It's like a community."

## Chapter 2: Prison Experiments

People say a lot of negative things about CCA," the head of training, Miss Blanchard, tells us. "That we'll hire anybody. That we are scraping the bottom of the barrel. Which is not really true, but if you come here and you breathing and you got a valid driver's license and you willing to work, then we're willing to hire you." She warns us repeatedly, however, that to become corrections officers, we'll need to pass a test at the end of our four weeks of training. We will need to know the name of the CEO, the names of the company's founders, and their reason for establishing the first private prison more than thirty years ago. (Correct answer: "to alleviate the overcrowding in the world market.")

To prepare us, Miss Blanchard shows a video in which CCA founders T. Don Hutto and Thomas Beasley playfully tell their company's origin story. In 1983, they recount, they won "the first contract ever to design, build, finance, and operate a secure correctional facility in the world." The Immigration and Naturalization Service gave them just ninety days to do it. Hutto recalls how the pair quickly converted a Houston motel into a detention center: "We opened the facility on Super Bowl Sunday the end of that January. So about ten o'clock that night we start receiving inmates. I actually took their pictures and fingerprinted them. Several other people walked them to their 'rooms,' if you will, and we got our first day's pay for eighty-seven undocumented aliens." Both men chuckle.

There is much about the history of CCA the video does not teach. The idea of privatizing prisons originated in the early 1980s with Beasley and fellow businessman Doctor Robert Crants. The two had no experience in corrections, so they recruited Hutto, who had been the head of Virginia's and Arkansas's prisons. In a 1978 ruling, the Supreme Court had found that a succession of Arkansas prison administrations, including Hutto's, "tried to operate their prisons at a profit." Guards on horseback herded the inmates, who sometimes did not have shoes, to the fields. The year after Hutto joined CCA, he became the head of the American Correctional Association, the largest prison association in the world.

To Beasley, the former chairman of the Tennessee Republican Party, the business of private prisons was simple: "You just sell it like you were selling cars, or real estate, or hamburgers," he told *Inc.* magazine in 1988. Beasley and Crants ran the business a lot like a hotel chain, charging the government a daily rate for each inmate. Early investors included Sodexho-Marriott and the venture capitalist Jack Massey, who helped build Kentucky Fried Chicken, Wendy's, and the Hospital Corporation of America.

The 1980s were a good time to get into the incarceration business. The prison population was skyrocketing, the drug war was heating up, the length of sentences was increasing, and states were starting to mandate that prisoners serve at least 85 percent of their terms. Between 1980 and 1990, state spending on prisons quadrupled, but it wasn't enough. Prisons in many states were filled beyond capacity. When a federal court declared in 1985 that Tennessee's overcrowded prisons violated the Eighth Amendment's ban on cruel and unusual punishment, CCA made an audacious proposal to take over the state's entire prison system. The bid was unsuccessful, but it planted an idea in the minds of politicians across the country: They could outsource prison management and save money in the process. Privatization also gave states a way to quickly expand their prison systems without taking on new debt. In the perfect marriage of fiscal and tough-on-crime conservatism, the companies would fund and construct new lockups while the courts would keep them full.

When CCA shares appeared on the NASDAQ stock exchange in 1986, the company was operating two juvenile-detention centers and two immigrant-detention centers. Today, it runs more than sixty facilities, from state prisons and jails to federal immigration-detention centers. All together, CCA houses at least 66,000 inmates at any given time. Its main competitor, the GEO Group, holds more than 70,000 inmates in the United States. Currently, private prisons oversee about 8 percent of the country's total prison population.

Whatever taxpayer money CCA receives has to cover the cost of housing, feeding, and rehabilitating inmates. While I work at Winn, CCA receives about thirty-four dollars per inmate per day. In comparison, the average daily cost per inmate at the state's publicly run prisons is about fifty-two dollars. Some states pay CCA as much as eighty per prisoner per day. In 2015, CCA reported $1.9 billion in revenue; it made more than $221 million in net income—more than $3,300 for each prisoner in its care. CCA and other prison companies have written "occupancy guarantees" into their contracts, requiring states to pay a fee if they cannot provide a certain number of inmates. Two-thirds of the private-prison contracts recently reviewed by the anti-privatization group In the Public Interest had these prisoner quotas. Under CCA's contract, Winn was guaranteed to be 96 percent full.

The main argument in favor of private prisons—that they save taxpayers money—remains controversial. One study estimated that private prisons cost 15 percent less than public ones; another found that public prisons were 14 percent cheaper. After reviewing these competing claims, researchers concluded that the savings "appear minimal." CCA directed me to a 2013 report—funded in part by the company and GEO—that claimed private prisons could save states as much as 59 percent over public prisons without sacrificing quality.

Private prisons' cost savings are "modest," according to one Justice Department study, and are achieved mostly through "moderate reductions in staffing patterns, fringe benefits, and other labor-related costs." Wages and benefits account for 59 percent of CCA's operating expenses. When I start at Winn, nonranking guards make $9 an hour, no matter how long they've worked there. The starting pay for guards at public state prisons comes out to $12.50 an hour. CCA told me that it "set[s] salaries based on the prevailing wages in local markets," adding that "the wages we provided in Winn Parish were competitive for that area."

Based on data from Louisiana's budget office, the cost per prisoner at Winn, adjusted for inflation, dropped nearly 20 percent between the late nineties and 2014. The pressure to squeeze the most out of every penny at Winn seems evident not only in our paychecks but in decisions that keep staffing and staff-intensive programming for inmates at the barest of levels. When I asked CCA about the frequent criticism I heard from both staff and inmates about its relentless focus on the bottom line, its spokesman dismissed the assertion as "a cookie-cutter complaint," adding that it would be false "to claim that CCA prioritizes its own economic gain over the needs of its customers" or the safety of its inmates.

*The Escape*

Two weeks after I start training, Chase Cortez (his real name) decides he has had enough of Winn. It's been nearly three years since he was locked up for theft, and he has only three months to go. But in the middle of a cool, sunny December day, he climbs onto the roof of Birch unit. He lies down and waits for the patrol vehicle to pass along the perimeter. He is in view of the guard towers, but they've been unmanned since at least 2010. Now, a single CO watches the video feeds from at least thirty cameras.

Cortez sees the patrol van pass, jumps down from the back side of the building, climbs the razor-wire perimeter fence, and then makes a run for the forest. He fumbles through the dense foliage until he spots a white pickup truck left by a hunter. Lucky for him, it is unlocked, with the key in the ignition.

In the control room, an alarm sounds, indicating that someone has touched the outer fence, a possible sign of a perimeter breach. The officer reaches over, switches the alarm off, and goes back to whatever she was doing. She notices nothing on the video screen, and she does not review the footage. Hours pass before the staff realizes someone is missing. Some guards tell me it was an inmate who finally brought the escape to their attention. Cortez is caught that evening after the sheriff chases him and he crashes the truck into a fence.

When I come in the next morning, the prison is on lockdown. Staff are worried CCA is going to lose its contract with Louisiana. "We were already in the red, and this just added to it," the assistant training director tells me. "It's a lot of tension right now."

CCA said nothing publicly about the escape; I heard about it from guards who had investigated the incident or been briefed by the warden. (The company later told me it conducted a "full review" of the incident and fired a staff member "for lack of proper response to the alarm." When I asked CCA about its decision to remove guards from Winn's watchtowers, its spokesman replied that "newer technologies . . . are making guard towers largely obsolete.")

Later that day, Reynolds and I bring food to Cypress, the segregation unit. It is dinnertime, but inmates haven't had lunch yet.

A naked man is shouting frantically for food, mercilessly slapping the plexiglass at the front of his cell. In the cell next to him, a small, wiry man is squatting on the floor in his underwear. His arms and face are scraped with little cuts. A guard tells me to watch him.

It is Cortez. I offer him a packet of Kool-Aid in a foam cup. He says thank you, then asks if I will put water in it. There is no water in his cell.

•     •     •

When inmates are written up for breaking the rules, they are sent to inmate court, which is held in a room in the corner of Cypress unit. One day, our class files into the small room to watch the hearings. Miss Lawson, the assistant chief of security, is acting as the judge, sitting at a desk in front of a mural of the scales of justice. "Even though we treat every inmate like they are guilty until proven innocent, they are . . . ?" She pauses for someone to fill in the answer.

"Innocent?" a cadet offers.

"That's right. Innocent until proven guilty."

This is not a court of law, although it issues punishments for felonies such as assault and attempted murder. An inmate who stabs another may end up facing new criminal charges. He may be transferred, yet prisoners and guards say inmates who stab others typically are not shipped to a higher-security prison. The consequences for less serious offenses are usually stints in seg or a loss of "good time," sentence reduction for good behavior. According to the DOC, Winn inmates charged with serious rule violations are found guilty at least 96 percent of the time.

"Inmate counsel, has your defendant appeared before the court?" Miss Lawson asks a prisoner standing at the podium.

"No, ma'am, he has not," he replies. The inmate counsel represents other inmates in the internal disciplinary process. Every year, he is taken to a state-run prison for intensive training. Miss Lawson later tells me that inmate counsel never really influences her decisions.

The absent inmate is accused of coming too close to the main entrance. "Would the counsel like to offer a defense?"

"No, ma'am."

"How does he plead?"

"Not guilty."

"Mr. Trahan is found guilty." The entire "trial" lasts less than two minutes.

The next defendant is called.

He is being considered for release from segregation. "Do you know your Bible?" Miss Lawson asks.

"Yes, ma'am."

"Do you remember in the Gospel of John when the adulteress was brought before Jesus? What did he say?"

"I don't remember that, ma'am."

"He says, 'Sin no more.'" She points for him to leave the room.

The next inmate, an orderly in Cypress, enters. He is charged with being in an unauthorized area because he took a broom to sweep the tier during rec time, which is not the authorized time to sweep the tier. He starts to explain that a CO gave him permission. Miss Lawson cuts him off. "How would you like to plead?"

"Guilty, I guess."

"You are found guilty and sentenced to thirty days' loss of good time."

"Man! Y'all—this is fucked up, man. Y'all gonna take my good time!?" He runs out of the room. "They done took my good time!" he screams in the hall. "They took my good time! Fuck them!" For removing a broom from a closet at the wrong time, this inmate will stay in prison an extra thirty days, for which CCA will be paid more than $1,000.

*True Colors*

One day in class we take a personality test called True Colors that's supposed to help CCA decide how to place us. Impulsive "orange" people can be useful in hostage negotiations because they don't waste time deliberating. Rule-oriented "gold" people are chosen for the daily management of inmates. The majority of the staff, Miss Blanchard says, are gold—dutiful, punctual people who value rules. My results show that green is my dominant color (analytical, curious) and orange is my secondary (free and spontaneous). Green is a rare personality type at Winn. Miss Blanchard doesn't offer any examples of how greens can be useful in a prison.

The company that markets the test claims that people who retake it get the same results 94 percent of the time. But Miss Blanchard says that after working here awhile, people often find their colors have shifted. Gold traits tend to become more dominant.

Studies have shown that personalities can change dramatically when people find themselves in prison environments. In 1971, psychologist Philip Zimbardo conducted the now-famous Stanford Prison Experiment, in which he randomly assigned college students to the roles of prisoners and guards in a makeshift basement "prison." The experiment was intended to study how people respond to authority, but it quickly became clear that some of the most profound changes were happening to the guards. Some became sadistic, forcing the prisoners to sleep on concrete, sing and dance, defecate into buckets, and strip naked. The situation became so extreme that the two-week study was cut short after just six days. When it was over, many "guards" were ashamed at what they had done and some "prisoners" were traumatized for years. "We all want to believe in our inner power, our sense of personal agency, to resist external situational forces of the kinds operating in this Stanford Prison Experiment,"

Zimbardo reflected. "For many, that belief of personal power to resist powerful situational and systemic forces is little more than a reassuring illusion of invulnerability."

The question the study posed still lingers: Are the soldiers of Abu Ghraib, or even Auschwitz guards and ISIS hostage takers, inherently different from you and me? We take comfort in the notion of an unbridgeable gulf between good and evil, but maybe we should understand, as Zimbardo's work suggested, that evil is incremental—something we are all capable of, given the right circumstances.

.        .        .

One day during our third week of training I am assigned to work in the chow hall. My job is to tell the inmates where to sit, filling up one row of tables at a time. I don't understand why we do this. "When you fill up this side, start clearing them out," the captain tells me. "They get ten minutes to eat." CCA policy is twenty minutes. We just learned that in class.

Inmates file through the chow line and I point them to their tables. One man sits at the table next to the one I directed him to. "Right here," I say, pointing to the table again. He doesn't move. The supervisor is watching. Hundreds of inmates can see me.

"Hey. Move back to this table."

"Hell nah," he says. "I ain't movin'."

"Yes, you are," I say. "Move." He doesn't.

I get the muscle-bound captain, who comes and tells the inmate to do what I say. The inmate gets up and sits at a third table. He's playing with me. "I told you to move to that table," I say sternly.

"Man, the fuck is this?" he says, sitting at the table I point to. I'm shaky with fear. *Project confidence. Project power.* I stand tall, broaden my shoulders, and stride up and down the floor, making enough eye contact with people to show I'm not intimidated, but not holding it long enough to threaten them. I tell inmates to take off their hats as they enter. They listen to me, and a part of me likes that.

For the first time, for just a moment, I forget that I am a journalist. I watch for guys sitting with their friends rather than where they are told to. I scan the room for people sneaking back in line for more food. I tell inmates to get up and leave while they are still eating. I look closely to make sure no one has an extra cup of Kool-Aid.

"Hey, man, why you gotta be a cop like that?" asks the inmate whom I moved. "They don't pay you enough to be no cop."

"Hey Bauer, go tell that guy to take his hat off," Collinsworth says, pointing to another inmate. "I told him and he didn't listen to me."

"You tell him," I say. "If you're going to start something, you got to finish it." A CO looks at me approvingly.

## The Dog Team

Out in the back of the prison, not far from where Chase Cortez hopped the fence, there is a barn. Miss Blanchard, another cadet, and I step inside the barn office. Country music is playing on the radio. Halters, leashes, and horseshoes hang on the walls. Three heavyset white COs are inside. They do not like surprise visits. One spits into a garbage can.

The men and their inmate trusties take care of a small herd of horses and three packs of bloodhounds. The horses don't do much these days. The COs used to mount them with shotguns and oversee hundreds of inmates who left the compound every day to tend the grounds. The shotguns had to be put to use when, occasionally, an inmate tried to run for it. "You don't actually shoot to kill; you shoot to stop," a longtime staff member told me one day. "Oops! I killed him," she said sarcastically. "I told him to stop! We can always get another inmate, though."

Prisoners and officers alike talk nostalgically about the time when the men spent their days working outside, coming back to their dorms drained of restless energy and aggression. CCA's contract requires that Winn inmates are assigned to "productive full time activity" five days a week, but few are. The work program was dropped around the same time that guards were taken out of the towers. Many vocational programs at Winn have been axed. The hobby shops have become storage units; access to the law library is limited. The big recreation yard sits empty most of the time: There aren't enough guards to watch over it. (Asked about the lack of classes, recreation, and other activities at Winn, CCA insisted "these resources and programs were largely available to inmates." It said the work program was cut during contract negotiations with the DOC, and it acknowledged some gaps in programming due to "brief periods of staffing vacancies.")

"Things ain't like they used to be," Chris, the officer who runs the dog team, tells us. "It's a frickin' mess."

"Can't whup people's ass like we used to," another officer named Gary says.

"Yeah you can! We did!" Chris says. He then sulks a little: "You got to know how to do it, I guess."

"You got to know *where* to do it also," Miss Blanchard says, referring, I assume, to the areas of the prison the cameras don't see.

"We got one in the infirmary," Chris says. "Haha! Gary gassed him."

"You always using the gas, man," the third officer says.

"If one causes me to do three or four hours of paperwork, I'm go' put somethin' on his ass," Gary says. "He's go' get some gas. He's go' get the full load. I ain't go' do just a light use of force on him; I'm go' handle my business with him. Of course, y'all the new class. I'm sitting here telling y'all wrong. Do it the right way. But sometimes, you just can't do it the right way."

With no work program to oversee, the men's main job is to take the horses and the packs of bloodhounds anywhere across thirteen nearby parishes to help the police chase down suspects or prison escapees. They've apprehended armed robbers and murder suspects.

When we step inside the kennel, the bloodhounds bay and howl. Gary kicks the door of one cage and a dog lunges at his foot. "If they can get to him, they go' to bite him," he says. "They deal with 'em pretty bad."

Back in the barn office, Gary pulls a binder off the shelf and shows us a photo of a man's face. There is a red hole under his chin and a gash down his throat. "I turn inmates loose every day and go catch 'em," Chris says, rubbing the stubble on his neck. "And that was the result to one of 'em."

"A dog, when he got too close to him, bit him in the throat," Gary says.

"That's an inmate?" I ask.

"Yeah. What we'll do is we'll take a trusty and we'll put him in them woods right out there." He points out the window. The trusty wears a "bite suit" to protect him from the dogs. "We'll tell him where to go. He might walk back here two miles. We'll tell him what tree to go up, and he goes up a tree." Then, after some time passes, they "turn the dogs loose."

He holds up the picture of the guy with the throat bite. "This guy here, he got too close to 'em." Christian walks in the door.

"That looks nasty," I say.

"Eh, it wasn't that bad," Christian cuts in. "I took him to the hospital. It wasn't that bad." (CCA says the inmate's injuries were "minor.")

Gary, still holding out the picture, says, "He was a character."

"He was a piece of crap," Christian says. "Instigator."

"I gave him his gear and he didn't put it on correctly. That's on him," Chris says with a shrug.

*"Part of the bid'ness"*

"I would kill an inmate if I had to," Collinsworth says to me during a break one day. We are standing around outside; most cadets are smoking cigarettes. "I wouldn't feel bad about it, not if they were attacking me."

"You got to feel some kinda remorse if you a human being," Willis says.

"I can't see why you'd need to kill anyone," Miss Stirling says.

"You might have to," says Collinsworth.

"I do what needs to get done," says a forty-something, chubby-faced white officer. He wears a baseball cap low over his eyes. "I just had a use of force on an inmate who just got out of open-heart surgery. It's all part a the bid'ness." (CCA says it cannot confirm this incident.)

The officer's name is Kenny. He's been working here for twelve years, and he views inmates as "customers." While teaching class, he lectures us on CCA's principle of "cost-effectiveness," which requires us to "provide honest and fair, competitive pricing to our partner and deliver value to our shareholders." A part of being cost-effective is not getting sued too often. "One thing the Department of Corrections does is they give us a certain amount of money to manage this facility," Kenny explains. "They set a portion of money back for lawsuits, but if we go over budget, it's kind of like any other job. We got sixty-something-plus facilities. If they not making no money at Winn Correctional Center, guess what? We not go' be employed."

Kenny is detached and cool. He says he used to have a temper but he's learned to control it. He doesn't sit in bed at night writing up disciplinary reports while his wife sleeps, like he did years ago. Now, if an inmate gives him a smart mouth or doesn't keep a tidy bed, he'll throw him in seg to set an example. There are rules, and they are meant to be followed. This goes both ways: When he has any say, he makes sure inmates get what they are entitled to. He prides himself on his fairness. "All them in-mates ain't bad," he reminds us. Everyone deserves a chance at redemption.

Still, we must never let inmates forget their place. "When you a inmate and you talk too much and you think you free, it's time for you to go," he says. "You got some of these guys, they smart. They real educated. I know one and I be talkin' to him and he smarter than me. Now he might have more book sense, but he ain't got more common sense. He go' talk to me at a inmate level, not at no staff level. You got to put 'em in check sometimes."

Kenny makes me nervous. He notices that I am the only one in class who takes notes. One day, he tells us that he sits on the hiring committee. "We don't know what you here for," he says to the class. He then glances at me. "There might be somebody in this room here hooked up wit' a inmate." Throughout the day, he asks my name on several occasions. "My job is to monitor in-mates; it's also to monitor staff. I'm a sneaky junker." He turns and looks me directly in the eyes. "I come up here and tell you I don't know what your name is? I know what your name is. That's just a game I'm playing with you." I feel my face flush. I chuckle nervously. He has to know. "I play games just like they play games. I test my staff to test their loyalty. I report to the warden about what I see. It's a game, but it's also a part of the bid'ness."

## Mail Call

Over Christmas week, I am stationed in the mail room with a couple of other cadets to process the deluge of holiday letters. The woman in charge, Miss Roberts, demonstrates our task: Slice the top of each envelope, cut the back off and throw it in the trash, cut the postage off the front, staple what remains to the letter, and stamp it: *Inspected*.

Miss Roberts opens a letter with several pages of colorful child's drawings. "Now, see like this one, it's not allowed because they're not allowed to get anything that's crayon," she says. I presume this is for the same reason we remove stamps; crayon could be a vehicle for drugs. There are so many letters from children—little hands outlined, little stockings glued to the inside of cards—that we rip out and throw in the trash.

One reads:

> I love you and miss you so much daddy, but we are doing good. Rick Jr. is bad now. He gets into everything. I have not forgot you daddy. I love you.

Around the mail room, there are bulletins posted of things to look out for: an anti-imperialist newsletter called *Under Lock and Key*, an issue of *Forbes* that comes with a miniature wireless internet router, a CD from a Chicano gangster rapper with a track titled "Death on a CO." I find a list of books and periodicals that aren't allowed inside Louisiana prisons. It includes *Fifty Shades of Grey*; *Lady Gaga Extreme Style*; *Surrealism and the Occult*; *Tai Chi Fa Jin: Advanced Techniques for Discharging Chi Energy*; *The Complete Book of Zen*; *Socialism vs Anarchism: A Debate*; and *Native American Crafts & Skills*. On Miss Roberts's desk is a confiscated book: Robert Greene's *48 Laws of Power*, a self-help book favored by 50 Cent and Donald Trump. Other than holy books, this is the most common text I see in inmates' lockers, usually tattered and hidden under piles of clothes. She says this book is banned because it's considered "mind-bending material," though she did enjoy it herself. There are also titles on the list about black history and culture, like *Huey: Spirit of the Panther*; *Faces of Africa*; *Message to the Blackman in America*, by Elijah Muhammad; and an anthology of news articles called *100 Years of Lynchings*.

"That's the craziest girl I ever seen," Miss Roberts says of the woman who wrote the letter she holds in her hand. She is familiar with many of the correspondents from reading about the intimate details of their lives. "She's got his whole name tattooed across her back, all the way down to her hip bone. When his ass gets out—*whenever* he gets out, 'cuz he's got 30 or 40 years—*if* he ever gets out, he ain't going to her."

I feel like a voyeur, but the letters draw me in. I am surprised at how many are from former inmates with lovers still at Winn. I read one from a man currently incarcerated in Angola, Louisiana's infamous maximum-security prison:

> Our anniversary is in 13 more days on Christmas and we could have been married for 2 years why can't you see that I want this to work between us? . . . Bae, [remember] the tattoo on my left tittie close to my heart that won't never get covered up as long as I have a breath in my body and I'm about to get your name again on my ass cheek.

Another is from a recently released inmate to his lover:

> Hope everything is going well with you. Very deeply in love with you . . .
>
> I won't be able to spend x-mass with my family either. Baby my heart is broken and I am so unhappy. I always had a great fear of being homeless . . . And even if I did find a job and had to work nights or work the evening shift, then I wouldn't have anywhere to sleep because the shelter won't let you in to sleep after hours. In order to get my bed every night I have to check in before 4pm. After that you lose your bed so the program is designed to keep you homeless. It don't make sense . . .
>
> I bet that this is a sad letter. I wish that I had good news. This will be a short letter because I don't have a lot of paper left.
>
> Merry Christmas baby. Very deeply in love with you.

The front of one card reads, "Although your situation may seem impossible . . ." and continues on the inside, "through

Christ, all things are Him-possible!" It contains a letter from the wife of an inmate:

> Here I am once again w/ thoughts of you. I hate it here everything reminds me of you. I miss u dammit! It's weird this connection we have its as if I carry you in my soul. It terrifies me the thought of ever losing you. I pray you haven't replaced me. I know I haven't been the most supporting but baby seriously you don't know the hell I've been through since we got torn apart And I guess my family got fed up w/ seeing me kill myself slowly I attempted twice 90 phenobarb 2 roxy 3 subs. I lived. 2nd after I hung up w/ you 60 Doxepin 90 propananol i lived WTF? God has a sense of humor i don't have anyone but u, u see no one cares whether I live die hurt am hungry, well, or safe . . . So I've been alone left to struggle to survive on my income in and out mental wards and running from the pain of you bein there . . .
>
> Your my everything always will be
> Love your wife.

This note and its list of pills haunt me all weekend. What if no one else knows this woman tried to commit suicide? I decide I need to tell Miss Roberts, but when I return to work, I sit in the parking lot and have a hard time summoning the courage. What if word gets out that I'm soft, not cut out for this work?

After I pass through the scanner, I see her. "Hey, Miss Roberts?" I say, walking up behind her.

"Yes," she says sweetly.

"I wanted to check with you about something. I meant to do it on Friday, but, uh . . ." She stops and gives me her full attention, looking me in the eyes. "When we had a class by the mental health director, she told us to report if there was any kind of suicidal—"

She cuts me off, waving her hand dismissively, and starts walking away.

"No, but it was like a letter thing—"

"Yeah, don't even worry about that," she says, still walking toward her door.

"Really?"

"Mmmhmmm. That's if you see something going on down there," she says, pointing toward the units. "Yeah, don't worry about it. All right." She enters the mail room.

.      .      .

After Christmas, we take our final test. It is intimidating. The test was created by CCA; we never take the qualification exam given to the state's guards. Ninety-two questions ask us about the chain of command, the use-of-force policy, what to do if we are taken hostage, how to spot a suicidal inmate, the proper way to put on leg irons, the color designation for various chemical agents. We went through most of these topics so cursorily there's no way I could answer half of them. Luckily, I don't need to worry. The head of training's assistant tells us we can go over the test together to make sure we get everything right.

"I bet no one ever doesn't get the job because they fail the test," I say.

"No," she says. "We make sure your file looks good." (CCA says this was not consistent with its practices.)

About a third of the trainees I started with have already quit. Reynolds is gone. Miss Doucet decides she can't risk an asthma attack, so she quits too. Collinsworth goes to Ash on the night shift. Willis works the night shift too; he will be fired after he leaves the prison suddenly one day and a bunch of cell phones are found at his post. Miss Stirling gets stationed in Birch on the day shift. She won't last either. Two and a half months from now, she will be escorted from the prison for smuggling contraband and writing love letters to an inmate.

## Chapter 3: "The CCA Way"

It's the end of December, and I come in at six a.m. for my first of three days of on-the-job training, the final step before I become a full-fledged CO. The captain tells an officer to take me to Elm. We move slowly down the walk. "One word of advice I would give you is never take this job home with you," he says. He spits some tobacco through the fence. "Leave it at the front gate. If you don't drink, it'll drive you to drinking."

Research shows that corrections officers experience above-average rates of job-related stress and burnout. Thirty-four percent of prison guards suffer from post–traumatic stress disorder, according to a study by a nonprofit that researches "corrections fatigue." That's a higher rate than reported by soldiers returning from Iraq and Afghanistan. COs commit suicide two and a half times more often than the population at large. They also have shorter life spans. A recent study of Florida prison guards and law enforcement officers found that they die twelve years earlier than the general population; one suggested cause was job-related stress.

The walk is eerily quiet. Crows caw, fog hangs low over the basketball courts. The prison is locked down. Programs have been canceled. With the exception of kitchen workers, none of the inmates can leave their dorms. Usually, lockdowns occur when there are major disturbances, but today, with some officers out for the holidays, guards say there just aren't enough people to run the prison. (CCA says Winn was never put on lockdown due to staffing shortages.) The unit manager tells me to shadow one of the two floor officers, a burly white marine veteran. His name is Jefferson, and as we walk the floor an inmate asks him what the lockdown is about. "You know half of the fucking people don't want to work here," Jefferson tells him. "We so short-staffed and shit, so most of the gates ain't got officers." He sighs dramatically. (CCA claims to have "no knowledge" of gates going unmanned at Winn.)

"It's messed up," the prisoner says.

"Man, it's so fucked up it's pitiful," Jefferson replies. "The first thing the warden asked me [was] what would boost morale around here. The first two words out of my mouth: pay raise." He takes a gulp of coffee from his travel mug.

"They *do* need to give y'all a pay raise," the prisoner says.

"When gas is damn near four dollars a gallon, what the fuck is nine dollars an hour?" Jefferson says. "That's half yo' check fillin' up your gas!"

Another inmate, whom Jefferson calls "the unit politician," demands an Administrative Remedy Procedure form. He wants to file a grievance about the lockdown—why are inmates being punished for the prison's mismanagement?

"What happens to those ARPs?" I ask Jefferson.

"If they feel their rights have been violated in some way, they are allowed to file a grievance," he says. If the captain rejects it, they can appeal to the warden. If the warden rejects it, they can appeal to the Department of Corrections. "It'll take about a year," he says. "Once it gets to DOC down in Baton Rouge, they throw it over in a pile and forget about it. I've been to DOC headquarters. I know what them sonsabitches do down there: nothin'." (Miss Lawson, the assistant chief of security, later tells me that during the fifteen years she worked at Winn, she saw only one grievance result in consequences for staff. )

I do a couple of laps around the unit floor and then see Jefferson leaning against the threshold of an open tier door, chatting with a prisoner. I walk over to them. "This your first day?" the prisoner asks me, leaning up against the bars.

"Yeah."

"Welcome to CCA, boy. You seen what the sign say when you first come in the gate? It says, 'The CCA Way.' Know what that is?" he asks me. There is a pause. "Whatever way you make it, my boy."

Jefferson titters. "Some of them down here are good," he says. "I will say dat. Some of 'em are jackasses. Some of 'em just flat-out ain't worth a fuck."

"Just know at the end of the day, how y'all conduct y'all selves determines how we conduct ourselves," the prisoner says to me. "You come wit' a shit attitude, we go' have a shit attitude."

"I have three rules and they know it," Jefferson says as he grips the bars with one hand. "No fightin'. No fuckin'. No jackin' off. But! What they do after the lights are out? I don't give a fuck, 'cuz I'm at the house."

.        .        .

The next day, I'm stationed in Ash, a general population unit. The unit manager is a black woman who is so large she has trouble walking. She is brought in every morning in a wheelchair pushed by an inmate. Her name is Miss Price, but inmates call her the Dragon. It's unclear whether her jowls, her roar, or her stern reputation earned her that name. Prisoners relate to her like an overbearing mother, afraid to anger her and eager to win her affection. She's worked here since the prison opened in 1991, and one CO says that in her younger days, she was known to break up fights without backup. Another CO says that last week an inmate "whipped his thing out and was playing with himself right in front of her. She got out of her wheelchair, grabbed him by the neck, threw him up against the wall. She said, 'Don't you ever fucking do that to me again!'"

In the middle of the morning, Miss Price tells us to shake down the common areas. I follow one of the two COs into a tier and we do perfunctory searches of the TV room and tables, feeling under the ledges, flipping through a few books. I bend over and feel around under a water fountain. My hand lands on something loose. I get on my knees to look. It's a smartphone. I don't know what to do—do I take it or leave it? My job, of course, is to take it, but by now I know that being a guard is only partially about enforcing the rules. Mostly, it's about learning how to get through the day safely, which requires decisions like these to be weighed carefully.

A prisoner is watching me. If I leave the phone, everyone on the tier will know. I will win inmates' respect. But if I take it, I will show my superiors I am doing my job. I will alleviate some of the suspicion they have of every new hire. "Those ones who gets along with 'em—those ones are the ones I really have to watch," SORT commander Tucker told us in class. "There is five of y'all. Two and a half are gonna be dirty."

I take the phone.

Miss Price is thrilled. The captain calls the unit to congratulate me. The other COs couldn't care less. When I do count later, each inmate on that tier stares at me with his meanest look. Some step toward me threateningly as I pass.

Later, at a bar near my apartment, I see a man in a CCA jacket and ask him if he works at Winn. "Used to," he says.

"I just started there," I say.

He smiles. "Let me tell you this: You ain't go' like it. When you start working those twelve-hour shifts, you will see." He takes a drag from his cigarette. "The job is way too fucking dangerous." I tell him about the phone. "Oh, they won't forget your face," he says. "I just want you to know you made a lot of enemies. If you work in Ash, you gonna have a big-ass problem because now they go' know, he's gonna be the guy who busts us all the time."

He racks the balls on the pool table and tells me about a nurse who gave a penicillin shot to an inmate who was allergic to the medicine and died. The prisoner's friends thought the nurse did it intentionally. "When he came down the walk, they beat the shit out of him. They had to airlift him out of there." (CCA says it has no knowledge of this incident.) He breaks and sinks a stripe.

### Suicide Watch

On my first official day as a CO, I am stationed on suicide watch in Cypress. In the entire prison of more than 1,500 inmates, there are no full-time psychiatrists and just one full-time social worker: Miss Carter. In class, she told us that a third of the inmates have mental-health problems, 10 percent have severe mental health issues, and roughly a quarter have IQs under 70. She said most prison mental health departments in Louisiana have at least three full-time social workers. Angola has at least eleven. Here, there are few options for inmates with mental-health needs. They can meet with Miss Carter, but with her caseload of 450 prisoners, that isn't likely to happen more than once a month. They can try to get an appointment with the part-time psychiatrist or the part-time psychologist, who are spread even thinner. Another option is to ask for suicide watch.

A CO sits across from the two official suicide-watch cells, which are small and dimly lit and have plexiglass over the front. My job is to sit across from two regular segregation cells being used for suicide watch overflow, observe the two inmates inside, and log their behavior every fifteen minutes. "We never document anything around here on the money," Miss Carter taught us a month ago. "Nothing should be nine, nine-fifteen, nine-thirty, because the auditors say you're pencil-whipping it. And truth be known, we do pencil-whip it. We can't add by fifteen because that really puts you in a bind. Add by fourteen. That looks pretty come audit time." One guard told me he just filled in the suicide-watch log every couple of hours and didn't bother to watch the prisoners. (CCA's spokesman says the company is "committed to the accuracy of our record keeping.")

For one inmate, Skeen, I jot down the codes for "sitting" and "quiet." For the other, Damien Coestly (his real name), the number for "using toilet." He is sitting on the commode, underneath his suicide blanket, a tear-proof garment that doubles as a smock. "Ah hell nah, you can't sit here, man!" he shouts at me. Other than the blanket, he is naked, his bare feet on the concrete. There is nothing else allowed in his cell other than some toilet paper. No books. Nothing to occupy his mind.

The sparse conditions are intended to be "a deterrent as well as protection," Miss Carter said. Some inmates claim to be suicidal because, for one reason or another, they want out of their dorms and don't want to go to protective custody, where they would be labeled as snitches. Inmates on suicide watch don't get a mattress; they have to sleep on a steel bunk. They also get worse food. The official ration is one "mystery meat" sandwich, one peanut butter sandwich, six carrot sticks, six celery sticks, and six apple slices per meal. Assuming this meal contains no nutritional supplements, I calculate that eating it three times a day provides at least 250 calories less than the U.S. Department of Agriculture's daily recommendation for sedentary adult men younger than forty-one years old. (CCA says suicide-watch meals are of "equivalent nutritional value" to general-population meals. It also says suicide watch "is designed for the safety of the inmate and nothing else.")

Nowhere else does a single guard oversee one or two inmates. If more than two inmates are on constant watch for more than forty-eight hours, the prison has to ask the regional corporate office for permission to continue, Miss Carter tells us. (CCA says this is inaccurate.) Sometimes the regional office says no, she says, and the prisoners are put back on the tiers or in seg.

"Come on, man, get the fuck out of here," shouts Coestly. "You know what I'm about to do is, get up on top of this bed and jump straight onto my motherfucking neck if y'all don't get the fuck out from the front of my cell."

I look over to the cell to the right and see Skeen sitting on his metal bed, staring at me and masturbating under his suicide blanket.

I tell him to stop.

"Move your chair, then. I'm just doing my thing." He keeps going.

I get up and grab a pink slip to write him up, my first disciplinary report.

"You making a mistake," he says. "You fuck with me like that, I'm gonna go all night."

"All right," I say.

"Write that bitch. I don't give a fuck. I'm on extended lockdown." He tells me he's been in Cypress for three years. He starts singing and dancing in his cell. *"All night, all niiiiiight."* Prisoners down the tier laugh. "I'll add that to my collection. I have about a hundred write-ups. I don't give a fuck!"

Someone down the tier calls for me. He's not on suicide watch, just regular segregation. "I'm having some mental-health issues, man," he says. He has a wild look in his eyes and he speaks intensely, but quietly. "I'm not suicidal or homicidal necessarily, but it's hard for me to be around people." There is another man in his cell with him, sitting on the top bunk, shaving his face. "And, and, and the voices, demons, whatever you want to call them, want me to wait till y'all come down here and throw defecation or urine or something. I don't want to do that, okay?" He says he wants to go on suicide watch as a preventive measure. "Until I figure out what's going on here"—he taps the sides of his head with his index fingers—"then that's where I need to be." His request is denied by the unit manager. With four inmates on suicide watch, we are already over capacity.

"We are gonna have a Mexican standoff," Coestly says. "Ever seen one of those? I get off the bed, jump off that mothafucker headfirst." He says he's having a mental-health emergency, which I am required to report. When I tell the key officer, she rolls her eyes. In class, Miss Carter told us that "unless he's psychotic and needs a shot to keep him from doing the behavior, then I just let them get it out of their system." It takes six hours for a psychiatrist to show up.

One of the other inmates on suicide watch, who's been silent until now, starts yelling through his food slot. "World war!" he shouts. "I got some niggas who need to tell the CIA something, since they already got their eye in the sky, the satellite orbiting in space processing global information." His voice has a demonic quality to it and he occasionally hits the plexiglass to punctuate his sentences. The CO sitting directly across from him twiddles his thumbs and gazes ahead blankly.

In the neighboring cell, Skeen is staring at me, completely naked, masturbating vigorously. I tell him to stop. He gets up, comes to the bars, and strokes himself five feet in front of me. I leave and come back with the pink sheet and he shouts, "Stop looking like that 'cuz you making my dick hard!" I don't respond. "Stop looking like that 'cuz you making my dick hard! Stop looking like that 'cuz you making my dick hard!" The seemingly schizophrenic man next to him hits the plexiglass over and over. "That's what the devil's doing to you, in the invisible world— sticking his invisible dick in your white or black ass and *fucking* you with it." My heart is pounding. For an hour, I stare at a cup on the floor and study the blotches in the concrete.

A few hours later, a SORT officer walks a cuffed man onto the tier. The man's eyes are tightly closed and snot is dripping off his upper lip. He was pepper-sprayed after punching my old instructor Kenny in the face as Kenny sat in his office doing paperwork. Kenny's in the hospital now—after he confiscated another inmate's cell phone, the prisoner put a paid hit out on him.

*Building Rapport*

Kenny is gone for days, recovering from his busted nose. The message his assailant sent was clear: Keep your hands off our phones. Meanwhile, the fact that I took the phone in Ash showed Miss Price that I'm a strong officer who plays by the rules, so she asked the warden if I could be posted there permanently. Now I work there, on the floor, almost every day. I immediately try to smooth over the phone thing with the inmates. I tell a few of them that I took it because I didn't have a choice and suggest they should try to hide their contraband better. "You ain't no police?" one asks me. "Nah. I ain't here to be police," I reply. "If people ain't fucking with me, I ain't got a problem with them."

Don't be like your partner Bacle, they tell me. In some units and on some shifts, the pairing of floor officers changes day to day, but for whatever reason Bacle and I become a regular pair. (He has allowed me to use his real name.) I tell the inmates I'll never be like him, all that shouting and hollering.

The truth is, Bacle's temper tantrums make us laugh. One inmate asks him for his Social Security number every day just to set him off. If he were not a squat, hobbling sixty-three-year-old, Bacle's occasional fantasies about putting shock collars on inmates or shoving his keys down their throats might not seem so harmless. But he hates the company too. "All you are is a fucking body to 'em. That's the way I feel," he says. He counts the days until his Social Security kicks in and he no longer needs to work here to supplement his retirement checks from the Coast Guard.

Every day, I come to know him more and more. He is a reader of old westerns and an aficionado of Civil War reenactments. He uses words like "gadzooks" and phrases like "useful as tits on a boar hog." Back before the hobby shops closed, he liked to buy his wife gifts made by prisoners. Once, he bought her a handmade saddle for her toy unicorns. "When she seen it, she was tickled pink. We are still fat, dumb, and happy over it!" His breath smells perpetually of menthol chewing tobacco, a fleck of which is always stuck in the corner of his mouth.

Bacle becomes a teacher of sorts. "You got to have what I call a *rapport* with some of the inmates," he says. Mostly, he is referring to the orderlies, the prisoners selected for special roles inside each unit. When an orderly passes out toothpaste, Bacle tells me to follow the inmate's lead. "I just kind of modify it from when I was in the service. I might have rank over someone, but I don't want to step on their toes."

Without the orderlies, the prison would not function. Each unit has a key orderly, whose job is to keep the key clean and pack up the property of any prisoner sent to seg. Count-room orderlies deliver the tallies from each unit to the room where they're tabulated. Tier orderlies, floor orderlies, yard orderlies, walk orderlies, and gym orderlies keep the prison clean. Orderlies typically maintain a friendly relationship with the guards but take every opportunity to make it clear to other inmates they are not snitches. And they rarely are. It is much more likely for them to be movers of contraband. They cozy up to guards who will bring it in, and their freedom of movement allows them to distribute the goods. I will see some of the most trusted orderlies get busted while I'm here.

Bacle regularly gives his lunch to the muscular key orderly. We are not allowed to do this, so he does it discreetly. "It's a habit I got into when I started," he says. Bacle isn't afraid to bend the rules to keep things under control. When one inmate starts marching around angrily, saying "fuck white people" and we're too afraid to try to get him into his tier, Bacle buys cigarettes from another inmate, gives them to the agitated prisoner, and says, "Why don't you go have a smoke on your bed to calm your nerves?" And it works. When Miss Price isn't watching, Bacle lets a guy called Corner Store off his tier so he can run deodorant and chewing tobacco and sugar and coffee between inmates on different tiers. They aren't allowed to trade commissary items, but they do anyway, so when we let Corner Store handle it, they stop pestering us with ploys to get off the tier, like faking medical emergencies.

Corner Store is a thirty-seven-year-old black man who looks fifty-five. His hair is scraggly, his uniform tattered, his face puffy.

He walks with the clipped gait of a stiff-legged old man who is late for a meeting he doesn't really want to attend. He's been in prison for half his life, though I don't know what for. I rarely know what anyone is in for. I do know that he used to sell crack, that he saw his friend get shot to death when he was eight, and that he once had a firefight with some white men in Mississippi who called him a "nigger." At least that's what he tells me. Fourteen of his eighteen years behind bars have been at Winn.

Corner Store does not inspire fear, yet he is confident. He tells COs to open the tier door for him; he does not ask. On his pluckier days, he flaunts his status by sitting in the guards' chairs and smoking. He talks to us as if we are office colleagues from different departments. And unlike the floor orderly who protects his reputation by loudly proclaiming that rats deserve to get stabbed, Corner Store doesn't need to make a show of his loyalty to inmates, yet it is unwavering. When I ask him to teach me some prison lingo, he refuses gently.

The first time I meet Corner Store, he walks through the metal detector at the entrance of the unit. It beeps, but neither Bacle nor I do anything; its sound is one of the many we tune out. The device was installed not long before I started working here, in an effort to cut down on the number of inmates carrying shanks, but functionally it is a piece of furniture. We never use it since it takes at least two officers to get inmates to line up, walk through it, and get patted down whenever they enter or exit the unit, which leaves no one to let inmates into their tiers. When Corner Store makes it beep, he calls over to me: "Hey, watch this here! I'm going to go back through this thing and it won't go off." He jumps through it sideways, and it doesn't make a sound. I laugh. "This is something my granddaddy taught me years ago," he says. "Anything that a man makes can always be altered. Always."

He had to learn to hustle because he has no money and no support from his family. For his courier services, inmates kick him cigarettes, coffee, and soup. He doesn't take charity; he learned early that little comes without strings in prison. Sexual predators prey on needy inmates, giving them commissary or drugs, seemingly as gifts, but eventually recalling the debt. If you don't have money, the only way to pay is with your body. "When I first come to prison, I had to fight about five times for my ass," Corner Store says. "This is how it starts: You're scared of being in prison because of the violence or whatever. You go to people for protection. But this is the No. 1 thing you don't do. You have to be a man on your own." He tries to discourage vulnerable inmates from seeking help and says he's gotten into fights to stop new prisoners from being sexually assaulted. "It just hurts me to see it happen. A kid who really don't even understand life yet, you turn and fuck his life up even more?"

He says there have been periods when he's had to pack a shank. "Sometimes it's best, because you got some bullheaded people in prison who don't understand nothin' *but* violence. When you show them you can get on the same level they gettin' on, they leave you the fuck alone."

"They always talking about how prison rehabilitates you," he says. "Prison don't rehabilitate you. You have to rehabilitate yourself." When Miss Price is around, Bacle and I are careful not to make it obvious we are letting Corner Store out, and he makes sure to stay out of her sight.

Instructors like Kenny preached against giving concessions to inmates, but in reality most guards think you have to cooperate with them. Frankly, there just aren't enough staff members to do otherwise. Bacle and I don't have time, for example, to keep watch over the corrections counselor when she is in her office, where there are no security cameras, so she uses two inmates as her bodyguards. (CCA says this went against its policy.) COs are always under pressure to impress on the supervisors that everything is under control. We rely on inmates for this, too, letting some stand out in front of the unit to warn us when a ranking officer is coming so we can make sure everything is in order.

It can be a slippery slope. In 2007, a Tennessee inmate, Gary Thompson, sued CCA, claiming that guards, including a captain, periodically ordered him to beat up other inmates to punish them, giving him the best jobs and privileges as a reward. On one occasion, he claimed, guards called him the "largest nigger," put him with a mentally ill inmate who'd cut a swastika into his arm, and ordered Thompson to "rough [him] up." When Thompson filed a complaint, he was put in the hole. CCA denied his allegations but settled the case.

In Idaho, CCA was accused of ceding control to prison gangs to save money on wages. A lawsuit filed in 2012 by eight inmates at the Idaho Correctional Center alleged there was effectively "a partnership between CCA and certain prison gangs," in which gang members were used to discipline inmates. A subsequent FBI investigation found that employees had falsified records and understaffed mandatory positions. A confidential Idaho Department of Correction memo shared with CCA that was disclosed in the case showed that by August 2008, inmate-on-inmate assaults and other incidents of violence had "steadily increased to the point that there are four incidents for every one that occurs in the rest of the Idaho state operated facilities combined." (CCA points to a later analysis by an independent monitor that concluded that the rate of violence at ICC over the entire first eight months of 2008 was not disproportionate to that of other facilities.) No charges were brought against CCA, nor were any sanctions levied against it. But the state ended automatic renewal of its contract, and reopened it to bidders. CCA did not bid. "It was a lot better than this place," an out-of-state guard who worked in Idaho at the time told me.

There are no gangs at Winn, but that has more to do with Louisiana prison culture than the management of the prison. In most prisons around the country, the racial divide is stark and internal politics are determined by racialized prison gangs like the Aryan Brotherhood and the Mexican Mafia. But Louisiana is an anomaly. Here, there are no prison gangs. In a prison that is 75 percent black and less than 25 percent white, people of different races sit together in the chow hall, hang out on the yard, and sleep in the same dorms.

Throughout my time at Winn, I meet guards from CCA prisons around the country who talk up the benefits of gangs. Two SORT members filling in from Oklahoma speak to each other in Sureño sign language that they learned from prisoners transferred from California. The influx of gang members is a "good thing," one of the SORT guys tells me, because gang culture is highly disciplined. "With their politics, they *have* to clean their cells. They *have* to maintain cleanliness. If they don't, they get stabbed. If they acted the way these guys act, they'd get stabbed."

•　　　•　　　•

I quickly learn it's no longer possible to be the silent observer I was in training, so I try to find the middle ground between appearing soft and being draconian. When I write up one inmate after he runs off the tier against my orders, I think about it all weekend, wondering if he will get sent to Cypress. I feel guilty and decide I will only write up inmates for two things: threatening me and refusing to get on their tier after they enter the unit. The floor is where most assaults happen, and if a lot of inmates are out there, things can get out of hand. That's not why I choose to write them up for it, though. I write them up because my main job is to keep inmates off the floor, and if I don't establish authority, I end up having to negotiate with each prisoner over how long he can wander the unit, which is exhausting.

I spend free moments leaning up against the bars, making chitchat with prisoners about their lives. I tell one, Brick, that I am from Minnesota. He says he has friends there. "We got to hook up!" he says. I cultivate these relationships; having gray-haired, charming inmates like him in my good graces helps me because younger, harder prisoners follow their lead. I do favors for others— I let a cop killer outside when it's not yard time because he seems to have influence over some of the inmates. Guys like him and Corner Store teach me how to win inmates' respect. They teach me how to make it in here.

I try to address every request and respond to every inmate who yells "Minnesota," my new nickname. The microwaves on some tiers are broken, so I help out by carrying cups of water for soup or coffee to Brick's tier, where he heats them up. When Corner Store isn't working and people ask if I can let them off the tier for a minute so they can run and exchange a honey bun for a few cigarettes, I unlock the door. "You're cool," one inmate says to me. "Real laid-back." I let people out to see the corrections counselor when they need a mattress or need to call their lawyers, even when she tells me she doesn't want to field these requests, which is most of the time.

Brick can see that I get tired striking across the unit from one place to the next for twelve hours a day. He sees that by the end of the day my feet and back hurt and I start to ignore the inmates. He knows that two people aren't enough to run this floor. "This shit don't work," he says to me. We bump fists.

## Chapter 4: "You Got to Survive"

There is a looming sense of crisis at Winn. Shortly after Cortez escaped, the warden decreed that the security staff should meet at the start of every shift. So at six a.m. each day, everyone is shepherded into a conference room, where they brood over coffee and Monster Energy drinks. "I apologize if it seems as though we're coming down on y'all all the time," says Assistant Warden Parker, who introduced himself to me in Cypress four weeks ago. He's sitting on a table, the picture of a guy-next-door, we're-in-this-together type of boss. "Unfortunately, due to a series of events that took place over 2014, culminating with that escape, there is a high, high level of scrutiny on how you do your job."

He doesn't get into specifics, but guards tell me there was a rash of stabbings over the summer that CCA didn't report to the Louisiana DOC. (The company's spokesman says it reported all assaults.) "Someone said this place has slid downhill for a long time," the assistant warden says to us. "Here's what we have before us: We have to climb up that hill extremely fast."

The DOC, which has ultimate authority over all prisons in the state, has been taking a closer look at Winn's day-to-day operations. (According to DOC documents I later obtained, the department had just written to CCA about "contract compliance" and areas where Winn's "basic correctional practices" needed improvement.) Wardens from publicly run state prisons have appeared out of nowhere, watching over COs as they work, asking them questions. The newer guards fret about losing their jobs. Old-timers shrug it off—they say they've seen Winn weather tough times before.

At each morning meeting, we are given a new "game plan": keep inmates off the bars of the tiers, move them quicker out to chow, keep them off the floor, finish count faster. We never discuss the problem that both guards and inmates complain about most: There aren't enough employees. Corporate has tried to mitigate the problem by bringing officers in from out of state. The economics of this are never clear to me—it seems far more expensive to pay for their transportation and lodging than to hire more locals or raise wages. In addition to the SORT members, there are an average of five guards filling in for a month or so at a time from places like Arizona and Tennessee.

According to CCA's contract with Louisiana, thirty-six guards are expected to show up for work at six a.m. every day. Twenty-nine of them fill mandatory twelve-hour positions that require a body in them at all times—these include unit floor officers, front-gate officers, perimeter patrol, supervisors, and infirmary officers.

I make a habit of counting the number of security staff at the meetings. Some days there are twenty-eight, some days twenty-four, but there are almost always fewer than twenty-nine.

It's possible that employees working overtime from the night shift aren't there or that others trickle in late. But it still appears there are often fewer people on the shift than contractually required to keep the prison open, let alone running smoothly. CCA's spokesman later tells me I was too low on the totem pole to have an accurate understanding of staffing at Winn. (He adds that "security is everyone's job" and a "team effort" involving even employees who are not guards.) Correspondence between CCA and the DOC shows that in early 2015 Winn had forty-two vacancies for regular guards and nine vacancies for ranking officers. Miss Lawson, the assistant chief of security, says that when officials from the DOC were scheduled to visit, "we would be tripping over each other, but it was just because we were paying people overtime to come in and work extra."

Often, the only guards in a 352-inmate unit are the two floor officers and the key officer. There is supposed to be an officer controlling the gate that connects each unit walk to the main walk, but often there isn't. From nine a.m. to five p.m. on weekdays, every unit should have two case managers, who manage rehabilitation and reentry programs, two corrections counselors, who are in charge of resolving inmates' daily issues, and a unit manager, who supervises everything. Not once do I see all these positions filled in a unit.

During my time at Winn, I witness corners cut daily. Key officers, who are charged with documenting activities in the units, routinely record security checks that do not occur. I hear that these logbooks are audited by the state and are the only evidence of whether guards walk up and down the tiers every half-hour. I almost never see anyone do such a security check unless DOC officials are around. Collinsworth tells me that when he worked in the key he was told repeatedly to record security checks every fifteen to thirty minutes, even though they weren't being done. Miss Lawson later says she was once reprimanded by a warden for refusing to log checks that did not occur. "I'm just going to write down that you are doing your security checks every thirty minutes," a ranking officer once told me. "That's just how it's been done, so until someone up top tells me different, that's how we'll do it." (CCA's spokesman says the company had no knowledge of security checks being skipped or logbooks being falsified.)

Even with the guards filling in from out of state, we are required to work extra days, which means that for up to five days in a row, I have just enough time to drive home, eat, sleep, and come back to the prison. Sometimes I have to stay longer than twelve hours because there is no one to take over for me. A guard I relieve one morning is ending a four-day stretch; in a forty-eight-hour period he worked forty-two hours at the warden's insistence, he says. He didn't sleep the whole time. (CCA says no such incident occurred.)

Assistant Warden Parker tells us the DOC has required CCA's corporate office in Nashville, Tennessee, to report what CCA is doing to fix the mess at Winn. An obvious remedy would be to raise the pay of nonranking officers to the level of DOC officers—which starts at $12.50 per hour, $3.50 more than ours—and reinstate rehabilitative and recreational programs for inmates. Miss Lawson says such requests hit a roadblock at the corporate level. "There were years that the wardens would beg for more money, and it was like, 'Okay, on to the next subject,'" she tells me.

Instead, corporate takes a different approach to show it means business: A few days after I worked suicide watch, it removed the local officers from Cypress and turned the unit entirely over to members of the company's national SORT team. These are guys who "use force constantly," Assistant Warden Parker says at a morning meeting. "I believe that pain increases the intelligence of the stupid, and if inmates want to act stupid, then we'll give them some pain to help increase their intelligence level." DOC data shows that during the first ten months of 2015, which includes part of the time I worked there, Winn reported twice as many "immediate" uses of force as the eight other Louisiana prisons combined. ("CCA expressly forbids retaliatory force," its spokesman tells me.)

Over the next four months, Winn will report using chemical agents seventy-nine times, a rate seven times higher than that reported by Angola. Collinsworth recalls an inmate who insulted a SORT officer's mother. The officer cuffed him, stood him in his underwear out of view of the cameras, and covered his whole body with pepper spray for "about eight seconds or so." When Collinsworth filed a report, standard procedure following a use of force, he says he was ridiculed by members of the SORT team, who told him "that I should have said I didn't see anything." He says an assistant supervisor admonished him for "tattling." (CCA says the officer who sprayed the inmate was fired.)

I enter Cypress briefly after SORT takes over. At six-thirty in the morning, the air is so saturated with pepper spray that tears stream down my face. The key officer is doing paperwork in a gas mask. A man screams and flails naked in a shower, his body drenched with pepper spray. Cockroaches run around frantically to escape the burning.

## Sex and Violence

One day, as prisoners go to chow, Bacle runs past me shouting, "Code Blue outside!" I dash out the front door of Ash, through a crowd of inmates. A couple of prisoners are pinning each other up against the fence, and a frail-looking, young white guy is rolling around on the ground.

I run to him. He rolls from side to side, whimpering and heaving in panic, grasping at small cuts and lumps on his arms. They are not deep like stab wounds; they are shallow and there are many.

Under them there is a multitude of tiny scars, cut crosswise—
the trademark self-mutilation of the sexually abused.

"Calm down, man," I say, leaning over him. "We are going to
take care of you. Just calm down." He keeps rolling and crying.

"He didn't get nothing he ain't deserve!" someone shouts from
down the walk.

A sergeant and the captain come and cuff the inmate who's
been pinned to the fence. When the crowd around him clears, I am
shocked. It's Brick. The guy on the ground is probably about
twenty-five years old. As Brick is taken off to Cypress, he calls the
man a "bitch."

A couple of officers look down at the young man disdainfully,
pull him off the ground, and take him away. Brick beat him with
a lock in a sock. He was angry because the young man had stayed
in Cypress for seven months, partly by his own choice. He was
supposed to come back to Brick. He is Brick's punk.

There are many things about this incident that I don't know—
intimacy and rape in prison are complex issues. Did the young
man stay in Cypress to escape Brick? Does he belong to Brick like
a sex slave? Or would he say the relationship is consensual in the
way a battered woman might say she stays with her husband because she loves him? Did he agree to exchange sex for protection?
Did he understand that once he crossed that bridge, there would
be no going back?

*Once a punk, always a punk.* Miss Carter, the mental-health
director, told us she's seen just two inmates reverse their punk
status in the eight years she's been here, and both cases involved
stabbing a lot of people. Guards here do not turn a blind eye to
overt rape, but the more subtle abuse of punks is accepted. Inmates and COs know a punk when they see one. He will do menial tasks when someone demands it. He is expected to keep his
face clean-shaven at all times. He has to pee sitting down or by
backing up to the urinal with his penis tucked between his legs.
He must shower facing the wall.

Since 2003, the federal Prison Rape Elimination Act (PREA) has required prisons to take measures to prevent sexual assaults. At Winn, this includes teaching new cadets about the law. "Why is the law so important?" our instructor Kenny asked us during training. "Liability." It was never fully clear whether the goal was to eliminate rape or to suppress homosexuality in the prison. Even consensual sex could lead to time in seg. "Don't even go there and entertain nicknames," Kenny said. "There's homosexuals down here got nicknames: Princess, Malibu, Tiki, Coco, Nicki. By calling them nicknames, that's entertainment. They think they got you goin' along with what they got goin' on. We can't stop 100 percent of the homosexuality that goes on down there, but we try to prevent and slow it down as much as possible."

Nationwide, as many as 9 percent of male inmates report being sexually assaulted behind bars, but given the anti-snitch culture of prison, the real number might be higher. According to the Louisiana budget office, Winn reported 546 sex offenses in the 2014 fiscal year, a rate 69 percent higher than that of Avoyelles Correctional Center, a publicly operated prison of comparable size and security level.

A survey by the federal Bureau of Justice Statistics (BJS) showed that in 2011 the rate of substantiated rapes and other "nonconsensual sexual acts" between inmates in a sampling of CCA prisons was similar to that of public prisons. CCA prisons reported less serious incidents of "abusive sexual contact" at more than twice the rate of public prisons. CCA says this data may be inaccurate because it predates the final implementation of the PREA standards. The company states it has "a zero-tolerance policy with regard to sexual abuse."

Prison has a reputation as a place of homosexual predation, but it's not that simple. Inmates like Brick rarely see themselves as gay and typically go back to pursuing women once they get out. Self-identified gay or transgender prisoners are, however, often on the receiving end of abuse: Federal data shows that

39 percent of gay ex-prisoners reported being sexually assaulted by another inmate. One study found that 59 percent of transgender women in California's prisons for men reported being assaulted.

But not all sex in prison is violent; many of the letters from male lovers I read in the mail room were full of tenderness and longing. Take, for example, this one from a man in Angola, written to one of the most flamboyant men at Winn:

> You are the only same sex person in my life. So you have to never worry about anyone taking your place, not even a female . . . Sweetie, you are a good wife. I don't give a damn what anybody said because I saw the good in you; the true you. That's why when we had sex I'd always look you in the eyes. To truly understand you was my hardest goal but when I did our relationship got so good.

An hour after the young man who was attacked went to the infirmary, he walks into Ash, his arms still bleeding. It's not clear whether Brick's absence is good or bad for him. Now, he has no protection. A couple of well-muscled inmates stand at the bars and look at him lustfully, telling him to try to get placed on their tier. He speaks with Miss Price and she abruptly tells me to put him on B1—Brick's dorm. Inmates have complained to me about this sort of thing; even people who have stabbed each other are sometimes put back in the same dorm. I open the gate and watch him walk down the tier.

Minutes later, he asks me to let him out. I do. He talks to Miss Price, telling her that he is in danger. People think he's a rat. Maybe they think he snitched on Brick to get away from him. Miss Price doesn't give it a moment of consideration, telling him to get back on the tier. When I open the door, a large, bearded man inside pushes him back out onto the floor. "You was asking her to put you on another tier?" he says. "If you think you can't live in here, you can't live in here. We don't need that kind of shit on the tier anyway." He slams the bars behind him.

The young man has two options: Go back on the tier or go to the count room, where they will assign him to another unit.

Miss Price tells me to take him out.

"You gotta go," I tell him halfheartedly.

"I don't want to go on no PC, man," he says to me. He thinks they are going to put him in protective custody.

"I don't know what to tell you," I say. I really don't.

Consider the options swirling in his mind: He could go back to his tier, where a man twice his size has made it very clear he is not welcome. There, he would risk nights as a punk without a protector. He might get robbed. He might get raped. He might get stabbed.

Then there is the alternative, the only one that Winn, like many other prisons, offers to inmates like this: the protective-custody wing in Cypress. He would be put in a cell, maybe alone, maybe with another man, for twenty-three hours a day. He would be branded a snitch just for going there, which means that when he eventually left, the odds of getting stabbed would be high.

He storms past me, back to the key. "I ain't going on no PC, man," he shouts at Miss Price. "I just came from Cypress!" He paces back and forth, working himself up. "Y'all go' have to drag me out this bitch, man. Real talk. I ain't trippin' on what the fuck y'all fixing to do to me," he says, pointing at Bacle and me. "Real talk! 'Cuz I ain't going on no PC." Miss Price screams for him to get out.

"Man, I can live on any fucking tier you put me on!" he shouts. I escort him out of the unit; he's eventually placed in another one.

·　　·　　·

During our training, Kenny warned us how easy it was to be manipulated into sex by inmates. Even male guards "fall victim to bein' involved in a relationship wit' a inmate," he said. "We got some folks come in here with relationships on the outside, and it just blows my mind how these inmates get in that ear and they wind up falling victim. That's just the way it is. They don't call 'em cons for no reason." He warned us to be vigilant because even in a consensual relationship, the guard could be classified as a sex offender. He told us about one captain at Winn, Charlie Roberts (his real name), who got "involved wit' a inmate. Havin' oral sex wit' him. So guess where he is sittin' at? A federal institution."

This story came up several times as an example of a guard who had to face the consequences of his weak will. Nothing was ever said about the inmate who gave Roberts blow jobs. When I looked at the files from Roberts's case, I learned the inmate was a transgender woman who went by the name China. She had identified as a girl from age eleven. Her father beat her repeatedly, and by the time she turned thirteen she had left home and begun stripping on Bourbon Street in New Orleans. In 2000, she was sentenced to four years in prison for a "crime against nature"—oral sex for pay—and sent to Winn. During her first year, she was serving a stint in seg for a dirty urine test when, she later testified, Roberts shackled her, brought her to an office, and told her to give him a blow job. If she didn't, he said he would put her in a cell with an inmate who would "handle" things. When she later told two administrators what had happened, one allegedly told her that if she ever lied about one of his guards again, he would "plant [her] ass under Cypress."

Over the next two years, China said, she was raped several times by inmates, but she kept it to herself. "I was ridiculed and picked on by the staff, and that made it to where I couldn't go to the staff for help at all," she said in a deposition. "If an inmate did want to rape me . . . who could I turn to?" She became another inmate's punk. One day in 2003, Miss Price sent her to the count room for having an "outrageous" feminine haircut. There, an officer ordered her to take another urine test by peeing in a cup while standing. China had been through this with him before—she'd told him she couldn't pee standing up. After a long standoff, Roberts showed up and told her she could sit on the toilet. The other guards left. As she peed, Roberts entered the bathroom and closed the door behind him. He told her that if she didn't give him oral sex again, he would taint her urine test and send her back to Cypress.

"Stop playing," China said. Roberts slapped her in the face. She dropped to her knees and did what he asked. When she finished, he said, "Bitch, you better swallow."

"I would die before I ever fucking swallowed anything he put in my mouth," she later recalled. She held the semen in her mouth and spit it out onto her shirt. After she filed a grievance and contacted the American Civil Liberties Union, she called the FBI. An agent came to the prison, took the shirt, and interviewed Roberts. The next day, CCA shipped China off to a publicly operated state prison, where she was held in a solitary cell "no bigger than a broom closet" and never let out for exercise. She was released from prison eleven months later.

"If I knew that the prison was going to shave me bald and send me to another prison and put me on maximum-security lockdown," she later testified, "I would have swallowed." Even harder than the solitary was knowing that, had she swallowed, she would have been able to finish her auto-body class, which might have kept her from having to live on the streets and going back to sex work when she got out. "I would have swallowed and I would have kept on swallowing until I got that piece of paper."

CCA denied all of China's allegations, but it settled the case out of court for an undisclosed amount. Roberts also denied her allegations when the FBI interviewed him, but the bureau found that the semen on her shirt was his. Roberts ultimately pleaded guilty to sexually assaulting China and making false statements to the FBI, and he was sentenced to six years in federal prison and a $5,000 fine. I have not been able to track down China. Roberts served his sentence and was released in 2012.

Nearly half of all allegations of sexual victimization in prisons involve staff. In the 2011 BJS survey, CCA prisons reported a rate of substantiated staff-on-inmate sexual assault similar to that of public facilities. However, CCA prisons' rate of reported staff-on-inmate sexual harassment was five times higher. Another federal report found that former inmates of private state prisons are twice as likely to report being sexually victimized by staff members as inmates who were in public prisons.

Prisoners also sexually harass and abuse officers. A recurring issue is inmates standing at the bars and masturbating at women guards sitting in the key. I see some women's reports of sexual abuse by prisoners handled swiftly, but I hear other female guards complain that their sexual-harassment charges have gone nowhere. (CCA says it "takes any allegation of sexual harassment very seriously and has strong policies and practices in place for investigating such claims.") I once write up an inmate for masturbating in front of a nurse, a violation that should cause him to be moved to Cypress, but he isn't. I regularly see the macho culture of prison transcend the division between guards and inmates—male officers routinely ignore the harassment of their female colleagues. "Some of them staff, they'll wear clothes so tight you can see everything they got," Kenny lectured in class. "They'll walk down there and they just struttin' they stuff. We got one, shoot, trying to sue the company 'cuz an inmate touched her on the butt. Man, you was down here every day shaking your stuff! If you do all this trying to draw attention to yourself, you go' get some, and if you ain't mindful, you'll get more than what you asked for."

In a class on "inmate manipulation," Kenny told us that when he was a unit manager, there was a female officer he didn't like. Many prisoners didn't like her either, and one in particular was "bound and determined to get this girl fired." One night, the woman fell asleep in a chair on a unit floor, he said. She had also left the inmate's tier door open. The inmate crept out of his tier, pulled his penis out, and "went to town wit' it" inches from her head. Not long afterward, the inmate was released, and he sent a letter to the prison, telling them to look at the surveillance footage from that night. CCA fired the guard for sleeping on the job and for leaving the tier door open, Kenny recalled.

"Ain't nuttin' we could do to him," Kenny said of the inmate. "That's over wit'. He gone home." (CCA says it is unaware of such an incident and that it would have reported the inmate to law enforcement.) "I laughed, but it's also kind of scary. I don't want nothing bad to happen to nobody." But, he added, "We was lookin' to get her too. He got her for us. It worked out on both ends."

## Cracking Down

In the morning meeting, the supervisor and Assistant Warden Parker admonish us about the topic they've been lecturing about all week—cracking down on sagging pants and homemade clothing. They are frustrated because no one is doing it. In private, the officers grumble that if the supervisors don't want inmates to wear bleach-stained jeans instead of their "CCA blues," they should confiscate the pants themselves. Why should the guards put themselves on the line? Parker seems to be aware of this, and he's keen to show he's not a front-office kind of guy. His personal goal is to become "lord of the do-rags," taking the prohibited head coverings whenever he sees them.

"Does anybody know why we don't want them to individualize their uniform?" Parker asks us. "We want them *institutionalized*. You guys ever heard that term? We want them institutionalized, not individualized. Is that sort of a mind game? Yup. But you know what? It's worked over the couple hundred years that we've had prisons in this country. So that's why we do it. We do not want them to feel as though they are individuals. We want them, for lack of a better term, to feel like a herd of cattle. We're just moving 'em from point A to point B, letting them graze in the dining hall and then go back to the barn. Okay?"

Parker says the DOC wardens have been pestering him. "Are they scared, Mr. Parker?" he mimics. "Are you not providing the adequate training that your staff members need, Mr. Parker, to be strong enough to take clothing away from an inmate? Are they that scared, Mr. Parker?"

His tone softens. "I don't know when it last dawned on me in the last couple weeks—I actually care about this institution and I care about all of you. I'm tired of people telling me that people at Winn aren't doing their jobs. A term that was used a couple of weeks ago that was very embarrassing to me was: They don't even understand basic prison management at Winn." Some of the guards shake their heads. "Anybody feel good about that one? I know I sure as hell don't."

After the meeting, everyone moves slowly down the walk. Edison, a big white CO with a bull neck, says he's tired of this " 'Kumbaya' bullshit." He was removed from his post in Cypress when the SORT team took it over. Suggesting he can't handle his own is about the worst insult you could give him. "I'm sick and tired of doin' this shit," he says. "The security in this place is pathetic. They need to tighten up on the tier doors, re-man the towers, and reinstitute the inmate work out in the field and the inmate programs, and give these fools something to do besides sit in their beds, eat, watch TV, and figure out how to fuck with us." He blames the "ivory tower" in Nashville—CCA's corporate headquarters—for Winn's problems. "Those fools ain't got nothing in their mind but the bottom line."

Today, the supervisor tells Edison to join Bacle and me in Ash. Having a new guard come to Ash is like having a visitor to our twisted household. This morning, standing around, waiting for the day to begin, Bacle complains about the most mundane of issues: Some inmates don't sit on their bunks during count like they are supposed to.

"How's your fighting skills, Bauer?" Edison asks. The question makes me nervous. This is the opposite of the approach I'm trying to take in here.

"All right," I say.

"You're with me," he says. "We're going to give these motherfuckers an eye-opener today. I don't play that bullshit. You get your ass on the bunk."

"You're not into this playing shit," Bacle says sympathetically.

"That's right," Edison says.

"You're a grade A1 asshole when it needs to be," Bacle says.

"I'm a grade A1 drill instructor when I have to be."

"That's what this place needs!"

"I know it does," Edison says. "It needs to go back to about 1960. Give a goddamn PR-24"—a police baton—"and hand a can of gas to everybody. You get stupid, you get beat down. You get big and stupid, you get gassed and beat down. Either way, you learn your fucking place."

Edison has been here for a year and a half. "With my skill set, and with where I moved to, it was the only fuckin' thing open," he says. He is an Army Rangers veteran and was once a small-town police chief. He says he retired when "the city council got afraid of me." "When I was a cop, I knew damn well that I would shoot your ass. I didn't carry two extra clips, I carried four. When I went to work, I went to war. When I got off, I still went to war. I carried two clips on me regardless of what I was wearing. I carried *at least* my Glock 40 underneath my arm, and usually I had a Glock .45 on my ankle. Go ahead, play with me."

We walk the floor. He stops. We stop. "You know what is stupid?" he says. "I see murderers. I see rapists. I see robbers. And then I see, the vast majority is in here for bein' stupid enough to smoke a joint too close to a school. Twenty-five years, federal mandatory. Then you got somebody that slaughtered a whole

fucking family gets twenty-five to life and he's out in six to eight."
(About one-fifth of Winn inmates are in for drug-related crimes.
Getting busted with a joint near a school will typically land you
about six years, not twenty-five.) Edison's indignation about drug
criminalization surprises me. "Now, where's the fucking justice
in that? And we're paying how much per inmate per day?"

"Count time!" the woman in the key yells. I unlock the door
of B1 tier and Edison walks in. An inmate is standing at the sink,
brushing his teeth. "Get on your bunk," Edison barks. The inmate keeps his back turned to Edison. "Or would you like to do
it in Cypress?" Edison steps in toward him. "Step out!" Edison
shouts, pointing to the door. He's seriously sending a prisoner to
seg for this?

The inmate walks out, still brushing his teeth. "This man is
going on about some bullshit," he says, waving his toothbrush
around. A spot of toothpaste lands on Edison's jacket, which is
hanging on a nearby chair.

"Go ahead! Be dumb! Let's go!" Edison yells, turning his hat
backward. "*Please* be stupid enough to touch me. I'm already taking your ass to Cypress." The inmate continues to brush his teeth.

I walk down the tier and do count. "That Crip boy go' to tear
his ass up," one inmate says as I pass. "Your work partner going
to get stabbed."

I can't keep count straight in my head. I just want to get off
the tier.

When we leave the tier everyone comes up to the bars and
yells at Edison. "You want to go next?" he shouts. "Behind the
wall!" They don't budge. "Every one of y'all is going to Cypress."

"Suck my dick!"

The captain and a sergeant enter the unit. The captain tells
Edison to step aside so he can talk to the inmates and try to ease
the tension. "This pacification bullshit," Edison mutters to me.
"Yeah, we knew how to pacify 'em in Vietnam. We dropped a
fuckin' 500-pounder on 'em. That pacifies." The captain tells

Edison to come with him. "It's not warm and fuzzy enough," Edison says to me as he leaves.

The sergeant, whose name is King, pulls me aside. "I'm here for you, bro," he says. In the past, I've heard him complain that the supervisors don't back the line officers enough. "Don't ever think I'm against you. 'Cuz I'm gonna knock one of 'em out if I have to. And we go' to write that report like he was trying to kill me and it was self-defense. Hahahaha!"

King has only been working at Winn for five months, but he's been in corrections for eight years. As a kid, he spent time in juvenile hall. Like Edison, he is an army vet, and he credits the military for correcting his delinquent ways. After twenty-two years in the service, he got a job in a juvenile-correctional facility in Texas. One day, he told a boy to get off the basketball court and the kid grabbed his throat and tried to strangle him. "I damn near beat the piss out of him. Sixteen years old, six-foot-three. As soon as you put your hands on me, you're not a teenager, you're a man. I put that uppercut on his ass and the superintendent said, 'I strongly suggest that you resign, sarge.' I fucked him up pretty good."

"Oh well!" Bacle says.

"All of this I shattered," he says, pointing to his jaw and mouth. "Oh well!"

## Pink Shades

During count, I tally bodies, not faces. If I look at faces, it means I have to keep the numbers straight while constantly calibrating sternness and friendliness in my eyes for each individual. When I go down the tier, I make a point to walk in a fast, long stride with a slight pop in my left step, trying to look tough. I practiced this in the mirror because inmates comment every day on a twist in my walk that I never knew existed. Sometimes prisoners whistle at me as I pass. In my normal life, I try to diffuse any macho tendencies. Now, I try to annihilate anything remotely feminine about me. As I walk and count, I tighten my core to keep my hips from moving.

I steel myself for A1 tier. For some reason, inmates on this tier are always testing me, and as I walk down one side, someone makes a comment about my "panties" as I pass. "You like that dick. You like that dick," someone sings as I go by. I ignore it. Another comments that I look like a model. I pretend I don't hear him. On my way back toward the front, I hear again, "You like that dick. You like that dick."

This has been going on for weeks, but this time something snaps. I stop count and march back to the guy calling out to me, a thirty-something black man with pink sunglasses and tattoos crawling up his neck. "What did you say to me?" I shout.

"I ain't said nothin'."

"Why are you always saying shit like that? You are always focusing so much on me, maybe you like the dick! Bitch ass!"

"Say that again?"

"Maybe you like the dick!" I shout. I am completely livid.

"He doesn't know how big a mistake he just made," another inmate says as I storm out.

When we finish count, I go back to Pink Shades's tier. "Give me your ID," I say to him. He refuses. "Give me your ID! *Now!*" I shout at the top of my lungs. He doesn't. I get his name from another officer and write him up for making sexual comments. He says he's going to file a PREA grievance on me.

I try to cool down. My heart is still hammering ten minutes later. "Are you all right, sarge?" a prisoner asks me. Slowly, my rage turns to shame and I go into the bathroom and sit on the floor. Where did those words come from? I rarely ever shout. I am not homophobic. Or am I? I feel utterly defeated. I go back to A1 and call Pink Shades to the bars.

"Look, I just want you to understand I don't have a problem with any of y'all," I tell him. "I think a lot of you are in here for sentences that are too long. I'm not like these other guys, all right?"

"All right," he says.

"But, you know, when people disrespect me like that for no reason, I can't just take that—you know what I mean?"

He tries to deny taunting me, but I won't back down. "Look, you going to have inmates talkin' crazy," he says.

"But you don't want me talking crazy to you, right?" There are inmates staring at us in astonishment.

"I feel you," he says. "You came here and talked to me like a man. And I apologize. I ain't got nothing against any of y'all officers. You feel me? I understand that you gotta live. You got to survive. Those words hurt you. I feel you. I mean I was singing a song, but you probably took it the wrong way. It triggered something in you." He's right. Something about being here reminds me of being in junior high, getting picked on for my size and the fact that I read books, getting called a faggot.

I tear up his disciplinary report and throw it in the trash. When I walk back down the tier for the next count, no one pays any attention to me.

*Man Down*

One day in Ash, a few inmates shout, "Man down! Man down!" A large man, Mason, is lying on his bed in C2, his right hand over his bare chest. His eyes are closed and his left leg is moving back and forth slowly.

"We just put him on his bed. He had fell off this side of his fucking bed just now, bro," an inmate says to me. "He's fucked up." I radio for a stretcher.

Mason starts to cry. His left hand is a fist. His back arches. "I'm scared," he mouths. Someone puts a hand on his arm for the briefest moment: "I know, son. They finna come see you now."

A stretcher finally arrives. The nurses and their orderlies move slowly. "They weren't supposed to send that man back down here," an inmate says to me. Earlier today Mason was playing basketball and fell to the ground in pain, he explains. He went to the infirmary, where they told him that he had fluid in his lungs.

Three inmates pick up Mason in his sheet and put him on the stretcher. His hands are crossed over his chest like a mummy as two prisoners wheel him away.

Within a few hours he is sent back to the tier.

Days later, I see Mason dragging his feet, his arms around his chest. I tell him to take my chair. He sits and hunches over, putting his head in his lap. It feels like a "throbbing pain in my chest," he says. We call for a wheelchair. "They told me I got fluid on my lungs and they won't send me to the hospital," he says. "That shit crazy."

A nurse happens to be in the unit, passing out pills. I tell her they keep sending Mason to the infirmary but won't take him to the hospital. She insists "nothing serious" is wrong with him.

"When I saw him last week, he was almost passed out," I say. "He was in a lot of pain."

She looks at me sidelong. "But the doctor still ain't going to send him to the hospital just 'cause of that."

If he were sent to the hospital, CCA would be contractually obligated to pay for his stay. For a for-profit company, this presents a dilemma. Even a short hospital stay is a major expense for an inmate who brings the company about thirty-four dollars per day. And that's aside from the cost of having two guards keep watch over him. Medical care within the prison is expensive, too. CCA does not disclose its medical expenses, but in a typical prison, health-care costs are the second-biggest expense after staff. On average, a Louisiana prison puts 9 percent of its budget toward health care. In some states it can be much higher; health care is 31 percent of a California prison's budget. Nearly 40 percent of Winn inmates have a chronic disease such as diabetes, heart disease, or asthma, according to Louisiana's budget office. About 6 percent have a communicable disease such as HIV or hepatitis C.

One day, I meet a man with no legs in a wheelchair. His name is Robert Scott. (He consented to having his real name used.) He's been at Winn twelve years. "I was walking when I got here," he tells me. "I was walking, had all my fingers." I notice he is wearing fingerless gloves with nothing poking out of them. "They took my legs off in January and my fingers in June. Gangrene don't play. I kept going to the infirmary, saying, 'My feet hurt. My feet hurt.' They said, 'Ain't nothin' wrong wicha. I don't *see* nothin' wrong wicha.' They didn't believe me, or they talk bad to me—'I can't believe you comin' up here!'"

His medical records show that in the space of four months he made at least nine requests to see a doctor. He complained of sore spots on his feet, swelling, oozing pus, and pain so severe he couldn't sleep. When he visited the infirmary, medical staff offered him sole pads, corn removal strips, and Motrin. He says he once showed his swollen foot, dripping with pus, to the warden. On one of these occasions, Scott alleges in a federal lawsuit against CCA, a nurse told him, "Ain't nothing wrong with you. If you make another medical emergency you will receive a disciplinary write-up for malingering." He filed a written request to be taken to a hospital for a second opinion, but it was denied.

Eventually, numbness spread to his hands, but the infirmary refused to treat him. His fingertips and toes turned black and wept pus. Inmates began to fear his condition was contagious. When Scott's sleeplessness kept another inmate awake, the inmate threatened to kill him if he was not moved to another tier. A resulting altercation drew the attention of staff, who finally sent him to the local hospital.

"But when I got my legs cut off they didn't come back and say, 'Robert, I'm sorry.' I done taked my lickin'. Part of being locked up." He is now suing CCA for neglect, claiming that inmates are denied medical care because the company operates the prison "on a 'skeleton crew' for profitable gain."

"Where do you think is one of the number-one areas that we get hit on as a confinement business?" Assistant Warden Parker asks us at a staff meeting. "Medical! Inmates have this thing that if they have a sniffle they are supposed to be flown to a specialist somewhere and be treated immediately for that sniffle." His tone becomes incredulous. "Believe it or not, we are required by law to take care of them."

It's true: Under Supreme Court rulings citing the Eighth Amendment, prisons are required to provide inmates with adequate health care. Yet CCA has found ways to minimize its obligations. At the out-of-state prisons where California ships some of its inmates, CCA will not accept prisoners who are over sixty-five years old, have mental-health issues, or have serious conditions like HIV. The company's Idaho prison contract specified that the "primary criteria" for screening incoming offenders was "no chronic mental health or health care issues." The contracts of some CCA prisons in Tennessee and Hawaii stipulate that the states will bear the cost of HIV treatment. Such exemptions allow CCA to tout its cost-efficiency while taxpayers assume the medical expenses for the inmates the company won't take or treat.

In 2010, the company and Immigration and Customs Enforcement settled a federal lawsuit brought by the ACLU that asserted immigration detainees at a CCA-run facility in California were routinely denied prescribed medical treatment. (CCA admitted no wrongdoing.) In a rare case that made its way to trial in 2001, the company was found to have violated the Eighth and Fourteenth Amendments and ordered to pay $235,000 to an inmate whose broken jaw was left wired shut for ten weeks. (He removed the wires himself with nail clippers while guards watched.) The jury wrote they hoped the message sent by the ruling would "echo throughout the halls of your corporate offices as well as your corporate housing facilities." (CCA appealed and settled for an undisclosed amount.)

CCA has also been the subject of medical malpractice cases involving pregnant inmates. In 2014, it settled a case for $690,000 over the death of a prisoner's baby at a county jail in Chattanooga, Tennessee. When the inmate went into labor, she was put in a cell with no mattress and left there for three hours as she bled heavily onto the floor. CCA employees did not call an ambulance until approximately five hours after the prisoner asked for help. Her newborn baby died shortly thereafter. In court proceedings, the warden testified that surveillance footage showed no signs of an emergency. But before the footage could be reviewed, CCA claimed it had been accidentally erased. The court sanctioned the company for destroying evidence.

CCA settled another case for $250,000 after a pregnant woman being held in a jail in Nashville complained of vaginal bleeding and severe abdominal pain. She said medical staff demanded "proof," so they put her in solitary and turned off the water so her blood loss could be "monitored." She claimed they did nothing to alleviate her pain as she endured contractions, filling the toilet with blood. The next morning, the inmate was shackled and taken to a hospital, where doctors found that she was already dilated. While prison guards watched, she gave birth and was immediately sedated. When she woke up, medical staff brought her the dead baby. She said she was not allowed to call her family and was given no information about the disposal of her son's body.

At least fifteen doctors at Winn have been sued for delivering poor medical care. The prison hired several of them even after the state had disciplined them for misconduct. One, Aris Cox, was hired in the nineties, after his license was temporarily suspended for writing prescriptions to support his tranquilizer addiction. While Mark Singleton was at Winn, the Louisiana board of medical examiners discovered that he had failed "to meet the standard of care" at his previous position in New Mexico. He was put on probation, but CCA kept him on. Winn hired Stephen Kuplesky after his license had been temporarily suspended for prescribing painkillers to a family member with no medical condition. Robert Cleveland was working at Winn when he was put on medical probation for his involvement in a kickback scheme with a wheelchair company. He was later disciplined for prescribing narcotics from his home and vehicle. (It's not clear if he was working at Winn at the time. CCA says all doctors at Winn had "appropriate credentials.")

Data collected by *Prison Legal News* on more than 1,200 state and federal suits against CCA shows that 15 percent of them were related to medical care. (This sample is not a complete list of complaints against the company; in 2010 alone, CCA faced more than 600 pending cases. Between 1998 and 2008, the company settled another 600 cases.) Since most inmates can't afford legal counsel, it's nearly impossible for them to prevail in court. When I made public-records requests in a couple of states for a more recent accounting of lawsuits settled by CCA, the company intervened, arguing that a list of settlements involving claims of medical malpractice, wrongful deaths, assaults, and the use of force "constitutes trade secrets."

· · ·

My reconciliation with Pink Shades encouraged me. Every time I have a problem with a prisoner, I try the same approach and eventually we tap knuckles to show each other respect. Still, these breakthroughs are fleeting. In the moment, they feel like a glimmer of a possibility that we can appreciate each other's humanity, but I come to understand that our positions make this virtually impossible. We can chat and laugh through the bars, but inevitably I need to flex my authority. My job will always be to deny them the most basic of human impulses—to push for more freedom. Day by day, the number of inmates who are friendly with me grows smaller.

There are exceptions, like Corner Store, but were I to take away the privileges Bacle and I have granted him, I know that he, too, would become an enemy.

My priorities change. Striving to treat everyone as human takes too much energy. More and more, I focus on proving I won't back down. I am vigilant; I come to work ready for people to catcall me or run up on me and threaten to punch me in the face. I show neither fear nor compunction. Sometimes prisoners call me racist, and it stings, but I try as hard as I can not to flinch because to do so would be to show a pressure point, a button that can be pressed when they want to make me bend.

Nearly every day the unit reaches a crescendo of frustration because inmates are supposed to be going somewhere like the law library, GED classes, vocational training, or a substance-abuse group, but their programs are canceled or they are let out of the unit late. Inmates tell me that at other prisons, the schedule is firm. "That door would be opening up and everybody would be on the move," an inmate who's been incarcerated throughout the state says. Here, there is no schedule. We wait for the call over the radio; then we let the inmates go. They could eat at eleven-thirty a.m. They could eat at three p.m. School might happen, or maybe not. It's been years since Winn has had the staff to run the big yard. Sometimes we let the inmates onto the small yard attached to the unit. Often we don't. Canteen and law-library hours are canceled regularly. There just aren't enough officers to keep everything going.

Guards bond with prisoners over their frustrations. Prisoners tell us they understand we are powerless to change these high-level management problems. Yet the two groups remain locked in battle like soldiers in a war they don't believe in.

Whenever I open a tier door, I demand that everyone shows me his pass, and I use my body to stop the flood of people from pouring out. Some just push through.

I catch one. "Get back in!" I shout. "I'm writing you up right now if you don't get back in there right now. You hear me?"

He walks back in, staring me down. "White dude all on a nigga's trail, man," he says. I shut the door, ignoring him. "You better get the fuck from down here before I end up hurtin' one of y'all," he shouts at me. "You green as a motherfucker!"

I'm tired.

An inmate comes around the key. Bacle is following him and calls for me to stop him. I stand in the inmate's path. I know him, the one with the mini-dreads. I feel threatened, frankly, whenever I see him. "This way," I say, pointing back to where he came from. He tries to walk past me. I lock eyes with him. "This way!" I command. He turns back and walks slowly away. I walk behind him. He stops, spins around, throws his hands in the air, and shouts, "Get the fuck off my trail, dog!" I know he's testing me. I open his tier door. He walks in, stands just inside, and stares me down hard. I grab the door and slam it shut—*bang!*—in his face.

I turn and step back into the throng of inmates milling around the floor. "Motherfucker's going to end up dead!" he shouts after me. I stop and turn around. He just stares. I grab the radio on my shoulder, then pause. Was I ever taught what to do when something like this happens? I know how to press the button and speak into the radio, but whom do I call? I think of King, the officer who smashed the kid's jaw. "Sergeant King, could you come down to Ash?" I say into my shoulder.

"En route."

When he arrives, I take him into B1 tier. I find Mini-Dreads.

"He needs to get locked up," I say, looking him in the eyes.

King cuffs him. I tell King he threatened my life. He needs to go to seg.

"What happened?! I ain't said nuttin'!" the inmate shouts. I walk away.

I go back to chasing the others into their tiers. "What you lock that dude up for?" an inmate asks me. "Dude was 'bout to go home," another says. "He ain't go' go home now." I walk away, unyielding. In the back of my mind, however, there is a voice: *Did you see him say anything? Wasn't your back turned? Are you sure what you heard?* It doesn't matter, really. He wanted to intimidate me and it was about time I threw someone in the hole. They need to know I am not weak.

.    .    .

One morning, Ash smells like feces. On D2, liquid shit is oozing out of the shower drain and running down the tier. "It's been here over twelve hours," one inmate says.

"Man, you got worms and everything on the floor. Real talk."

"This is a health and safety violation!"

"Man, this is cruel and unusual punishment!"

We let inmates out to go to the small yard. As they flow out of the tiers, I see a large group run to A1 tier. Bacle pushes the tier door shut and calls a Code Blue over the radio. Inside the tier, two prisoners are grappling, their bodies pressed up against the bars. Each is gripping a shank in one hand while holding the other's arm to keep him from swinging. Drops of blood spatter the floor. The surrounding scene is oddly calm. Inmates stand around and watch, not saying anything.

"Break it up," Bacle says indifferently. "Break it up."

The two combatants are speaking to each other quietly, almost at a whisper.

"Come on," one says. "Come on with it, big dog."

"I'ma do you like you did me."

They grapple some more.

"Break it up!" Bacle yells.

"Come on!" I shout, feeling utterly impotent.

Bacle, Miss Price, a CCA employee from out of state, and I stand just two feet from them, separated by the bars, and watch the two try to press their knives into each other.

One man breaks his hand free, swings it up, and jams his shank into the side of the other man's neck. My breath stops for a moment, and I utter a gagging sound. "It ain't sharp enough, big dog," says the guy who was just stabbed. "Let me show you where the sharp one is."

Bacle reaches through the bars and grabs the stabber by his hood as the other inmate struggles to break loose. For the first time, the other prisoners make noise. "Hey, man, you're gonna get him killed like that!" one shouts at Bacle. Bacle lets go, and the two men tumble across the floor, landing in a heap by the toilet, blocked from our view by a short wall. They keep scuffling. An arm swings up and jabs down. One prisoner walks over to the urinal two feet from them and pees as they keep stabbing.

The fight lasts nearly four minutes, until a SORT member comes in with a can of pepper spray. "Don't fucking move," he barks. "Everybody lay the fuck down." He sprays the men as they try to stab each other. One, who's had a bit of his ear sliced off, is taken to the hospital. The other goes to seg.

The smell of pepper spray fades, but the smell of shit does not. It's not until the afternoon that someone comes in to fix the toilets and finds a shank stuck in the plumbing.

Later, I recount to a sergeant how one of the inmates was poking the knife into the other guy's neck. "Did you learn something from that?" he asks me.

"Not really."

The inmate could have slit the other guy's throat if he wanted to, he says. But he didn't. "Both of 'em scared. That's the reason for havin' them shanks in the first place, 'cuz they are scared."

### The Audit

At the end of my shift, I stride briskly down the dark walk. I am relieved to be going home, but after two weeks on the job as a full-time CO, I'm afraid in a way I wasn't at first. The longer I work here, the more people have grudges against me. As I head down the walk, inmates are coming and going from various parts of the prison and I can't see any other guards around. I don't have a radio—I am required to give it to the officer who relieves me. I've seen the surveillance footage, and I doubt it would be clear enough to identify anyone who might jump me in this darkness.

The gate before the exit is locked and I am routed through the visitation area. There, twenty or so officers from my shift are sitting at the tables, frowning. Two inmates are serving pizza. We've been trapped in a company meeting. Assistant Warden Parker is there. The chief of security. HR. I grab some pizza and sit down, frustrated.

"How many people here got less than a year in?" Parker asks. I raise my hand. "You've probably seen a lot of bad days, okay? We're gonna change that. And it takes all of us working together. It really, really does. As long as we stay as a decent team and we remember that the bad guys are the guys who stay here twenty-four/seven and don't get to leave."

On the wall is a painting of a black kid and a white kid lying on their bellies on a grassy hillside, looking at a rainbow. Next to it is another mural of a lion and a tiger tearing through an American flag with a bald eagle flying overhead. "The CCA Way" is written above it.

"The company took a look at things and they realized that we need to do a little bit better for the staff here at Winn. I'm not going to say that we've waved a magic wand and everybody's walking out of here, gonna go buy new cars, but the hourly wage for a correctional officer is going to go up to ten dollars an hour. So congratulations to everybody sitting inside this room." He starts clapping and a few people join unenthusiastically. "This is going to be one of those proud moments," he says.

"Does anybody know what the ACA is?" Parker asks. "Have you been hearing about 'We got ACA coming up. Ooooh! ACA's coming. We gotta panic! Hit the panic button!'"

"The American Correctional Association," someone volunteers.

"Okay, why do we care about ACA?" Parker asks.

"We need our jobs. We need to pass."

"That's a theme that goes with it. Years and years and years ago, I think it was 1870, there was a governor upset with what he thought was cruel and unusual punishment," he lectures. "So he started drafting up a little group of people that would go around and they would check on prisons and prison conditions to ensure that the people who were confined were not being treated cruelly. After time they started developing a sophisticated auditing process. So, a third-party person who has no dog in the fight, so to speak, comes in and they take a look at how are we treating our inmates. And they give us a stamp of, 'You're treating them with proper care.'

"That way when we go to court and the inmate says, 'Oh, they made me eat Pizza Hut pizza! That's cruel and unusual punishment! It should have been Domino's!'—when it goes to court, we pull up our ACA files and say, 'Hey, look, here's how we prepare our food in the kitchen. We prepare the food in our kitchen under these standards.'"

The ACA is a trade association, but it's also the closest thing we have to a national regulatory body for prisons. More than 900 public and private correctional facilities and detention centers are accredited under its standards. Winn was the first prison to be accredited in Louisiana. Shortly after T. Don Hutto cofounded CCA, he became the president of ACA.

Over the next few weeks, inmates repaint every unit in preparation for the ACA audit. The maintenance man is run ragged as he tries to fix busted vents, plumbing, and cell and tier doors. ("We didn't own the facility," CCA's spokesman told me, noting that major maintenance issues at Winn were the DOC's responsibility. CCA's contract states that it was responsible for routine and preventive maintenance.)

In anticipation of the audit, I read the ACA standards. How will the auditors deal with the fact that the cells in segregation are at least twenty square feet smaller than required? Or that inmates only get ten minutes to eat, not the mandated twenty? There are many other ACA standards and recommendations Winn does not appear to meet: We rarely have the required number of positions staffed; guards' pay is not comparable to the pay of state corrections officers; guards rarely ever use the metal detectors at the entrances to the housing units; prisoners often don't get one hour of daily access to exercise space; suicide-watch meals are below caloric requirements; there aren't enough toilets in the dorms. (The ACA did not respond to a request for comment.)

Then again, Winn passed its last ACA audit, in 2012, with a near-perfect score of 99 percent, the same score it received in its previous audit three years earlier. In fact, CCA's average score across all its accredited prisons is also 99 percent.

On the morning of the audit, we wake everyone up and tell them to make their beds and take any pictures of women off their lockers. Two well-dressed white men enter Ash unit and do a slow lap around the floor. The only questions they ask Bacle and me are what our names are and how we're doing. They do not examine our logbook, nor do they check our entries against the camera footage. If they did, they would find that some of the cameras don't work. They do not check the doors. If they did, they would see they need to be yanked open by hand because most of the switches don't work. They don't check the fire alarm, which automatically closes smoke doors over the tiers, some of which must be jimmied back open by two guards. They do not ask to go on a tier. They do not interview any inmates. They do a single loop and they leave.

.    .    .

After nearly two decades, Corner Store is about to be free. He has just six weeks to go before he qualifies for early release with the "good time" he's earned. How does someone reenter the world after two decades behind bars, with no friends on the outside and no money to his name? His first step, he says, will be to stay in a shelter until he can get on his feet. He doesn't know where he will go yet. He tells me he doesn't want to count the days. "It stresses me out. Anxiety sets in. Your mind goes, working and thinking about stuff. How am I going to do this? How am I going to do that? It causes a panic attack. When I walk, I walk."

But fantasies creep into his mind. "I'ma get me a big bottle of Kaopectate, a big German chocolate cake, five-gallon thing of milk," he says. "Just get out the way, that's all I'ma tell you." We are outside, talking through the fence; he's on the small yard and I'm on the Ash walk. "After that, I want me a seafood platter, a *real* seafood platter about the size of the kitchen table, just for me and Mom. It's all about Mom when I go home."

He puts his hand on the fence and leans in. "What I'm sayin' is this here, man: I just wanna go have fun, boy. And fun does not mean me-gettin'-in-trouble fun. Fun means just enjoying life. I wanna be able to take my mothafuckin' shoes off and socks off and walk in the sand. I wanna be able to just go outside in my shorts and just my house slippers and stand in the rain and just—" he spreads his arms, points his face to the sky, and opens his mouth. "Them thangs I miss. You can't do that in here. Alls I'm sayin' is this here: When I get out, I don't want to have to poke my chest out any longer. It hurts to poke my chest out. It's a weight on my shoulders I've been toting for the last twenty-some-thin' years, and I'm ready to drop that weight because the load is heavy."

## Chapter 5: Lockdown

On my fifth week on the job, I'm asked to train a new cadet. He is a short white man in his forties with peppered black hair. He says he worked as a security contractor in Iraq and Afghanistan for Triple Canopy and Blackwater. He is hoping to go back to

Afghanistan soon. "I had terrorists who blew up schools and shit that I had to take care of. It wasn't all PC like it is here." Prisoners here, he says, get treated with kid gloves. "They got rights and all this crap. Fuck that."

I show him how to open the doors and do callouts, and I tell him we are going to start letting people out for chow soon. "What do you mean?" he says, suddenly looking frightened. "You are just going to open the doors and let them out? I can't believe that!"

He doesn't think they should go out at all. "Fuck 'em. Not unless you have absolutely an emergency. Or you're on a work plan or some shit like that. I'd make prison so bad that you would never want to come back. When I was growing up, my mom used to live in Mississippi. They had all the work gangs and they were all in orange and all chained up. Chain gangs and shit like that. That's how it should be. Make it so bad, you'd never want to come back."

"It's pretty bad in here," I tell him. "People get stabbed here all the time." At least seven inmates have been stabbed in the last six weeks. As people come in from chow, I hear on the radio, "Code Blue in Elm! Code Blue in Elm!" A CO is frantically calling for a stretcher. Several inmates are stabbing each other; they can't count how many.

"Everyone on the tier!" Bacle shouts to the prisoners milling about. "Fuck all that," one says. "We'll have another Code motherfucking Blue." Bacle blows his whistle. We get everyone in and I head out onto the Ash walk to see what is happening.

A minute later, a bleeding man is wheeled by on a work cart and I return inside. Several people were injured, and I hear one was stabbed about thirty times. Miraculously, no one dies.

Three days later, I see two inmates stab each other in Ash.

A week after that, another inmate is stabbed and beaten by multiple people in Elm. People say he was cut more than forty times. During this time, Miss Price quits after nearly twenty-five years of service. She says she's tired of this work. (We will go without a unit manager in Ash for weeks.) Not long after she leaves, someone is beaten unconscious and stabbed through the cheek in Birch and another inmate is stabbed in Cypress.

It is difficult to imagine how someone gets stabbed in segregation. How do shanks get in? How do inmates get to each other? The morning after the stabbing in Cypress, I hear Assistant Warden Parker call over the radio for maintenance to come and fix the cell doors there. A month ago, he told us that inmates in the unit could pull some cell doors off their tracks. A month before that, Mr. Tucker, the SORT commander, told us something similar. Apparently this problem still hasn't been fixed.

Miss Calahan (her real name), the Ash key officer, tells me they had the same problem in the unit before I started. She points at D1 tier and says that for two months, she and Bacle told the higher-ups to fix the door. At least one inmate filed a grievance about it. "I popped it several times using my foot," Bacle says. He even showed the warden how it was done. Then, one evening, two inmates shook the tier door open from the outside, apparently unnoticed by the floor officers. One was carrying an eight-inch knife, the other an ice pick. According to a legal complaint, the two inmates found another inmate who lived on the tier and stabbed him twelve times in the head, mouth, eye, and body. One of the attackers warned that he would kill anyone who alerted the guards, so the victim lay bleeding, waiting for a CO to come through for the mandatory half-hour security check. Unsurprisingly, no one did. He bled for an hour and a half until a guard came by for count. He spent nine days in the infirmary.

"Child, next day they was out here fixing that door!" Miss Calahan says.

Bacle says he wishes an investigative reporter would come and look into this place. He complains about how, in other prisons, inmates get new charges for stabbing someone. Here, they are put in seg, but they rarely get shipped to another prison with tighter security. "CCA wants that fucking dollar!" Bacle says through clenched teeth. "That's the reason why we play hell on getting a damn raise, because all they want is that dollar in their pocket."

High levels of violence have been documented at several CCA prisons. At Ohio's Lake Erie Correctional Institution, which CCA bought in 2011, inmate-on-inmate assaults increased 188 percent and inmate-on-staff assaults went up more than 300 percent between 2010 and 2012, according to a state report. (A 2015 report by the state prison inspector, provided by CCA, noted that Lake Erie had "drastically improved" and said the facility was "outperforming some of the state institutions.") In 2009, Kentucky declined to raise CCA's per diem rate at one facility because the company's prison was twice as violent as its state-run counterpart and because a suicidal employee smuggled in a gun and shot herself in the warden's office. There is no current data on how violence in public prisons compares with violence in private ones. The last study released by the Department of Justice was in 2001, and it found that the rate of inmate-on-inmate assaults was 38 percent higher at private prisons than at public prisons.

But are any of these numbers accurate? If I were not working at Winn and were reporting on the prison through more traditional means, I would never know how violent it is. While I work here, I keep track of every stabbing that I see or hear about from supervisors or eyewitnesses. During the first two months of 2015, at least twelve people are shanked. The company is required to report all serious assaults to the DOC. But DOC records show that for the first ten months of 2015, CCA reported only five stabbings. (CCA says it reports all assaults and that the DOC may have classified incidents differently.)

Reported or not, by my seventh week as a guard the violence is getting out of control. The stabbings start to happen so frequently that, on February 16, the prison goes on indefinite lockdown. No inmates leave their tiers. The walk is empty. Crows gather and puddles of water form on the rec yards. More men in black are sent in by corporate. They march around the prison in military formation. Some wear face masks.

.　　　.　　　.

The new SORT team, composed of officers from around the country, shakes down the prison bit by bit. The wardens from the DOC continue to wander around, and CCA also sends in wardens of its own from out of state. Tension is high. No inmates except kitchen workers can leave the tiers. Passing out food trays becomes a daily battle. Prisoners rush the food cart and take everything.

"CCA is not qualified to run this place," an inmate shouts to me a day into the lockdown. "You always got to shut the place down. You can't function. You can't run school or nothing because you got everybody on lockdown."

Another inmate cuts in. "Since I been here, there's been nothing *but* stabbings," he says. "It don't happen like this at other prisons because they got power. They got control. Ain't no control here, so it's gonna always be something happening. You got to start from the top to the bottom, you feel me? If [the warden] really want to control this prison—goddamn!—why ain't you go' call and get some workers? But you know what it's all about? It's about the money. 'Let them kill theyselves.' They don't give a fuck."

One day, a former public-jail warden visits Ash. "I don't know what's going on down here, but it's not good," he says to me. "There's something fucked up, I can tell you that."

I ask if Winn seems different from publicly operated prisons. "Oh, hell yeah," he says. "Too lax." If this were his prison, he says, there would be four officers on the floor, not two. At his public facility, officers start at $12.50 an hour. When they go to police academy, they get another $500 a month. Every time they pass a quarterly fitness test, they get $300. The initial training is ninety days. I tell him it was thirty days here. "This is a joke," he says.

"I been doing this for sixteen years. This is a free jail to me. Too much shit going on down here. Not no consequences." He says CCA could lose its contract.

One day, the visiting SORT team comes to Ash. One masked officer keeps watch over everyone with a pepper-ball gun. Other SORT members stand around, eating Twinkies and Oatmeal Creme Pies and drinking Mountain Dew. They tear up the tiers, throwing things out, slicing up mattresses. They find drugs and cell phones. Bacle tries to stop them from taking inmates' coffee or destroying their matchstick crafts. Their overzealousness riles him. "Some people here think just because they're locked up they're a bunch of shitheads. I look at it, they fucked up and they're doing their damn time."

As soon as SORT leaves, inmates scream over each other to tell me what was taken, cursing me for not standing up for them.

·        ·        ·

During the lockdown, Corner Store asks me to let him out of his tier. With the canteen closed, his services are badly needed. Everyone's commissary is getting low; many inmates are in search of cigarettes. They ask me to ferry things from one tier to the next, but I refuse, mostly because I know that once I do, the requests will never stop. I don't let Corner Store out. I tell him it's too risky with all these eyes around. For days, he just lies on his bed, staring at the ceiling.

His release date is five days away, but he still doesn't know where he's going when he gets out.

"Isn't it Tuesday you are getting out?"

"Supposedly," he says. Louisiana law doesn't allow early release unless the inmate has an address to go to. New parolees have to stay in the state, and his mother doesn't live in Louisiana. With no one outside to assist him, he has to rely on CCA to make arrangements with a shelter. The prison's coach was trying to help, but Corner Store says he got "roadblocked" by the administration.

"So they just keep you here?" I say, incredulous.

"Yeah, basically. I'm not even angry, man. I just know my day is coming. I've waited years for this. I'm not mad."

I ask Corner Store's case manager what is happening with him. "He might be supposed to be getting out," he says, but "as long as he don't have that [address], his feet will not hit outside that gate. It ain't nothin' I can do for him."

"They don't want nobody to leave," Corner Store tells me. "The longer they keep you, the more money they make. You understand that?"

.　　　.　　　.

One of the SORT members tells me they'll be at Winn for months. Yesterday, they found fifty-one shanks in Elm, roughly one for every seven men. DOC records show that during the first four months of 2015, CCA reported finding nearly 200 weapons at Winn. That made it the state's most heavily armed prison, with more than five times more confiscated weapons per inmate than GEO's similarly sized Allen Correctional Center, and twenty-three times more than Angola. "They getting ready to start a war," one officer says in a morning meeting.

Sergeant King stops by Ash. As he makes to leave, people start shouting from their tiers. "What's up with the fuckin' store?" It's been three weeks since anyone here went to canteen. Inmates are up at the bars, looking angry. "You 'bout to start a whole riot," one says to King.

Bacle seems nervous. "If they start throwing shit, you step right up here where they can't gitcha," he tells me, pointing toward the entrance. Less than a week ago, inmates rioted in a privately operated immigrant detention center in Texas. I saw prisoners here watching it on the news.

I walk over to one of the tiers.

"There ain't go' be no count or no nothing!" one shouts at me.

"Ain't no COs coming in this bitch until we go to canteen."

"That's what's up. We all standing behind that."

"We gonna put this bitch on the channel eight news."

"Y'all risking your fucking life around here playing these fucking games!"

"Fuck the count! Bring the warden down here."

King comes over to one of the tiers. "Y'all gotta give me an opportunity. Before y'all start bucking. Before y'all start refusing. Because here's what's going to happen: They're gonna bring the SORT force down here."

"We don't give a fuck!"

"I ain't got no fucking soap! No nothing! No deodorant! No fucking cigarettes! This place is shit!"

I don't want to give the impression we are afraid, so I walk the floor. Everyone, everywhere, is pissed. I feel an explosion coming and I want to flee. "I'm surprised ain't nobody got you yet," a white inmate with a shaved head says to me, his eyes cold and focused. "They go' get you."

A few years ago, a riot erupted in a low-security CCA prison in Mississippi over what inmates saw as inadequate health care and poor food. A guard was beaten to death. When Alex Friedmann, a former CCA inmate and a company shareholder, asked for a moment of silence for the guard at a corporate meeting in 2013, the board chair refused to honor the request. (At the time, CCA said it had "honored his memory a number of ways.")

King calls Bacle and me to the door. "Listen, it's a lot of tension down here," he says.

"No shit," Bacle says.

"They found seventy-five shanks in two days. These sonsabitches is dangerous, y'all. I don't want y'all goin' in them tiers. I don't want y'all lettin' nobody out. As of right now, if this shit don't get handled, y'all going to have a fuckin' riot on y'all hands.

All the black suits ain't going to do nothin' but pepper-ball and gas all of they asses." He leaves.

A while later, a CCA warden from Tennessee comes and talks to the inmates. "Y'all saying that y'all are being mistreated. I got plenty of people here. If we want to act like refugees and animals, then we can do it that way." The prisoners don't back down.

A couple of hours later, SORT comes and escorts the inmates to the canteen.

### A Drastic Change

The lockdown lasts a total of eleven days. When it ends, Corner Store stands at the bars, waiting for me to let him out to work the floor. I ignore him. He pleads, but I am unbending. I have become convinced that he thinks he has influence over me, though I can't articulate why. I become suspicious of his friendliness and wonder if he is manipulating me. I start to talk to him like every other inmate and he looks at me with confusion. When he lingers too long as I hold the gate open for chow, I slam it shut and let him stew. He calls my name as I walk away. I feel a twinge of guilt, but it lasts only momentarily.

His release date comes and goes. When I do count, I see him lying on his bunk. Eventually, he stops making eye contact as I pass.

An inmate orderly corners me. "Listen, what's the problem?" he says, leaning against his broom.

"What problem?" I say curtly.

"Listen, be cool. Be cool. We talking. Relax. Why you so aggressive when I talk to you? You're too snappy."

"I'm not aggressive, man!"

"No, no, no. There's been a drastic change in you. What the fuck went wrong?"

I tell him we are under pressure from management to tighten up. This is true, but there is more. I see conspiracies brewing.

Things I used to view as harmless transgressions I now view as personal attacks. When a physically disabled man doesn't leave the shower in time for count, I am certain he is testing me, trying to break me down, to dominate me. The same is true when I see prisoners lying under their blankets during the daytime or standing at the bars. I don't care about the rules, per se; many of them seem arbitrary. But I become obsessed with the notion that people are breaking them in front of me to whittle away at my will. I write inmates up all day long. One paper after another, I stack them, sometimes more than twenty-five disciplinaries in a day. Some inmates are clever; they know how to get under my skin without breaking the rules. So I shake down their beds and look for a reason to punish them.

I carry all this with me. Some days, when I stop for gas on the way home from work I notice myself, for a split second, casing the black men who enter the gas station. When I shoot pool at the local bar, I imagine—I hope—that the white man in hunting camouflage who's playing against me will do something to spark a fight.

One day, the key officer tells me to go to the captain's office. I am nervous; this has never happened before. He is sitting alone at his desk. "I think you are a very strong officer," he says. I relax—it's my employee evaluation. "I think you are a very detailed officer. You got a knack for this. You got a 'it' factor for this. It's just who you are as a person. So, like you went down there to Ash and you just took the bull by the horns and just ran with it. It seems like them guys are starting to understand now—this is how this unit is go' run. This is how CO Bauer go' run it."

The computer screen in front of him reads, "He is an outstanding officer. He has a take-charge attitude. He is dependable and stern. He would be an excellent candidate for promotion."

"That's how we feel about you. I just think that you need to stay consistent with what you are doing. Don't break." Despite myself, I crack a smile.

•     •     •

Even after the lockdown ends, SORT does not leave. They patrol the walk, frisking random inmates, and shake down tiers relentlessly. One morning, I spot white buses parked outside the prison as I pull in for work. At the morning meeting, there are about fifteen wardens and COs from public prisons across the state. The Winn warden steps up to the podium. "Our friends here from the Louisiana Department of Corrections have come to help us out," he says. This is the moment everyone has feared. Are they taking over? Will we lose our jobs?

A warden and a couple of officers from Angola follow Bacle and me to Ash. One tells us they are taking inmates who are too friendly with staff and shipping them to other prisons. He also says they've been administering lie detector tests to officers. Several have already refused to take one and walked off the job. When he says this, I get nervous. I go into the bathroom and flip through my notebook. I rip out my notes. I throw them in the toilet and hold the handle down for a good ten seconds.

When it's count time, the COs from Angola blow a whistle and bark for everyone to sit up straight on their bunks. We've never done this. They tell us that if we get used to counting people sleeping under their blankets, we might eventually count someone who is dead. All the inmates sit up without hesitation. As long as the DOC officers are here, everything is quiet and smooth. They make inmates walk through the metal detector as they enter the unit, and Bacle and I put them in their tiers. I feel less worried about getting attacked, and some inmates tell me things are better for them, too. But others say that as soon as the DOC is gone, things will go back to the way they were. "It's like Mommy and Daddy back home," one prisoner says. "But when they go back on vacation, the kids is back out."

The Winn COs are deferential to the DOC officers, but in private they describe them as elitist pricks. It feels like incompetence has been replaced with overzealousness. The DOC officers chide us for letting inmates smoke inside, and when they spot someone smoking on camera, they find him and strip-search him in front of everyone. When I sit on a chair to take a break, a DOC officer, staring at the monitor inside the key, tells me to go into the TV room in one of the tiers. There is an inmate in there whose pants are sagging. He orders me to tell the man to pull them up.

### "It gets in your blood"

Three days later, the DOC officers leave, and the order they imposed vanishes with them. COs slide back into their old routines and prisoners resist more than usual. Assistant Warden Parker, however, is jubilant: CCA has hung onto the prison. "The great state of Louisiana came in with both guns a-blazing," he tells us during a morning meeting. "They were ready to tear Winn apart." In interviews with staff, the DOC learned that staff members had been "bringing in mountains and mountains of mojo"—synthetic marijuana—and having sex with inmates. "One person actually said that they trusted the inmates more than they trusted me, the warden. One staff member said, 'The inmate made me feel pretty. Why wouldn't I love him? Why wouldn't I bring him things he needs because you all won't let him have it?'"

Later that morning, I clench up when my old instructor Kenny enters the unit and approaches me. "The warden told me to find somebody that's knowledgeable and ready for leadership," he says, smiling slightly. "Out of all y'all's crew down here, I'm gonna handpick you. If you are interested in moving on up, I'm go' make it happen. I'm going to train you for the next level." I've been on the job for two months.

In the following days, I walk up and down the tiers at count time, barking at inmates to sit up on their bunks. If they are asleep, I kick their beds. Some refuse to obey, so I write them up.

At the end of a long day, I head down the walk. On my way out, I meet Miss Carter, the mental-health director.

"How do you like it so far?" she asks.

"It's okay. It can be exciting," I say.

"It gets in your blood, doesn't it? Someone asked me if we were pretty picky about who we hire," Miss Carter continues as we pass through the front gate. "I said, 'Well, I'd love to tell you yes, but we take 'em six-legged and lazy.' We take whatever we can get!" she says with a laugh. "When you get down like this, you'll take whatever. But then we come across a few good people like yourself. That's not the norm."

Outside, there is a chorus of frogs and crickets. The air is sweet and balmy. Like I do every night when I get off work, I take a breath and try to remember who I am. Miss Carter is right. It is getting in my blood. The boundary between pleasure and anger is blurring. To shout makes me feel alive. I take pleasure in saying "no" to prisoners. I like to hear them complain about my write-ups. I like to ignore them when they ask me to cut them a break. When they hang their clothes to dry in the TV room, an unauthorized area, I confiscate the laundry and get a thrill when they shout from down the tier as I take it away. During the lockdown, when Ash threatened to riot, I hoped the SORT team would come in and gas the whole unit. Everyone would be coughing and gasping, including me, and it would be good because it would be action. All that matters anymore is action.

Until I leave. When I drive home, I wonder who I am becoming. I feel ashamed of my lack of self-control, my growing thirst for punishment and vengeance. I'm getting afraid of the expanding distance between the person I am at home and the one behind the wire. My glass of wine with dinner regularly becomes three. I hear the sounds of Ash unit as I fall asleep. I dream of monsters and men behind bars.

.    .    .

Late one night in the middle of March, my wife wakes me. James West, my *Mother Jones* colleague who's recently come to Louisiana to shoot video for my story, has not returned from trying to get a nighttime shot of the outside of Winn. Something is wrong. The sheriff of Winn Parish answers James's phone. James, he says, will be in jail for a while. I feel the blood drain from my face. Then I wonder, "Will they come for me?" We scramble to pack up everything that has anything to do with my reporting and check into a hotel at two a.m. A few hours later, I call in sick.

The same morning, James tells the sheriff he needs to make a call. "You can tell them we didn't shoot you at dawn!" the sheriff says. James is later taken in leg irons into a room for questioning. "We don't care if you are doing an exposé on CCA," a deputy tells him. "We have nothing to do with them. They have given us trouble in the past." A state trooper adds, "I don't care if that guy works in the prison." James assumes he is referring to me but says nothing.

James is charged with trespassing. By evening, a $10,000 bond is posted and he is released. "Send me a copy of the article when it's done," one of the cops tells him.

We pick up James at a gas station at the edge of Winnfield and drive out of town. The next morning, as I get coffee in the hotel lobby, I see a SORT officer standing outside in a black uniform, flex-cuffs hanging from his belt. Are they looking for me? We exit through a side door, and as I pull my truck out I see another man I recognize from the prison. We go back to the apartment, hurriedly throw everything in plastic bags, and leave. We drive across the border to Texas. I feel, oddly, sad.

A couple of days later, I call HR at Winn. "This is CO Bauer. I'm calling because I've decided to resign."

"Oh! Mr. Bauer, I hate to hear that!" the HR woman says. "I hate to lose you. Your evaluation looked good and it looked like you were willing to hang in there and hopefully promote. Well, I hate it, Mr. Bauer. I truly do. In the future, if you decide to change your mind, you know the process."

## Epilogue

When Bacle pulled into Winn's front gate after I left town, the guard told him the assistant warden wanted to see him. "What the hell did I do?" he thought. In his office, Assistant Warden Parker asked Bacle what he knew about me. "He was a good partner," Bacle told him. "I enjoyed working with the dude. He has no problem writing 'em up." He asked what was wrong, but Parker wouldn't say. On his way out, Bacle asked the officer at the front gate, "What's going on with Bauer?"

"You ain't heard?" the officer said. "He was an undercover reporter!"

Bacle recounted this to me on the phone ten months later. "Oh, I *laughed*," he said. "I don't know if you remember, but I told you once that it would be nice to have an investigative reporter out there."

Word about me got out quick. The day after I quit, the Winnfield newspaper reported that I had been working at the prison. National media picked up the story and CCA issued a statement saying my approach "raises serious questions about his journalistic standards." A couple of guards I worked with reached out to me right away. Miss Calahan, who'd quit before me because she thought the job was getting too dangerous, wrote to me on Facebook: "Hey boy you got they ass lol." Another sent me an e-mail: "Wow, Bauer! I'm honored. I don't even know what to say."

I attempted to contact everyone who's mentioned in this story to ask them about their experiences at Winn. Some refused outright. Others didn't respond to my phone calls and letters, and a few I could not track down. A surprising number, however, were eager to talk. Corner Store insisted he and other inmates knew something was up all along. "I just don't know no CO to pull out his pad every five minutes," he told me. "Everybody's like, 'Oh man, I knew it, I knew it, I knew it.'" Collinsworth said that when he found out I was a reporter, he "thought it was cool." Christian thought "pretty much what most people thought: Can't wait to read the story!"

Some people whom I would never have expected spoke to me. One was Miss Lawson, who'd been the assistant chief of security. "They were scared to death of who you were," she told me. "After they found out you were a reporter, it was like, 'Oh my God. Oh my God.'" The DOC quickly required the staff to undergo fresh background checks. CCA's corporate office sent people to Winn to open what she described as an "extensive" investigation on me. They gathered "everything that had your name on it," Miss Lawson said. Ironically, the investigation narrowed in on the item that, in my mind, had symbolized my transformation from an observer into a real prison guard: the cell phone I had confiscated in Ash. "I got called like four or five times for that one phone from corporate," Miss Lawson said. "It was like they were insinuating that you brought the phone in or there was some information in the phone. I'm like, 'No, he found it in a water fountain.'"

After I'd filled out the paperwork about the phone and handed it off to Miss Price, it had disappeared somewhere in the chain of command. The mystery of the missing cell phone grew into a broader probe in which Christian and Miss Lawson were fired for allegedly selling phones to inmates. Both deny it, and CCA did not pursue legal action against them.

Miss Lawson also told me that Assistant Warden Parker texted her a photo of me, asking if she knew who I was. After she identified me, Miss Lawson says, Parker told her to delete the photo and "forget I sent it to you." She kept it, however, and e-mailed it to me. The image was a shot of a laptop screen on which a video of me was playing. I recognized the footage immediately: James had filmed it on the afternoon before he was arrested.

When James was detained, he was careful to protect his camera and the footage on it, even as he was surrounded by SORT officers from the prison and Winn Parish deputies. Police body-cam footage that I later obtained shows one deputy grabbing James's camera as James struggles to hang on to it, telling the officer that searching his camera and memory cards would be illegal. After James was cuffed and put in a police cruiser, two officers left their body cameras on. The video shows a SORT member scrolling through the images on James's camera. The sheriff never obtained a search warrant for my colleague's belongings, but someone apparently searched them anyway. Geolocation data on the photo Miss Lawson sent me points to the sheriff's office. (The Winn Parish sheriff says he was "not aware" of anyone searching James's things.)

In April 2015, about two weeks after I left Winn, CCA notified the DOC that it planned to void its contract for the prison, which had been set to expire in 2020. According to documents that the DOC later sent me, in late 2014 the department had reviewed CCA's compliance with its contract and asked it to make immediate changes at Winn. Several security issues were identified, including broken doors and cameras, and unused metal detectors. The DOC also asked CCA to increase inmate recreation and activities, improve training, hire more guards, hire more medical and mental-health employees, and address a "total lack of maintenance." Another concern raised by the DOC, CCA's chief corrections officer acknowledged, was a bonus paid to Winn's warden that "causes neglect of basic needs." The DOC also noted that CCA had charged inmates for state-supplied toilet paper and toothpaste and made them pay to clip their nails. In a message to its shareholders, the company gave no hint of any problems at Winn; it only said the prison wasn't making enough money. LaSalle Corrections, a Louisiana-based company, took over in September.

Some guards stayed on with the new company, but many left. Bacle got a job at a lumber mill. Miss Calahan became a CO at a local jail. One went on to army basic training. Another took a security-guard job in Texas. Some are still unemployed. Assistant

Warden Parker took a similar position at another CCA prison. Some Winn prisoners have been transferred across the state and some have been released. Robert Scott is still suing over his amputated legs. I still don't know what most of them were in for, but I was shocked to find out that Corner Store was in for armed robbery and forcible rape.

One inmate's mother read about me in the news and asked an attorney to connect us. When the lawyer told me her son's name—Damien Coestly—it took me back to my first day on the job, when I was working suicide watch. It had been a year since I'd pulled my chair across from him as he sat on the toilet, his entire body hidden under his suicide blanket. He had told me to "get the fuck out of here" and threatened that if I didn't he would "get up on top of this bed and jump straight onto [his] mother-fucking neck." He had gone on hunger strike repeatedly to protest the limited dietary options and inadequate mental-health services. In June 2015, he hanged himself. His autopsy said he weighed seventy-one pounds.

.    .    .

Five months after I left Winn, *Mother Jones* received a letter from a law firm representing CCA. The letter dropped hints that the company had been monitoring my recent communications with inmates and was keeping an eye on my social-media presence. CCA's counsel claimed I was bound by the company's code of conduct, which states, "All employees must safeguard the company's trade secrets and confidential information." Since guards are not privy to confidential business information, the implication is that what I experienced and observed inside Winn should remain secret.

CCA insisted on receiving a "meaningful opportunity to respond" to this story prior to its publication. Yet when I asked for an in-person interview, the company refused. CCA did eventually reply to the more than 150 questions I sent; its responses are included throughout this article. In one letter to me, CCA's spokesman scolded me thirteen times for my "fundamental misunderstanding" of the company's business and "corrections in general." He also suggested that my reporting methods were "better suited for celebrity and entertainment reporting."

•        •        •

In March 2016, Corner Store walked free. He stayed in prison a full year while CCA was supposed to help him find a place to go. A lawyer eventually tracked down his father's address and arranged for him to stay there. He rode a Greyhound bus to Baton Rouge. His mother drove from Texas to see him. He got his seafood platter. He walked in the rain. He got a job detailing cars. Sometimes he would hop on a bus, any bus, and ride the entire route just to see the city.

Two weeks after he gets out, James and I visit him at his house on a quiet street near the airport. His father invites us in.

"You all taking [him] somewhere?" his father asks us as we sit on the couch waiting for Corner Store to get ready.

"Yeah, we were going to see if he wants to go anywhere," I say.

"You all ain't come here to arrest him?"

Corner Store comes out of his room and walks directly outside. He tells us to get straight in the car—no talking in the street. He's tense.

"Hey, this no names involved, huh?"

"What are you worried about?" I ask.

"Let's just say something happens and I go back."

"Who would you be worried about?"

"The free people." He means the guards.

"Do you think you might go back?"

"Anything is possible," he says. The smallest parole violation could land him back in prison. "If they were ever to see me again, they wouldn't have too much of a liking for me. They feel like you shouldn't even be talking about this."

When we pick up Corner Store the next day, he tells me he hasn't seen the Mississippi yet. He used to fish in it, growing up. We head to the river. After we sit and talk awhile, he stops scoping out everyone who passes by, and he stares out at the glistening surface. A tugboat chugs past. He walks down to the bank, scoops up some water, brings it to his nose, and breathes in deep.

## Harper's Magazine

**WINNER—COLUMNS AND COMMENTARY**

*The first woman to write "The Easy Chair" since the column was introduced in Harper's Magazine in 1851, Rebecca Solnit was first nominated for the Ellie for Columns and Commentary in 2016. The three pieces that won the Ellie this year included a meditation on the film* Giant, *an examination of the link between isolation and modern conservatism, and a portrait of an African American writer living on death row. "Because her touch with reported material is humble and light and her writing so able, it can appear that Solnit arrives at her insights with little effort," said the Ellie judges, "yet there is nothing 'easy' about her work. Each of these pieces tells an important story with curiosity and care."*

Rebecca Solnit

# Bird in a Cage
# *and* The Ideology
# of Isolation *and*
# Giantess

## Bird in a Cage

There are two things I think about nearly every time I row out into San Francisco Bay. One is a passage from Shankar Vedantam's *The Hidden Brain*, in which he talks about a swim he once took. A decent swimmer in his own estimate, Vedantam went out into the sea one day and discovered that he had become superb and powerful; he was instantly proud of his new abilities. Far from shore, he realized he had been riding a current and was going to have to fight it all the way back to shore. "Unconscious bias influences our lives in exactly the same manner as that undercurrent," Vedantam writes. "Those who travel with the current will always feel they are good swimmers; those who swim against the current may never realize they are better swimmers than they imagine."

Most mornings I row out against the current, and the moment when I turn around is exhilarating. Strokes that felt choppy and ineffectual are suddenly graceful and powerful. I feel very good at what I do, even though I know that the tide is going my way.

Rowing is the closest I will ever come to flying. On calm, flat days my battered old oars make twin circles of ripples that spread out until they intersect behind the stern of the boat. I'm forever retreating from that gentle disturbance, the water smoothing itself into glass again as I go. On the calmest days, when the bay is a mirror, these oars pull me and my scull through reflected clouds in long glides, the two nine-foot oars moving together like wings in that untrammeled space.

The birds are one of the great joys, the terns and pelicans and gulls, the coots and stilts and cormorants, who dive and fly and float, living in the air and the water and the plane between them. The freedom of rowing is enlarged by the freedom of the birds. I set out from the estuary of Corte Madera Creek as it pours into San Francisco Bay. En route I pass Point San Quentin, and San Quentin Prison.

•　　　•　　　•

When I row past the prison I think about currents and I think about Jarvis Jay Masters, who's been on my mind for a long time. We were born eight months apart and are both children of coastal California. We're both storytellers. But he has been in San Quentin since he was nineteen, more than a third of a century ago, and has swum against the current all his life. For the past twenty-five years, he's been on death row, though the evidence is on the side of his innocence.

Until he turned twenty-three, Masters's story could have been that of any number of poor inner-city boys: his father missing in action; his mother drawn into the vortex of heroin; his early neglect; and a ride through the best and worst of the foster-care system, which dropped him straight into the juvenile-prison system. At nineteen, he was sent to San Quentin for armed robbery. Four years later, on June 8, 1985, Howell Burchfield, a prison guard and father of five, was murdered. Two members of a black prison gang were convicted of planning and carrying out the crime. They were given life sentences. Masters was accused of conspiring in the murder and of sharpening the weapon that was used to stab Burchfield in the heart. He received the death penalty.

In books and movies, resourceful lawyers or investigators find a subtle detail, possibly two, to undermine an otherwise credible case. But in Masters's case there aren't merely one or two weak links. So far as I can tell, the whole chain is rotten.

Major witnesses changed their testimony, and several of the prisoners who testified against Masters recanted. Some testified that they had been offered incentives to incriminate him. One star witness was so unreliable and so widely used as an informant that dozens of cases in the state had to be thrown out because of his involvement. He has recanted his testimony about Masters. The man convicted of carrying out the murder said in 2004 that Masters was innocent and that all three men on trial were "under orders from [gang] commanders that, under threat of death, none of us could discuss the [gang] in any way." Meaning that Masters faced two death penalties, and one set him up for the other.

I first read about Masters in *Altars in the Street*, a 1997 book by Melody Ermachild Chavis, who was the defense investigator for his murder trial. They have remained close for thirty years. Chavis and I later became friends ourselves. "It was obvious working on it even way back then, between 1985 and 1990, that they had a lot of suspects and a lot of theories," she told me earlier this year. "The big mistake they made was: they destroyed the crime scene. They bagged it all up and threw it in the Marin County dump."

She described the way prisoners and prison officials got rid of hundreds of notes that had been exchanged between prisoners, as well as a large collection of prison-made knives, which had been thrown out of the cells when the prisoners realized that they were going to be searched. According to one account in Masters's mountain of legal documents, guards collected two different potential murder weapons, which they say they put into envelopes as evidence. Both disappeared before the trial.

Masters was a gang member at the time of the killing, but the gang's leaders eventually gave many reasons why it was impossible that he had sharpened the missing weapon. One was that he had voted against killing Burchfield, an act of insubordination for which he had been stripped of responsibilities. Another was geography; he was on the fourth tier of a cell block, and the murder took place on the second tier. Moving a weapon back and forth would have been difficult and dangerous, and a witness testified that the weapon never left the second tier. Most critically, someone else admitted to making it.

Masters's attorneys filed the opening brief of his appeal in 2001, after which his case progressed slowly. It was not until November of last year that the California Supreme Court heard oral arguments on the appeal. Even by the standards of California's glacial appeals process, this is an unusually long time.

.        .        .

Though only 6.5 percent of Californians are black, African Americans make up 29 percent of the state's incarcerated and 36 percent of those condemned to death. They are more likely than others convicted of similar crimes to receive the death penalty, and assailants of any race who kill a white person are far more likely to be sentenced to death than killers of other victims. There are those who swim with the current and those who swim against it, and then there are those who have firehoses turned on them.

The first time I saw Masters was at a session of a 2011 evidentiary hearing. There, in the small courtroom, stood a tall, gracious man in shackles and an orange jumpsuit. A dozen or so friends and supporters were present, most of them from the Buddhist community. Since his sentencing, Masters had become a devoted Buddhist practitioner. He told me that he meditates daily and tries to incorporate teachings about compassion into his daily life among prisoners and guards. In 1989, he took vows from Chagdud Tulku Rinpoche, an exiled Tibetan lama and distinguished teacher who died in 2002. (The first vow was "From this day forward I will not hurt or harm other people even if it costs my life.") Pema Chödrön, a writer and abbess who is perhaps the best-known Buddhist in the West after the Dalai Lama, speaks of Masters with admiration, and she visits him every year.

When we began talking on the phone, a few months ago, Masters told me how much prisoners crave connection with the outside world. Buddhism allowed him to join a community of ethical and idealistic people with practical ideas about how to respond to suffering and rage. It took him outward and inward. "Meditation has become something I cannot do without. I see and hear more clearly, feel more relaxed and calm, and I actually find my experiences slowing down," he wrote in 1997. "I'm more appreciative of each day as I observe how things constantly change and dissolve. I've realized that everything is in a continual process of coming and going. I don't hold happiness or anger for a long time. It just comes and goes."

He's also connected to the outside world through his writing. He's the author of two books and many magazine essays. He told me that his essays "go out on their own wings and some of them fly back to me." It's not the first time he's used flight as a metaphor for his own reach; the title of his memoir comes from an incident when he stopped another prisoner from nailing a seagull with a basketball in the prison yard. Asked why, he said off the top of his head, "That bird has my wings," and so the gripping, moving narrative of his early years is titled *That Bird Has My Wings*.

"You know, it's really hard to get in," I told Masters about my attempts to figure out how to move through the prison system. "It was easy for me," he replied, and we laughed. From the time I first wrote him, it took me approximately two months of bureaucratic wrangling to be able to visit him. Finally, on a cold Sunday in January, I showed up at the visitors' entrance wearing the permitted clothing and carrying what few articles I was allowed: a key, a state-issued ID, some coins and bills for the vending machines, and a few pages of fact-checker's questions and quotes to verify, sealed inside a clear ziplock bag. I passed through something much like airport security, and on the other side, I stepped out to face a shabby jumble of sinister architectural styles. I was suddenly left alone to find my way to the visiting rooms a couple hundred yards away.

There were more doors to go through, operated by a young woman in the guard booth who let me in and took my license and pass. I entered a room in which everything except the vending machines was painted a pale buttery yellow. There were fifteen cages in which prisoners were locked with their visitors, a U-shaped arrangement with guards on the inside (where prisoners entered) and outside (where the visitors entered). Each cage was about four by eight feet, just slightly smaller than the cells the prisoners live in, and was furnished with two plastic chairs and a tiny table.

A guard wearing a heavy belt with keys dangling on steel chains locked me in the cage closest to the door through which the prisoners entered and exited. Masters arrived with his hands cuffed behind him. Once inside the cage he offered them up to the guard to be unlocked, a gesture both had apparently engaged in so many times that it appeared utterly routine. Thus began my first face-to-face meeting with Masters. Soon afterward a stocky white man with gray hair passed by on his way out of the visiting room, and he and Masters shouted something at each other. It was a little unclear whether this was animosity or friendship, but Masters said it was the latter. The two men had known each other since being in foster care together. It was as though they'd been groomed for death row since they were little boys.

Another prisoner passed by and said that his daughter was on break from college and coming to see him. After a brief discussion with the man, Masters told me that he'd become a confidant, someone who, because of his writings and the way he conducted himself, was trusted with things that prisoners might not ordinarily share. He reminded me that he's been in prison since before some of the younger inmates and guards were born.

"I have been so blessed because I was thinking about all that could have gone wrong, that could've affected me," he told me. "All the things that didn't go wrong. I have seen a lot of tragedy, and all of those things could've been me. I've seen the violent heart, and I count my blessings that I haven't had that kind of hatred. Being on death row, I have a front-row seat on what suffering is. I'm not damaged, not had this place tear me up like I've seen a hundred times. I'm probably crazy for not being crazy. I count my blessings every day."

. . .

When I started rowing, I thought it would be a meditation practice of sorts because so much concentration goes into the single gesture that moves you across the water. That repetitive movement requires the orchestration of the whole body, and it contains a host of subtleties in timing and positioning and force. You could spend a lifetime learning to do it right, but even as you're learning you can go miles across the water. Gradually the gestures became second nature, and I could think about other things.

Though I don't get lost in thought much. It's too beautiful.

I want to keep rowing, to keep relishing that freedom on the open water under the changing weather, going with and against the tides, but I don't need so much freedom that I can't go inside a prison on occasion. Buddhism calls for the liberation of all beings, and it's a useful set of tools for thinking about prisons and what we do with our freedoms.

We are all rowing past one another, and it behooves us to know how the tides move and who's being floated along and who's being dragged down and who might not even be allowed in the water. I bought Masters some things from the vending machines just outside the cages, which I could access and he couldn't. He asked whether I was going to eat, and I said maybe I'd get a taco after. He said, "That's freedom." He was right. Freedom to eat tacos on my own schedule, to pursue the maximum freedom of rowing, to enter the labyrinth of San Quentin and leave a couple of hours later, to listen to stories and to tell them, to try to figure out which stories might free us.

It was stories, written down by Melody Ermachild Chavis; by Alan Senauke, a Zen priest; and by Jarvis Masters himself that made me care about him and think about him and talk to him and visit him. And it was these stories that made me hope to see him leave that cage on his own wings. Meanwhile, there is a way Jarvis is already free; as a storyteller he's escaped the narratives about himself he's been given and he's made his own version of what a life means.

"Whatever the outcome, I want to be in a position to deal with that," he told me. "There are a lot of people who say, 'Jarvis, you gonna win this case.' It's the same way the other way," meaning people who say he won't win. "I'm scared both ways; I'm scared to think this way and scared that way. Do I lose sleep? Of course I lose sleep. I do have some faith in this system, I just have to. The possibility of them coming to the right decision is there. I do have faith in the outcome of this system. History doesn't give you a lot of good reasons for it. That's just my bottom line."

# The Ideology of Isolation

If you boil the strange soup of contemporary right-wing ideology down to a sort of bouillon cube, you find the idea that things are not connected to other things, that people are not connected to other people, and that they are all better off unconnected. The core values are individual freedom and individual responsibility: yourself for yourself on your own. Out of this Glorious Disconnect come all sorts of illogical thinking. Taken to its conclusion, this worldview dictates that even facts are freestanding items that the self-made man can manufacture for use as he sees fit.

This is the modern ideology we still call conservative, though it is really a sort of loopy libertarianism that inverts some of the milder propositions of earlier conservative thinkers. "There is no such thing as society," Margaret Thatcher said in 1987. The rest of her famous remark is less frequently quoted:

> There is [a] living tapestry of men and women and people and the beauty of that tapestry and the quality of our lives will depend upon how much each of us is prepared to take responsibility for ourselves and each of us prepared to turn round and help by our own efforts those who are unfortunate.

Throughout that interview with *Woman's Own* magazine, Thatcher walked the line between old-school conservatism—we are all connected in a delicate tapestry that too much government meddling might tear—and the newer version: "Too many children and people have been given to understand, 'I have a problem, it's the government's job to cope with it.'" At some point in the decades since, the balance tipped definitively from "government aid should not replace social connections" to "to hell with others and their problems." Or as the cowboy sings to the calf, "It's your misfortune / And none of my own."

The cowboy is the American embodiment of this ideology of isolation, though the archetype of the self-reliant individual—like the contemporary right-wing obsession with guns—has its roots less in actual American history than in the imagined history of Cold War–era westerns. The American West was indigenous land given to settlers by the U.S. government and cleared for them by the U.S. Army, crisscrossed by government-subsidized railroads and full of water projects and other enormous cooperative enterprises. All this has very little to do with Shane and the sheriff in *High Noon* and the Man with No Name in Sergio Leone's spaghetti-western trilogy. But never mind that, because a cowboy silhouetted against a sunset looks so good, whether he's Ronald Reagan or the Marlboro Man. The loner taketh not, nor does he give; he scorneth the social and relies on himself alone.

.     .     .

*Him*self. Women, in this mode of thinking, are too interactive, in their tendency to gather and ally rather than fight or flee, and in their fluid boundaries. In fact, what is sometimes regarded as an inconsistency in the contemporary right-wing platform—the desire to regulate women's reproductive activity in particular and sexuality in general—is only inconsistent if you regard women as people. If you regard women as an undifferentiated part of nature, their bodies are just another place a man has every right to go.

Justice Clarence Thomas's first public questions after a decade of silence during oral arguments at the Supreme Court came this February, when he took an intense interest in whether barring those convicted of misdemeanor domestic violence from owning guns violated their constitutional rights. That there is a constitutional right for individuals to own guns is a gift of Antonin Scalia's radically revisionist interpretation of the Second Amendment, and it's propped up on the cowboy ethos in which guns are incredibly useful for defending oneself from bad guys, and one's right to send out bullets trumps the right of others not to receive them. Pesky facts demonstrate that very few people in this country successfully use guns to defend themselves from bad people—unless you count the nearly two-thirds of American gun deaths that are suicides as a sad and peculiar form of self-defense. The ideologues of isolation aren't interested in those facts, or in the fact that the majority of women murdered by intimate partners in the United States are killed with guns.

But I was talking about cowboys. In *West of Everything*, Jane Tompkins describes how westerns valued deeds over words, a tight-lipped version of masculinity over communicative femininity, and concludes:

> Not speaking demonstrates control not only over feelings but over one's physical boundaries as well. The male . . . maintains the integrity of the boundary that divides him from the world. (It is fitting that in the Western the ultimate loss of that control takes place when one man puts holes in another man's body.)

Fear of penetration and the fantasy of impenetrable isolation are central to both homophobia and the xenophobic mania for "sealing the border." In other words, isolation is good, freedom is disconnection, and good fences, especially on the U.S.-Mexico border, make good neighbors.

Both Mitt Romney and Donald Trump have marketed themselves as self-made men, as lone cowboys out on the prairie of the free market, though both were born rich. Romney, in a clandestinely videotaped talk to his wealthy donors in 2012, disparaged people "who are dependent upon government, who believe that they are victims, who believe that government has a responsibility to care for them, who believe that they are entitled to health care, to food, to housing, to you name it."

Taxes represent connection: what we each give to the collective good. This particular form of shared interest has been framed as a form of oppression for more than three decades, at least since Ronald Reagan, in his first inaugural address, bemoaned a "tax system which penalizes successful achievement."

The spread of this right-wing hatred of taxes has been helped along by the pretense that taxes go to loafers and welfare queens who offend the conservative idea of independence, rather than to things conservatives like (notably, a military that dwarfs all others) or systems that everyone needs (notably, roads and bridges).

.　　.　　.

I ran into this hatred for dependency in an online discussion of the police killing of a homeless man in San Francisco in April. More than a hundred messages into a fairly civil discourse started by a witness to the shooting, a commenter erupted,

> I'm sick of people like you that think homeless people who can't take care of themselves and their families have left them for us taxpaying citizens to care for think they have freedom. Once you can't take care of or support yourself, and expect others to carry your burden, you have lost freedom. Wake up.

The same commenter later elaborated, "Have you ever owed money? Freedom lost. You owe someone. It's called personal responsibility."

Everyone on that neighborhood forum, including the writer, likely owed rent to a landlord or mortgage payments to a bank, making them more indebted than the homeless in their tents. If you're housed in any American city, you also benefit from a host of services, such as water and sanitation and the organizations overseeing them, as well as from traffic lights and transit rules and building codes—the kind of stuff taxes pay for. But if you forget what you derive from the collective, you can imagine that you owe it nothing and can go it alone.

All this would have made that commenter's tirade incoherent if its points weren't so familiar. This is the rhetoric of modern conservatives: freedom is a luxury that wealth affords you; wealth comes from work; those who don't work, never mind the cause, are undeserving. If freedom and independence are the ideal, dependence is not merely disdained; it's furiously loathed. In her novelistic paean to free enterprise *Atlas Shrugged*, Ayn Rand called dependents parasites and looters. "We don't want to turn the safety net into a hammock that lulls able-bodied people to lives of dependency and complacency," said one of Rand's admirers, Speaker of the House Paul Ryan, the man lately charged with saving the soul of conservatism from Trumpist apostasy.

The modern right may wish that every man were an island, entire of himself, but no one is wholly independent. You can't survive without taking air into your lungs, you didn't give birth to or raise yourself, you won't bury yourself, and in between you won't produce most of the goods and services you depend on to live. Your gut is full of microorganisms, without which you could not digest all the plants and animals, likely grown by other people, on which you rely to survive. We are nodes on intricate systems, synapses snapping on a great collective brain; we are in it together, for better or worse.

.     .     .

There is, of course, such a thing as society, and you're inside it. Beyond that, beneath it and above and around and within it and us, there is such a thing as ecology, the systems within which our social systems exist and with which it often clashes.

Ecological thinking articulates the interdependence and interconnectedness of all things. This can be a beautiful dream of symbiosis when you're talking about how, say, a particular species of yucca depends on a particular moth to pollinate it, and how the larvae of that moth depend on the seeds of that yucca for their first meals. Or it can be a nightmare when it comes to how toxic polychlorinated biphenyls found their way to the Arctic, where they concentrated in human breast milk and in top-of-the-food-chain carnivores such as polar bears. John Muir, wandering in the Yosemite in 1869, put it this way: "When we try to pick out anything by itself, we find it hitched to everything else in the universe."

This traditional worldview—for a long time, it was called conservative and stood in contrast to liberal individualism—could be seen as mystical or spiritual, but the accuracy of its description of natural systems within what we now call the biosphere is borne out by modern science. If you kill off the wolves in Yellowstone, elk populations will explode and many other plant and animal species will suffer; if you spray DDT on crops, then the stuff does the job you intended of killing off pests, but it will also, as Rachel Carson told us in 1962, kill the birds who would otherwise keep many insects and rodents in check.

All this causes great trouble for the ideology of isolation. It interferes with the right to maximum individual freedom, a freedom not to be bothered by others' needs. Which is why modern conservatives so insistently deny the realities of ecological interconnectedness, refusing to recognize that when you add something to or remove an element from an environment, you alter the whole in ways that may come back to bite you. The usual argument in defense of this pesticide or that oil platform is that impact does not spread, that the item in question does not become part of a far-reaching system, and sometimes—often, nowadays—that that far-reaching system does not itself exist.

No problem more clearly demonstrates the folly of individualist thinking—or more clearly calls for a systematic response—than climate change. The ideologues of isolation are doubly challenged by this fact. They reject the proposed solutions to climate change because they bristle at the need for limits on production and consumption, for regulation, for cooperation between industry and government, and for international partnership. In 2011, Naomi Klein attended a meeting at the Heartland Institute, a libertarian think tank, and produced a landmark essay about why conservatives are so furiously opposed to doing anything about climate change. She quotes a man from the Competitive Enterprise Institute who declared, "No free society would do to itself what this agenda requires. . . . The first step to that is to remove these nagging freedoms that keep getting in the way." "Most of all, however," she reported, "I will hear versions of the opinion expressed by the county commissioner in the fourth row: that climate change is a Trojan horse designed to abolish capitalism and replace it with some kind of eco-socialism."

On a more fundamental level, the very *idea* of climate change is offensive to isolationists because it tells us more powerfully and urgently than anything ever has that everything is connected, that nothing exists in isolation. What comes out of your tailpipe or your smokestack or your leaky fracking site contributes to the changing mix of the atmosphere, where carbon dioxide and other greenhouse gases cause the earth to retain more of the heat that comes from the sun, which doesn't just result in what we used to call global warming but will lead to climate chaos.

As the fact of climate change has become more and more difficult to deny, the ideologues of isolation deny instead our responsibility for the problem and the possibility that we are capable of acting collectively to do anything about it. "Climate change occurs no matter what," Paul Ryan said a few years ago. "The question is, can and should the federal government do something about it? And I would argue the federal government, with all its tax and regulatory schemes, can't." Of course it can, but he prefers that it not do so, which is why he denies human impact as a cause and human solutions as a treatment.

•    •    •

What keeps the ideology of isolation going is going to extremes. If you begin by denying social and ecological systems, then you end in denying the reality of facts, which are after all part of a network of systematic relationships between language, physical reality, and the record, regulated by the rules of evidence, truth, grammar, word meaning, and so forth. You deny the relationship between cause and effect, evidence and conclusion, or rather you imagine both as products on the free market, which one can produce and consume according to one's preferences. You deregulate meaning.

Absolute freedom means you can have any truth that you like, and isolation's ideologues like truths that keep free-market fundamentalism going. You can be like that unnamed senior adviser (probably Karl Rove), who in a mad moment of Bush-era triumphalism told Ron Suskind, "We're an empire now, and when we act, we create our own reality." Reality, in this worldview, is a product subject to market rules or military rules, and if you are dominant in the marketplace or rule the empire, your reality can push aside the other options. "Freedom" is just another word for nothing left to limit your options. And this is how the ideology of isolation becomes nihilism, trying to kill the planet and most living things on it with the confidence born of total disconnection.

# Giantess

The radical is so often imagined as the marginal that sometimes the truly subversive escapes detection just by showing up in a tuxedo instead of a T-shirt or a ski mask. Take *Giant*, the 1956 film directed by George Stevens. It stars Elizabeth Taylor and features three queer men, Rock Hudson, James Dean, and Sal Mineo, who uneasily orbit one another in ways that seem only partly about their cinematic roles.

This is what caught my eye the first time I saw *Giant*. It was the thirtieth-anniversary screening at San Francisco's Castro Theatre, the great 1,400-seat dream palace where, from my midteens on, I learned from the sighs and groans and snickers of the gay men around me in the dark to notice homoerotic subtext, to delight in women with verve, and to appreciate camp and bitchiness and cliché.

In the film, Elizabeth Taylor plays that rarest of joys, a woman who breaks the rules, triumphs, and enjoys herself rather than winding up dead or deserted or defeated, as too many female rebels have in too many movies. The year before my first viewing, Hudson had died of AIDS, and Taylor had begun advocating and fund raising for those with the then-untreatable and horrifically stigmatized disease. Her outspoken heroics in real life made her a little like the unconquered heroine she was in the movie.

Whenever I see a woman like that onscreen, I get revved up in a way that men who identify with Hollywood's endless stream of action heroes must be all the time. Just watching Jennifer Lawrence walk down a Texas street like a classic gunslinger in the 2015 biopic *Joy* gave me a thrill I get maybe once a year. Lawrence's Katniss Everdeen was the hard drugs. Beyoncé's recent videos have offered some of the same satisfaction, of a woman who slays and doesn't stay down. *Distaff invictus*, lady with agency.

·　　　·　　　·

The second time I saw the film on the Castro's huge screen, for its fortieth anniversary, I brought my own superb source of low-volume commentary, the performance artist Guillermo Gómez-Peña. He was dressed all in black leather and slumped down in his seat with a hangover. He kept murmuring, almost from the start, "Rebecca, I do not *believe* what I am seeing."

Early in the film, Taylor's Maryland debutante Leslie Lynnton simultaneously captivates and annoys Jordan Benedict II, the West Texas rancher played by Rock Hudson, the former by being a flirtatious and lovely woman, the latter by speaking her mind. Freudian motif alert: he's come to buy a stallion—a gleaming black horse that she rides magnificently in the opening scene—

from her father. At breakfast the morning after they meet, she tells him that she's been up all night reading about his home state. He prepares to be flattered when she adds, "We really stole Texas! . . . I mean away from Mexico."

It's a demurely outrageous scene, complicated by the handsome African American butler whose nonplussed expression gets some camera attention along with Hudson's choke on his toast. The film, made the year after *Brown v. Board of Education* and its little-remembered parallel case, *Hernandez v. Texas*, takes on race in Texas, a white and brown affair, though it leaves out the politics of being black in the South. It's not a perfect polemic and falls within the suspect genre of racial justice as seen from the perspective of a white ally, but it's nevertheless extraordinary for a blockbuster filmed while Martin Luther King Jr. was finishing graduate school and Rosa Parks was still giving up her seat.

*We really stole Texas.* It's an amazing thing to say even now, and as an observation Elizabeth Taylor offers over breakfast to a cattle baron besotted with his homeland, it's astonishing. The year that Guillermo and I watched *Giant* turn forty—1996—California was in the midst of an era of immigrant bashing, driven by various myths that shifted the burden of a brutal new economy from its lords and masters to its underclass. That year was also the 150th anniversary of the beginning of the Mexican War, which ended two years later with the United States seizing Mexico's northern half, the rich expanse from New Mexico to California that, had it remained in Mexican hands, might have led to a wildly different global geopolitics and, perhaps, poor Yankees sneaking across the border for jobs in the superpower to the southwest. (Texas, of course, had been stolen earlier.) Amnesia has long been an important component of the ideology of demonizing Latino immigrants and residents, from the Gold Rush to California governor Pete Wilson in the 1990s to the current Republican presidential nominee.

But anyway: Jordan Benedict II survives the truth from the mouth of a beautiful woman, and a scene or two later they're newlyweds speeding home in his private railcar. First seen riding to hounds across the rolling green countryside of the Mid-Atlantic, Leslie is shocked by life on the scorched grasslands of west Texas. But she adjusts to her surroundings. And makes adjustments to them: she starts meddling with the treatment of Latino workers on the half-million-acre ranch, having found herself in not only an arid country but an apartheid one. There her husband rules like Abraham in the land of Canaan. Mighty are his herds, vast his lands. Among other things, the film seems to propose that the great division in the United States is not necessarily the famous Civil War configuration of North-South but rather East-West, with differences of manners, histories, ecologies, and scale. It's clear that Leslie thinks that meeting people who speak Spanish means she's arrived in another country.

The horse Leslie rode with confidence in that opening scene has come with her, so she's identified with the stud, the stallion, the wild force—a nice subversion of the idea that the East represents ethereal inaction. In an early scene, her husband and sister-in-law insist she's too delicate to stay on her spirited steed or out on the roundup under a broiling sun. They dispatch her in a vehicle driven by James Dean's character, layabout handyman Jett Rink. Of course, he falls for her, in part because she treats him with gracious respect (in part because she's the most gorgeous thing the world has ever seen).

Leslie's brusque sister-in-law, who lives and breathes ranching and bullying, manages to kill herself and the stallion by digging in her spurs and fighting the power of a horse used to kinder riders. She breaks his leg; he breaks her skull; she expires on a sofa; he is put down off camera. But before the film gets to her death scene, a resurrection thread starts. Leslie gets Jett to stop the car at the barrio of shacks in which the ranch's Latino workers live, and there she finds a sick mother and baby. When the doctor comes to tend to her dying sister-in-law, Leslie violates the segregation of the place by making him do something more useful—save the life of an infant named Ángel Obregón.

It's a freak: a wildly successful mid-1950s Technicolor film about race, class, and gender from a radical perspective, with a charismatic, unsubjugated woman at the center. True, there were other left-wing movies made back then. *Salt of the Earth*, also told from the perspective of a strong woman, had been released in 1954, but it was a diligent, black-and-white film about a New Mexico miners' strike that Hollywood soon blacklisted; the lavishly colorful *Giant* was nominated for numerous Oscars, won for best director, and raked in huge box office. It reached a lot of people, which is what we would like propaganda and advocacy to do; *Giant* suggests that pleasure helps (as do budgets).

.    .    .

Works of art that can accompany you through the decades are mirrors in which you can see yourself, wells in which you can keep dipping. They remind you that what you bring to the work of art is as important as what it brings to you. They can become registers of how you've changed. If *Giant* is a different film with each decade, perhaps that's because I am a different person, focused on different things in the world around me.

It took another decade for me to recognize that *Giant* is also about a marriage, one that is strong but not easy, between two people who survive profound disagreements with forbearance and persistence. It's called *Giant* after the scale of things in Texas, and Rock Hudson is a mountain of a man who looms over everyone, but it could have been called *Giantess*. Taylor's Leslie Benedict possesses a moral stature and a fearlessness that overshadow all else: she tells off powerful men, acts on behalf of the people who are supposed to be invisible, and generally fights authority. She doesn't lose much, either, though she accommodates. Her husband mostly reacts and tries to comprehend. Virginia Woolf once remarked that Mary Wollstonecraft's lover Gilbert Imlay had, in involving himself with the great feminist revolutionary, tried to catch a minnow "and hooked a dolphin, and the creature rushed him through the waters till he was dizzy." Jordan Benedict is often dizzy, but unlike Imlay he never unhooks himself.

Watching Jordan absorb the impact of this relationship—the realization that you might not get what you want or know what to do next or agree with the person you love—is sobering, and Hudson plays it well, with complex emotions moving across his big smooth slab of a face like clouds moving across the prairie. "You knew what a frightful girl I was when you married me," Leslie tells Jordan at one point. There are a lot of movies about how to get into a relationship, about falling in love, and some about falling out, but not many about keeping at it through the years.

How long does it take to see something, to know someone? When we put in years, we realize how little we grasped at the start, even when we thought we knew. We move through life mostly not seeing what is around us, not knowing who is around us, not understanding the forces pressuring us, not understanding ourselves. Unless we stay with it, and maybe this is really a movie about staying with it. This year, at the sixtieth anniversary, the familiar joys remained, but I noticed nuances of the plot that had escaped me before.

The worst thing imaginable happens to our protagonists: they have a son who grows up to become Dennis Hopper. Jordan Benedict III is a red-haired, uneasy, shifty, anxious man who as a child feared horses and as an adult wants to be a doctor and seems to become one remarkably quickly. Without his parents' knowledge, he also marries Juana Guerra, a Latina nurse, played by the Mexican actress Elsa Cárdenas.

As Juana draws her white in-laws into a series of charged battles, the film marks the shift from widely tolerated segregation and discrimination to a nascent civil-rights era. First she's turned away from a new hotel, where the hairdressers refuse to style her, then from the diner where she stops with her son, her husband, and her in-laws on their way home. An ostentatiously humble Latino trio (the actors look as though they rode with Pancho Villa) is ejected from the establishment. Hudson, decades into the story line (hours into the movie), finally rises to the occasion and punches the diner's huge chef, who punches him back more effectually. Hudson loses the fight but wins Taylor's admiration for slugging his way into civil-rights activism, a rebel with a cause.

Hopper's character refuses to contemplate taking over the ranch, and though one of his two sisters is a born rancher, she breaks her father's heart by telling him that she wants a small place where she and her cowhand husband can try out new scientific methods. In the scene where Hudson's character realizes that he has begotten children but no dynasty or heirs, Mineo's Ángel Obregón, acknowledged a few scenes earlier as the best man in the place, lingers in the background.

The film seems to suggest that if only Hudson's character could overcome his racism, a true heir is at hand, the man his wife had saved from death years before. Instead, Ángel goes unrecognized and unacknowledged and comes home from the Second World War in a coffin.

This time around I realized that gently, slowly, the movie has denied the patriarch every form of patriarchal power; his wife does not obey and often does not respect him, his children refuse his plans for them. Ranching itself ceases to be the great pivotal industry that defines Texas; oil has changed everything, and Jett Rink, the surly ranch hand he despised, has become a tycoon. Jordan Benedict II, one of the biggest ranchers in Texas, has been denied all the forms of power that matter to him, the film tells us, and that's just fine, for him as much as anyone, once he gets over it. The shift is not just from cows to crude but from patriarchy to some kind of negotiated reshuffling of everything, the beginning of our contested contemporary era. The film also points to the rise of Latinos from a small minority to a powerful force in the United States—nearly 20 percent of the population, and twice that in Texas.

Part of the astonishment, I realized as I watched *Giant* this year, is that this is a film about a man who finds he can't control anything at all, and yet he's not Job and this is not a jeremiad. That would presume that he should control things and that it's sad when he doesn't. It would propose that kings should not be deposed. This film postulates the opposite: the king has fallen—as he does, literally, in the diner—and everything is fine. That's what makes it radical. I've always seen the film as being about Taylor's outsized character, but maybe it's an anti-bildungsroman about the coming of middle age and the surrendering of illusions, including the illusion of control. The disobedient son, Jordan Benedict III, presents his father with a grandson to carry on the family name, Jordan Benedict IV, a brown child whose big brown eyes, I finally noticed, are the closing shot of the film. This, says *Giant*, is the future; get used to it.

## The Hedgehog Review

FINALIST—ESSAYS AND
CRITICISM

In an essay described by the Ellies judges as "carefully argued yet emotionally raw," Becca Rothfeld delivers an unexpected answer to the universal question, "What is love?" Love, Rothfeld tell us, is waiting. Rothfeld graduated from Dartmouth in 2014 and received her master's degree from Cambridge in 2016. She is now a Ph.D. candidate in philosophy at Harvard. Founded in 1999, The Hedgehog Review is published thrice annually by the Institute for Advanced Studies in Culture at the University of Virginia. Borrowing its name from Archilocus' aphorism "The fox knows many things, but the hedgehog knows one big thing," the publication says its mission is to achieve "the breadth of the fox and the depth of the hedgehog."

Becca Rothfeld

# Ladies in Waiting

Your absence has gone through me
Like thread through a needle.
Everything I do is stitched with its color.

—W. S. Merwin[1]

In the most memorable scene of the 2002 film *Secretary*, nothing happens. The protagonist, Lee, sits as still as possible, her hands planted firmly on the desk in front of her. She has been instructed by her lover, who is also her sexually sadistic employer, to hold this position until he returns. For over ten minutes, a period that represents entire days in the movie's internal timeline, Lee remains faithfully immobile, wetting herself in the process.

Lee offers up her violent passivity as proof of her love, and her physical humiliations are like religious devotions. Hoping to gratify her lover by depriving herself of food, she declines into hunger-induced delirium in which she experiences a hallucinatory vision of her therapist. He explains, "There's a long history of this in Catholicism. The monks used to wear thorns on their temples, and the nuns wore them sewn inside their clothing."[2] Like centuries of monks, nuns, and mystics before her, Lee transforms her inertia and hunger into an active occupation through the performance of sacrificial pain.

Hunger is a particularly intensified iteration of waiting: acute wanting directed toward a palpably absent object. The literal hunger of mystics like Catherine of Siena, who famously fasted for much of her life, corresponds to a greater hunger, necessarily insatiable, for communion with God. When Lee's lover comes to her rescue, he resuscitates her with a protein shake, and their relationship adopts the familiar, flagellatory rhythm of feeding and hungering, deprivation and indulgence. Lee's grand gesture, the gift of her famished waiting, is its origin and its core.

Waiting seems central to the experience and practice of masochistic piety's messianic successor, romantic love, the force that is supposed to redeem twenty-first-century women as religious salvation once redeemed their forebears. But how exactly does waiting figure into contemporary romance? In his 1977 treatise *A Lover's Discourse*, Roland Barthes argues that waiting is constitutive of love:

> "Am I in love?—Yes, since I'm waiting." The other never waits. Sometimes I want to play the part of the one who doesn't wait; I try to busy myself elsewhere, to arrive late; but I always lose at this game: whatever I do, I find myself there, with nothing to do, punctual, even ahead of time. The lover's fatal identity is precisely: *I am the one who waits*.[3]

In Barthes's view, love is centrally defined by the transfiguration of neutral lack into conspicuous vacancy, of emptiness into absence: Love is waiting, and waiting is love. For Catherine of Siena, perennially ravenous, the absence is God's. For Lee, delectably paralyzed with submission, it is her boss's. For the lover, the beloved's absence is always acute. Distance is not a redistribution of presence but an evasion or a thwarted expectation, like a phantom limb.

In *Secretary*, Lee has fled the premise of what would have been her wedding to a banal boyfriend, and as she awaits her boss's return she wears a crumpled wedding dress. This image might seem to undermine the usual marital tropes: A sort of inverse Miss Havisham, Lee deserts her conventional lover at the altar in favor of a sexually deviant relationship. She is the abandoning, not the abandoned, party, and her passivity is chosen, not imposed.

But despite this, she represents yet another variation on the familiar figure of the woman waiting. Initially, this woman wove while her husband went off to war; later, she donned a wedding dress and waited at the altar for a man who would never come; finally, she settled behind her telephone or her mailbox, first analog, then digital, to wait for men who would probably never call or write. As Barthes elaborates,

> Historically, the discourse of absence is carried on by the Woman. . . . It is Woman who gives shape to absence, elaborates its fiction, for she has time to do so. . . . It follows that in any man who utters the other's absence *something feminine* is declared: this man who waits and who suffers from his waiting is miraculously feminized. A man is not feminized because he is inverted but because he is in love.[4]

Barthes suggests that waiting is constitutive of love—the lover is "the one who waits." If waiting, even for men, is an essentially female posture, then love proves to be a fundamentally feminine exercise. The figure at the desk, with her tattered wedding dress, her throbbing hunger, her clenched hands, could only have been a woman.

## The Day-After Text

At first, everything was good, as it tends to be in the early stages, after the first bouts of effortless intimacy, when your body fits so neatly into a foreign body that it seems to have returned to a familiar place. I received his day-after text promptly, approximately seven hours after I left his bed. The text was a ritual gesture, and its content mattered less than its arrival within the allotted twenty-four hours, before the possibility of future interaction expired. In its immediate aftermath I did not wait. But as our conversation acquired momentum and settled into a comfortable cadence, I found the distribution of my attention shifting. Some part of it was withheld, repurposed, devoted to measuring the increasing lengths of his silences. He was beginning to recede, and I was beginning to wait.

As long as he was the unanswered party and I could imagine *him* in a state of painful expectation, I felt invulnerable. I fantasized about never replying, about savoring my silence and his presumed anxiety for the rest of my life, but I never managed to go very long without answering and reverting to my habitual state of waiting. ("I try to busy myself elsewhere, to arrive late; but I always lose at this game . . .")

Before I met him, I spent most of my time at the British university where I was studying "abroad" taking prolonged showers, checking Facebook in the library, and thinking haltingly about the essays I was writing for my master's program. In the library, I sat next to a young man with preternaturally red cheeks—they looked painful, scraped—who seemed to be conducting a survey of eighteenth-century botanical atlases. For hours, he sat hunched over his laptop, scrutinizing archival documents that somebody, perhaps he, had laboriously scanned. Sometimes he took notes by hand. Not once did I ever see him check his e-mail or Facebook, as I often did, only to find that no one had contacted me since the last time I checked, five minutes before.

At the pub, where the beleaguered members of my course congregated once a week to "talk about their 'work,'" no one talked about their work. The botany boy, to whom I had never spoken, was never in attendance. Maybe these sessions occurred when he did his laborious scanning. I lamely sipped sparkling water while my peers, who drank beer, speculated endlessly about the weather, which was so stubbornly noncommittal (never torrential but never fully sunny) that it left little to the predictive faculties.

After I met him, however, I spent much of my time waiting for him. This was more engaging than one might imagine. Immediately after receiving messages from him, I felt a sense of amazed, vertiginous relief that he had answered—yes, he had answered—and this lasted for several seconds at a time before it reverted to muted panic that soon he would answer at greater and greater intervals and then would cease to answer at all. I experienced a cumulative total of maybe five minutes of joy during the week before I saw him again, not counting sleeping hours.

There is an eroticism to waiting: Sexual fulfillment requires that one urgently desire what is necessarily, torturously delayed. Romantic waiting is, like certain shades of pain, delicate enough to hint teasingly at future gratification but never disagreeable enough to preclude it. But at a certain point, gratification has been so thoroughly warded off that waiting becomes unendurable, and it wasn't long after our second meeting that I began to wait in earnest. What had at first been surprised delight that he existed was transformed, without my noticing it, into fear that his privacy would close back over him. His silences began to stretch longer and longer, often for days. I wondered, relentlessly and futilely, what this portended. When I confronted him about what I could only describe as a "tonal shift"—what seemed to me to be a cruel infliction of waiting—he purported to have no idea what I was talking about.

This shift (tonal or otherwise) in patterns of waiting represented a shift in power: Expectation is a form of subjugation. What is the opposite of waiting: the imposition of waiting on someone else? I wished it on him, ineffectually, like a curse. As his communications petered out, I felt increasingly powerless, besieged. I recalled the medieval conception of God as sustaining us, actively willing us into existence second by second, and I felt that his silence was at every moment draining me of myself.

## Depression, Too, Is a Form of Waiting

In *Iris*, the literary critic John Bayley's tragic account of his brilliant wife, the novelist and philosopher Iris Murdoch, and her descent into the fog of Alzheimer's, he quotes clergyman Sydney Smith's advice to a depressive: "Take short views of the human life—never further than dinner or tea."[5] Depression, too, is a form of waiting, for deliverance or vindication or a sudden onslaught of meaning that fails, devastatingly, to arrive. Waiting is a manipulation of time—it is "enchantment," as Barthes writes, a spell that stills and silences its victims—and its antidote is to make time pass at the usual rate once again. (In *Great Expectations*, Miss Havisham's abandonment and subsequent waiting arrest time completely: She stops the clocks at 8:40, the moment at which she received the letter breaking off her engagement.)

Smith exhorts the depressive to throw herself entirely into some proximate thing, to repopulate the vast stretches of undifferentiated blankness with something like events. One tries to foist sequences back onto a slop of time that has come to consist in the recurring, harping note of absence. So one lives, one tries to inhabit the minutiae of the activities one performs, one tries to externalize oneself and ultimately to lose one's sense of one's selfhood altogether, so that one can become the objects one rearranges on the dresser and forget that one is waiting, that none of one's activities are complete without some additional element that is wretchedly, unforgettably elsewhere.

Why did I obey the unspoken imperative to wait? Was I trying, like Lee, to prove my affection through my mute endurance? Was my inability to revert my experience of duration to its former state, when his silence was not perceived as a continual laceration, indeed was not perceived at all, somehow masochistic? Or perhaps I felt waiting was better than mourning.

"The woman was then lied to, cheated on, tormented, and often not called. She was intentionally left up in the air about his intentions. One or two letters went unanswered. The woman waited and waited, in vain. And she did not ask why she was waiting, because she feared the answer more than the waiting," writes Austrian author Elfriede Jelinek in *The Piano Teacher*.[6] To be "not called," this phrasing intimates, is to be actively wounded: "Not calling" is a transitive offense, like "tormenting." But Jelinek's conclusion seems wrong: Waiting, which renders everything provisional, which suspends progress or conclusion of any kind, is worse than clarity. It is waiting that keeps one captive at the desk, determined to see things through until he returns or one starves, whichever comes first.

## Waiting Is the Rule

There is, of course, a simpler answer to the question of the role waiting plays in contemporary courtship than Barthes's convoluted philosophical one. It is that women wait for men: They wait for their Tinder matches to initiate contact, for men to propose to them after years of dating or to ask them on dates at all, for the decisive day-after text (a custom that I realized with some surprise has antecedents in classical Japan; in *The Tale of Genji*, noblewomen anxiously await morning-after haikus in the wake of their nocturnal exploits).

The messages that I answer immediately, without inserting a buffer of delay calculated to give the (erroneous) impression that I'm busy or unavailable, come from my female friends, and they often constitute an agonized refrain: How soon should I reply? Can I say something yet? Should I call? I know I shouldn't text him, but. . . . My advice, ingrained in me by years of comparable counsel from comparably responsive female friends, is always to wait. Waiting is the rule, the convention, tacitly enforced by men who retreat from female aggression and actively perpetuated by women who self-police. This is the agreement we opt into when we receive the first day-after texts with such awed gratitude, as if we didn't deserve them.

Literature bears out Barthes's claim and my experience: In books, it is always women who wait. In the *Odyssey*, Penelope awaits the return of her husband for twenty years, weaving a funeral shroud for her father during the day and unraveling it during the night to put off intermediary suitors, one of whom she will wed when the interminable tapestry is finally complete. Penelope is the product of an oral lyrical tradition that excluded women, and it is only fitting that a male authorship relegated her to the sort of maddening inactivity that waiting so often entails. Like Miss Havisham, condemned to tread the same obsessive mental routes over and over again, Penelope is doomed to weave and unweave the same tired designs to no discernable end.

Centuries later, Walt Whitman would open his 1856 poem "A Woman Waits for Me" with a succinct expression of breathtaking entitlement: "A woman waits for me" as if it were simply and irrefutably so. Later still, in Raymond Carver's poem "Waiting," a male speaker makes his way to

> the house where the woman
> stands in the doorway
> wearing the sun in her hair. The one
> who's been waiting
> all this time.
> The woman who loves you.
> The one who can say,
> "What's kept you?"[7]

There is a fond condescension to this poem: It is tender, but it takes the woman's love and patience—her presence in the door, her mounting fear—for granted. To the male narrator, the waiting woman is a comforting inevitability. The woman's anxious and vaguely accusatory question does not come from a comparable place of security—not that Carver bothers to investigate.

Of course, waiting women have also spoken for themselves. Gaspara Stampa, a sixteenth-century Italian poet often regarded as the iconic jilted lover, anticipates Barthes's equation of waiting with love in her seminal poem "By Now I Am So Tired of Waiting":

> By now I am so tired of waiting,
> so overcome by longing and by grief,
> through the so little faith and much forgetting
> of whom of whose return I, weary, am bereaved,
>
> that she who makes the world pale, whitening
> it with her sickle, and claims the final forfeit—
> I call on her often for relief,
> so strongly sorrow wells within my breast.
>
> But she turns deaf ears unto my plea,
> scorning my false and foolish thoughts,
> as he to his return stays also deaf.
>
> And so with weeping whence my eyes are filled,
> I make piteous these waters and this sea;
> while he lives happy there upon his hills.[8]

Stampa's poem is, at its core, an indictment of indifference: She denounces the man to whom it is addressed because he fails to suffer from her absence, and thus fails to conceive of the passage of their time apart as an exercise in waiting. Stampa, in contrast, is excruciatingly aware of her lover's absence, and she can be described as *waiting* precisely because she experiences separation as pain. This is what waiting is: the transformation of time into misery.

Dorothy Parker's short story "A Telephone Call," a two-thousand-word exercise in agonized anticipation, echoes Stampa's initial figuration of apathy as the inverse of waiting. The work follows a woman waiting for a telephone call (not, we presume, forthcoming) from a man she loves:

> I mustn't. I mustn't do this. Suppose he's a little late calling me up—that's nothing to get hysterical about. Maybe he isn't going to call—maybe he's coming straight up here without telephoning. He'll be cross if he sees I have been crying. They don't like you to cry. He doesn't cry. I wish to God I could make him cry. I wish I could make him cry and tread the floor and feel his heart heavy and big and festering in him. I wish I could hurt him like hell.[9]

The story ends inconclusively, as it must. Resolution would be too relieving: It is inimical to the uncertainties and frustrations of waiting. With a gesture that mirrors Penelope's in its contrived futility, the narrator begins to count by fives, hoping that her beloved will call her before she reaches five hundred. "Five, ten, fifteen, twenty, twenty-five, thirty, thirty-five. . . . " "A Telephone Call" concludes without concluding.

Waiting is sustained by the possibility of fulfillment yet to be decisively precluded. The woman in Parker's story is capable of waiting because she is capable of hope. If she believed with any certainty that the call in question would never come, then her orientation would change: She might grieve, but she would no longer wait. The man who neglects to telephone is certain that a woman is waiting on the other end of the line, and this is why he is not waiting, why he feels no urge to confirm that she is still there with her hands placed, as instructed, on the desk.

As in *Secretary*, waiting—a nonevent—constitutes the crucial narrative force in "A Telephone Call." Parker eschews conventional plot arcs, in which ends represent marked departures from beginnings. The woman waiting by the phone follows Penelope in performing activities that represent a particularly poignant kind of stasis. For every image she weaves, there is a countervailing un-weaving: for every advance, a retreat. There is no progression, just endless circling around the same fixed point of obsession. Waiting itself is her occupation and preoccupation. "Absence becomes an active practice, a *business* (which keeps me from doing anything else)," writes Barthes.

If women historically have been the ones who wait, it is at least in part because most cultures have confined them to state of involuntary idleness. (Penelope is not permitted to leave home to participate in the war effort, and Lee is the secretary, not the boss.) The gendered distribution of waiting assumes a hierarchy of time and activity in which men set the terms and fix the schedules. To be waited for is to assert the importance of one's time; to wait is to occupy a position of eternal readiness in which one can be called on at male convenience. Waiting amounts in this sense to "waiting on": Waiting women exist provisionally and subserviently, in the service of an absent element.

In his book *Interruptions*, the critic Hans-Jost Frey writes, "To understand waiting as expectation is to think of it from the point of view of totality. One who waits is in a state of incompleteness and waits for completion."[10] (This formulation vindicates Jelinek's cleverly transitive phrasing: If waiting is an active occupation, then absence is an active cruelty.) There emerges a metaphysical dependence: If togetherness is completion, then separation is fragmentation. The integrity of the lover is conditional upon the beloved, the eternally awaited. If waiting constitutes love, as Barthes suggests, it is because waiting is the ultimate act of vulnerability: It requires a willingness to endanger one's wholeness, to halve oneself.

## Jolted Out of the Self

Barthes makes two suggestions, both radical. First, he suggests that love is a question of waiting, and second, that waiting is essentially feminine. From this it follows that to fall in love is to become "feminized"—to wait, and thereby take up a traditionally and stereotypically feminine project. But Barthes goes further, proposing that the object of love is absent in a stronger sense: What it means to love, he writes, is for "an always present I" to be defined "only by confrontation with an always absent *you*." *A Lover's Discourse* is structured as a series of one-sided declarations, "the site of someone speaking within himself, *amorously*, confronting the other (the loved object), who does not speak."[11] The lover waits, speaks, entreats, but the beloved is constitutionally silent.

To love is to be jolted out of the self by the strangeness of another person, and the beloved entrances precisely because of his unutterable difference—the most basic and insuperable absence. He is absent even when he is present because he is other, situated outside of myself: "But isn't desire always the same, whether the object is present or absent? Isn't the object *always* absent?" As Barthes reminds us, there are two concepts in Greek for desire, one for the missing someone who's left, and a second for the more curious sensation of missing someone beside me, someone who is with me but who remains less than fully accessible to me: "*Pothos*, desire for the absent being, and *Himéros*, the more burning desire for the present being."[12]

Maybe love is the recovery of some former, half-remembered unity, and what we experience is just the aftermath of a prior separation. In the poem "Misery and Splendor," Robert Hass writes of a couple mid-coitus that "they are trying to become one creature, and something will not have it."[13] But do they really want to become "one creature," to collapse into each other? Wouldn't this just expand the sphere of a single loneliness? Love and sex must honor difference: The beloved must continue to resist assimilation into the self, must remain apart, elusive, an adored, if tonally inconstant, mystery.

## The Art of Elective Waiting

Waiting is consuming. At times it is terrible, a wound that cannot be mitigated but must instead be mutely survived. There are days when making it to dinner or tea, as per Sydney Smith's sage advice, is a feat. And sometimes waiting is an insult, an indignity, as pointlessly pathetic as refusing to take off the wedding dress in which you were abandoned years ago by someone who no longer cares and probably doesn't remember.

But waiting in some form is necessary. In his essay "Penelope Waiting," literary critic Harold Schweizer argues that narrative itself is a specialized kind of waiting: "What constitutes a literary text or a work of art," he writes, "is not its formal closure or sensuous completeness but rather its complicated extension in our own time of waiting."[14] Stories require displaced elements, problems that plague us enough to keep us reading and caring. Investment is diffuse, and present enjoyment is predicated on the projection of future fulfillment. Narrative obeys erotic laws: This is why the seeming nonstories of *Secretary* and "A Telephone Call" absorb us. Just as delay intensifies narrative and deferral intensifies orgasm, difference intensifies love.

The alternative to dejected waiting, then, is patience, the art of elective waiting: a capitulation that women author, a passivity over which we assert ownership and which we might come to more comfortably inhabit. When we identify with it, even the worst of it, waiting becomes an end in itself. Frey writes, "There is a waiting without expectation. It can set in when one has waited for something for so long, without seeing any signs of imminent fulfillment, that the object of expectation gradually begins to fade, and yet one does not stop waiting."[15] Waiting without expectation is like prayer, devotion undertaken without the expectation of immediate reward or acknowledgment.

There is no true not-waiting, anyway. What seems like fullness is just an intimation of filling, a preview of a more complete dissolution. What I want—to not wait, to converge—is impossible. I want everything, all at once, every part of myself touching every part of you at every moment. An intimacy as absolute as this could only be violent, a rupture. It would conceive of flesh as no more than barrier. It would hurt. I have wanted to admit you into my privacy: I have craved a feast of trespass and violation. And at times I have wanted you to wrench me apart and enter into me until the only life I remember is your life and the only word I remember is your name.

But this isn't possible, and I don't really want it, anyway. If I were a part of you, I would not be apart from you and there would be no me in opposition to you, no you to elude me. Instead, I choose my waiting and the joy I find in surrender, in flinging myself at everything I encounter with the brutality of adoration. Catherine of Siena understood this: The whole purpose of adoring God to the point of such delicious abjection is that he is by nature unattainable. He never arrives with a protein shake, prizing hunger apart from filling, or pleasure apart from pain. He never defiles the purity of agony with the weakness of relief. He hurts without mercy. He is a story that never ends.

## Notes

1. W.S. Merwin, "Separation," in *The Second Four Books of Poems* (Port Townsend, WA: Copper Canyon Press, 1993), 15. Retrieved from Poetry Foundation website: https://www.poetryfoundation.org/poetrymagazine /poems/detail/28891.

2. Steven Shainberg (director), Erin Cressida Wilson (screenwriter), *Secretary* (motion picture), distributed by Lions Gate Films (2002).

3. Roland Barthes, *A Lover's Discourse*, trans. Richard Howard (London, England: Vintage Classics, 2002), 40.

4. Ibid., 14.

5. John Bayley, *Iris: A Memoir of Iris Murdoch* (London, England: Duckworth, 1998), 44.

6. Elfriede Jelinek, *The Piano Teacher*, trans. Joachim Neugroschel (London, England: Serpent's Tail, 2009), 75.

7. Raymond Carver, "Waiting," in *All of Us: The Collected Poems* (New York, NY: Vintage Books, 2000). Retrieved from Writer's Almanac, http://writersalmanac.publicradio.org/index.php?date=2001/05/25.

8. Gaspara Stampa, "By Now I Am So Tired of Waiting," in *The Defiant Muse: Italian Feminist Poems from the Middle Ages to the Present*, ed. Beverly Allen, Muriel Kittel, and Keala Jane Jewell (New York, NY: Feminist Press, 1986), 15.

9. Dorothy Parker, "A Telephone Call," in *The Portable Dorothy Parker*, intro. Brendan Gill (New York, NY: Viking Press, 1973): 121.

10. Hans-Jost Frey, *Interruptions*, trans. Georgia Albert (Albany, NY: State University of New York Press, 1996), 57.

11. Barthes, *A Lover's Discourse*, 3.

12. Ibid., 15.

13. Robert Hass, "Misery and Splendor," in Human Wishes (New York, NY: HarperCollins, 1989). Retrieved from Poetry Foundation website: https://www.poetryfoundation.org/poems-and-poets/poems/detail/49593.

14. Harold Schweizer, "Penelope Waiting," *Soundings: An Interdisciplinary Journal* 85, nos. 3–4 (2002), 280.

15. Frey, *Interruptions*, 57.

## Texas Monthly

FINALIST—COLUMNS AND
COMMENTARY

The publication of "The Reckoning" marked the fiftieth anniversary the University of Texas Tower shooting—the first mass murder of its kind. The victims included eighteen-year-old Claire Wilson and her unborn son. This is her story. Based on more than one hundred hours of interviews, "The Reckoning" is only the latest example of Pamela Colloff's extraordinary skill as a reporter and writer. Colloff's work for Texas Monthly was nominated for Ellies in Public Interest in 2001 and 2011; in both Reporting and Feature Writing in 2013; and again in Feature Writing in 2015. Her two-part series "The Innocent Man" won the award for Feature Writing in 2013. Earlier this year Colloff joined ProPublica as a senior reporter and the New York Times Magazine as a writer at large.

Pamela Colloff

# The Reckoning

## I.

In the spring of 1967, when Claire Wilson was a freshman at the University of Texas, she went to the library one afternoon to track down an old copy of *Life* magazine. Thumbing through a stack of back issues, she scanned the dates on their well-worn covers. Finally, she arrived at the one she was looking for, and she slid it off the shelf. On the cover was a stark black and white photograph of a fractured store window, pierced by two bullet holes; in the distance loomed the UT Tower. Above the university's most iconic landmark were three words in bold, black letters: "The Texas Sniper."

Claire sat down and studied the large, color-saturated pictures inside, turning the pages as if she were handling a prized artifact. She read how Charles Whitman, an architectural engineering major, had brought an arsenal of weapons to the top of the Tower on August 1, 1966, and trained his rifles on the students and faculty below, methodically picking them off one by one. She pored over the images of people crouching behind cars as the massacre unfolded, and the aerial photo of campus dotted with red *X*'s showing where Whitman had hit his intended targets.

On the list of those killed, she located the name of her boyfriend, Thomas Eckman. Her gaze fell on Tom's picture, in which he sat in the formal pose of all midcentury yearbook photos, smiling broadly, his tie tucked into his V-neck sweater. Claire stared into his eyes, tracing the contours of his face. Holding the magazine in her hands, she felt some reassurance that what she had witnessed on campus that day had actually happened.

Not that she needed proof: above her left hip was a gnarled indentation, not yet healed, where one of Whitman's bullets had found its mark. She had been hospitalized for more than three months after the killing spree, spending what was supposed to have been the fall semester of her freshman year learning how to walk again. But by the time she returned to UT, in January, the tragedy had become a taboo subject on campus. Absent were the protocols that would later come to define school shootings: the grief counselors, the candlelight vigils, the nationwide soul-searching. Whitman's crime—decades before Columbine, Virginia Tech, and Newtown became shorthand for on-campus depravity—was unprecedented, and there was no language for it yet. The mass shooting was an obscenity whose memory stained the university, an aberration to be forgotten, and in the vastness of that silence, Claire found herself second-guessing what she remembered. The few times her friends tiptoed around the subject, they referred to it as "the accident."

The person Claire longed to talk with most was gone. She had known Tom for only a few months, but they had been inseparable. They had met as summer-school students in May 1966, when she was five months pregnant and single—a scandalous state of affairs for a middle-class girl from Dallas, though Claire had never cared much for social conventions. Tom, who was also eighteen and new to Austin, had moved in with her on the spot. Claire had had no interest in getting married—the institution was an anachronism, as far as she was concerned—and Tom, whose parents had divorced when he was little, felt the same way.

Like her, Tom attended Students for a Democratic Society meetings and saw himself as a foot soldier in the civil rights movement, once driving with her to the Rio Grande Valley to stand in solidarity with striking farmworkers. The two passed whole afternoons on the screened-in porch they used for a bedroom in their house off campus, quoting favorite passages to each other from the novels they were reading: he, Joyce Cary's *The Horse's Mouth* and she, Lawrence Durrell's *The Alexandria Quartet*. Sometimes Tom pressed his hand to her belly to see if he could feel the baby move.

In the wake of the shooting, Claire tried to hold moments like these in her mind. But her thoughts often wandered back to that August morning, when she and Tom had set out across the South Mall—and then she would be there again, on that blisteringly hot day, walking on the wide-open stretch of concrete beside him.

·　　·　　·

The anthropology class they were taking had let out early, sometime after eleven o'clock. Claire and Tom walked to the Chuck Wagon, the cafeteria inside the Student Union where campus leftists and self-styled bohemians held court, and happened to run into an old friend of Tom's from junior high. Eager to catch up, the ex-classmate suggested that they go to the student lounge to shoot some pool. Tom explained that he and Claire had to feed the parking meter first; downing his coffee, he promised they would be right back.

Tom and Claire stepped out into the thick, midday heat and headed east under a canopy of live oak trees. Tom was sporting a short-sleeved plaid shirt and his first mustache. Claire was wearing a brand-new maternity dress he had picked out, a beige shift with a flowery ribbon around the yoke. She was eight months along by then, and she could feel the weight of the baby as she walked. When they reached the upper terrace of the South Mall, the live oaks receded, and they were suddenly out in the open, exposed under the glare of the noon sun.

To their left stood the Tower, the tallest building in Austin after the Capitol; to their right stretched the mall's green, sloping lawn. As was often the case, they were deep in conversation; they had just begun a discussion about Claire's spartan eating habits and Tom's concern that the baby was not getting proper nutrition. Claire was in the middle of saying that she had, in fact, had a glass of orange juice that morning when a thunderous noise rang out. An instant later, she was falling, her knees buckling beneath her. Bewildered, Tom turned toward her. "Baby," he said, reaching for her. "What's wrong?" Then he too was knocked off his feet.

The two teenagers collapsed onto the pavement beside each other. Claire was flat on her back, the arc of her abdomen rising up in front of her. She felt as if a white-hot electric current was coursing through her. Tom lay to her left, close enough to touch, his head turned away from her. She called out to him, but he did not answer.

At first, no one on the South Mall seemed to realize what was happening. A man in a suit and tie ordered Claire and Tom to get up, ignoring her pleas for a doctor as he breezed by. She realized he thought it was a stunt—guerrilla theater or an antiwar protest, maybe, judging from his contempt. Moments later, she heard screams and the frantic cries of other students as they scattered, ducking for cover.

Bullets rained down from above, dinging balustrades, shattering windows, kicking loose concrete. A dozen yards from her and Tom, a physics professor was felled in midstride as he descended the stairs to the mall's lower terrace; his body would remain there, sprawled across the steps beside the bronze statue of Jefferson Davis, as students crouched behind the trees and hedges nearby. On the lawn, a young woman in a blue dress with nowhere to hide cowered behind the concrete base of a flagpole. Claire looked up at the Tower, where every now and then the nose of a rifle edged over the parapet, followed by the crack of gunfire and a wisp of smoke. She wondered if the Vietnam War had somehow come to Texas.

Every fifteen minutes, the Tower's bell would chime, but it was nearly half an hour before the sound of sirens neared, and even then, no help came. A police officer who was advancing behind a stone railing, service revolver drawn, was swiftly shot in the neck. Unable to lift herself, Claire remained where she had fallen, marooned. Blood pooled beneath her, saturating her dress. She played dead as the sound of gunshots reverberated around her, echoing off the red tile roofs and limestone walls. Dozens of students had run home to retrieve their deer rifles, and the echo of return fire rang out as they came back to take aim at the gunman.

It was nearly one hundred degrees by then, and she ached to get off of the concrete, which scorched her bare legs. When the heat became unbearable, she bent her right knee just enough to lift her calf, half expecting to be torn apart by gunfire. She did not know whether to feel relief or dread when she was not. She feared that Tom was dead, and that her child was lost too; instead of the thrumming energy she usually felt inside her, the baby had become still.

A young woman with long red hair suddenly ran into her field of vision, offering to help. "Lie down quick so we don't get shot," Claire pleaded. The woman dropped to the pavement and, from the spot where she lay, a few feet away, tried to keep Claire conscious by peppering her with questions. *What classes are you taking? Where did you grow up?* Claire whispered a few words back, struggling to answer.

Finally, more than an hour after the shooting had begun, three young men bolted from their hiding places and sprinted toward her and Tom. One grabbed Claire's arms, the other her ankles, and together they ran as her body dangled between them. The third man hoisted Tom's wilted frame into his arms, steadying himself under the weight of the teenager's lifeless body before following close behind.

As they raced across the mall, Claire did not feel the penetrating pain of her injuries or realize that she was losing copious amounts of blood. She could not make sense of what had just happened, much less begin to fathom how the jagged path of one bullet had, in a single moment, redrawn her life's course forever. She knew only that if she were lucky, she might live.

## II.

Growing up, Claire had never thought of guns as something to fear. As a kid she had taken riflery at summer camp in East Texas, where she had delighted in the thrill of target practice. Her parents kept guns in their house in East Dallas—her father, a bird hunter and ex-marine, stashed his long guns in the closet, where they leaned up casually against the wall. Guns were intertwined in her family history; they had made Texas passable for her Tennessee-born ancestors, who received a land grant from Stephen F. Austin in the 1820s. At age twelve, her maternal grandfather had used the proceeds from his initial cotton harvest in Brazoria County to buy his first rifle.

Even when President Kennedy was assassinated, Claire did not blame gun violence but rather the culture of intolerance that gripped her hometown. She knew all too well what it meant to be an outsider in Dallas: at a time when the John Birch Society and archconservative oil magnate H. L. Hunt held sway over the city, her father, John, had dedicated his legal career to representing clients, many of them black, in worker's compensation cases. Her mother, Mary, was the local precinct chair for the Democratic party, so consumed by her work championing various liberal causes that Claire came to measure time in election cycles.

Though the Wilsons lived only one block from the Lakewood Country Club, they refused to join, leaving Claire and her four siblings to make the long walk to the municipal pool—which was also closed to blacks but at least welcomed their Jewish friends.

Not wanting Claire, the eldest, to be oblivious to the injustices beyond their privileged, all-white enclave, her father drove her on more than one occasion through West Dallas, then home to a toxic lead smelter and slums that lacked sewage systems and running water. When she was twelve, her father took her to see Martin Luther King Jr. speak at the Majestic Theater, in Fort Worth, where few whites were present; at a private reception afterward, he led her up to the young minister to shake his hand.

At the time, in the late fifties, the unspoken rules of segregated society seemed immutable to Claire. When her parents went out to dinner one night with a black couple they knew, she watched, frozen, as the four drove off in her parents' Cadillac, convinced they would all be murdered. By the time she was a teenager, however, she had grown impatient with the pace of change. Each day for a month during the summer of 1964, she donned a dress, hat, and white gloves and headed downtown with her mother to take part in the protests outside the Piccadilly Cafeteria, a popular restaurant that refused service to blacks. Claire was arrested and booked into the city jail, but the charges were dismissed. She was ridiculed for being a "nigger lover" when she returned that fall to Woodrow Wilson High School, an epithet she doubled down on when she spent the following summer in the Mississippi Delta working as a volunteer with the Student Nonviolent Coordinating Committee. So immersed did she become in the SNCC's effort to get black residents registered to vote that she stayed on until October, content to miss her senior year.

Late that fall, she ran into John Muir, an acquaintance who had come home to Dallas unexpectedly from his sophomore year at Columbia University. Muir was wrestling with whether to drop out of college and devote himself to the civil rights movement. A graduate of the elite St. Mark's School of Texas, Muir was charismatic and well read, and though he was white, he had served as vice president of the local NAACP Youth Council. Claire had gotten to know him during the summer of the Piccadilly protest, when a multiracial group of teen activists had regularly gathered at her parents' house. During those unhurried afternoons, Muir had introduced her to the works of E. E. Cummings and Joseph Heller and played her the first Bob Dylan album she had ever heard, but it was not until Christmas week in 1965, after Claire had returned from Mississippi, that they slept together.

Muir decided to return to Columbia after the holidays, but first he agreed to help Claire move to Austin. Her parents, whose marriage had been foundering for years, had recently divorced, and she saw no compelling reason to stay in Dallas. Before long, Claire had landed a job waiting tables in her new city and enrolled for night classes at Austin High. She felt at home in the sleepy capital, a place of cheap rent, psychedelic rock, and nascent political activism. Her involvement in the civil rights movement quickly won her respect and friends, and she fell in with a group of like-minded UT students who were ablaze with new ideas.

It was in the midst of this happy-go-lucky time—when she was finally free from the judgments of racist classmates and the near-constant threat of violence she had felt in Mississippi—that Claire discovered she was pregnant. Muir dutifully made a trip to Austin after she told him the news, but during their discussions about how to move forward, he never suggested they make a life together. While she had no desire to get married, Claire felt bruised by the rejection. Muir returned to Columbia, leaving behind the then-considerable sum of $200 so she could have an abortion.

On the advice of friends, Claire met with a woman who knew how to procure the illegal—and, at that time, often perilous—procedure. But she could not bring herself to go any further. Though her decision to keep the baby would have meant certain exile from most social circles, in her group of free-thinking friends, her pregnancy was of little concern. Privately, the idea of having a child thrilled her, but it was not until she met Tom that May that someone shared in her joy.

"I was really, truly happy for the first time in my life," Claire told me. "I was out on my own, and I was in love, and I had so many friends. We were revolutionizing the world, and Tom and I were at the front of it."

. . .

Whitman hit his targets with terrifying precision. Across a crime scene that spanned five city blocks, the former marine sharpshooter managed to strike his intended victims with ease, felling them from distances well beyond five hundred yards. His arsenal included a scoped 6 mm Remington bolt-action rifle; a .35-caliber pump rifle; a .357 Magnum Smith & Wesson revolver; a .30-caliber M1 carbine; a 9 mm Luger pistol; a Galesi-Brescia .25-caliber pistol; a twelve-gauge shotgun with a sawed-off barrel; and about seven hundred rounds of ammunition. His rampage dragged on for more than an hour and a half before Austin police officers Ramiro Martinez and Houston McCoy reached him on the Tower's observation deck and shot him dead. By the time it was all over, Whitman had succeeded in killing sixteen people and wounding thirty-one.

Claire's rescuers miraculously avoided being hit as they ran headlong toward the western edge of the mall, spiriting her to the shelter of the Jefferson Davis statue. From there, five bystanders took over, carrying her to Inner Campus Drive, where they loaded her into a waiting ambulance.

She would be one of thirty-nine gunshot victims delivered to Brackenridge Hospital's emergency room in the span of ninety minutes. Many of them were bleeding out quickly, and doctors and nurses shouted back and forth as they tried to discern who should be sent into surgery first. Claire and a seventeen-year-old high school student named Karen Griffith, who had been shot in the lung, were lying on gurneys beside each other, waiting to be X-rayed, when a doctor intervened. "There's no time for X rays," he yelled, directing his staff to prep them both for surgery.

Claire was still conscious when a medic began cutting off her blood-soaked dress, and she begged him to stop, not wanting to lose the garment Tom had picked out for her. Though she clung to the delusion that she had only been shot in the arm, her magical thinking did not extend to Tom, whom she felt certain was dead. She had seen his inert body as she was lifted away.

Claire was put under general anesthetic, and her doctors set to work. The full extent of the damage was not evident until they made a lengthy incision down her torso, from sternum to pubic bone. The bullet had torn into her left side just above the hip, splintering the tip of her pelvis, puncturing her small intestine and uterus, lacerating an ovary, and riddling her internal organs with shrapnel. A C-section was performed, but the baby—a boy—was stillborn. A bullet fragment had pierced his skull.

The operation took twelve hours. Not long after Claire regained consciousness, she was wheeled down a corridor to the ICU. Standing along the walls on either side were her friends, who had waited at the hospital until past midnight to learn if she had made it out of surgery. "We love you, Claire!" they called out.

She spent the next seven weeks in the ICU in a fog of Demerol and Darvon. All told, she would endure five operations at Brackenridge to repair the damage done to her. To distract herself from the pain, she would belt out protest songs from her bed, delivering renditions of "Which Side Are You On?" and "We Shall Overcome" at the top of her lungs. With no TVs or even visitors, besides family members, allowed inside the ICU, she had few distractions and little information about life outside Brackenridge. Despite being a victim in a tragedy that had made headlines around the world, she never saw or heard a single news report about the shooting.

Her life narrowed to her hospital bed and the green floor-to-ceiling curtains the nurses drew tightly around her, past which she could sometimes catch sight of a tree and a sliver of sky. Intravenous lines extended from all four of her limbs, and her left leg, which was in traction, was suspended above her. Every two hours, in an excruciating ritual she came to dread, a nurse would turn her, rolling her onto one side and then the other. Her mother, who tried to project an image of strength, often sat at her bedside, chatting with the doctors and offering Claire words of encouragement. Refusing to give in to the chaos that the shooting had wrought, she was always immaculately dressed, often wearing a two-piece knit suit from Neiman Marcus, her blond hair pulled into a French twist.

If Claire's mother or her doctors ever explicitly told her that her baby was stillborn, she struck it from her memory. No one, as far as she could recall, ever spoke aloud the fact that her child had died. That the baby was a boy and that a burial plot had been secured for him were the only details she gleaned. Claire did not ask questions because she already knew; she felt his absence. She was startled when her milk came in days after the C-section, leaving her breasts engorged, and relieved when it dried up and her baby weight fell away. Her body settled back into its old contours, her belly flat, as if the pregnancy had never happened.

Without the chance to hold the baby in her arms, Claire did not know how to mourn his loss; she had not yet chosen a name, and he felt like an abstraction, his face unknowable. But her grief for Tom, and their abbreviated summer together, only metastasized once the fall semester got under way. She was tormented by the fact that she had not been able to attend his funeral. "I learned more in those [months with Tom] than perhaps in any other period of my life," she wrote in a four-page condolence letter to his father. "The sort of things that were between Tom and me happen so rarely in this world that most people don't even understand the language."

Most of the shooting victims who had been admitted to Brackenridge were discharged; some, like Karen Griffith, did not survive. Only Claire stayed on, her presence noted every now and then in the local paper, which ran a two-sentence squib on September 16 announcing that she was the last of Whitman's victims to remain hospitalized.

The myriad complications of abdominal gunshot wounds, including the threat of infection and sepsis, made Claire's condition tenuous. By the time her surgeries were complete, several feet of her intestine had been removed, as well as an ovary and the iliac crest of her pelvic bone. Daily physical therapy sessions allowed her to gradually regain the ability to walk. After she was moved out of the ICU, she became adept at using a cane, and at night, when she was unable to sleep, she would maneuver her way to the nurses' station to visit with the women in starched white uniforms who cared for her, some of whom were not much older than she was.

Claire was finally released the first week of November. She was nineteen by then, though she felt a thousand years old. She returned to campus in January, and in the early spring, she made the first of several visits to the library to page through the August 12 issue of *Life*. She had no pictures of Tom, and though the yearbook photo featured in the magazine failed to capture his spirit, she liked to study it all the same.

The confirmation she sought about the massacre—that she had not dreamed or invented it—was muddled by the fact that *Life*, like most publications at the time, omitted her preterm baby from the official tally of the dead. And so rather than avoid the South Mall on her way to class each day, she purposely walked past the spot where she and Tom had been hit, intensely curious, as if her proximity to the crime scene would render it more vivid. When the Tower's observation deck was reopened that June, she visited it by herself, riding the elevator to the twenty-seventh floor and then taking three short flights of stairs to the top, just as Whitman had with his arsenal. She looked over the balustrade down at the mall, as he had, and crouched down to peer through the downspouts where he had rested the barrel of his gun.

Austin was a place that had brought her so much happiness, but as she surveyed campus and the city that spread out beyond it, she felt an overwhelming sense of dislocation. How would she ever recover from the enormity of her loss, she wondered, or navigate the years ahead? "I was so lonely and so longing for some sort of physical contact," Claire said. "All I wanted right then was for somebody to put their arms around me and hold me tight."

## III.

Ten years after the shooting, on a warm July afternoon in 1976, Claire stood in a phone booth in northern Colorado, not far from the rugged peaks of the Continental Divide, with the receiver pressed to one ear. She had agreed to speak to an *Austin American-Statesman* reporter named Brenda Bell who was interviewing survivors of the shooting for an article that would mark its ten-year anniversary. With the help of Claire's father, Bell had tracked Claire down in the foothills of the Rocky Mountains, outside the small town of Loveland. Claire had never spoken about the shooting publicly, and her voice was soft as she answered the reporter's questions.

After she had been shot, she told Bell, she was "basically mixed up—confused about life in general." Only once she started reading the Bible in the years that followed had she found some peace. Scripture, she explained, "started effecting a lot of changes in my life." She had found a group of Seventh-day Adventists who worked as medical missionaries around Loveland, where they tried "to help other young people physically, mentally, and spiritually," she said. Her time there, immersed in nature and the gospel, had been restorative. "I'm so thankful," she told Bell before she hung up. "I'm glad to be alive."

Claire had spent five years living and working at the Eden Valley Institute, a spiritual retreat accessible only by unpaved roads and bounded by jaw-dropping panoramas of the snow-capped Rockies. Its clean-living, Adventist doctrine rejected not just smoking, drinking, and sex outside marriage but also the distractions of popular culture. In an era defined by the loosening of social mores, it was a monastic existence; Claire did not watch the evening news, listen to the radio, or go to the movie theater. While some women worked on the institute's farm, which yielded much of their food, or helped with the cooking and childcare, her main occupation was teaching the residents' school-age children. (Her father approvingly told her on his first visit that the self-sustaining community was "the closest thing to Red China" he had ever seen.) Though newspapers could be found at Eden Valley, Claire steered clear of them, preferring to spend her free time taking long walks through the backcountry. She was unaware of the Watergate hearings or the fall of Saigon. "It was very healing to be way out, deep in the mountains, apart from the rest of the world," Claire told me.

She had tried at first to heal herself in more conventional ways, visiting UT's Student Health Center as early as 1967 for the talk therapy she believed she urgently needed. But after her first session, during which she felt that the psychologist had made a pass at her, Claire abandoned the idea. At her father's urging, she transferred to the University of Colorado at Boulder that fall, leaving the near-constant reminders of the shooting behind, but she was homesick there, and she returned to UT the following year.

To her friends, she had seemed fine—"nice and sunny," recalled one—but not long after her return, she landed at the Student Health Center again when she abruptly stopped eating. The psychiatrist who evaluated her, Claire thought, showed more interest in her admission that she had taken LSD before than in her obvious depression. He put her on Thorazine, a powerful antipsychotic, and though her hair began falling out and she struggled to concentrate in class, her treatment was not adjusted. "Questioning doctors was just not done then, so I was an obedient patient," she told me. "There never was any talk therapy. He only wanted to discuss my past drug experiences, which were so few." In 1969, at the end of her spring semester, she dropped out and moved back to Colorado.

It was that same year that Claire began to feel the stirrings of belief. "After the shooting, I'd started wondering what forces were at work in the universe," she said. "I felt strongly that there was a force I couldn't see, and I was interested in finding out what it was." She escaped to the mountains outside Boulder with a University of Colorado student named Ernie, with whom she lived in a rough-hewn house in the woods with no indoor heat or plumbing. They immersed themselves in nature and back-to-basics living, warming themselves by a coal stove and hauling water from a well.

Just down the road from them and the other hippies who had taken up residence in Lefthand Canyon was an eighty-two-year-old woman named Emma Spencer, whom her neighbors called "Ma." A Seventh-day Adventist, she grew her own food, wove rugs by hand, and strictly observed the Sabbath. To Claire, the child of nonbelievers, she was a source of fascination. Ma gave her a Bible, which she began to read, and one afternoon, Claire found herself kneeling in prayer beside the older woman, searching for words as she tried to communicate with God. She had cried for Tom many times, but as she knelt on the knobby rag rug in Ma's log cabin, she felt, as she would later recall, an "unbidden and unexpected" grief surface for the baby. For the first time, Claire began to weep for her lost son.

Her desire for "a sincere, authentic, Christian life," as she called it, took her to Eden Valley in 1971. She would remain there until she was thirty, not striking out on her own until the winter of 1977. Her friends in Texas and Colorado, who heard from her infrequently during this time, if at all, were stunned that the girl they knew, who delighted in skinny-dipping and challenging the status quo, had suddenly gotten religion. "I don't know what combination of PTSD, spiritual yearning—which was very much of the moment—depression, and epiphany led her to the strict regime of the Seventh-day Adventist utopia," observed Tim Coursey, a childhood friend. "But I do remember thinking, 'Well, how about that? She walked right through the looking glass.'"

·　　·　　·

The dream, which Claire first had in her twenties, always began the same way: she would look down and discover her baby, bright-eyed, in her arms. He was never as small as a newborn—he would be a few months old, perhaps, or a toddler, even, old enough to meet her gaze—and she would be flooded with relief as she stared back at him in wonder. Then she would glance away, or walk into another room, her attention wandering for no more than a second, and when she looked back, her son would be gone.

Claire did not have the dream frequently, but when she did, in the peripatetic years that followed her time at Eden Valley, she awakened with a start, a deep ache in her chest. As she moved from Colorado to other states in the West—New Mexico, Texas, and Wyoming—she would occasionally stop in a public library to see if she could find the old *Life* magazine, anxious for something concrete upon which to anchor her longings. In those analog days, before it was possible to conjure up information about anything with a few keystrokes, her personal history was relegated to microfilm reels and hardbound magazine volumes, and there, alone among the stacks, she would scrutinize Tom's photo again. People she met had sometimes heard she was the victim of gun violence—one rumor at Eden Valley placed her at the 1970 Kent State shootings—but she rarely shared her story.

After Eden Valley, Claire made a brief sojourn to another religious community in upstate New York and then headed to New Mexico, where her sister, Lucy, was working as a psychologist at a residential facility for developmentally disabled adults. It was there that Claire met her first husband—an easygoing teacher who ran the facility's art-therapy program—and they wed in 1979. She never discussed the shooting with him, and he never showed any interest in discussing it. "I really just wanted to be married and have a baby, and that was more important to me than whether we were a good match," Claire said. They were not, and within two years they had divorced.

Claire packed her belongings and headed to Stephenville, Texas, where she moved in with her grandmother and enrolled in Tarleton State University, determined to finally finish college. She did so two years later, in 1983, with honors, when she was thirty-five years old. Armed with a degree in education, she then made her way to Wyoming, where she taught at a private Seventh-day Adventist school in the town of Buffalo, in the shadow of the Bighorn Mountains. Like many rural Adventist schools, it was modeled on a one-room schoolhouse, and she was its only teacher. Her life in Wyoming suited her well—the school was out in the country, and she had fewer than a dozen students, ranging in grades from first to eighth—but even as she devoted herself to the children, Claire found she could not shake her recurring thoughts about her baby. She wanted to have a child of her own, before she ran out of time, and her dreams about holding her son took on a new intensity.

Claire had sought psychological help at Tarleton with little success, and two years after moving to Wyoming, she tried again. Soon she met a bright, empathetic local therapist who listened without judgment as she described the anger that sometimes felt as if it might consume her. She began to see him in twice-weekly sessions in his comfortable office just off Main Street, where she finally spoke freely—nearly two decades after the fact—about having lost Tom and the baby. "It was the first time I'd been given permission to talk about what had happened and to mourn in any sort of meaningful, sustained way," said Claire.

Her therapist told her about post–traumatic stress disorder, a then-new medical diagnosis that he said described the array of symptoms some trauma victims, many of them veterans of war, experienced in the wake of catastrophic violence. PTSD, he explained, was characterized by nightmares, emotional detachment, rage, and a strong desire to avoid people and places that might trigger memories of the trauma. It was a diagnosis Claire reflexively resisted because to accept it "felt cheap, since I hadn't earned it," she said. "I had never seen the horrors of Vietnam."

The incremental progress she was making was cut short when, six months into counseling, her therapist transferred her into group therapy, and Claire found herself surrounded by people with substance-abuse problems—many of whom had been mandated, by court order, to attend—who had little insight into her state of mind. At loose ends, she abandoned the group and took up with a nineteen-year-old ranch hand and Wyoming native named Brian James. Then thirty-eight, she had little in common with the soft-spoken high school graduate, but in him she saw a kindred spirit with a curious and unconventional mind. Each afternoon, after she had dismissed her students, they talked for hours, hiking through the canyons and dry creeks that he had grown up exploring. Eight months after they met, they decided to get married.

When they wed, in August 1986—a full twenty years after the UT tragedy—Brian was just two years older than Claire had been when she was shot. "I think she was still trying to recover all that she had lost at eighteen," her sister, Lucy, told me. They moved to Arizona, where Lucy had already put down roots, and rented a house in Patagonia, near the border town of Nogales. Claire taught elementary school and Brian worked construction jobs, and their marriage was a happy one at first, though they would never delve into the defining event of her life. "I knew Claire had been shot, and that she had lost her boyfriend and her baby, but we never had a deep conversation about it," Brian told me. "It wasn't something I asked her about, and it wasn't something she seemed eager to discuss."

Instead, Claire tried to get pregnant, but she was met with disappointment. Though her doctors in 1966 had assured her that she would still be able to have children despite being left with one ovary and a uterus that had been stitched back together, she often wondered if Whitman, who had already robbed her of so much, had also stolen her ability to conceive.

She had all but given up by 1989, when she was forty-one, and her mother called with an improbable offer. Mary Wilson was by then on her third marriage and had reinvented herself as a successful New York City real estate agent. She was animated on the phone as she laid out her proposal for Claire: a realtor who worked for her, who had emigrated from Ethiopia, had introduced her to a good friend of his from Addis Ababa. The friend had been allowed into the United States a year earlier so that his young son could undergo emergency surgery for a congenital heart defect that had left him near death. The boy had remained in the States so he could receive follow-up medical care, but he and his father had overstayed their visas, and if they returned to Ethiopia, he would not have access to the pediatric cardiologists he needed.

The father had already embarked on the long and complex process of seeking asylum, her mother continued, but his and his son's legal status was precarious. Would Claire and Brian consider adopting the boy, she asked, so he could remain in the country? The first step would be to take legal guardianship of him, an effort that his father supported. The boy was four years old, added her mother, and his name was Sirak.

That June, after Claire had studied every book she could find at the library on the subject of adoption, she and Brian packed up their hatchback and embarked on a cross-country road trip to New York to meet the little boy who would become their son. "He was an incredible gift," Claire said. "A gift I didn't expect."

## IV.

Sirak had not seen his mother since he had left Addis Ababa as a toddler, and from the moment he caught sight of Claire in her mother's house in Riverdale, he brightened. "I can't remember a time when I didn't know her," Sirak told me. On their first day together, his father and Brian set out to go sightseeing around the city, leaving Sirak and Claire to become acquainted with each other. For the next three days, she fed him, bathed him, sang to him, read to him, and tucked him in at night. He was cheerful and playful in return, and from the first day, he called her Mommy in his accented English.

When it was finally time to load his meager belongings—two shirts, two pairs of shorts, and a toy school bus—into the hatchback and head home to Arizona, his father walked him to the car and buckled him in. "His dad was very loving, but he didn't make a big deal out of saying goodbye," Claire said. "He made it seem like Sirak was going on a long trip, on a big adventure." Sirak's father could travel inside the United States while his application for asylum was under review, and he promised the boy that he would come see him soon.

As Brian drove, Claire and Sirak sat together in the back seat, watching as the Manhattan skyline faded from view. The boy cried quietly to himself for a few minutes, but he became more animated as they moved farther from the city, and he was insistent on Claire's undivided attention. If she pulled her book out and started to read—she was in the middle of James Michener's *Alaska*—he would stick his head between her and the page, grinning. If she lay down and stretched out across the back seat, he would sprawl on top of her until his face hovered just above hers. They remained that way for hours, talking and laughing and staring up at the flat, blue summer sky.

Though they could not have looked any more different, they each bore a similar scar: a long, vertical line along the torso where a surgeon's scalpel had once traced a path. Hers began below the sternum, while his was located higher up, closer to his heart. Years later, when he was old enough to understand, Claire would tell him what had happened to her in 1966 and he would listen, carefully considering her story, before adding that he would always think of the baby she had lost as his brother.

Despite the fact that Sirak had been born with a ventricular septal defect, or a hole in his heart, he thrived. He was a healthy if slight little boy, and when Claire took him to see his pediatric cardiologist every three months for his checkups, he was usually given a clean bill of health. As the only dark-skinned person in their community, he was a source of fascination to the kids who reached out to touch his hair. But Sirak embraced the very thing that set him apart, beaming when his father—who made biannual visits to Arizona—stood before his classmates and spoke about their African heritage. From the start, Sirak was quick to make friends and an exuberant presence. "Teach me!" he exhorted one teacher the summer before he started kindergarten.

Claire and Brian formally adopted him when he was six years old, shortly after they moved west to the unincorporated community of Arivaca. Sirak's father continued to make the trek out to see them, and each time he left, the boy would take the snap-brim cap his dad had worn during his visit and bring it to bed with him, resting it on the pillow. On nights when the stars shone so brightly above their desert outpost that they illuminated the canyons below, Claire, Brian, and Sirak would roll out their sleeping bags on the flat portion of their roof and lie side by side, staring up at the constellations.

Still, the area between the two lower chambers of Sirak's heart remained fragile, and at the age of seven, he was rushed into surgery after an echocardiogram suggested that his aorta had narrowed and was impeding blood flow to his brain. (The operation was called off after another round of tests.) Afterward, Claire found herself preoccupied with the possibility that something cataclysmic might happen. Even a nick in the mouth—sustained during a dental exam, say, or while playing with other kids—could allow bacteria into his bloodstream and have fatal consequences. Claire girded herself, carrying supplies of antibiotics in her purse at all times, but she could not shake her fear that, at any moment, she could lose Sirak. Once, she dreamed that she watched him board a bus that then abruptly pulled away, and she chased after it, calling out for the boy and waving her arms wildly, before losing sight of him.

Claire did her best to keep her worry to herself. Harder to hide was the anguish she had carried since the shooting, which would surface unpredictably despite how fortunate she felt about finally having a family. "I still had so much anger," Claire told me. She was moody and short-tempered, often lashing out at Brian, who grew distant, spending more and more time away from home. In 1996, when Sirak was eleven, Claire accepted a teaching position at a Seventh-day Adventist school in Virginia and took their son with her. Three years later, she and Brian divorced.

And then, just like that, Claire was a single mother, scratching out a living, ashamed by her cardinal failure, as she saw it, to keep her family intact. Her restlessness ensured that she and Sirak did not stay in Virginia long; they moved to Nebraska in 1999, when he started high school, and then to Kansas two years later. Though her pay as a teacher was barely enough to get by on, she and Sirak were resourceful, baking their own bread and gathering windfall apples. In Virginia, where they lived next to a public housing project, Claire sometimes treated herself to a twenty-five-cent copy of the *Washington Post*, and she and Sirak took turns reading the restaurant reviews aloud at the kitchen table, imagining that they, too, were dining in a white-tablecloth establishment.

What little Claire scraped together she put into piano lessons for her son, who was captivated by classical music. Once, when she reached to turn down the volume of a Beethoven symphony they were listening to in the car, Sirak had signaled for her to stop. "No," he said, smiling, as if transported. "We were just getting to the exciting part." He spent hours at the piano each day practicing Chopin's Études, and he played wherever he could find an audience, from their church to local nursing homes.

Then one day, at age fourteen, he started complaining of blinding headaches. His physician initially believed he had meningitis, but after further testing, he was diagnosed with Guillain-Barré syndrome, a rare disorder in which the body's immune system attacks the nervous system, often causing temporary paralysis. Sirak was rushed to the hospital, where he soon found himself unable to walk. Seeing Sirak confined to a hospital bed—so weak, at first, that he could not play the keyboard his teacher had brought him—Claire was seized by terror. As she sat vigil at his bedside, she closed her eyes and bowed her head, silently pleading with God not to take this son from her too.

The syndrome, exotic-sounding and mercurial, eventually ebbed with treatment, and Sirak returned to the ninth grade a month later, shuffling behind a walker. No sooner was his body strong again than he faced another ordeal; during his hospitalization, doctors had discovered he needed open-heart surgery to repair his aorta, this time unequivocally. The operation, performed in the spring of 2000, was a success, though it would be another three years—when his cardiologist told Claire that his heart had fully healed—before she felt any sense of relief. Sirak, who was eighteen by then, would be a healthy adult, the doctor explained.

Sometimes, in those days after Sirak's recovery, Claire thought back to an epiphany she'd had years before, while on a hike in Wyoming. She had come across a tree whose trunk bent at a dramatic angle at its midway point, forming a curvature that resembled the letter C. Something catastrophic—lightning? drought?—had diverted it from its path, but the tree, resilient, had righted itself and grown straight again.

## V.

Claire was still living in Virginia in the spring of 1999 when one word—Columbine—became synonymous with mass murder. Because she did not own a TV, she was not subjected to the disturbing footage that seemed to play on every channel, in which petrified teenagers streamed out of their suburban Denver high school, hands over their heads, frantic to escape the carnage inside. Still, when she saw the headlines, she felt her pulse race. She scoured the newspaper for details—about the pair of teenagers who had come to school armed with bombs and guns; about the twelve students and the teacher who had been slaughtered; about the twenty-one gunshot victims who had survived. Even as she grieved for them, Claire was taken aback by the attention the shooting commanded. As the victim of a crime that was still cloaked in silence and shame, she felt strangely envious. "So much of what had happened to me was still a mystery," she said. "Every single detail that revealed itself was precious."

In fact, Claire had begun to reconstruct parts of her story the previous Thanksgiving. That week, she had stopped in a bookstore in Washington Dulles International Airport, where she was waiting for a flight that would take her to Arizona to see her sister. Sirak was staying with friends for the holiday, and Claire, who was rarely apart from him, was on her own. Someone she knew had recently mentioned an item in the *Washington Post* on a new book called *A Sniper in the Tower*, by Texas historian Gary Lavergne, and Claire, who was curious to see it, eyed the shelves. Though pop culture had elevated Charles Whitman to near-mythic status in the intervening decades through both film and music—Harry Chapin's 1972 song "Sniper" cast him as a misunderstood antihero—the tragedy itself had received scant attention, save for the obligatory anniversary stories that ran in Texas newspapers.

Claire finally spotted the book, whose cover featured an old black and white yearbook photo of Whitman wearing a wide grin. Rather than start at the beginning, she flipped to the end and scanned the index, where she was startled to see her name. Turning to the first citation, on page 141, she skimmed the text and then came to a stop. "Eighteen-year-old Claire Wilson . . . was walking with her eighteen-year-old boyfriend and room-mate, Thomas F. Eckman," she read. "Reportedly, both were members of the highly controversial Students for a Democratic Society. She was also eight months pregnant and due for a normal delivery of a baby boy in a few short weeks."

Claire could feel her heart thumping in her chest at what came next:

Looking down on her from a fortress 231 feet above, Whitman pulled the trigger. With his four-power scope he would have clearly seen her advanced state of pregnancy. As if to define the monster he had become, he chose the youngest life as his first victim from the deck. Given his marksmanship, the magnification of the four-power scope, an unobstructed view, his elevation, and no interference from the ground, it can only be concluded that he aimed for the baby in Claire Wilson's womb.

Claire stood still, the frenetic energy of her fellow travelers receding into the background. What astonished her more than the notion that Whitman had deliberately taken aim at her child—an idea she could not yet fully grasp—was the simple fact that what had happened to her more than three decades earlier was written down in a book that she could hold in her hands. Though she had no money to speak of at that particular moment—her father had purchased her plane ticket for her—she did not hesitate before handing over her last twenty dollars to buy the book, which she devoured on her flight to Tucson.

The act of reclaiming her history would come afterward in fits and starts, beginning one summer night in 2001, when Claire sat at her computer and used a search engine for the very first time, carefully typing out the words "UT Tower Shooting." She had only a dial-up connection, and the results were slow to load, but the first link that appeared led to a blog written by an Austin advertising executive named Forrest Preece, who had narrowly escaped being shot by Whitman. Preece had been standing across the street from the Student Union, outside the Rexall Drug Store, on the morning of the shooting, when a bullet had whizzed by his right ear. As Claire read his account of the massacre—"Every year, when August approaches, I start trying to forget . . . but as any rational person knows, when you try to forget something, you just end up thinking about it more"—she felt strangely comforted. Each detail he described—the earsplitting gunfire, the bodies splayed on the ground, the onlookers who stood immobilized, wild with fright—was one she had carried with her all those years too.

Claire initiated a sporadic correspondence with Preece as she continued her itinerant existence—first heading to New York, to take care of her ailing mother after Sirak left for college, and then moving back to Colorado, in 2005, and Wyoming, two years later, to teach in Adventist schools. In each place, she felt the strange pull of the shooting tug at her. Once, in a sporting goods store in the Rocky Mountains, she decided to stop at the gun counter and ask the clerk if she could look at a .30-06. (Whitman had in fact shot her with a 6 mm bolt-action rifle, but Claire had been told otherwise.) The clerk laid the .30-06 out on the glass counter and Claire studied the weapon, finally reaching out to touch its stock, before pulling her hand back a moment later, unsure what she had come to see. Another time, while driving through the Denver area, she chose to take a detour through Columbine, even circling around the high school. She could not say exactly what she had gone looking for "except for some deeper understanding," she told me, that went unsatisfied.

Claire had stayed away from Austin for nearly forty years, but in 2008, when Preece asked her to attend a building dedication for the law-enforcement officers and civilians who had helped bring Whitman's rampage to an end, she felt compelled to return. The previous year, a student at Virginia Tech had armed himself and opened fire, killing thirty-two people and injuring seventeen, and Claire, rattled by yet another tragedy, craved human connection.

At the ceremony, which took place at a county building far from campus, she fumbled for the right words as she tried to convey her thankfulness to Houston McCoy, one of the police officers who had shot Whitman. When she later joined him, Preece, and several former officers on a visit to UT, she was dismayed to find that the only reference to the horror that had unfolded there was a small bronze plaque on the north side of the Tower. Set in a limestone boulder beside a pond, it was easy to miss. As Claire surveyed the modest memorial, an industrial air conditioning unit that sat nearby cycled on and a dull roar broke the silence. "I had heard about the memorial and had taken solace in thinking that it was a lovely place," she told me. "I was so disappointed to find no mention of Tom, the baby, or any of the victims."

Afterward, at his home, Preece showed her old news footage that TV cameramen had shot on the day of the tragedy, looking out onto the South Mall. As she watched, Claire was startled to realize that she was looking at a grainy image of her younger self, lying on the hot pavement. When she saw two teenagers dash out from their hiding places and run headlong toward her, she leaned closer, dumbstruck. Local news stations had aired the footage in the aftermath of the shooting and on subsequent anniversaries, but Claire had never seen any of it, and witnessing her own rescue was revelatory. She had always known the name of one of the students who saved her; James Love, a fellow freshman, had been in her anthropology class, and she had stopped him on campus once in 1967 to thank him for what he had done, but he had seemed ill at ease and eager to break free from the conversation. His partner, a teenager in a black button-down shirt and Buddy

Holly glasses, had remained unknown to her, so much so that she had half wondered, until she saw the black and white footage, if he had been an angel.

Preece helped her solve the mystery in 2011, after he spotted a headline in the *American-Statesman* that read "Man Who's the Life of the Party Has Brush With Death." Below it, the article detailed how a local performance artist named Artly Snuff, a member of the parody rock band the Uranium Savages, had survived a near-fatal car accident. Born John Fox, Snuff had graduated from Austin High and been weeks away from starting his freshman year at UT when Whitman opened fire. Though the article never referenced the shooting, the mention of Snuff's name jogged Preece's memory, and he recalled a *Statesman* column on Snuff years earlier in which he was praised for having helped carry a pregnant woman in the midst of the massacre.

Preece tracked down Snuff on Facebook, and in 2012, he put him and Claire in touch. "To finally hear her voice was stunning, because I'd wondered what had happened to her so many times," Snuff told me of their first phone call, which spanned hours. "For both of us, just talking was a catharsis. I'd seen things no seventeen-year-old should ever have to see, and I'd carried those memories with me, and Claire understood."

Snuff told Claire how he had crouched behind the Jefferson Davis statue with Love—a friend of his from high school whose life was later cut short by bone cancer—as gunfire erupted around them. They had agonized about what to do, he explained, as they looked onto the South Mall and saw her lying there, still alive. Too terrified to move, they had initially stayed put—Snuff's own cowardice, as he saw it, measured in fifteen-minute increments whenever the Tower's bells chimed on the quarter hour. In a voice thick with emotion, he told her that he had always regretted taking so long to work up the courage to help her.

Claire assured him that he owed her no apologies, saying that she loved him and would always think of him as her brother. She said so again when they saw each other in Austin in 2013, wrapping her arms around him in the entrance of the Mexican restaurant where they had agreed to meet. Oblivious to everyone else, they embraced for several minutes. "It was so affirming to finally say thank you," Claire told me.

Around them, a national debate about gun control had just erupted with new force. Three months earlier, in Newtown, Connecticut, a disturbed young man had fatally shot twenty children, none more than seven years old, and six adults, at Sandy Hook Elementary School. In a forceful speech at a memorial service for the victims, President Barack Obama had pushed for tighter regulation of firearms, warning that the cost of inaction was too great. In response, many gun owners had bristled at the notion that fewer licensed weapons, and more government regulation, would keep anyone safe. In Texas, where the Legislature was in session that spring, lawmakers had proposed several "campus carry" bills, which sought to upend the long-standing state law banning firearms at public universities. If passed, concealed handguns would be permitted on university grounds, in dorms, and in college classrooms.

Claire had returned to Austin because Jim Bryce, a lawyer and gun-control activist whom she had met when they were both students at UT, had asked if she, as a victim of campus gun violence, would testify at the Capitol. Though she had not engaged in any activism since the sixties—the Seventh-day Adventist Church advocates strict political neutrality—she felt that she could not turn down Bryce's invitation. And so on March 14, 2013, Claire appeared before the Homeland Security and Public Safety Committee, one among scores of people who had come to voice their support or opposition to the bills. No longer the campus radical she had once been, she did not stand out in the overflow crowd; at sixty-five, everything about her—from her chin-length silver bob to the reading glasses she slid on when it was her turn to speak to her comfortable shoes—was muted and sensible.

Like the other speakers, Claire was allotted three minutes. Compressing the totality of her experience into a few sound bites seemed impossible, but once at the microphone, she tried. "I never thought about somebody using a gun to kill themselves or others until August 1, 1966, when I was walking across the campus of the University of Texas," she said, her voice clear and steady. She sketched out what had happened to her in a few unadorned sentences—"I was eighteen and eight months pregnant"—and when she reached the end of her story, she added, "I was not able ever again to have a child."

She expressed her reservations, as both an educator and a sixth-generation Texan who had grown up around guns, about the proposed bills, arguing that the Legislature's objective should be to prevent future attacks, not arm more civilians. "A campus is a sacred place," she said. Then her time was up.

.  .  .

That fall, Claire received an e-mail from Gary Lavergne, with whom she had met and corresponded after reading *A Sniper in the Tower*. The e-mail told of an astounding discovery. "My Dear Friend, Claire," it began. "A few years ago, while working on my last book, I downloaded a database of grave sites located in the Austin Memorial Park. (My purpose was to locate the graves of some of the persons I had written about in *Before Brown*.) It wasn't until this past weekend that, while browsing among the almost 23,000 entries in that dataset, I noticed an entry for a 'Baby Boy Wilson.'"

Lavergne went on to explain that the burial date for the child was listed as August 2, 1966—the day after the massacre. Records showed that the unmarked plot had been purchased by a Lyman Jones, a man whose name Lavergne did not recognize. Claire did, immediately; a veteran journalist who had written for the *Texas Observer* during the fifties and sixties, Jones was her mother's second husband, and Claire's stepfather, at the time of the shooting.

Claire had always been aware that the baby had received a proper burial, but she had not pressed her mother for details until her later years, when her mother's memory was failing and she could no longer summon them. The small plot, she now learned from Lavergne, was located in a section of the cemetery mostly devoted to infants and stillborn babies. "Claire, I hope this gives you comfort," he wrote, explaining that he had gone to Austin Memorial Park to find the burial place. "Attached is a picture I took of the grave site. Your son is buried beneath the flowers I placed there so that you can see the exact spot."

Claire read and reread the e-mail in silence, brushing away tears. *Your son. Buried beneath the flowers.*

She would visit the cemetery the following August, after Lavergne and his family had a headstone made, with Claire's blessing. Below the image of a cross, it read:

Baby Boy Wilson
August 1, 1966

It stood near the perimeter of the cemetery, on a sunburned stretch of grass near a single hackberry tree. When Claire found it, she knelt down and gathered a handful of soil, placing it inside a folded sheet of paper, for a keepsake. Then she prostrated herself, pressing her forehead against the marble marker, which was cool even in the blazing August sun. She thought about Tom and about the baby's father, John Muir, whom she had called and spoken with, after a decades-long estrangement, before he had passed away that June. As she lay there, she was acutely aware of the baby's presence, of the molecules somewhere below the earth's surface that belonged to him. Claire stayed for a long time and prayed. "I felt not so hollow," she said. "I felt close to God."

## VI.

Claire lives in Texas now, having finally, after all her years of wandering, come home. Six years ago, she moved to Texarkana—which, with some 37,000 residents, is the most densely populated place she has lived for some time. An Adventist school had needed a teacher, and so, as she had done more than a dozen times before, she started over. Not since Eden Valley has she remained in one place for so long.

When I went to visit her earlier this year, we met at her white double-wide trailer, which sits on the pine-studded, western edge of town. Her bedroom window looks out onto a pasture, and though the view lacks the grandeur of the Rockies or the Great Plains, it allows her to imagine that she still lives in the wilderness, far from civilization. A few steps from her front door, in raised beds she built herself with wood, she had planted a winter garden. Collard greens and kale flourished next to fat heads of cabbage, and despite a recent freeze, a few stalwart strawberry plants thrived. As we talked, Claire bent down and tore off a few sprigs of mint, handing me some to taste. "Isn't it wonderful?" she said, her pale blue eyes widening.

When Claire told friends about her life in Texarkana, she focused on the happy things: her garden; the Nigerian family she had befriended; her students, many of whom lived below the poverty line, who hugged her waist and called her Miss Claire. She did not share her worry about Sirak, who was standing beside her on that January morning. He wore a cheerless expression, a black wool hat pulled down to his eyebrows, his shoulders squared against the cold. He had moved back in with her in August, not long after his thirtieth birthday, but he bore little resemblance to the young man she had sent off to college. Unless prodded to talk, he said little, and his speech was slow and leaden. Every now and then, as Claire and I chatted, he would smile at the mention of a childhood friend or a story about his and Claire's days in the Arizona high desert. Except for those moments, he seemed to have taken up residence in a world of his own.

For Claire, the first clue that something was not right with Sirak came in 2007. Then a month shy of graduating with a music degree from Union College, in Nebraska, Sirak had called her late one night. "Mom, my thoughts are racing and I can't make them stop," he confided, adding that he had not been sleeping much. Claire offered reassurance, certain these were the typical jitters of a graduating senior. But that July, shortly before he was set to begin a prestigious teaching fellowship in the University of Nebraska's music program, he called again and begged her to take him home. Rather than try to reason with him, she made the ten-hour drive from Colorado. When she arrived, she found Sirak standing in the parking lot of his apartment complex, wide-eyed and on edge. He refused to step foot inside his apartment by himself. "He was terrified, shaking, talking so fast," she told me. "That's when I knew something was really wrong."

At home, his behavior only grew more erratic. Sirak, usually a modest person, would walk to the mailbox at the end of their driveway in nothing but his underwear. He slept little and was reluctant to venture far from the house. Once, after he and Claire ate out, he told her he was sure that the restaurant's staff had put laxatives in their food. She took Sirak to see a series of mental-health professionals, but no one could offer a definitive diagnosis; a prescription for Lexapro, a popular antidepressant, did little to lessen his anxiety. Sometimes he would slip into a manic state, and Claire would coax him into her car and head for the emergency room. "At the hospital, I always got the same question: 'Is he threatening you or trying to hurt himself?'" she said. "And I would say, 'No,' and they would tell me that they couldn't help me."

Rather than face his descent into mental illness alone, Claire reached out to his biological father, who had been granted asylum in 1999. (Her ex-husband, Brian, had remarried and largely receded from Sirak's life.) The rest of Sirak's family—his mother, two brothers, and two sisters—had immigrated when Sirak was thirteen and settled with his father in Atlanta. Sirak had visited them nearly every summer since, and he and his siblings had forged an easy bond. Claire believed that Atlanta, with its big-city mental-health resources, would be a better place for him than rural Colorado, and in 2008, it was agreed that he would go live with his Ethiopian family.

In Atlanta, a psychiatrist finally diagnosed Sirak with bipolar disorder and prescribed him lithium, a mood stabilizer. During long, discursive phone conversations with Claire, Sirak assured her that he was taking his medication, but despite his sincere longing to get well, he never consistently followed his treatment protocol. Though he managed to hold a number of menial jobs—he bagged groceries, worked as a drugstore clerk, cleaned out moving trucks, delivered auto parts—his employment was often cut short when a manic episode overtook him. By 2012, during one of many voluntary commitments to Georgia Regional, a large, state-run hospital with a psychiatric ward, his diagnosis was modified to reflect his worsening condition. "I have Bipolar One, manic severe, with psychotic features," Sirak explained to me matter-of-factly, referring to the most severe form of the disorder.

When Claire saw Sirak on a visit last July, she was stunned. His doctors had put him on a powerful antipsychotic drug to keep his most serious symptoms in check, but it was plain that he was overmedicated. Sirak absently raised his feet, walking in place where he stood, and looked unfocused, his clothes rumpled, his hair uncombed. When he sat, he sometimes drifted off to sleep, and when he spoke, his voice was a curious monotone. "I'm not enjoying being alive very much right now," he told her. Eager to find a way to dial back his medications, she moved him to Texarkana the following month and gave him her spare bedroom. She found a psychiatrist to fine-tune his prescriptions and arranged for weekly talk therapy sessions. The change of scenery seemed to help him, at least at first. "Today Sirak told me he no longer wants to die," Claire e-mailed a handful of close friends in late August. "Rejoice with me."

By the time of my visit, he had lapsed back into a depression, and he announced that he wanted to return to Atlanta. (Several weeks later, he did.) Though he had once devoted hours each day to the piano—in 2012 he even went to New York to audition for the master's program at Juilliard—he had stopped playing, he told me, because he had lost his passion for music. "My doctor said I have something called anhedonia," he said. "It's like hedonism, but the opposite. It means I don't feel pleasure anymore."

He brightened only when he changed the subject to an obsession of his: his conviction that he will one day be reborn as a "child of prophecy," or a sort of modern-day messiah. As he described the superpowers he would possess when the prophecy came to fruition, he grew elated, his face alight. Beside him, Claire sat in silence, staring down at her clasped hands.

·      ·      ·

What if Whitman's bullet had never found her? Claire sometimes thinks about the intricate calculus that put her in his sights that day. What if her anthropology class had not let out early? What if Tom had lingered over his coffee one minute longer before they had gone to feed the parking meter? Such deliberations have never satisfied her, because each shift in the variables sets in motion other consequences. If she had not been shot, she might never have found God. If she had given birth, she would not have known the exhilaration, at forty-one, of becoming a mother, or the hard-won joy of raising Sirak. Sometimes she finds herself calculating the age of her first child, had he lived, and the number always astonishes her. She wrote it in my notebook one afternoon, carefully forming each numeral: forty-nine. He would probably be a father by now, she observed, and she a grandmother.

She rarely gives much thought to Whitman, who remains, in her mind, remote and inscrutable. "I never saw his face, because we were separated by so much distance," Claire said. "So it's always been hard to understand that he did this—that a *person* did this—to me." Paging through *Life* on her library visits all those years ago, she studied the photos of him, and one particular image—taken at the beach when Whitman was two years old—has always stayed with her. In the picture, he is standing barefoot in the sand, grinning sweetly at a small dog. Two of his father's rifles are positioned upright on either side of him, and Whitman is holding on to them the way a skier grips his poles.

"That's how I see him—as that little boy on the shore, still open to the world, just wanting his father's love and approval," Claire said. She cannot grasp how, in such a short span of time, "he became so twisted and decided to do what he did," she said. "But I've never felt it was personal. How could I? He didn't know me, I didn't know him."

It will have been fifty years since the shooting this summer, an anniversary that, for Claire, has brought the tragedy into clearer focus. A documentary that tells the story of the day of the massacre from the perspective of eyewitnesses and survivors, with an emphasis on Claire's ordeal, premiered at the South by Southwest Film Festival in Austin in March; directed by Austin-based filmmaker Keith Maitland, *Tower* will air nationally on PBS later this year. (The documentary is loosely based on a 2006 *Texas Monthly* oral history; I served as one of its executive producers.) The film, and recent efforts to plan a memorial for August 1, have reconnected Claire to people she thought she would never see again. "I felt so isolated by the years of silence," she wrote to Maitland during filming. "Now I feel restored to the community from which I was ripped."

Last spring, Claire found herself at the Capitol once again to testify against legislation that would allow concealed handguns on college campuses. While the bills she opposed in 2013 had ultimately failed, this time her testimony did little to deter gun-rights advocates, who succeeded in passing a campus carry bill by a two-to-one margin. Though supporters argued that the measure would make universities safer, Claire was heartened when protests erupted at UT, where an overwhelming majority of students, professors, and administrators balked at the Legislature's actions. In what Claire sees as a grotesque insult, the law will go into effect on August 1, half a century to the day that Whitman walked onto the Tower's observation deck and opened fire.

Like many survivors of the shooting, Claire will return to campus to mark the anniversary. The university, now a sprawling, multi-billion-dollar institution whose shiny new research facilities dominate the landscape, is drastically different from the one she entered in 1966, but the unsettled legacy of that summer remains. Though the gaping bullet holes left by Whitman's rampage were quickly patched over, not every scar was filled, and anyone who takes the time to look closely at the limestone walls and balustrades that line the South Mall can still make out tiny divots where his bullets missed their mark.

Claire longs to lie down, in the shadow of the Tower, on the precise spot where she was shot. "It's beyond me why I would feel comforted there," she told me. "But I want to lie down, and remember the heat, and remember Tom, and remember the baby." That wide-open stretch of concrete is the last place they were all together.

## Oxford American

FINALIST—ESSAYS AND CRITICISM

*"Daddy had a blues all his life that I couldn't begin to know, though I had so desperately tried to understand it": so writes Zandria F. Robinson as she begins looking for her late father in the music that he loved: church choirs, radio waves, the heartache of Bobby "Blue" Bland. In the end she finds insight but also something perhaps more valuable—hope. The Ellie judges used just one word to describe this extraordinary essay: "transporting."* The author of This Ain't Chicago: Race, Class, and Regional Identity in the Post-Soul South, *Robinson now blogs at newsouthnegress.com.* Oxford American *describes itself as "dedicated to featuring the best in Southern writing." The magazine won the Ellie for General Excellence in 2016.*

Zandria F. Robinson

# Listening for the Country

Wwhen I finally cranked the truck, WDIA came in raspy but sure over the insistent roar of the hemi. Together, the engine and the r&b made a Monday-morning kind of sound—time for coffee and work. I adjusted the mirrors, preparing to put the truck in gear. My feet were still swollen from wandering sticky-thighed downtown through packed Memphis parking lots as I looked for the truck in the spring's first real, wet heat. The swelling was useful, I thought, so my foot could lay heavy on the gas pedal without much flexing and force. I thrust it forward in search of the brake and hit it before I expected; Arthur Lee Robinson was taller than me, but I didn't have to adjust the seat. In thirteen years, I had never driven his truck, which he bought when he found out I was pregnant with his first grandchild.

Daddy would have fetched his own truck the Friday prior, but he flew away to heaven in the early morning hours of the last day of his jury service. His launching pad had been the sequester hotel on the other side of town, where Shelby County had been holding him and eleven others who would decide if Ricky Patton had murdered Terrance Covington a few Julys back. One juror had been dismissed for discussing the trial. Another had injured himself on the way to the jury box. Daddy's death, an apparent heart attack from diabetes complications and poor medication adherence, was the third strike. It triggered a mistrial and a brief wave of click-bait infamy, as local and national news-aggregating outlets picked up the story from our paper of record and included all of the facts: Arthur Robinson, sixty-four, was found on the bathroom floor of the sequester hotel by his fellow juror and roommate. The local paper quoted the judge as saying she'd never heard of such an occurrence. She wrote Mama a letter of condolence.

Daddy's truck was one of those places—like a grandmother's house, a real and actual soul food restaurant, or a barbershop owned by an older black man who guards the radio by silent threat of the revolver in his drawer next to the good clippers—where one could reliably expect to hear either (and only) 1070 WDIA or 1340 WLOK. It was the other side of sound, the other side of Southern blackness, a steady if muffled undercurrent that persisted and quietly buoyed new generations. I left the radio on WDIA, listening for what he might have heard when he parked his truck in that lot the previous week.

Daddy was country complex. You had to listen for the undercurrent, the Delta lower frequencies, to hear who he was. I knew he wouldn't be the type to haunt me and offer answers to my many questions from the beyond; he wouldn't come if I called him forth with my altar of rainbow candles, stones, and cowries. I pictured him in the Hereafter, seated at his table eating a sausage link on a rolled-up piece of white bread, raising an eyebrow in the direction of my summons.

No, Daddy couldn't be conjured in life, so he certainly couldn't be conjured in death. Instead, I tried to listen for him, as I had learned to do when I embraced countryness—my father's, my father's people's, black people's, and my own—as an adult. WDIA. WLOK. The various gospel compilations Daddy had somebody burn onto CDs, now thoroughly scratched from neglect. Songs he sang in the three choirs of which he was a member at St. John Missionary Baptist Church. Field hollers. B. B. King. My investigation was sensory, and I had to just catch the feeling of it, because I could never know for sure. With Daddy, you could only suppose and reckon.

·       ·       ·

Mama was and is no mystery. As she reminded everyone often, she was born an entire twenty days before Daddy and raised in the city. She said "country" with a deep, monstrous snarl one might use to say "from a can" in reference to vegetables at a family dinner. Country was dirt and rudeness and Delta and blues and double-wides and pig intestines and outhouses and racial repression. It was also violence and hurt and infidelity and excess spilling everywhere and onto everything. Mama was raised in Orange Mound, a historically black neighborhood in the middle of Memphis. She took the city bus while Daddy ran the dirt roads of Glendora, Mississippi, and was baptized in the Tallahatchie. Mama was a teetotaler dedicated to V8 until NPR said it contained too much sodium. Daddy's whiskey water and pills mangled our home lives until the rehab finally took. Daddy said "nigga." Mama, "the N-word." Daddy was Stax and Bobby "Blue" Bland. Mama was Motown. She had preached a quiet and dignified resistance, while I found *The Autobiography of Malcolm X* in Daddy's bathroom when I was eleven and read it with baby insurgent interest; I made the tiniest dog ears and mentally charted Daddy's and my separate progress before absconding with it altogether. Mama went to the doctor more than she went to Sunday service and had the blood pressure of the most unbothered house cat. In the truck, I found at least a month's worth of Daddy's diabetes and hypertension medicine strewn about, still in the baggies Mama had carefully packed. Together for more than four decades—most of their lives, until Daddy's death—my parents were baked chicken and chitlins, wheat and white. Mama was fact; Daddy, feeling. WKNO and WDIA.

•     •     •

Although the Delta was only a ways down Highway 61, my sister and I didn't visit until we were eight and nine. That was where Daddy's mama, our country grandmother, Celia Mae, lived, along with the brothers and sisters and cousins with whom Daddy had spent twenty-one years of his life before migrating to Memphis in 1972. He came then to introduce himself to his father, Jack Rose. Granddaddy Jack's affair with Celia Mae begot Daddy and Daddy's older brother, his only "whole" sibling. Within five years of coming to Memphis, Daddy had met and married Mama, and we came, starting with me, five years later. In the Delta, we discovered a whole world that we hadn't seen or heard or known, a world where Daddy had already spent a majority of his life when we came along. A world we could only imagine through stories Daddy told playfully to aggravate Mama; he loved when she fussed and cussed in response. A world we knew from stories Mama told us to cope with hurt and to warn us not to get country dirty. I became an ethnographer in part to understand that world empirically, with facts, so I could translate it for Mama and they could get along better. I always listened, and am still listening, for that world, the formative one that made Daddy. The one that Mama would say made her a widow too soon.

Mama didn't want that country to get on my sister and me. We knew the mechanics of their country mouse–city mouse skirmishes, deftly navigating around what signified which side. Mama didn't even want the *sound* of the country in our house. She was explicit about her disdain for the B. B., Robert Johnson, and Bobby "Blue" Bland blues Daddy played in defiance on our living room radio on the Saturdays he had off. Things that went wrong—Daddy's alcohol and drug addiction, his infidelities, his son, their hoarding—were country.

Daddy wasn't warring for our souls, but Mama was. And for a time, she won handily. A black Tiger Mother, she contained us in the relative urban privilege of a two-child, two-parent, two-car home in a lower-middle-class neighborhood in Memphis. We began classical violin lessons before we began elementary school because she loved the sound of the studio strings on Motown recordings. My sister and I were always enrolled in accelerated and gifted programs, and each graduated valedictorian of our respective classes. In our house, getting a B was like not voting—we knew people had died for us to get A's. My sister grew up to be a Japanese interpreter, and I am a college professor. Our careers are racially and regionally indistinguishable from those of any other children of middle-class Americans.

But country always has a way of sneaking and winning, and with two children, there was liable to be a split decision. Mama's mama said I should have been named Arthurine because I looked so much like Daddy when I came out. All my life, when I did something that painfully reminded Mama of him—like let money burn a hole in my pocket or shamelessly two-time on a boyfriend—she called me Arthurine with the same kind of malice she said "country." I thought my sister was the favorite because she was impeccably city. She is measured and reserved and probably still has money saved from childhood. Mama would say I should save like my sister, advising her not to lend me money for the candy lady when I had spent my own. I still borrow money from my sister to this day. Country.

Daddy died a month after Prince, in May 2016. I switched off "Sometimes It Snows in April," versions of which I had been listening to constantly, and spent the days following Daddy's death trying to listen for that country. I was trying to find that blues, wanting to know what songs he had sung in the choir, thinking about which were his favorites, wondering if we could have the choir sing one at the service. I wanted my own songs, too, something I could sing to myself to help soothe and release and make sense of things before the visitors started pouring in and I knew I would need to plaster some happy on my face. I rambled in my memory, my few little records, scrolling through my iTunes, trying to find a stick pin in a junk drawer. Asking myself that question so many of us ask ourselves every day—*What would Beyoncé do?*—I put on *Lemonade*, preparing for the funeral visitors, cleaning the kitchen and the bathrooms and the living room with "Daddy Lessons" floating through the house on repeat. The song, a reflection on a black girl's Southern-tough raising, narrates the lessons a Daddy, "with his gun and his head held high," gives to his daughter before his death. He tells her to take care of her mother and sister, and to shoot whenever trouble comes to town. My Daddy had definitely said "shoot," too, and I know one time for sure I should have followed that advice. It was the Mama in me, the nonviolence, the city sophisticate, the talk and stick it out, that had made me take more from men than I should have. It's always been hard to parse which of the country lessons and which of the city lessons I should adhere to and when.

I tried to think of some gospel songs, the kinds that make you holler and cry and reach for God when all those voices rise up together. But I didn't know any such songs offhand because I'm a heretic and also a cultural Christian fraud—perhaps even a Southern fraud because of this combination of spiritual and cultural heresy. Mama never made us go to Sunday service, only Sunday school, because she didn't believe fidgeting children should be bothering grown people trying to get the Word. As a child, I read the Bible like I read all other books, hot with King James for thinking he could challenge me with his long-ass book, determined to show him I could read *any* book cover to cover. The old people at church always said there was magic in the Bible, and I tried to unlock it, sneaking and skipping to Revelations to see who was going to hell in the end. On the phone with her friends, Mama said Daddy needed to get in the Word and maybe he'd stop drinking and drugging and ho'ing. I was confused about how the Word was going to do that for Daddy.

Bible men were a mess, constantly being smote and swallowed by fish and cheating on their wives.

At seventeen, I got baptized so I'd be eligible for the church scholarship. Three older black women surrounded me like the witches of *Macbeth* as I tried to sneak to the car after Sunday school one week. They explained that the deepest understanding of the Word comes after you get saved. *Don't you want to set a good example? Don't you want to be saved and not burn for eternity?* Mama did believe in hell, so I thought maybe I should get saved so I wouldn't burn. And so I could be eligible for the scholarship. I got it, but then I felt like a fraud because I thought I hadn't been saved long enough to cash in on Jesus, even for school books.

Mama taught us to fiercely question race, class, gender, our status as Southerners—but she did not want us to question too loudly in church, where she had faced rampant patriarchy and sexism over the years. She was no Bible scholar, but she scoured it for things to help her deal with Daddy, combining its teachings with what she learned in Al-Anon and Overeaters Anonymous, generating her own New Age Christianity before it was hip. This spiritual study and practice helped her suffer the most insufferable humiliations. I thought her marriage trapped her. But she stayed, she said, because the quality of our lives would have been severely diminished if they had divorced. She had not been confident that Daddy would have supported us and feared being plunged into poverty with two little black girls. At the height of his addiction, she managed to keep the lights, cable, and phone on with her substitute-teacher pay, and the violin lessons continued uninterrupted. Still, Daddy once hotwired Mama's car; another time he pawned our instruments. We had discovered they were missing after we were dressed and greased and headed out the door to play a concert with white people for white people. I'm not sure what Mama prayed for during that time, but

I know in those last years with her and Daddy, bitterness and Daddy's perpetual incorrigibility had made her too tight to pray right for anything. If she was praying, it wasn't reaching the Lord the way she intended. After he died, she told me she stayed because the Holy Spirit never moved her to leave.

.     .     .

Granddaddy Jack's wife, Grandma Lula Mae, had welcomed Daddy when he came to Memphis in 1972. At ninety-eight, she still remembers every time she opened her door to her husband's progeny from other women—she told me she welcomed them all when they showed up on her doorstep. I imagine "welcomed them all" is a euphemism born of temporal distance and dementia. Daddy called her Mrs. Rose, and he reigned as her favorite outside child. When he had his own country child, he brought the baby to Grandma Lula and Granddaddy Jack's house all the time. Mama eventually put two and twenty-two together and confronted him about it. Mama never said who gave her the math, but Daddy figured out the clue-giving snitch and grumbled about her the rest of his life. Mama often wondered aloud how Mrs. Rose must have felt being put in the position of harboring an outside child. Our brother, whose mother Daddy met in treatment, was nearly two when Mama found out. She told Daddy not to tell us until she was ready.

Eldest children, especially eldest girls—especially eldest Southern black girls—know things they shouldn't, try to be double agents in grown folks' fights, and never know that they can't win until it's too late. So when Daddy showed my sister and me a picture of a big-headed little toddler boy at a drum set and asked us who he was, I responded without hesitation: "our brother." Curious about the outside child, I became Daddy's accomplice. With Daddy, I snuck to my brother's kindergarten graduation and sat across from my brother's mother at a Pizza Hut afterward. I was sixteen, and she offered me a car, a Jeep, a country Trojan horse from the outside meant to aggravate the fragile stasis inside. When Mama found out and asked me why were we sitting up at some restaurant like we were a family, I said the woman hadn't done nothing to me, heaping a hurt on Mama. I wasn't grown enough then to know just how fundamentally untrue that was.

But I wanted to forge a relationship of some sort with my brother. Our meetings felt like a betrayal of Mama, and they were a country secret I kept well into adulthood. Later, when I was a mother, I coordinated, sometimes clumsily, the times when my brother, my daughter's uncle, would come to her birthday parties, and the times when Mama, her grandmother, would come. Once I messed up, and my brother and my mother were at my daughter's birthday party at the same time. Mama told me she didn't have to come next year.

.     .     .

I didn't mess up any more timing; over the years, I became a better country accomplice. Four years or so back, Daddy was clearly drinking again, slurring his words and laughing so hard at his own jokes that he might have shook the earth if something deep hadn't interrupted that joy. I consulted with my siblings. My brother confirmed that he couldn't help but notice Daddy's inebriation the last couple of times he had seen him. My sister, home from Japan and living with Mama and Daddy, said she had spied discarded beer cans on the back porch where Mama never looked. I thought he was going to die. I scheduled an intervention with Mama, my sister, and Daddy at my house. Through tears that came from nowhere I told them I wanted them to be happy, together or apart, trying to fix it all right there at the dining room table. Something calmed down after that, and I didn't see him drunk anymore. As a reward, I sometimes gave him whiskey when he visited.

He had been my accomplice, too, in the way daddies can be on their best days. My daughter's father, DeMadre, loved him. He always begged Daddy to tell him a story about "a time they whupped the white folks' ass." From San Francisco, DeMadre came to the South in the late 1990s after having been wooed by the LeMoyne-Owen recruiter on an HBCU college tour, and I met and started dating him in my second year of college. He wanted to know about the country just like I did. When he would visit us, Daddy would tell a story about when he and his brother borrowed a white boy's bike with no intention of giving it back and rode it until dark and kept it the next few days, too. "When did you give it back, Daddy?" I would ask on cue. "Shit, when I felt like it," he would say, and we would try to fill up the world with that small bit of laughter in the context of all that repression. DeMadre, himself an outside child with one other "whole" brother, a fraternal twin, had a fraught relationship with his father. He looked to Daddy as his own. Daddy was an example of the possibilities for outside children, and daddies with outside children.

One August, on the day our daughter turned fourteen months old, DeMadre called my father and asked him to come pick up a two-wheeler he had let us borrow. Daddy was the first on the scene to find him. He talked to the police, and made sure they got DeMadre's body out after he shot himself. DeMadre had called Daddy so I wouldn't find him when I got home. In his carefully written note to me, he said I should tell Daddy that he loved him.

At DeMadre's Memphis memorial, somebody whispered that the coroner had to identify him by his dental records because he had used buckshot instead of duck ammo. I didn't think this could be true, but everything was so unsure then. I couldn't shake that nightmare vision out of my head. I finally told Daddy and asked him to tell me the truth. Daddy replied like he had been called to death scenes for terminally sad outside children all his life: "Naw. He jus' had a li'l hole in his head."

DeMadre died about a week before school was to start. I was entering the second year of my master's program at Memphis, preparing to teach my own class for the first time, and starting some fieldwork—and I was scrambling to find care for my still-nursing toddler. Daddy changed his work schedule to keep my daughter on Monday, Wednesday, and Friday mornings that year. Each morning, he took her for a breakfast of grits, sausage, eggs, and toast across the street from where I had moved into student family housing. My daughter had walked on her first birthday but quickly decided walking was overrated. Daddy held her hand and made her walk baby-bowlegged around the family-housing playground until she felt confident enough to do it on her own. She was running in no time. He gave her sips of coffee at those breakfasts, too. "In the country, babies always usta drank coffee to get ready to pick cotton," he said. You never could tell if Daddy was serious.

When Daddy went to theology school and got a degree, started reading the Bible more than I had as a little girl (and for seemingly religious rather than vengeful purposes), joined Mama's church and three of its choirs, began leading the Nurture for Baptists group, took over leading the holiday family dinner prayers, and became assistant superintendent of the Sunday school on the fast track to take over as superintendent—I didn't know if he was playing a major joke on us or if he had seen his life flash before his eyes. He had grown up in church, but, by all accounts, he had hell in him as a child, despite his baptism.

If Mama's faith had been on a steady utilitarian hum, Daddy seemed to now be really in search of God's Word and the truth and the light. In his truck I found spiral notebooks full of scripture notes. Mama used to say she wished all that Bible and church would make him a better husband. He was a complicated country contradiction.

·    ·    ·

Mama was temporarily devastated when I eloped, but Daddy was delighted. He found the whole thing amusing. It had been ten years since DeMadre's death, and after suffering through raggedy partners that I had refused to marry in the interim, Daddy was glad to have a decent and official son-in-law with whom he could talk shit and fix shit.

The January before Daddy died, it had gotten down to forty-two degrees in my husband's and my house, and Daddy couldn't figure out why. We had been ordering parts for the furnace, swapping things around, waiting for other parts to come in, and nothing was working. He thought it might be the valve and brought one in from the truck to change it. Our valve was old and stuck, and he insisted on turning the large cracked red wrench himself to take it off. He was tired and had been moving more slowly, as I had commented several times. He said he was all right. But watching him try to get the torque on that thing was torture. I joked, "I been working out, you know, I'm pretty strong," and my husband nearly jumped in at one point, equally tortured by the sounds of work coming from Daddy's body. But it finally gave, and he quickly got the other valve on. We went to test the system again, sure we had it fixed. It didn't work. "Aww, gotdamn," Daddy said. We trudged back up from the basement. He was so disappointed, and I was far sadder for him than I could have ever been about the cold. He said he'd be back the next day after work.

Exhausted and frustrated that night, Daddy dreamed of his grandmother Rosie Robinson, whose surname her daughter Celia Mae inherited, which Celia Mae gave to Arthur because she was not married to his father, Jack Rose, when Arthur was born. Daddy gave the name to my brother as his first name—a reverse junior. In the dream, Daddy was with his older sister and saw Big Mama—as he called his grandmother—on top of a hill, looking as young as ever. He was scared of Big Mama, subconsciously goading his sister into asking a question that might have earned him a dream whipping. "Big Mama," she had asked her up the hill, "why'd you discipline him so?" Big Mama responded, "Because the Lord showed me." He awoke with the answer to the heating conundrum, a temporary solution while we waited on a new circuit board to arrive, and told us about the dream over whiskey in a warming living room after he got the system going.

The next week, he went out and bought Mama all new appliances. They still had the avocado green stove from when they had moved into the house in 1976, and the oven hadn't worked in months. The refrigerator door had never closed properly since they switched the side it opened on to accommodate Mama's left-handedness. And the washer had been flooding the kitchen whenever it felt like it. You could hear the steam whistling out of Mama's ears as she fumed about the money he had spent as well as the fact that he had not consulted with the person who most uses the appliances. He also hadn't measured the space for the refrigerator, and as a result, Mama repeatedly referred to it as "the big black dick in the living room" until they swapped it out. Mama, the practical one, had never owned a new car or had a car note, and Daddy had been telling people he was going to get rid of her aged clunker and buy her an Impala. It was the car he had when they had first met. He didn't get to buy her the Impala.

• • •

Prince was gone and a month later so was my daddy, but the world did not care—not one bit. It continued on unbothered, the zodiac clicking right on over to Gemini and reminding me that I was still alive, even if Daddy and Prince weren't, and I would have a birthday soon. Mama and I were sitting at my dining room table planning the funeral program. I asked her if she knew Daddy's favorite song. She didn't know, she said, mentioning that she liked "Come Ye Disconsolate," but that she ain't want nobody messing up Donny and Roberta. I wondered if I could sing it, but I wasn't going to have her mad at me because she didn't think anybody but Aretha and Luther and one of the Temptations could really sing. Funerals are for the living.

Daddy had a blues all his life that I couldn't begin to know, though I had so desperately tried to understand it as his first-born and accomplice. He sang in three choirs at the church; surely there were songs. What were his favorite songs to sing in the choir? What were his go-to shower songs, or caterwauls, as Mama and my sister would call them? What songs had he stolen away and hummed and moaned in the quiet?

I put on my ethnographer hat and went back to the CDs that I had found in the truck. There was the first album my brother's jazz-fusion band released. A specially burned prerelease of my husband's hip-hop EP. B. B. King's greatest hits. Disc 3 of Prism Leisure's essential jazz collection. The 2010–2015 St. John Missionary Baptist Church—Barron Street, not Vance Avenue—Gospel Choir anniversary CDs. A 2011 St. John Missionary Baptist Church—Barron Street, not Vance Avenue—Male Chorus CD. And CDs with Mama's left-handed writing on them: three annual compilations she made for everybody she knew at Christmastime with both secular and Christian songs; the soundtrack to *The Preacher's Wife*; and a compilation of women singing gospel songs with Whitney and Aretha. There was a CD I had burned for him years back with Bobby "Blue" Bland, B. B. King, and some Lee Williams spirituals on it.

Daddy had given me a list of requests for Bobby "Blue" Bland. "Ain't No Love in the Heart of the City" was first. Then there was "I Wouldn't Treat a Dog (The Way You Treated Me)," "Steal Away," "Three O'Clock Blues" with B. B. King, "I'm Too Far Gone to Turn Around," "You Did Me Wrong," and more. When I first saw the list, I thought it was mighty narcissistic of Daddy to be having the blues with all he had done to Mama. But listening to that music in the wake of Daddy's death some ten years later, I was compelled to consider for the first time the shape of Daddy's hurt—and his right to it. He had hurt Mama and the rest of us, but I had not given him space to hurt, not about anything, really, beyond a stubbed toe. His upbringing in Jim Crow Mississippi with disappearances and violences and the concomitant beatings from Big Mama Rosie. A missed scholarship opportunity because a racist counselor hadn't turned in a form. His visit to Memphis that was only supposed to be a stop on the way to St. Louis that turned out to be an entire life and abrupt death. His guilt about what he had done to Mama, or to us. His mama's death, the only time I saw him cry, and all the other people he loved who had died or gone missing. Having to tell his daughter about the hole in her child's father's head. And those women who weren't Mama. I wondered if Daddy was thinking of them when he listened to Bland sing:

> I'll never fall in love again
> If I should live three hundred years
> I'll never give my heart to another woman
> No matter who she is
> You did me wrong, baby
> That's why I'm singing this song.

Had they broken my daddy's heart while he was breaking Mama's? Did he hear Mama's city pain in Bland's declaration that he had a "hole where [his] heart used to be"? Or was he thinking of his own heart, and how he had turned Mama mean? I wondered if Daddy was listening for the country in Bland, or if he just needed someone who sonically and ontologically knew his regret and guilt and sorrow and heartbreak. Like Bland, Daddy had "felt so bad" and found places to "steal away and moan sometimes." If I couldn't know where he stole away, I wished I could know what or why he moaned.

To triangulate and make sure my research was robust, I started listening to WDIA incessantly. I listened to the parade of voices, newcomers and regulars, weighing in on the day's events, half hoping Daddy would call in and say "psych!" and laugh and laugh and laugh until tears came. I tried to recall those snippets of songs I used to hear on the way to Sunday school, the only time Mama would switch from the oldies station to WLOK. All those years listening weekly on the fifteen-minute ride to Orange Mound, and I only came up with enough memory matter to Google two songs. "A witness? Can I get a witness? For Jesus? Somebody know Jesus? Won't he make a difference in your life?" That one turned out to be "You Brought the Sunshine," a Clark Sisters song originally recorded the year before I was born. I listened to all of the available versions, watching those four Detroit Clark Sisters singing and shining and glittering with their spectacular hair. Without that AM crackle and on-the-way-to-Sunday-school anxiety, I couldn't catch whatever it was I was looking for.

The other lyric I recalled was "I lift my hands in total praise to you." I remembered the song's concluding chorus of amens because that was the snippet WLOK would play between tracks. Atlanta-born, Chocolate City–raised Richard Smallwood had written that song—"Total Praise."

> Lord, I lift mine eyes to the hills
> Knowing my help is coming from you.
> Your peace you give me in time of the storm.
> You are the source of my strength.
> You are the strength of my life.
> I lift my hands in total praise to you.
> Amen, amen, amen, amen, amen, amen, amen, amen.

I listened to it over and over and over and got nothing.

· · ·

There was business to tend to. My sister and I were grown daughters for real now, and we made plans and helped Mama make plans like grown daughters do. That Monday, the day after I found the truck, we met with the funeral director at my dining room table. Her wig was a carefully manicured synthetic helmet of sorrow, jet black with blond highlights. Both ancient and from the future, it swooped gently across her forehead, framing her face. I figured she must have worn it to communicate how sorry she was about Daddy's death.

She knew Daddy and demonstrated how she would pull his face into his signature smile. We were going to put him in a red tie, and the theme color would be red. Mama and Daddy's pastor was there, too. He pulled my sister and me aside to warn us not to let this light-eyed lady with her Sorrow Wig trick our grieving Mama out of money. He admonished us to tell the lady we only had $3,000. Later, I told Mama what the pastor said, and she said Daddy would have gotten up from the dead and said, "Bitch, why you put me in this wooden box?" if she had given him a $3,000 funeral. She tickled herself with the truth and absurdity of the prospect. There was some longing there, too.

My sister and I worked tirelessly on the program, she on the format, me on the obituary. Mama tried to get the order of the siblings from both sides straight so no one would be offended. She wouldn't let me put my brother in the obituary, but he was in the list of survivors and in the funeral car, our fragile family making small talk and nitpicking over funeral details. I was a weary country accomplice.

By the day of the visitation, I had cried, but I still had not been carried away like I needed to be to clear my system before the show. Walking into the church, I saw the red tie first. I went straight to the casket. The diabetes got his body. The barber was terrible. They hadn't cut his nails again. The makeup was too light. They hadn't pulled the wires hard enough for the smile. I touched the tie, careful not to mess up the delicate but grotesque system that held his body there propped up for us to see. I had cleaned his signature cap—it said ROB in white lettering on a black surface with a red rim, something he had specially made with a gift card I got him. I had intended to place it in the casket, but I changed my mind and kept it, withholding it from this body I didn't recognize.

The break did not come at the wake or the next day at the funeral, not even when the casket was reopened because my "whole" uncle from St. Louis got lost and was late. The pastor said a few words about Daddy, and Mama whispered to us even though she is biologically incapable of whispering. ("He should have seen the hell in him before he got to church every week.") The pastor then launched into the kind of homophobic and sexist tirade that made me hate the church as a child, managing to condemn Caitlyn Jenner before opening the doors of his Father's house to receive new members. The choir, sparse because it was Memorial Day weekend, didn't sing anything of particular note. I was fidgeting for a break, but I would not get it there.

Mama had designated one friend, one church member, one coworker, and one family member to speak at the funeral. She wanted to prevent infighting about who in the family had the most right to speak. There had already been a squabble about who was the oldest of his sisters. To settle the argument, they drew out their driver's licenses and compared.

The coworker who spoke had worked alongside Daddy for years without knowing his full name; everyone knew him as Rob. A frail man with glasses, he said he had once told Daddy about his rheumatoid arthritis, and how his doctor said he wasn't going to be able to work anymore before long and that he was going to have to get a cane. Daddy told him, "Get an umbrella." The man replied that an umbrella was fine for the rain, but what would he do when it was sunny out? Daddy said, "Use it to keep the sun off ya face." So the man got an umbrella, and held it up for the church to see. With his umbrella cane still raised, he concluded, "He loved his whiskey, and he loved his family. And I'm gon' miss him." No one could ever tell if Daddy was serious.

After everyone was gone, when the lights were off, I thought release would come. It didn't. I just kept listening for things.

What did come was a windstorm that shook the house and knocked down the two trees in my backyard. I heard the crack like lightning and got up from the dining room table and walked into the kitchen in time to see a massive branch fall and take out the east fence. I stood there waiting for the rest. *Just take me on out, then, if you wanna, shit.* But my daughter screamed at me to move and get to the basement. She had already been upstairs to fetch her baby brother from his crib. I was still staring when she commanded me again: *Move, Mom.*

No power lines down, no structures damaged but the fence. The second tree had been plain snatched up at the roots like a giant had plucked it up to floss with and dropped it when he was done. There was nothing left but heat, so much sun now where there once had been shade. It hurt. I had grown so accustomed to the shade that I had forgotten where it was coming from all these years.

.　　　.　　　.

The last piece of business was Daddy's car, a red Oldsmobile 98, the same shade as his truck. It had been given to him by his brother, and he planned to drive that car when he retired. He kept it in storage, spending thousands of dollars over the years, awaiting that day. Since he had turned fifty-five, he had been threatening to retire at sixty-two. Mama couldn't bear the thought of his not getting the full Social Security benefit. Even though she knew he could get the full benefit at sixty-six, she wanted him to wait until sixty-six-and-a-half, perhaps for good measure. Well.

We had to cut the storage unit's lock because none of Daddy's three dozen keys fit. I squatted down as far as possible to have enough force to lift the door. Seemed like ages since it had been raised. And there was the car. It had three flat tires and part of the unit's ceiling had caved in on it. But there it was. Still proud. Hidden away in a tight, musty space and entombed with cancerous stuff crumbling around him, but there he was. Arthur Lee Robinson. There were two air-conditioning motors inside, too. A Mama size and a Daddy size.

I had driven over in the truck, and WLOK was on the radio when I returned to head to the other side of town. I had just left it on in there. "Lord, I lift mine eyes to the hills, knowing my help is coming from you," said the voices from the speaker. "Your peace you give me in time of the storm. You are the source of my strength. You are the strength of my life. I lift my hands in total praise to you."

Halfway down Park in Orange Mound, "Total Praise" came on. It finally got through to me—catharsis came so hard and fast I could not see. My eyes were raining and there were no damn windshield wipers. I just pulled in the turning lane and parked and waited for the rain to pass but knew it wouldn't. There came that chorus of amens, one on top of the other, and I wailed until I was afraid I was being sealed away, too.

Sometimes I'm still there in that lane, facing east, hands lifted, unable to get out and back home to myself until somebody brings the right key.

•    •    •

Daddy liked to tell Mama that when they retired, he was moving them to some land in Mississippi and giving her a truck patch to garden. Mama would balk, saying proudly that all the plants would die if she were in charge. When any of us would sing, he would ask if we sang in parts, though we were all better singers than he was, with or without a choir. He ran us out of rooms with his flatulence and paid us a dollar to scratch his dandruff and a dollar for each A we earned. He always brought money right on time when I hadn't asked, and we knew he was so proud of us. He loved sausage links and chitlins and peanut M&M'S, and had his absolute favorite—ribs—for his last dinner of jury duty. He loved Mama the best way he knew how. He was sorry he hurt her, though he didn't ever say so except for with the Bobby "Blue" Bland, and the appliances, and the new car he wanted Mama to have. She finally got it after he died.

Mama still finds things of Daddy's that she thinks my brother would like, and in my accomplice role, I get them from her and give them to him. Watches, shirts with "Rob" on them, caps. She asks me what my brother has said about these things. She's said his name or referred to him as my brother more in the few months since Daddy died than she did in his entire life. In the end, Mama did right by Daddy's son.

I will always wonder what songs of comfort he sang to himself, what he hummed alone before he flew home in the end. "This old world is so lonely. This old town is so sad. This old room is so cold and empty," Bland had sung. Daddy must have felt so bad. What of his gospel? When he lay on that cold tile to rest and prepare for flight, was DeMadre there with a warm laugh and his own caterwauling, returning the favor? When he at last no longer had to steal away into himself to moan, what was his solace? Did he take his final right to cry? Did he lift his eyes to that hill where he saw Big Mama, knowing help was coming from her, and from the Lord? What did he pray?

In the end, I hope there was a chorus of rising amens to free him, lifting him in total praise for a life well led.

I hope he had all the amens. Amen, amen.

Amen, Daddy, amen.

Amen. Amen.

# Permissions

# Contributors

**SHANE BAUER** is a senior reporter at *Mother Jones* and recipient of numerous awards, including the 2017 National Magazine Award for Reporting, the Goldsmith Award for Investigative Reporting, and the Hillman Prize for Magazine Journalism. He is also the coauthor, with Sarah Shourd and Joshua Fattal, of *A Sliver of Light*, a memoir of his two years as a prisoner in Iran.

**PAMELA COLLOFF** joined the staff of *Texas Monthly* in 1997. She is a six-time National Magazine Award finalist and won the Feature Writing award in 2013 for her story "The Innocent Man." Her work has also appeared in *The New Yorker* and has been anthologized in *Best American Magazine Writing, Best American Crime Reporting, Best American Non-Required Reading*, and *Next Wave: America's New Generation of Great Literary Journalists*. In 2014 the Nieman Foundation for Journalism at Harvard University awarded her the Louis M. Lyons Award for Conscience and Integrity in Journalism. She is currently a senior reporter at *ProPublica* and a writer-at-large at the *New York Times Magazine*.

**JEFFREY GOLDBERG** was a Middle East correspondent and the Washington correspondent for *The New Yorker* before joining *The Atlantic* in 2007. He was previously a correspondent for the *New York Times Magazine* and *New York* magazine. He has also written for the *Jewish Daily Forward* and was a columnist for the *Jerusalem Post*. Goldberg's book *Prisoners* was hailed as one of the best books of 2006 by the *Los Angeles Times*, the *New York Times*, the *Washington Post, Slate, The Progressive, Washingtonian*, and *Playboy*. He received the 2003 National Magazine Award for Reporting for his coverage of Islamic terrorism and the 2005 Anti-Defamation League Daniel Pearl Prize. He is also the winner of the International Consortium of Investigative Journalists prize for best international investigative journalist; the Overseas Press Club award for best human-rights reporting; and the Abraham Cahan Prize in Journalism. In 2001, Goldberg was appointed the Syrkin Fellow in Letters of the Jerusalem Foundation, and in 2002 he became a public-policy scholar at the Woodrow Wilson International Center for Scholars in Washington, D.C.

**NIKOLE HANNAH-JONES** is a domestic correspondent for the *New York Times Magazine* focusing on racial injustice. She has written on federal failures to enforce the Fair Housing Act, the re-segregation of American schools, and policing in America. Her extensive reporting in both print and radio on the ways segregation in housing and schools is maintained through official action and policy has earned a National Magazine Award, a Peabody, and a Polk Award. Ms. Hannah-Jones earned her bachelor's degree in history and African American studies from the University of Notre Dame and her master's degree in journalism and mass communication from the University of North Carolina at Chapel Hill. Ms. Hannah-Jones lives in Brooklyn with her husband and very sassy daughter.

**MAC MCCLELLAND** is an award-winning journalist and the author of *Irritable Hearts: A PTSD Love Story* and *For Us Surrender Is Out of the Question: A Story From Burma's Never-Ending War,* which was a finalist for the 2011 Dayton Literary Peace Prize. She's written for *Rolling Stone,* Reuters, *Mother Jones, New York,* and the *New York Times Magazine,* among other publications, and corresponded for PBS and *Vice News Tonight* on HBO. She's been nominated for three National Magazine Awards for Feature Writing. Her features have been translated and reprinted around the world.

**SIDDHARTHA MUKHERJEE** is the author of *The Emperor of All Maladies: A Biography of Cancer,* winner of the 2011 Pulitzer Prize in general nonfiction, and *The Laws of Medicine*. He is the editor of *Best Science Writing 2013*. Mukherjee is an assistant professor of medicine at Columbia University and a cancer physician and researcher. A Rhodes scholar, he graduated from Stanford University, the University of Oxford, and Harvard Medical School. He has published articles in *Nature, The New England Journal of Medicine*, the *New York Times*, and *Cell*. He lives in New York with his wife and daughters. Visit his website at: SiddharthaMukherjee .com

**DAVID QUAMMEN** is an author and journalist whose fifteen books include *The Song of the Dodo* (1996), *The Reluctant Mr. Darwin* (2007), and *Spillover* (2012), a work on the science, history, and human impacts of emerging diseases (especially viral diseases), which was short-listed for eight national and international awards and won three (including the Merck Prize, given in Rome). More recently he published two short books, *Ebola* and *The Chimp and the River*, both drawn largely from *Spillover*. His latest book is *Yellowstone: A Journey Through America's Wild Heart*, which is an expanded version of the May 2016 special issue of National Geographic on the Greater Yellowstone Ecosystem, with text by Quammen and photos by a team of eight photographers. Quammen is a contributing writer for *National Geographic*, in whose service he travels often, usually to Africa. He has also written for many other magazines, ranging from *Harper's, The Atlantic*, and the *New York Times Book Review* to *Outside, Rolling Stone*, and *Powder*. He is a three-time recipient of the National Magazine Award for essays and other work in *Outside* and *National Geographic*. Much of his nonfiction is focused on ecology and evolutionary biology, frequently garnished with history and travel. He has received a Guggenheim fellowship, a Lannan Literary Award for nonfiction, and the Stephen Jay Gould Prize from the Society for the Study of Evolution. In addition he has published three novels and a book of short stories, one of which,

"Walking Out," has recently been adapted into an independent film, premiering in January at the Sundance Festival. Quammen has lived in Montana for forty-three years and in the Greater Yellowstone Ecosystem for most of that time. He is presently at work on a book on the *Tree of Life*. His home is in Bozeman, where he shares a house and a small lot with his wife, Betsy Gaines Quammen, a conservationist finishing a doctorate in environmental history, and their family of other mammals.

**ZANDRIA F. ROBINSON** is a writer and cofounder of the Center for Southern Literary Arts in Memphis. She is the author of *This Ain't Chicago: Race, Class, and Regional Identity in the Post-Soul South* and coauthor with Marcus Anthony Hunter of *Chocolate Cities: The Black Map of American Life*. Robinson blogs at *New South Negress* and tweets sundries at @zfelice.

**BECCA ROTHFELD** is a doctoral candidate in the department of philosophy at Harvard University.

**GEORGE SAUNDERS** is the author of nine books, including *Tenth of December*, which was a finalist for the National Book Award and won the inaugural Folio Prize (for the best work of fiction in English) and the Story Prize (for the best short-story collection). He has received MacArthur and Guggenheim fellowships and the PEN/Malamud Prize for excellence in the short story and was recently elected to the American Academy of Arts and Sciences. In 2013, he was named one of the world's hundred most influential people by *Time*. He teaches in the Creative Writing Program at Syracuse University.

**GABRIEL SHERMAN** was named *New York* magazine's national affairs editor in 2015, covering politics and business, having previously served as a contributing editor at the magazine since 2008. In 2016, he broke one of the most significant media stories in years—the downfall of Roger Ailes at Fox News, building on his biography of Roger Ailes, *The Loudest Voice in the Room* (2014), a New York Times best-seller, and previous reporting for the magazine. Sherman has written news-making features for *New York* on Donald Trump and his presidential campaign, Rupert Murdoch, Jared Kushner, NBC News, the *New York Times*, a Facebook scandal at Horace Mann School, Time Inc., Jeff Zucker, and Stuyvesant Town. He has written profiles of Michael Bloomberg, Sarah Palin, and New Jersey governor Chris Christie, among others. His 2010 cover story "Chasing Fox" won the Mirror Award from Syracuse University's Newhouse School for Best Single Article, and his Horace Mann piece was a finalist for the Livingston Award for young journalists. Since September 2016, he has served as a contributor to NBC News and MSNBC, and he has also appeared on *Charlie Rose*, CNN, Fox News, *CBS This Morning*, *ABC World News*, and National Public Radio. His journalism has appeared in the *New York Times*, the *Guardian*, *The New Republic*, *Slate*, *GQ*, *The Atlantic*, *Wired*, and *Outside* magazine, among other publications. He currently lives in New York City with his wife, Jennifer Stahl.

**REBECCA SOLNIT**, a writer, historian, and activist, is the author of twenty books on feminism, western and indigenous history, popular power, social change and insurrection, wandering and walking, hope, and disaster, including a trilogy of atlases and the books *The Mother of All Questions*; *Hope in the Dark*; *Men Explain Things to Me*; *The Faraway Nearby*; *A Paradise Built in Hell: The Extraordinary Communities That Arise in Disaster*; *A Field Guide to Getting Lost*; *Wanderlust: A History of Walking*; and *River of Shadows: Eadweard Muybridge and the Technological Wild West* (for which she received a Guggenheim, the National Book Critics Circle Award in criticism, and the Lannan Literary Award). A product of the California public education system from kindergarten to graduate school, she is a columnist at *Harper's*.

**SARAH STILLMAN** is a staff writer at *The New Yorker*. She is also the director of the Global Migration Program at Columbia University's Graduate School of Journalism, where she teaches a course on covering immigration and refugee issues. She has written on topics ranging from civil forfeiture to debtors prisons and from Mexico's drug cartels to Bangladesh's garment-factory workers. She won the 2012 National Magazine Award for Public Interest for her reporting from Iraq and Afghanistan on labor abuses and human trafficking on United States military bases and also received the Michael Kelly Award, the Overseas Press Club's Joe and Laurie Dine Award for international human-rights reporting, and the Hillman Prize for Magazine Journalism. Her reporting on the high-risk use of young people as confidential informants in the war on drugs received a George Polk Award and the Molly National Journalism Prize. Before joining *The New Yorker*, Stillman wrote about America's wars overseas and the challenges facing soldiers at home for the *Washington Post*, *The Nation*, newrepublic.com, *Slate*, and TheAtlantic.com. She cotaught a seminar at Yale on the Iraq War and also ran a creative-writing workshop for four years at the Cheshire Correctional Institution, a maximum-security men's prison in Connecticut. Her work is included in *The Best American Magazine Writing 2012*. She is a 2016 MacArthur Fellow.

**ANDREW SULLIVAN** joined *New York* as a contributing editor in 2016 before becoming a staff writer at large in 2017, writing features for the print magazine as well as commentary and live blogs for nymag.com. He was a finalist for the National Magazine Award in Essays and Criticism in 2017. Sullivan began his pioneering blog *The Daily Dish* in 2000, eventually hosting it at publications including *Time*, *The Atlantic*, and the *Daily Beast* before launching the *Dish* as an independent, subscriber-funded website in early 2013. In January 2015, he closed the site and stepped back from daily blogging. Sullivan was editor of *The*

*New Republic* from 1991 to 1996, a writer for the *New York Times Magazine* from 1996 to 2002, and a weekly columnist on America for the *Sunday Times of London* from 1996 to 2015. He is the author of several books, including *The Conservative Soul* and *Virtually Normal*, the first book to argue for marriage equality. A graduate of Oxford University, he received an MPA and a Ph.D. from Harvard University.

**MATT TAIBBI** has been a reporter for *Rolling Stone* magazine since 2003. He is also the author of seven books, the past four being *New York Times* best-sellers: *The Great Derangement*, *Griftopia*, *The Divide*, and *Insane Clown President*. He won the National Magazine Award for Commentary in 2008. Before his work in the United States, Taibbi lived in the former Soviet Union for eleven years and for a while edited his own English-language newspaper, the *eXile*, in Moscow. Matt is married and with his wife Jeanne has three young boys: Max, Nate, and Zeke. He is forty-seven.

**NICHOLAS THOMPSON** was named editor in chief of *Wired* in 2017. Before joining *Wired*, Thompson served as editor of *NewYorker.com* from 2012 to 2017, during which time monthly readership increased by 700 percent. He also oversaw the redesign of the website, the launch of the New Yorker Today app, and the introduction of an online paywall, which contributed to a 130 percent increase in annual subscriptions. Before *The New Yorker*, Thompson was a senior editor at *Wired*, where he assigned and edited the feature story "The Great Escape," which was the basis for the Oscar-winning film *Argo*. During his career, Thompson has written about politics, technology, and law for numerous publications. In 2009, his book *The Hawk and the Dove: Paul Nitze, George Kennan, and the History of the Cold War* was published to critical acclaim. Thompson is also a contributor for CBS News and regularly appears on *CBS This Morning* and CBSN. He is a cofounder of *The Atavist*, a National Magazine Award–winning digital publication. Thompson is a senior fellow in the American Strategy Program at the New America Foundation, a member of the Council on Foreign Relations, and a member of the Young Leaders Council on the National Committee on American Foreign Policy. He was a United States Truman Scholar and graduated from Stanford University.